Current Issues in Cross-Border Insolvency and Reorganisations

The International Bar Association Series

Other titles in this series:

(Please order by ISBN or title)

International Bar Association Series

Current Issues in Cross-Border Insolvency and Reorganisations

Editors

E. Bruce Leonard

and

Christopher W. Besant

Graham & Trotman

A member of Wolters Kluwer Academic Publishers

LONDON/DORDRECHT/BOSTON

and

International Bar Association

Graham & Trotman Limited
Sterling House
66 Wilton Road
London SW1V 1DE
UK

Kluwer Academic Publishers Group
101 Philip Drive
Assinippi Park
Norwell, MA 02061
USA

International Bar Association
2 Harewood Place
Hanover Square
London W1R 9HB
UK

ISBN 1 85333 958 X
Series ISBN 1 85333 096 5

i00037554 X

British Library Cataloguing in Publication Data is available

Library of Congress Cataloging-in-Publication Data

Current issues in cross-border insolvency and reorganisations /
    editors, E. Bruce Leonard and Christopher W. Besant.
        p. cm.— (International Bar Association series)
        ISBN 1-85333-958-X. — ISBN 1-85333-096-5 (series)
        1. Bankruptcy.   2. Corporate reorganizations. I. Leonard, E. Bruce. II. Besant, Christopher W.
III. Series.
K1375.4.C87   1994
346′.078 — dc20
[342.678]

94-7617
CIP

Typset in Times 10/11pt by EXPO Holdings, Malaysia.
Printed and bound in Great Britain by Hartnolls Ltd, Bodmin, Cornwall.

Contents

Preface

International insolvencies and reorganisations are being encountered at an ever-increasing rate. Just as the decade of the 1980s saw unprecendented levels of activity in international mergers and acquisitions and other commercial transactions, the decade of the 1990s has seen a similarly unprecendented wave of multinational and cross-border restructurings and insolvencies. Indeed, many of the businesses that were involved in the mergers and acquisitions of the 1980s have become involved in the international insolvencies and restructurings of the 1990s. Such cases as *Maxwell Communication*, *Olympia & York* and *Maruko* show that major insolvencies are now more international in scope than ever before. The current wave of cross-border insolvencies and reorganisations also shows that there is considerable scope and a very significant need for increased co-operation and co-ordination between countries in multinational reorganisations and insolvencies.

The legislatures of the major trading countries have shown a distinct and consistent disinclination to become involved on a country-to-country basis in insolvency treaties or agreements. There may be valid reasons for this widespread legislative failure to act but it seems difficult to explain this failure by concluding that, internationally, things are in a better condition now than they would be through co-operative action between major trading countries.

At the risk of over-generalising, it would seem that the courts of the major trading countries, taken as a whole, are demonstrating an increased willingness to co-operate with each other and to co-ordinate activities to secure commercially-oriented results in international restructurings. The courts seem to be more and more prepared to work toward frameworks that encourage co-ordination and co-operation between jurisdictions in multinational cases. The courts, however, need the active and innovative participation of the insolvency community to create structures that are conducive to increasing cross-border co-ordination in multinational cases.

The insolvency community, through the aegis of the International Bar Association, is in a unique and advantageous position to work toward achieving meaningful improvements in international insolvencies and reorganisations. The IBA is the world's foremost international association of lawyers. It comprises representation from over 150 Bar Associations and Law Societies representing a membership of over 2,500,00 lawyers. In addition, the IBA enjoys the membership of 16,000 individual lawyers in over 160 countries. The IBA provides a superb forum in which, and through which, to address important international commercial issues and to share and disseminate specialist knowledge and experience in all areas of the law.

vii

The IBA's Section on Business Law is the largest of the IBA's three sections with over 12,500 members. Its objectives are to promote the exchange of information and views among its members with regard to laws, practices and procedures that affect business, financial and commercial activities throughout the world. Committee J, the Insolvency and Creditors' Rights Committee, is one of the major committees of the Section on Business Law with a membership of over 1,000 insolvency and secured transactions lawyers from over 75 countries worldwide. Committee J's membership includes many of the world's most experienced and respected insolvency practitioners and authorities. Committee J, consequently, takes great pleasure in publishing *Current Issues in Cross-Border Insolvency and Reorganisations.*

This book has been made possible by the efforts of many of Committee J's most active and prominent members. The chapters have been contributed by leading practitioners and authorities who were actually involved in the cases they describe. Having authoritative accounts of some of the most noteworthy international restructurings in the past fifteen years is a significant and, perhaps, unique accomplishment and the collected materials in this volume, benefitting from the experience of exceptionally-qualified authors, should present a very valuable resource for anyone who is active in the insolvency community.

We hope that this book, by featuring the analysis and research of senior members of Committee J with active and direct experience in the areas in which they are writing, will make a significant contribution to the literature in the insolvency area and that it will be of interest and assistance to practitioners, academics and the judiciary who are concerned with, and involved in, the insolvency area.

E. Bruce Leonard
Co-Chair, International Bar Association
Committee on Insolvency and Creditors' Rights
Toronto, Canada
May, 1994

Further details of Committee J and the IBA and its Section on Business Law are available from:

International Bar Association
2 Harewood Place
Hanover Square
London W1R 9HB

Tel: +44 (0)71 629 1206
Fax: +44(0)71 409 0456

1

The Proposed European Community Insolvency Convention

Philippe Woodland Ph.D.*

Principal Administrator in the Legal Service of the Council of the European Communities, Brussels, Belgium

1.1 General Approach

The purpose of this paper is to analyse the proposed Insolvency Convention which is soon likely to bind the States belonging to the European Community (referred to as EC States). The law applying in such States to cross-border bankruptcies would be affected by the entry into force of multilateral conventions in a field where very few bilateral conventions already exist. In Europe only one multilateral convention has been adopted within the framework of the Council of Europe (*see* **1.3**), but it is far from being implemented. The draft Convention on Insolvency Proceedings currently being discussed in Brussels appears beyond doubt to be more ambitious and, if it were adopted in its present form, would lead to important changes in cross-border bankruptcy practice.

First of all, this paper will review some of the legal characteristics of the European Community (EC) together with the background to the negotiations on bankruptcy matters. Then, the main provisions of the draft Convention will be described, with a view to drawing out their consequences for a cross-border bankruptcy opened in an EC State (the situation arising from the opening of bankruptcy proceedings in a non-EC country will also be tackled). Finally, the text itself of the draft Convention (the 1992 version), is appended to the present paper as **Annex 1**.

1.2 Bankruptcy proceedings and European Community law

The European Community is, in fact, made up of three different Communities: ie the European Coal and Steel Community which appeared first in 1951 with the Treaty of

---

*The present paper, finished in March 1993, is based on a report presented to the International Symposium on Civil Justice (August 1992, Tokyo).

Current Issues in Cross-Border Insolvency and Reorganisations (E. B. Leonard, C. W. Besant, eds.; 1–85333–958–X; © International Bar Association; pub. Graham & Trotman/International Bar Association, 1994; printed in Great Britain), pp. 1–32.

Paris; the European Atomic Energy Community; and the European Economic Community, the latter two both established in 1957 by treaties signed in Rome. It is the last (referred to as the EEC Treaty) which is relevant as regards bankruptcy. Following an agreement reached in Maastricht at the end of 1991, a treaty on European Union is on its way with a view, among other aims, to amending the EEC Treaty, thus establishing "the European Community"; the official designation would therefore coincide with the one that has come to be used in practice. The aims of the Community, as set out in Article 1 of the EEC Treaty, are the establishment of a common market (later called the single or internal market) and the progressive approximation of the economic policies of the Member States, to which the Maastricht Treaty adds in particular the establishment of economic and monetary union. However no substantial changes will affect the provisions of the Treaty applying directly or indirectly to bankruptcy matters.

The European Community presently comprises 12 Member States: Belgium, Denmark, Germany, Greece, Spain, France, Ireland, Italy, Luxembourg, the Netherlands, Portugal and the United Kingdom (listed in alphabetical order of the Member States in their own languages). Some of the EFTA countries (European Free Trade Association) have also applied for EC membership (indeed the negotiations with Austria, Sweden and Finland have already begun). The draft Convention on Insolvency proceedings would therefore have an even more important impact, since it could become part of the *"acquis communautaire"* (ie EC Acts which have to be accepted by newcomers during accession negotiations). Another possibility is to extend the EC text to EFTA countries by means of a separate Convention having more or less the same provisions. Such a device has already been used with the Lugano Convention (1988) agreed between EC and EFTA countries to extend the EC Brussels Convention (1968) on jurisdiction and the enforcement of judgments in civil and commercial matters.

The latter Convention was based on Article 220 of the EEC Treaty which provides that:

> "Member States shall, so far as is necessary, enter into negotiations with each other with a view to securing for the benefit of their nationals: ... the simplification of formalities governing the reciprocal recognition and enforcement of judgments of courts or tribunals and of arbitration awards."

To implement Article 220, the EC institutions operate in a rather unusual way. They do not rely on regulations (which are directly applicable in all EC States) or directives (which are binding on each EC State as to the result to be achieved, but not as to the method of doing so), which represent proper Community legal instruments, but on reciprocal agreements. Instead of the Council (which represents the governments of the Member States) acting, often by a qualified majority, on a proposal from the Commission (which is a supranational body) with the intervention of the European Parliament (and possibly of the Economic and Social Committee), the proceedings have more in common with ordinary international negotiations. The draft agreements are not proposed formally by the Commission; they have to be adopted by the Council (acting unanimously) meeting as a "Conference of Representatives of the Governments of the Member States" and then ratified by all Member States.

Within the framework of Article 220 of the EEC Treaty, a convention has to be concluded amongst all EC States. Since it can prove difficult, at least in the first stage, to reach unanimous agreement on a convention, a possible solution lies in the one adopted for the Rome Convention (1980) on the law applicable to contractual obligations. The EC Court of Justice was given powers to interpret the latter through two separate protocols: the first covers interpretation of the Convention by the Court of Justice, for which ratification by only seven EC States (ie of the protocol and therefore of the Convention itself) is sufficient; the second actually confers powers on the Court of Justice and therefore needs ratification (but this would be a mere formality) by all EC States. Such a solution is now considered the most realistic one and it has been incorporated in the latest draft of the EC Bankruptcy Convention (*see* **Annex 1**). This solution would involve the deletion of the reference to Article 220 in the preamble of the Convention. This would allow the Convention to enter into force only between some EC States (at least seven, perhaps ten, since the legal particularities of the Irish and UK legal systems could prove difficult to overcome). But the Convention would then be kept within the EC legal framework, with the possibility (which is essential in practice) for the Court of Justice to rule on its interpretation.

1.3 The background to an EC draft Bankruptcy Convention

It was clear from the very beginning that bankruptcy matters have to be tackled separately from other kinds of court proceedings; they need to be governed by a convention of their own. Consequently, bankruptcy proceedings relating to the winding-up of insolvent companies or other legal persons, judicial arrangements, compositions with creditors and analogous proceedings were excluded from the scope of the "general Convention", or Brussels Convention (*see* **1.2**), by its Article 1, sub-paragraph 2. As far as such proceedings were concerned, a committee of experts met (within the Commission) between 1963 and 1980 to draw up a first and then (following the Community's enlargement from 1973) a second draft Convention. This latter draft Convention was studied within the EC Council from 1982 until 1985, when work was suspended for lack of sufficient agreement. The draft was based on the principle of the unity of bankruptcy proceedings, jurisdiction being given to only one court in the EC territory according to where the debtor's centre of administration was situated. But objections were raised about its excessive complexity, and in particular about the provisions which took account of safeguards and privileges existing in only one EC State or another. It also presupposed an ideal of certain uniform rules (compensation, reservation of title, etc) which were watered down, if not abandoned, in the course of the discussions.

In the meantime, negotiations had been initiated within the Council of Europe (an international organisation comprising some 25 European states, thus larger than the EC but with a more limited scope of competence). This finally led to a "European Convention on Certain International Aspects of Bankruptcy" prepared for signing in Istanbul on 5 June 1990 (referred to here as the Council of Europe Convention). However, as at 1 March 1993, only seven states have signed and none has ratified the Convention. Some EC States are obviously waiting for the outcome of the negotiations in Brussels. Furthermore, Article 40 of the Convention allows scope for reservations on Chapter II (exercise of certain powers of the liquidator) and Chapter III (secondary bankruptcies). This involves some risk of distortion between countries, which would have obvious disadvantages as between EC States. Chapter I contains general provisions and Chapter IV concerns information of the creditors and the lodging of their claims. Although a notable achievement in the field of international bankruptcy, the rules set out in this Convention do not go far enough to ensure the efficient handling of bankruptcies with an international dimension. To give but one example, it is based on indirect international jurisdiction (see Article 4), which is weaker with regard to domestic criteria of jurisdiction than a direct one. In this chapter, there is no intention to discuss the consequences of the possible application of the Council of Europe Convention to cross-border bankruptcies within the EC. It appears more likely that a Convention proper to the EC would apply in such a case, given the probable difficulties with ratifying the Council of Europe Convention. References could nevertheless be made to this Convention with a view to emphasising the links with the EC draft Convention.

The completion of the negotiations within the Council of Europe led to the resumption of negotiations within the EC. In an informal meeting held in San Sebastian in Spain in May 1989, the Ministers of Justice of the EC States decided that discussions should restart with a view to achieving an EC bankruptcy convention, which was required by the growing economic interdependence between the countries of the Community and the completion of the internal market. For this purpose, it was later decided to set up an *ad hoc* working party and to appoint a permanent chairman (Dr Manfred Balz of Germany). The work actually started in mid-1990. A questionnaire on guidelines for a bankruptcy convention was circulated among the delegations of experts representing EC governments. Following the answers given and after taking into account the results achieved in the Council of Europe, a preliminary draft Convention was drawn up by the permanent chairman with the assistance of the General Secretariat of the Council (this is a special case where the Commission participates in the discussions but without having the right of initiative to propose a draft for the basis of discussion). The draft text was supplemented by an explanatory memorandum which outlined its principles.

The preliminary draft Convention on Insolvency Proceedings has a total of 42 (now 45) articles divided into the following six (now five) chapters:

- Chapter I — scope and general provisions;
- Chapter II — recognition of the insolvency proceedings;
- Chapter III — secondary insolvency proceedings;
- Chapter IV — information of the creditors and the lodging of their claims;
- Chapter V — interpretation by the EC Court of Justice (now deleted and replaced by two protocols — *see* **1.2**); and
- Chapter VI — transitional and final provisions.

The draft Convention seeks to offer solutions that are as simple and flexible as possible in this complicated legal area. It does not attempt to create a "European" type of bankruptcy nor to harmonise the laws of the EC States. The purpose is rather to construct legal conditions for handling cross-border bankruptcies in the EC by settling conflicts of laws and jurisdictions. To this end, the main principles are those of universality of the bankruptcy and of direct international jurisdiction. The universality is, however, limited by the opening of one or more sets of secondary proceedings whose effects are, in such cases, confined to the territory of the EC State(s) in which they were opened. This is a clear deviation from the principle of unity which prevailed in the previous EC draft Convention.

The *ad hoc* working party was able to complete a first reading of the draft Convention by the end of January 1992. An amended version was issued in April (*see* **Annex 1**). Since then, a second reading has gone on with a view to reaching a final agreement by the end of 1993 or (more likely) in 1994.

1.4 Main lines of the draft EC Convention

1.4.1 Scope

The title of the draft Convention refers to "insolvency proceedings", which is obviously a broad concept. In Europe (and elsewhere) there is no uniform concept of insolvency; the notion varies from one country to another, as do the criteria applicable to the opening of insolvency proceedings. Therefore a definition broad enough to encompass such proceedings in all their diversity seems appropriate. Article 1 of the draft Convention is largely based on the corresponding provision of the Council of Europe Convention and it provides that:

> "This Convention shall apply to collective insolvency proceedings which entail the disinvestment of the debtor, [the constitution of a debtor's estate] and the appointment of a liquidator, and which may entail the liquidation of the debtor's assets."

It is to be noted that the nationality of the parties is irrelevant; therefore, companies, firms and individuals from countries outside the EC may be caught by the draft Convention. The disinvestment of the debtor is a classic condition, although not mandatory in new kinds of proceedings such as the French *redressement judiciaire* (judicial administration proceedings). It follows from these conditions that compositions with creditors are in principle excluded from the scope of the Convention. Nevertheless, a composition could open or close insolvency proceedings which are themselves covered by the Convention (see Article 3, paragraph 2). The same French law (Law of 25 January 1985 on judicial administration and liquidation) no longer makes any reference to the notion of a debtor's estate (*masse* in French). But the notion should be understood here in the sense (as, eg, in German and Dutch law) of debtors' assets to be used for the collective satisfaction of creditors' claims and not in the sense (traditional in French law) of a meeting of creditors. A precise definition is now given in paragraph 3 of Article 1a, the condition itself (ie the constitution of a debtor's estate) being omitted in the general definition.

The appointment of a liquidator seems self-evident, but this raises the question of proceedings which might not have such a requirement. For example, the draft Law on the Reform of Insolvency legislation (*Gesetzentwurf zur Reform des Insolvenzrechts*) which is under scrutiny in Germany provides for no such appointment, at least during the first stage of the proceedings. The final condition concerning the liquidation of the debtor's assets also leads to peculiar difficulties. Does it mean that the proceedings should inevitably result in the winding-up of the debtor's assets? Such a definition would be much too restrictive. The reforms recently adopted in a number of EC countries break down the proceedings into several stages, the first of which aims at reconstruction and the last at liquidation. A flexible interpretation of Article 1 ("proceedings which *may* entail the liquidation") would allow for the inclusion of all these proceedings. Nevertheless, given the inevitable doubts, it seems necessary to complete the definition by a specific list of the proceedings which would fall under the Convention in each EC State. The list will appear in Annex A of the Convention. Clearly, one of the issues at stake is whether to retain only liquidation proceedings in the narrow sense of the term or to include reconstruction proceedings either wholly or in part. The special case of credit institutions and insurance companies is excluded from the scope of the Convention; in fact specific instruments regarding them are under scrutiny within the EC institutions.

1.4.2 Principle of universality

The starting point of the draft Convention is a system of "controlled" universality (an expression coined by Professor Hans Hanish of Geneva). Proceedings opened in one EC State would have effect throughout the EC within the limits laid down by the Convention itself. When a system is based on the principle of territoriality, it prevents any recognition of a foreign judgment and limits the effects of bankruptcy proceedings to a single country. The disadvantages are obvious and, even if cross-border bankruptcies happen less frequently than purely local ones, the recent trend in a number of national laws is clearly towards universality. In accordance with this principle, the judgment opening the proceedings would be recognised *ipso jure* (without further formalities) in all EC States and would in all of them entail immediate disinvestment of the debtor and allow the bankruptcy to produce its other effects, in particular as regards the powers of the liquidator and the staying of individual creditors' actions. A controlled universality, however, would qualify these results, either by making the opening of proceedings subject to certain conditions such as the possibility of one or more secondary bankruptcies, or by permitting some classes of creditors to press their claims individually. Nevertheless, the principle of universality would result, first, in automatic recognition throughout the EC of the opening of proceedings in accordance with the terms of the Convention (see Article 9) and, second, in direct international jurisdiction (see Article 2). Thanks to this last option, the rules of jurisdiction laid down by the Convention would be mandatory for EC States and supplant national law.

The system of controlled universality involves making a distinction between a "main" bankruptcy and "secondary" ones. It differs from the "parallel bankruptcies" system in which separate insolvency proceedings of universal character could be opened in two or more States, thus being in competition with the situation in another State where no proceedings have been opened. In the system of the draft Convention the main bankruptcy would be the only one to become universal within the EC. The secondary ones would be limited in territorial scope, thus affecting only those of the debtor's assets which were situated in the EC State where the secondary proceedings are opened. But owing to their general recognition, the possibility exists that some effects will result in other EC States, for example if the liquidator in the secondary proceedings claimed assets which had been improperly moved to the territory of another EC State (see Article 9a, paragraph 2).

The criteria applicable to the opening of either a main or a secondary bankruptcy are set out in Article 2 of the draft Convention. The jurisdiction for the opening of a main bankruptcy is that of the centre of the debtor's main interests (this criterion was also used in the Council of Europe Convention). In the case of corporate entities, the registered or statutory office is presumed to be the centre of the main interests. But this presumption may be rebutted, for example where it is proved that the entity's management decisions are taken elsewhere. The courts of an EC State, other than that in which the centre of the debtor's main interests is situated, would only be able to open proceedings having territorial effect. However, this would only be possible if the debtor possesses an establishment (ie a branch without separate legal personality) or other assets in the territory of that EC State. It flows from the most recent draft of the text that secondary proceedings *stricto sensu* only occur when a main bankruptcy has been opened at the same time (or before) within the EC (see Article 2, paragraph 3). In other circumstances, it would be clearer to refer to "separate" proceedings also having territorial effect.

A special case arises where the debtor's centre of main interests lies outside the EC, the opening of a main bankruptcy under the Convention being then out of the question. The concept of "centre of main interests" is taken in a legal and not in an economic sense. In particular, the criterion for a subsidiary is to have its "seat" within the EC even if its parent company's seat is situated outside. But it will still be possible to open separate proceedings in an EC State where the debtor possesses an establishment or other assets. Furthermore, the draft Convention does not prevent an EC State from recognising the proceedings of universal character opened in a non-EC State since the effects of such proceedings are confined to the territory of the former State.

1.4.3 Applicable law

In accordance with the principle of universality, the recognition *ipso jure* of a bankruptcy opened by the court having jurisdiction logically involves the application of the *lex fori concursus* (ie the law of the State where bankruptcy proceedings are opened), for both procedural and substantive rules. The provisions of Article 3 of the draft Convention deal with the matter. Paragraph 1 of this article states the principle that the judge opening the proceedings is to apply his national law including the rules of private international law (PIL). This is true both for main and secondary bankruptcies. On the other hand, these PIL rules have no bearing on any procedural matters, as set out in paragraph 2. The same solution applies as regards paragraph 3, where reference is made to the "national law" (of the State of the court that has jurisdiction), in accordance with the terminology adopted by the Hague Conference on Private International Law. Paragraph 3 deals with some substantive questions, namely: the capacity for the debtor to be declared bankrupt; the composition of the debtor's estate; the determination of the effect of certain legal acts, in particular contracts, affecting the estate; the limits of the powers of the liquidator and the debtor respectively regarding the estate; and any other matter in which creditors may have an interest. As far as this latter aspect is concerned, the possibility of several proceedings (main and secondary ones) should be borne in mind; the ranking of the various debts, as determined by reference to the legal system governing the main proceedings, will be valid in another EC State only if no secondary proceedings have been opened there. This was a major difficulty as regards the unity system (*see* **1.3**). The whole of paragraph 3 is aimed at avoiding conflicts of laws in the main cases where the cross-frontier nature of the proceedings would give rise to uncertainties.

Articles 4 to 8a of the draft Convention result from a similar aim. Their provisions are designed for settling conflicts of laws in well-known tricky situations, for example where particular rights of third parties have to be protected adequately. Article 4, paragraph 1 protects the rights *in rem* of third parties over assets situated in States than other than the one in which the proceedings were opened, at the time when the proceedings were opened. The concept of a right *in rem* is used in a broad sense here: it encompasses special privileges, including the case where the privilege relates to assets (eg of a company) that may fluctuate with time. In other words, the "fixed and floating charges" known in particular in the laws of the United Kingdom are covered. A useful precision as regards registered assets, which are legally linked with the State of registration, is given by paragraph 2 of the same Article 4. According to paragraph 3, the right of a creditor to set off a claim against the debtor's estate is to be determined by the law applicable to the creditor's right and not by the law governing the opening of the bankruptcy proceedings. Article 5 deals with reservation of title clauses. They are treated in the same way as rights of guarantee *in rem* within the meaning of Article 4, paragraphs 1 and 2, which shall apply accordingly. Therefore, the law of the place where the asset is situated (*lex situs*) determines both the validity of the clause and the effects of insolvency on the buyer's property. The system is complemented by the uniform rule (a rare example) laid down in paragraph 2 of the same article (taken over from Italian law), which enables a sale to go ahead normally despite the fact that the seller has became insolvent since delivery; this will prevent the liquidator appointed in the proceedings against the seller from terminating the contract abruptly.

Article 6 states that the law applicable to the effects of the insolvency proceedings on the lessee or lessor in the case of leases of real estate is that of the *lex contractus*. But in the meantime, the tendency seems to revert to the provision set out in the first draft, namely to apply the law of the place where the property is situated along the lines of what Article 4 provides for rights *in rem*. According to Article 7, the effects of the bankruptcy proceedings on employment contracts and, more generally, employment relations between employers and employees is to be governed by the law which governs the contract in question. However, where the law of a non-EC State is involved, the law of the EC State where the proceedings are opened is to apply. Article 8 states that a legal act that is detrimental to the creditor is voidable, unenforceable against creditors or void only where provision is made for such action both under the law of the State in which proceedings have been opened (*lex fori concursus*) and under the law which determines the validity of the legal act (*lex causae*) provided that it is the law of a EC State (otherwise the *lex causae* is not taken into consideration). Finally, Article 8a lays down a conflict rule according to which the effects of insolvency proceedings on litigation are subject to the law of the court in which the litigation is pending (*lex fori*). That law also determines how, by whom and in compliance with which formalities the cases are to be continued. The aim is to avoid conflicts between insolvency and the relevant law of procedure.

1.4.4 Course of proceedings having universal effects (main bankruptcy)

For the sake of clarity, it seems appropriate in the first place to describe how proceedings having universal effects would work under the draft Convention. For these purposes it is to be assumed that only one bankruptcy is opened within the EC, where the debtor's main interests are located (*see* **1.4.2**). The peculiarities of secondary or separate bankruptcies will then be examined. Here the applicable law is mainly the *lex fori concursus* with the exceptions provided for in the draft Convention (*see* **1.4.3**). The first step in the proceedings is the appointment of the liquidator (or receiver), who plays a central role in most legal systems. According to the definition given in Article 1a, paragraph 2, "liquidator" is understood in a broad sense (a list of the professionals concerned in each EC State will be appended to the Convention). The liquidator (where there is only one bankruptcy opened) is permitted to exercise throughout the EC the powers conferred on him by the law of the State in which the proceedings are opened (Article 10, paragraph 1). He does not have to seek a court order in order to exercise these powers in any other EC State: it is sufficient for him to produce evidence of his appointment by an official certificate. The other EC States in which the liquidator is to exercise his powers may only request a translation of the certificate; no legalisation or other similar formality may be required (see Article 11 which reproduces the corresponding provision in the Council of Europe Convention).

This does not mean that third parties have no protection against a liquidator from another EC State misusing his powers. Not only may they ask him to provide evidence of his appointment, but they may also contest his substantive powers in compliance with the law applicable in the State where his powers are contested. Furthermore, in areas falling outside the scope of his powers, the liquidator must observe the rules of substance and procedure in force in the EC State where he wishes to intervene (Article 10, paragraph 3). The draft text cites (but without listing exhaustively) the special procedures for liquidating an asset forming part of the debtor's estate, for example the rules on advertising, the obligation to hold a public sale rather than a private one, etc. With a view to avoiding a potential difficulty, it is expressly stated (in paragraph 1 of Article 10) that the liquidator will have the power to remove the assets from the territory in which they are situated, except where those assets are encumbered by a right *in rem* or other charges (*see* **1.4.3**). Lastly, the liquidator may not perform in another EC State any act which is manifestly contrary to the public policy of that State (this is implied by Art. 18). On the whole, the powers of the liquidator appear much more effective than under the Council of Europe Convention which provides in particular for the suspension of these powers (subject to certain measures for preserving the debtor's estate) for a two-month period in order to allow for the possibility of opening a bankruptcy in other States where the debtor's assets are located.

Specific provisions apply to the situation of creditors, in particular to ensure that all creditors ranking equally are treated equally. Article 12, paragraph 1 makes it compulsory to return to the estate any of the debtor's assets which a creditor has obtained individually in an EC State other than that in which the proceedings were opened. This could have been by means of a payment by the debtor, or by judicial execution, etc (but for what is obtained under other bankruptcy proceedings, *see* **1.4.5**). This rule constitutes an enforcement measure against the creditor who must hand over the asset in kind (or its equivalent in money) to the liquidator. In the interest of creditors and third parties generally, the draft Convention also provides for rights to information. Chapter IV broadly reproduces the corresponding chapter of the Council of Europe Convention on the rights of creditors to be informed about insolvency proceedings and the lodging of their claims. Here, the scope extends more widely than the proceedings defined in Article 1 (*see* **1.4.1**) to include some proceedings which do not always involve a liquidation, in other words to include "reconstruction" proceedings (or "reorganisations"). To avoid any uncertainty, these proceedings will be listed in a specific annex of the Convention. It is compulsory to inform creditors "who have their usual abode, residence or head office" in another EC State of the opening of bankruptcy proceedings in a given State (indeed this could be extended to all foreign creditors). There are also provisions for the lodging of such creditors' claims. As regards languages, Article 34 seeks to reconcile, not without difficulty, the needs of the courts and liquidators on the one hand with the creditors' need for protection on the other hand. In short, each person or body may use their own language but the heading of the document has to be in all EC official languages. In addition, the liquidator may request the publication in any other EC State of "the substance of the judgment opening the insolvency proceedings" (Article 13) and register the proceedings in the land register, the trade register or other public registers (Article 14). It is for the liquidator to decide whether this best serves the interests of the debtor's estate or of legal certainty. But, according to paragraph 2 of both Articles 13 and 14, the possibility exists, subject to certain conditions, for publication to take place automatically without the need for a request from the liquidator.

1.4.5 Consequences of proceedings having territorial effects (secondary or separate bankruptcies)

The structure of the draft Convention is based on the possibility of opening one or more sets of secondary proceedings in addition to the main ones (*see* **1.4.2** on this distinction). Secondary proceedings can be opened in all EC States where establishments or assets of the debtor are situated (Article 20, paragraph 1). However, there are provisions to ensure that only one court has jurisdiction in a given State to open a secondary bankruptcy. It might happen that proceedings which subsequently had only territorial effect were opened before the primary (main) ones (Article 29). Incidentally, it is worth noting that when the debtor's centre of interests lies in a non-EC country, proceedings opened in an EC State could not be considered as secondary ones within the meaning of the draft Convention: they do not fall under the latter (*see* **1.4.2**). In other words, the secondary bankruptcy is characterised by a legal link (arising from the Convention) with the main one, this link being emphasised by using the adjective "secondary" in preference to "satellite" or "parallel" (the same reasons explain the same wording in the Council of Europe Convention; *see also* **1.4.2**).

The opening of the main proceedings *ipso facto* allows secondary proceedings to be opened in any EC State where the debtor has an establishment or assets. It is not necessary to prove the local insolvency of the debtor. According to Article 22, the liquidator in the main proceedings (hereafter, the "main liquidator") has the right to request the opening of secondary proceedings, together with the liquidator(s) appointed in secondary proceedings already opened in another (or other) Member State(s). The persons normally entitled to request the opening of bankruptcy proceedings in the State where the debtor has an establishment or assets also retains this entitlement. However, paragraph 2 of the same article limits the creditors' right to ask for the opening of such proceedings: the creditor must prove that he has a special interest in this regard. This provision is intended to maintain priority for the main proceedings, but it seems clear that preferential creditors in the State in question will always have an interest in requesting the opening of proceedings when their claims rank lower (or even have no preference at all) in the State of the main proceedings (*see* **1.4.3**). Another means of preventing secondary proceedings being opened unnecessarily is offered by the possibility of the court requiring an adequate advance payment on account of costs (or an adequate guarantee), if such a possibility exists under the *lex fori* (Article 23).

In principle, the draft Convention applies to secondary proceedings subject to the exceptions set out in Chapter III. In particular, it flows from Article 3 that application of the *lex fori concursus* is provided for all proceedings falling under the scope of the Convention. Examples have also been given of provisions concerning the liquidator which apply both to main and secondary proceedings. Chapter III provides for links between them which involve close co-operation between the liquidators, with some advantages for the main one. The liquidators are requested to communicate to each other all relevant information (Article 24, paragraph 1). Even if the emphasis is placed on measures designed to terminate the proceedings, this provision is meant to cover both the nature and the rank of the claims lodged, important decisions relating to the administration and disposal of the assets forming part of the estate, as well as any disputes entered into in connection with the proceedings. However, this is limited to legally admissible information since, for example, the communication may be prohibited under data protection rules. Furthermore, the liquidator in the secondary proceedings must consult the main liquidator on the use of the estate, particularly in the event of assets being realised (Article 24, paragraph 2). Therefore, decisions on such matters as whether to continue or cease operations or to put a major asset up for sale cannot be taken without consulting the main liquidator. More specifically, a composition with creditors will not be binding without the main liquidator's prior consent, even if he is obliged to give it where the interests of the creditors in the main proceedings would not be affected by the arrangement (Art. 27).

The main liquidator is also empowered to stay the secondary proceedings for up to three months. The matter is formally referred to the court which opened the secondary proceedings but that court does not have any discretionary powers in the matter, except for recourse to general principles such as the improper use of a right. In any event, the court may reject the stay "if the liquidator manifestly has no legitimate interest in this". Otherwise, the court is obliged to stay the proceedings for such initial period not exceeding three months as is requested by the main liquidator (Article 26, paragraph 1). The aim is to give him sufficient time to reorganise and preserve the affairs of the debtor. This does not necessarily constitute acceptance of reconstruction proceedings, but it is undoubtedly a step in that direction. Economic realities justify giving preference to the main proceedings, opened where the debtor's centre of interests is located, in order to avoid the disadvantages of a hasty liquidation and by providing the best opportunities for effective intervention on behalf of the debtor's undertaking or assets. This should benefit all creditors in the long run; in any case, their rights are simply frozen. The creditors having security *in rem* in the (suspended) secondary proceedings are entitled to receive interest continuously (ie when it is due) on their claims. The main liquidator is permitted to ask for an extension of the initial stay of proceedings for a further period of up to three more months (paragraph 2 of the same article). However, such an extension is not automatic and in order to persuade the court to grant it, the liquidator must establish that the stay of proceedings is in the interests of the estate where the main proceedings are being conducted, so that the estate may be sold off or reorganised. The financial rights of creditors who have lodged claims in the secondary proceedings cannot be prejudiced in any way apart from these additional delays. In this case, the main liquidator is obliged to provide guarantees for the preservation of the value of the estate in the secondary proceedings; he must also continue to pay interest to the same secured creditors. Finally, according to paragraph 3 of Article 26, the main liquidator as well as liquidators and creditors in secondary proceedings are given the right to request termination of the stay of proceedings where the need for it no longer exists.

The system applying to the exercise of creditors' rights in the various proceedings appears rather new. A simple way to deal with the question would have been to pay preferential creditors out of the assets of the debtor's estate who are situated in the territory of the EC State(s) where secondary proceedings are opened and to transfer the surplus assets (if any) to the main proceedings. Unsecured creditors could then be treated equally within the main proceedings. Beside the practical difficulties of this solution, however, it would involve (as in the Council of Europe Convention) drawing up a list of the claims which must firstly be satisfied in the secondary proceedings. In the absence of an agreed list, differences between legal systems would lead to unequal situations. With a view to getting around this difficulty, Article 25 of the draft Convention sets out a rule based on the principle of mutual representation of creditors in each type of proceedings by the liquidators. While lodging a preferential claim appears to be determined by the territory in which the claim is situated, there is no condition attached to lodging an ordinary claim. The creditor can select any of the sets of proceedings that have been opened. Therefore, both the liquidators in the main and secondary proceedings are empowered to lodge (unsecured) claims in the other proceedings. This gives the creditors the practical opportunity of lodging claims collectively through the liquidators. Nevertheless, a creditor can always withdraw the lodging of such a claim.

Equality between creditors remains the general rule (*see* **1.4.4**), in spite of the advantages provided by Articles 4 and 5 in favour of given categories of creditors (*see* **1.4.3**). But the system is also designed to give effective powers to the liquidator. The liquidator will be entitled to exercise the rights attached to claims in the other proceedings in which he represents the creditor. He will have the right to vote in the other proceedings, provided the creditor does not exercise the vote himself or through a specially appointed representative (Article 25, paragraph 2). Where a creditor has lodged his claim in several (main and secondary) proceedings, the various liquidators are required by the same provision to vote in the same way. This means that if a liquidator votes for a proposal and another votes against (or abstains), the voting right of the creditor concerned is not taken into account; the creditor is deemed to be absent. In any event, the liquidator has the right to attend creditor's meetings (Article 25, paragraph 3), irrespective of whether the creditor in question is also present. Nevertheless, in practice it would be no easy task to co-ordinate the proceedings in order to ensure equal treatment of creditors. In this connection, the "imputation rule" laid down in Article 12, paragraph 2 of the draft Convention (based on Art. 5 of the Council of Europe Convention) is helpful . It states that where at least two proceedings have been opened and a creditor has obtained part payment of his claim in one of them, account will be taken of that payment as regards the creditors of the estate in the other proceedings. He may not share in the distribution of the estate until the other creditors have obtained an equivalent dividend in percentage terms. Therefore, the flexible rules laid down as regards the lodging of the various claims could well lead in practice to complicated situations.

1.4.6 Final provisions of the draft Convention

The provisions set out in Chapter V are drawn extensively from the corresponding provisions in the previous Community draft of 1982. It does not seem necessary to comment upon them in this chapter. It is only to be recalled here that the Convention with its two complementary protocols might enter into force between less than 12 EC States, although at least seven ratifications would be required (*see* **1.2**).

Annex 1
Draft EC Bankruptcy Convention
[Text as it stands in 1992]

Preamble

The High Contracting Parties to the Treaty establishing the European Economic Community,

Desiring to implement the provisions of Article 220 of that Treaty by virtue of which they undertook to secure the simplification of formalities governing the reciprocal recognition and enforcement of judgments of courts or tribunals;

Anxious to strengthen in the Community the legal protection of persons therein established;

Considering that it is necessary for this purpose to determine the jurisdiction of their courts or authorities with regard to insolvency proceedings, to create certain uniform conflict rules for such proceedings, to ensure the recognition and enforcement of judgments given in such matters, to make provision for the opening of secondary insolvency proceedings and to guarantee information for creditors and their right to lodge claims;

Have decided to conclude this Convention and to this end have designated as their plenipotentiaries:

His Majesty the King of the Belgians

Her Majesty the Queen of Denmark

The President of the Federal Republic of Germany

The President of the Hellenic Republic

His Majesty the King of Spain

The President of the French Republic

The President of Ireland

The President of the Italian Republic

His Royal Highness the Grand Duke of Luxembourg

Her Majesty the Queen of the Netherlands

The President of the Portuguese Republic

Her Majesty the Queen of the United Kingdom of Great Britain and Northern Ireland who, meeting in the Council, having exchanged their full powers, found in good and due form,

Have agreed as follows:

Chapter 1   General provisions

Article 1   Scope

1. Without prejudice to Article 31, this Convention shall apply to collective insolvency proceedings which entail the disinvestment of the debtor and the appointment of a liquidator, and which may entail the liquidation of the debtor's assets.

2. This Convention shall be without prejudice to the provisions of Community law applicable to special categories of debtors, such as insurance companies and credit institutions.

[*Alternative*:

This Convention shall not apply to insolvency proceedings relating to insurance companies or credit institutions.][1]

Article 1a   Definitions

1. The collective proceedings referred to in Article 1(1), hereinafter referred to as "insolvency proceedings", are listed in Annex A[2], which is an integral part of this Convention.

2. Within the meaning of this Convention, the term "liquidator" means any person or body whose function is to administer or liquidate the debtor's estate or to supervise his activities; these persons or bodies are listed in Annex B (2), which is an integral part of the Convention.

3. Under this Convention the term "estate" covers the totality of the debtor's assets which are sequestrated through the opening of proceedings and which are administered or liquidated by a liquidator and are no longer at the debtor's disposal.

4. Under this Convention the term "court" covers the insolvency court or any other State body which has jurisdiction under the law of a Contracting State to open insolvency proceedings or proceedings within the meaning of Article 31.

Article 2   International jurisdiction

1. The courts of the Contracting State in whose territory the debtor has the centre of his main interests shall have jurisdiction to open insolvency proceedings. For companies and legal persons, unless the contrary is proved, the place of the registered or statutory office shall be presumed to be the centre of their main interests.

2. The courts of a Contracting State which do not meet the conditions of jurisdiction defined in paragraph 1 shall have jurisdiction to open insolvency proceedings the scope of which is confined to those of the debtor's assets which are situated in that Contracting State, where the debtor possesses an establishment or other assets in its territory. (...).

3. Proceedings defined in paragraph 2 shall be secondary insolvency proceedings within the meaning of Chapter III of this Convention if at the time of their opening proceedings are opened in another Contracting State. Where proceedings as defined

---

[1]The decision on the alternative could be made dependent on the progress of the discussions on the relevant Directives.

[2]It is proposed that the negotiations be based on the relevant Annexes to the Council of Europe Convention.

in paragraph 1 are opened after proceedings as defined in paragraph 2 have been opened, Article 29 shall apply.

Article 3 Applicable law

1. Except as otherwise provided in this Convention, the insolvency law applicable to insolvency proceedings and their effects is that of the Contracting State in whose territory those proceedings have been opened or are to be opened.

2. The law of the State where the insolvency proceedings have been opened shall determine the conditions for the opening and closure of those proceedings, in particular by a composition, as well as their administration.

3. In addition, the national law of the State in which proceedings have been opened shall determine in particular:

(a) whether insolvency proceedings can be brought against the debtor on account of his capacity;
(b) which part of the debtor's assets belongs to the estate and whether assets acquired after the opening of proceedings belong to that estate;
(c) the substantive and procedural powers and rights of the liquidator and the debtor respectively, vis-à-vis the estate;
(d) under which conditions set-offs may be enforceable vis-à-vis the estate;
(e) the effects of proceedings on current contracts to which the debtor is party;
(f) which claims shall be lodged as claims of creditors in bankruptcy or considered to be claims in respect of debts incurred by the debtor's estate;
(g) the distribution of the estate amongst the creditors, in particular according to the respective rankings of their debts and whether a creditor who obtains partial satisfaction after the proceedings have been opened on the basis of a right *in rem* or as a result of a set-off is taken into consideration on the basis of his original or the remaining part of his claim;
(h) the conditions for the closure of the insolvency proceedings, in particular the conditions for a composition closing the proceedings;
(i) creditors' rights after the closure of proceedings;
(j) the legal or official procedures and the rules applicable to the lodgement, verification and allowance of claims.

Article 4 Right *in rem* of third parties: set-off

1. The opening of insolvency proceedings shall not affect the rights *in rem* or other charges of third parties over assets which form part of the estate, where those assets are not situated in the territory of the State in which proceedings have been opened, at the time they were opened.

2. Where the asset is registered in a public register, it shall be deemed to be situated in the State in which the register is kept.

3. The opening of insolvency proceedings shall not affect the right of creditors to set off a claim against the estate where the law of a Contracting State other than that in which proceedings have been opened applies to that claim.

Article 5 Reservation of title

1. Article 4(1) and (2) shall apply accordingly in respect of the validity of reservation of title in insolvency proceedings concerning the buyer's assets and in respect of the effects of such proceedings on the buyer's property.

2. In the event of insolvency proceedings being brought against the seller after the thing sold has been delivered, the proceedings shall not be a ground for rescinding or terminating the contract and shall not prevent the buyer from acquiring ownership of the thing sold.

Article 6 Leasing of immovable property

The effects of the insolvency proceedings on a lease or tenancy or other contract for letting immovable property shall be governed solely by the law on insolvency proceedings of the State whose law is applicable to the contract.

Article 7 Contract of employment

The effects of the insolvency proceedings on employment contracts and relations shall be governed solely by the law on insolvency proceedings of the contracting State whose law is applicable to the contract of employment.

Article 8 Action to set aside

1. Where a legal act would be detrimental to creditors, that act, together with any contract establishing it, is only to be considered as voidable, unenforceable against creditors or void where provision is made for such action not only under the insolvency law of that State in which the proceedings were opened but also under that Contracting State's law which determines the validity of the legal act.

2. Where the insolvency proceedings are opened in a Contracting State whose courts have jurisdiction only by virtue of Article 2(2), action to void, declare unenforceable against creditors or void shall lie only insofar as the debtor's assets situated in that State have been injured.

Article 8a Effect of the insolvency proceedings on lawsuits

Solely the law of the State in which the lawsuit is pending shall apply as regards the effects of the insolvency proceedings on a lawsuit pending in connection with assets forming part of the estate.

Chapter II Recognition of the insolvency proceedings

Article 9 Principle

1. The opening of insolvency proceedings by the courts of a Contracting State which have jurisdiction pursuant to Article 2 shall be recognised and shall take effect on the territory of all the other Contracting States from the time that the judgment becomes effective in the State where the proceedings are opened. This shall also apply where on account of his capacity insolvency proceedings could not be brought against the debtor in the other Contracting States.

2. Recognition of insolvency proceedings opened by the competent courts of a Contracting State pursuant to Article 2(1) shall not preclude the opening of other insolvency proceedings by the competent courts in other Contracting States pursuant to Article 2(2). These insolvency proceedings shall be secondary insolvency proceedings within the meaning of Chapter III of this Convention.

Article 9a Effects of recognition

1. Except as otherwise provided in this Convention, recognition of insolvency proceedings opened pursuant to Article 2(1) shall result in the extension, with no further formalities, to the other Contracting States of the effects which the law of the

State where proceedings have been opened imputes to insolvency proceedings, provided that proceedings as defined in Article 2(2) are not opened in those States.

2. Recognition of insolvency proceedings opened pursuant to Article 2(2) shall mean that the effects of proceedings may not be challenged in other Contracting States. Where the debtor in such insolvency proceedings is granted a stay, discharge or other restriction of the creditors' rights, they shall have an effect on the assets situated in other Contracting States only in the case of those creditors who have expressly agreed to the restriction of their rights.

Article 10 Powers of the liquidator

1. The liquidator in proceedings opened pursuant to Article 2(1) has the right to exercise in the other Contracting States, provided that proceedings as defined in Article 2(2) have not been opened in those States, all the powers conferred on him by the law of the State in which proceedings have been opened. He may in particular remove the assets belonging to the estate from the territory of the State in which they are situated, except where those assets are encumbered by a right within the meaning of Article 4 or 5.

2. The liquidator in proceedings opened pursuant to Article 2(2) may in particular, in the other Contracting States, claim through the courts, or out of court that movable property situated there has been removed from the State in which proceedings have been opened after those proceedings started or that a legal act by the debtor is voidable, unenforceable against creditors or void pursuant to Article 8(2).

3. In exercising his powers, the liquidator shall comply with the law of the Contracting State in whose territory he wishes to take action. Should special procedures be required to liquidate an asset forming part of the estate, those procedures shall be determined by the law of the Contracting State in whose territory the asset is situated.

Article 10a Right of request of the liquidator

The liquidator in proceedings opened pursuant to Article 2(1) or (2) shall be empowered to request the opening of insolvency proceedings in another Contracting State.

Article 11 Proof of the appointment of the liquidator

The appointment of the liquidator shall be evidenced by a certified copy of the original decision appointing him or by an official certificate of appointment issued by the court which opened the insolvency proceedings. A translation in the official language or one of the official languages of the Contracting State where the liquidator exercises his powers may be required. No legalisation or other similar formality shall be required.

Article 12 Return: imputation

1. Where a creditor obtains out of the estate in proceedings opened pursuant to Article 2(1) part of the debtor's assets situated in a Contracting State other than that in which proceedings have been opened, by means of the debtor partially honouring his obligation, compulsory enforcement or in any other way after the start of those proceedings, he must return to the liquidator what he has obtained.

2. A creditor shall be entitled to keep what he has obtained under insolvency proceedings opened in another Contracting State. He shall not, however, participate in the distribution of the estate until the other creditors with the same ranking have obtained equivalent dividend; the distribution shall not take into account what the creditor has obtained in accordance with rights *in rem*, or by lawful set-off.

Article 13 Publication
1. At the liquidator's request, the substance of the judgment opening the insolvency proceedings and, where it is the subject of a separate decision, the substance of the judgment appointing the liquidator shall be published in the other Contracting States in due form as provided by each of them. The publication shall specify, in addition, whether the jurisdiction of the courts of the State in which proceedings are opened is based on Article 2(1) or Article 2(2).

2. The law of a Contracting State may provide that the publication take place automatically where the debtor has an establishment in that Contracting State and where proceedings as defined in Article 2(1) have been opened in another Contracting State insofar as the publication serves the interests of the bankrupt's estate or of legal certainty.

Article 14 Registration in a public register
1. At the liquidator's request, insolvency proceedings opened by a court in a Contracting State which has jurisdiction in accordance with Article 2(1) shall be registered in the land register, the trade register or other public registers in other Contracting States, insofar as this serves the interests of the bankrupt's estate or of legal certainty.

2. The law of a Contracting State may provide that the registration also take place automatically under the same conditions as those laid down in paragraph 1.

Article 14a Costs
The costs of the publication pursuant to Article 13 and of the registration pursuant to Article 14 shall be borne by the estate.

Article 15 Honouring of an obligation to the debtor
Where in the territory of a Contracting State an obligation to the debtor has been honoured when it should have been honoured to the liquidator concerned in insolvency proceedings opened in another Contracting State, the person honouring the obligation shall be given a discharge if, at the time of the obligation being honoured, he had not been informed of the opening of proceedings. If he honoured the obligation before the opening of proceedings was published in accordance with Article 13 he shall be presumed, unless the contrary is proved, not to have had knowledge of them. If he honoured the obligation after the publication, it shall be presumed, unless the contrary is proved, that he had been informed of the opening of proceedings.

Article 16 [*deleted, see Article 8a*]

Article 17 Enforceability of judgments
1. Judgments handed down in a Contracting State by the court whose judgment concerning the opening of proceedings is recognised in accordance with Article 9 and which concern the course and closure of the insolvency proceedings shall be recognised and enforced in the other Contracting States without any special procedure being required.

This shall apply in particular

(a) insofar as the judgment of a court which has jurisdiction in accordance with Article 2(1) regarding the opening of insolvency proceedings is, under the law of the State in which proceedings have been opened, also enforceable against the debtor, to that enforceable judgment;
(b) to the judgment of a court which has jurisdiction in accordance with Article 2 vis-à-vis the persons involved in the proceedings concerning the collecting of evidence or the obtaining of information;
(c) to compositions terminating insolvency proceedings which have been approved by a court which has jurisdiction in accordance with Article 2(1).

2. The recognition and enforcement of judgments other than those referred to in paragraph 1 are subject to the Convention on Jurisdiction and the Enforcement of Judgments in Civil and Commercial Matters, even if the judgment is delivered by the court which opened the insolvency proceedings.

This shall apply in particular to

(a) judgments concerning the voidability, unenforceability or voidness of a legal act which is detrimental to creditors;
(b) judgments concerning the liability of the liquidator or the managers or shareholders of the debtor undertaking;
(c) judgments in a lawsuit concerning assets forming part of the estate;
(d) the enforceable judgments obtained by creditors in insolvency proceedings after termination of the proceedings.

3. The Contracting States shall not be obliged to recognise and enforce a judgment concerning the freedom of the individual.

Article 18 Public policy

Recognition of insolvency proceedings or the enforcement of a judgment handed down in the context of such proceedings may be withheld by a Contracting State where its effects would be manifestly contrary to the public policy of that State.

Chapter III Secondary insolvency proceedings

Article 19

Where insolvency proceedings (main insolvency proceedings) opened by the courts of a Contracting State which have jurisdiction pursuant to Article 2(1) are to be recognised in another Contracting State, insolvency proceedings shall be opened at the admissible request of a person or body empowered to do so in all the other Contracting States the courts of which have jurisdiction pursuant to Article 2(2), in respect of the assets situated in those States (secondary insolvency proceedings), without the insolvency of the debtor or a place of jurisdiction for the insolvency being required in accordance with the law of the other Member States. These types of proceedings shall be governed by Articles 20 to 28 below.

Article 20 Territorial jurisdiction

1. The courts of the Contracting State within the jurisdiction of which an establishment or other assets belonging to the debtor are situated shall have territorial jurisdiction to open secondary proceedings.

2. Jurisdiction based on the presence of an establishment shall preclude that based on the presence of other assets.

3. Where a debtor possesses several establishments in a Contracting State, territorial jurisdiction shall fall exclusively to the court within the jurisdiction of which an establishment is situated, and before which the application was first brought. Where a debtor does not possess an establishment in a Contracting State but possesses other assets there, jurisdiction shall fall exclusively to the court within the jurisdiction of which an asset is situated, and before which the application was first brought.

Article 21 Applicable law [*deleted*]

Article 22 Right to request

1. The opening of secondary insolvency proceedings may be requested by:

(a) the liquidator in insolvency proceedings opened by one of the courts in a Contracting State which has jurisdiction pursuant to Article 2(1) or (2),

(b) any other person or authority granted the right to request the opening of proceedings by the law of the Contracting State within the territory of which the opening of secondary proceedings is requested.

2. A creditor's request shall be admissible only if that creditor has a specific interest in the opening of secondary proceedings, or in particular if he cannot be required to participate in the main proceedings, or if it seems probable that his position in the latter would be considerably less favourable than in the secondary proceedings.

Article 23 Advance payment of costs

Where the law of the Contracting State within the territory of which the opening of secondary proceedings is requested does not permit the opening of such proceedings unless the costs involved are wholly or partially covered by the estate, the courts of that Contracting State may require the applicant to make an adequate advance payment of costs or to provide an adequate guarantee.

Article 24 Duty to communicate information

1. The liquidators in the main and secondary insolvency proceedings shall promptly communicate to each other any legally admissible information which might be relevant to the other proceedings, in particular all measures aimed at terminating any insolvency proceedings.

2. The liquidator in the secondary insolvency proceedings shall give the liquidator in the main insolvency proceedings an opportunity of making proposals with a view to the liquidation or other use of the estate remaining in the secondary proceedings.

Article 25 Exercise of creditors' rights

1. The liquidators in the main and any secondary insolvency proceedings shall be empowered to lodge claims, with the ranking to be attributed to those claims, in the other proceedings when those claims have already been lodged in the proceedings for which they were appointed. The right of a creditor to withdraw such a lodgement of his claim shall not be affected.

2. Where the creditor does not exercise his right to vote in person or through a representative, the liquidator in each of the proceedings shall be empowered to exercise

the right to vote arising out of a claim lodged in the other proceedings. Where a creditor has lodged his claim in several secondary insolvency proceedings and where several liquidators in such proceedings simultaneously claim the right to vote in the main insolvency proceedings, the liquidators may exercise the right to vote only in the same way.

3. The liquidators shall be empowered to participate in the other insolvency proceedings on the same basis as a creditor and in particular to attend creditors' meetings.

Article 26 Stay of the liquidation

1. At the request of the liquidator in the main insolvency proceedings the court which opened the secondary insolvency proceedings shall stay the liquidation in the secondary insolvency proceedings for up to three months provided that the liquidator in the main insolvency proceedings accepts continuously to pay the interest to the creditors in the secondary insolvency proceedings affected by the stay insofar as their claims are secured *in rem*. The court may require the liquidator to provide an adequate guarantee. The court may reject the stay if the liquidator manifestly has no legitimate interest in this.

2. A liquidation may be stayed for a further period of up to three months at the request of the liquidator in the main insolvency proceedings where the latter establishes that it is in the interests of the estate in the main insolvency proceedings to do so, the purpose being to allow all or part of the debtor's undertaking to be sold or re-organised. The first and second sentences of paragraph 1 shall apply mutatis mutandis. Moreover, in such cases the liquidator shall provide adequate guarantees that the value of the estate in the secondary insolvency proceedings will not be reduced by the extension of the stay.

3. The stay shall be lifted by the court

— at the request of the liquidator in the main insolvency proceedings;
— at the request of a creditor or a liquidator in the secondary insolvency proceedings when the legitimate interest or the benefits to be expected for the estate from the stay no longer exist.

Article 27 Composition ending the insolvency proceedings

1. Where a composition in the secondary proceedings is provided for in the law applicable to those proceedings:

(a) it may not become final without the prior consent of the liquidator in the main proceedings; however, such consent is not required if the financial interests of the creditors in the main insolvency proceedings are not adversely affected by that composition;
(b) the liquidator in the main insolvency proceedings may himself propose a composition.

2. Should the composition provide that a stay, discharge or any other restriction of creditors' rights shall have effect in respect of the debtor's assets not belonging to the estate in the secondary insolvency proceedings, the composition may enter into force only with the agreement of all the creditors involved.

3. As long as the liquidation is stayed pursuant to Article 26, only the liquidator in the main insolvency proceedings may propose a composition; other proposals for compositions shall neither be put to the vote nor approved.

Article 28   Assets remaining in the secondary insolvency proceedings

1. If by distribution of the estate in the secondary insolvency proceedings it is possible to meet all claims in their entirety, the liquidator shall forthwith pass any asset or other surplus remaining from those proceedings to the liquidator in the main proceedings.

2. This shall also apply where, following a composition to terminate the secondary insolvency proceedings, a portion of the estate has not been used for the reimbursement of creditors in those proceedings.

Article 29   Subsequent opening of the main insolvency proceedings

Where proceedings are opened pursuant to Article 2(1) following the opening of other proceedings in another Contracting State pursuant to Article 2(2), Articles 24 to 28 shall apply to those opened first, insofar as the progress of those proceedings make it necessary to invoke these Articles.

Article 30   Preservation measures

Where in order to preserve the debtor's assets a temporary administrator (receiver) is appointed by the courts of a Contracting State competent to do so pursuant to Article 2(1) before the opening of the main proceedings, that temporary administrator shall be empowered to request in another Contracting State whose courts have jurisdiction to open proceedings pursuant to Article 2(2) that the measures admissible under the law of that Contracting State between the request for the opening of insolvency proceedings and the opening of such proceedings be taken to secure and preserve the debtor's assets.

Chapter IV Information of the creditors and lodgement of their claims

Article 31   Scope of Chapter IV

In addition to the proceedings referred to in Article 1(1), this Chapter shall also apply to collective insolvency proceedings which entail the appointment of a liquidator but which do not lead to the disinvestment of the debtor or entail the liquidation of his assets.

These proceedings are listed in Annex C, which is an integral part of the Convention.[3]

Article 32   Duty to inform the creditors

1. As soon as the proceedings referred to in Article 31 are opened in a Contracting State, the court of that State or the liquidator appointed in it shall promptly and individually inform the known creditors who have their usual abode, residence or head office in the other Contracting States.

2. The information shall be given by a notice containing the appropriate details, in particular as to time limits and measures to be taken. Such a notice shall also indicate whether creditors whose claims are preferential or guaranteed *in rem* need lodge their claims.

---

[3]See n. 2.

Article 33 Lodgement of claims

Any creditor who has his usual abode, residence or head office in a Contracting State other than the State in which the proceedings were opened may lodge his claim in writing with the court or liquidator. The creditor shall send copies of supporting documents, if any, and shall indicate the nature of the claim, the date on which it arose and its amount, as well as whether he is requesting a preference or a guarantee *in rem* in respect of the claim and which assets are covered by the guarantee.

Article 34 Languages

1. The information to be given to creditors in accordance with Article 32 shall be provided in the official language or one of the official languages of the State in which proceedings have been opened. For this purpose a form is to be used bearing the following heading in all the official languages of the Community. "Request to lodge a claim. Please observe any time limits."

2. Any creditor within the meaning of Article 33 may validly lodge his claim in the official language or one of the official languages of the Contracting State in which he has his usual abode, residence or head office. However, the lodgement shall bear the heading "Lodgement of a claim" in the official language or one of the official languages of the State in which proceedings have been opened. The court or the liquidator shall be obliged to provide, if necessary, a translation of the lodgement in the official language or one of the official languages of the State in which proceedings have been opened by the time that the claims are examined, with the costs being charged to the estate.

Chapter V Transitional and final provisions

Article 35 Duration of applicability

The provisions of this Convention shall apply only to proceedings opened after its entry into force. Acts done by a debtor before the entry into force of this Convention shall continue to be governed by the law which was applicable to them at the time they were done.

Article 36 Relationship to other Conventions

1. When this Convention applies, it shall, in respect of the matters referred to therein, supersede, as between the States which are party to it, the following conventions concluded between two or more of those States:

— the Convention between Belgium and France on Jurisdiction and the Validity and Enforcement of Judgments, Arbitration Awards and Authentic Instruments, signed in Paris on 8 July 1899;
— the Convention between Belgium and the Netherlands on Jurisdiction, Bankruptcy, and the Validity and Enforcement of Judgments, Arbitration Awards and Authentic Instruments, signed in Brussels on 28 March 1925;
— Enforcement of Judgments in Civil and Commercial Matters, signed in Rome on 3 June 1930;
— the Convention between the Kingdom of the Netherlands and the Federal Republic of Germany on the Mutual Recognition and Enforcement of Judgments and other Enforceable Instruments in Civil and Commercial Matters, signed in The Hague on 30 August 1962;

— the Convention between the United Kingdom and the Kingdom of Belgium providing for the reciprocal enforcement of judgments in civil and commercial matters, with Protocol, signed at Brussels on 2 May 1934;

— the European Convention on Certain International Aspects of Bankruptcy, signed in Istanbul on 5 June 1990.

2. The conventions referred to in paragraph 1 shall continue to have effect in relation to matters to which this Convention applies, so far as concerns proceedings opened before the entry into force of the latter.

3. This Convention shall not apply:

— in any Contracting State, to the extent that it is irreconcilable with the obligations arising in relation to bankruptcy resulting from another convention concluded by that State with one or more non-Member States before the entry into force of this Convention; and

— in the United Kingdom of Great Britain and Northern Ireland, to the extent that it is irreconcilable with the obligations arising in relation to bankruptcy and the winding-up of insolvent companies resulting from any Commonwealth arrangements which still remain in force at the time of the entry into force of this Convention.

Article 37 Territorial scope

— open —

Article 38 Ratification and entry into force

1. This Convention shall be ratified by the signatory States. The instruments of ratification shall be deposited with the Secretary-General of the Council of the European Communities.

2. This Convention shall enter into force on the first day of the sixth month following the deposit of the instrument of ratification by the last signatory State to take this step.

Article 39 Accession to the Convention

1. The Contracting States recognise that any State which becomes a member of the European Economic Community shall be required to accept this Convention as a basis for the negotiations between the Contracting States and that State necessary to ensure the implementation of the last paragraph of Article 220 of the Treaty establishing the European Economic Community.

2. The necessary adjustments may be the subject of a special convention between the Contracting States of the one part and the new Member State of the other part.

Article 40 Notification by the Council of the European Communities

The Secretary-General of the Council of the European Communities shall notify the signatory States of:

(a) the deposit of each instrument of ratification;
(b) the date of entry into force of this Convention.

Article 41 Protocol to the Convention

The Protocol(s) annexed to this Convention by common accord of the Contracting States shall form (an) integral part(s) thereof.

Article 42 Duration of the Convention

This Convention is concluded for an unlimited period.

Article 43 Revision of the Convention

Any Contracting State may request the revision of this Convention. In this event, a revision conference shall be convened by the President of the Council of the European Communities.

Article 44

1. The Contracting States may announce to the Secretary-General of the Council of the European Communities at any time that they wish to amend Annexes A, B or C.

2. The Secretary-General shall notify the signatory and the Contracting States of the content of that announcement. The desired amendment shall be deemed accepted if none of the notified States raises objections within three months of the date of notification. The amendment shall enter into force on the first of the following month.

Article 45 Deposit of the Convention

This Convention, drawn up in a single original in the Danish, Dutch, English, French, German, Greek, Irish, Italian, Spanish and Portuguese languages, all ten texts being equally authentic, shall be deposited in the archives of the Secretariat of the Council of the European Communities. The Secretary-General shall transmit a certified copy to the Government of each signatory State.

In witness whereof, the undersigned Plenipotentiaries have hereunto set their hands.

Done at   , this

First protocol

on the interpretation by the Court of Justice of the European Communities of the Convention on Insolvency Proceedings, opened for signature   in   on

THE HIGH CONTRACTING PARTIES TO THE TREATY ESTABLISHING THE EUROPEAN ECONOMIC COMMUNITY,

HAVE DECIDED to conclude a Protocol conferring jurisdiction on the Court of Justice of the European Communities to interpret that Convention, and to this end have designated as their Plenipotentiaries;

HIS MAJESTY THE KING OF THE BELGIANS:

HER MAJESTY THE QUEEN OF DENMARK:

THE PRESIDENT OF THE FEDERAL REPUBLIC OF GERMANY:

THE PRESIDENT OF THE HELLENIC REPUBLIC:

HIS MAJESTY THE KING OF SPAIN:

THE PRESIDENT OF THE FRENCH REPUBLIC:

THE PRESIDENT OF IRELAND:

THE PRESIDENT OF THE ITALIAN REPUBLIC:

HIS ROYAL HIGHNESS THE GRAND DUKE OF LUXEMBOURG:

HER MAJESTY THE QUEEN OF THE NETHERLANDS:

THE PRESIDENT OF THE PORTUGUESE REPUBLIC:

HER MAJESTY THE QUEEN OF THE UNITED KINGDOM OF GREAT BRITAIN AND NORTHERN IRELAND:

WHO, meeting within the Council of the European Communities, having exchanged their full powers, found in good and due form,

HAVE AGREED AS FOLLOWS:

Article 1

The Court of Justice of the European Communities shall have jurisdiction to give rulings on the interpretation of:

(a) the Convention on Insolvency Proceedings, opened for signature in   on   , hereinafter referred to as "the   Convention",

(b) the Conventions on accession to the   Convention by the States which have become Members of the European Communities since the date on which it was opened for signature,

(c) Annexes A, B and C thereto,

(d) this Protocol.

Article 2

Any of the courts referred to below may request the Court of Justice to give a preliminary ruling on a question raised in a case pending before it and concerning interpretation of the provisions contained in the instruments referred to in Article 1 if that court considers that a decision on the question is necessary to enable it to give judgment:

(a) — in Belgium:
   la Cour de cassation (het Hof van Cassatie) and le Conseil d'Etat (de Raad van State),
— in Denmark:
   Højesteret,
— in the Federal Republic of Germany:
   die obersten Gerichtshöfe des Bundes,
— in Greece:
   Τα ανφτατα Διυιαστηρια
— in Spain:
   el Tribunal Supremo,
— in France:
   la Cour de cassation and le Conseil d'Etat,
— in Ireland:
   the Supreme Court,
— in Italy:
   la Corte suprema di cassazione and il Consiglio di Stato,
— in Luxembourg:
   la Cour Supérieure de Justice, when sitting as Cour de Cassation,
— in the Netherlands:
   de Hoge Raad,
— in Portugal:
   o Supremo Tribunal de Justiça and o Supremo Tribunal Administrativo,
— in the United Kingdom:
   the House of Lords and other courts from which no further appeal is possible;

(b) the courts of the Contracting States when acting as appeal courts.

Article 3

1. Where a question of interpretation of the Convention or of one of the other instruments referred to in Article 1 is raised in a case pending before one of the courts listed in Article 2(a), that court shall, if it considers that a decision on the question is necessary to enable it to give judgment, request the Court of Justice to give a ruling thereon.

2. Where such a question is raised before any court referred to in Article 2(b) that court may, under the conditions laid down in paragraph 1, request the Court of Justice to give a ruling thereon.

Article 4

1. The competent authority of a Contracting State may request the Court of Justice to give a ruling on a question of interpretation of the provisions contained in the instruments referred to in Article 1 if judgments given by courts of that State conflict with the interpretation given either by the Court of Justice or in a judgment of one of the courts of another Contracting State referred to in Article 2. The provisions of this paragraph shall apply only to judgments which have become *res judicata*.

2. The interpretation given by the Court of Justice in response to such a request shall not affect the judgments which gave rise to the request for interpretation.

3. The Procurators-General of the Supreme Courts of Appeal of the Contracting States, or any other authority designated by a Contracting State, shall be entitled to request the Court of Justice for a ruling on interpretation in accordance with paragraph 1.

4. The Registrar of the Court of Justice shall give notice of the request to the Contracting States, to the Commission and to the Council of the European Communities; they shall then be entitled within two months of the notification to submit statements of case or written observations to the Court.

5. No fees shall be levied or any costs or expenses awarded in respect of the proceedings provided for in this Article.

Article 5

1. Except where this Protocol otherwise provides, the provisions of the Treaty establishing the European Economic Community and those of the Protocol on the Statute of the Court of Justice annexed thereto, which are applicable when the Court is requested to give a preliminary ruling, shall also apply to any proceedings for the interpretation of the instruments referred to in Article 1.

2. The Rules of Procedure of the Court of Justice shall, if necessary, be adjusted and supplemented in accordance with Article 188 of the Treaty establishing the European Economic Community.

Article 6

This Protocol shall be subject to ratification by the Signatory States. The instruments of ratification shall be deposited with the Secretary-General of the Council of the European Communities.

Article 7

1. To enter into force, this Protocol must be ratified by seven States in respect of which the   Convention is in force. This Protocol shall enter into force on the first day of the third month following the deposit of the instrument of ratification by the last such State to take this step. If, however, the Second Protocol conferring on the Court of Justice of the European Communities certain powers to interpret the Convention on Insolvency Proceedings opened for signature in   on   , concluded in   , on   , enters into force on a later date, this Protocol shall enter into force on the date of entry into force of the Second Protocol.

2. Any ratification subsequent to the entry into force of this Protocol shall take effect on the first day of the third month following the deposit of the instrument of ratification, provided that the ratification, acceptance or approval of the Convention by the State in question has become effective.

Article 8

The Secretary-General of the Council of the European Communities shall notify the Signatory States of:

(a) the deposit of each instrument of ratification;
(b) the date of entry into force of this Protocol;
(c) any designation communicated pursuant to Article 4(3);
(d) any communication made pursuant to Article 9.

Article 9

The Contracting States shall communicate to the Secretary-General of the Council of the European Communities the texts of any provisions of their laws which necessitate an amendment to the list of courts in Article 2(a).

Article 10

This Protocol shall have effect for as long as the   Convention remains in force under the conditions laid down in Article 38 of that Convention.

Article 11

Any Contracting State may request the revision of this Protocol. In this event, a revision conference shall be convened by the President of the Council of the European Communities.

Article 12

This Protocol, drawn up in a single original in the Danish, Dutch, English, French, German, Greek, Irish, Italian, Portuguese and Spanish languages, all ten texts being equally authentic, shall be deposited in the archives of the General Secretariat of the Council of the European Communities. The Secretary-General shall transmit a certified copy to the Government of each Signatory State.

Second protocol

conferring on the Court of Justice of the European Communities certain powers to interpret the Convention on Insolvency Proceedings, opened for signature in   , on

THE HIGH CONTRACTING PARTIES TO THE TREATY ESTABLISHING THE EUROPEAN ECONOMIC COMMUNITY,

WHEREAS the Convention on Insolvency Proceedings, opened for signature in   on   , hereinafter referred to as "the   Convention", will enter into force after the deposit of the seventh instrument of ratification, acceptance or approval;

WHEREAS the uniform application of the rules laid down in the   Convention requires that machinery to ensure uniform interpretation be set up; whereas to that end appropriate powers should be conferred upon the Court of Justice of the European Communities, even before the   Convention enters into force with respect to all the Member States of the European Economic Community,

HAVE DECIDED to conclude this Protocol and to this end have designated as their Plenipotentiaries:

HIS MAJESTY THE KING OF THE BELGIANS:

HER MAJESTY THE QUEEN OF DENMARK:

THE PRESIDENT OF THE FEDERAL REPUBLIC OF GERMANY:

THE PRESIDENT OF THE HELLENIC REPUBLIC:

HIS MAJESTY THE KING OF SPAIN:

THE PRESIDENT OF THE FRENCH REPUBLIC:

THE PRESIDENT OF IRELAND:

THE PRESIDENT OF THE ITALIAN REPUBLIC:

HIS ROYAL HIGHNESS THE GRAND DUKE OF LUXEMBOURG:

HER MAJESTY THE QUEEN OF THE NETHERLANDS:

THE PRESIDENT OF THE PORTUGUESE REPUBLIC:

HER MAJESTY THE QUEEN OF THE UNITED KINGDOM OF GREAT BRITAIN AND NORTHERN IRELAND:

WHO, meeting within the Council of the European Communities, having exchanged their full powers, found in good and due form,

HAVE AGREED AS FOLLOWS:

Article 1

1. The Court of Justice of the European Communities shall, with respect to the Convention, have the jurisdiction conferred upon it by the First Protocol on the interpretation by the Court of Justice of the European Communities of the Convention on Insolvency Proceedings, opened for signature in   , on   , concluded in   , on   . The Protocol on the Statute of the Court of Justice of the European Communities and the Rules of Procedure of the Court of Justice shall apply.

2. The Rules of Procedure of the Court of Justice shall be adapted and supplemented as necessary in accordance with Article 188 of the Treaty establishing the European Economic Community.

Article 2

This Protocol shall be subject to ratification by the Signatory States. The instruments of ratification shall be deposited with the Secretary-General of the Council of the European Communities.

Article 3

This Protocol shall enter into force on the first day of the third month following the deposit of the instrument of ratification of the last Signatory State to complete that formality.

Article 4

This Protocol, drawn up in a single original in the Danish, Dutch, English, French, German, Greek, Irish, Italian, Portuguese and Spanish languages, all ten texts being equally authentic, shall be deposited in the archives of the General Secretariat of the Council of the European Communities. The Secretary-General shall transmit a certified copy to the Government of each Signatory State.

2

A Comparison of Bankruptcy Reorganisation in the US with the Administration Procedure in the UK

Jay Lawrence Westbrook

Bernard J. Ward Professor of Law at The University of Texas, Austin, Texas, USA

The distinguished American judge Learned Hand once commented that being a litigant in our courts was worse than anything short of sickness or death. That remark may capture the feelings of a British lawyer, accountant, or business person ensnared in a Chapter 11 reorganisation proceeding in the United States. Yet the United Kingdom has recently adopted its own salvage procedure, administration, which is based in significant part on the Chapter 11 experience in the United States.

During my recent appointment as a visiting member of the faculty of Queen Mary and Westfield College, I had the unique opportunity to compare Chapter 11 reorganisation and UK administration. I taught an LL M course in comparative and international corporate insolvency with a fine scholar and exemplary teacher, Harry Rajak of King's College. At his suggestion, under the able chairmanship of Mr Justice Hoffmann, I gave a lecture comparing the two systems. The editors have asked me to summarise here the principal points presented. What follows is necessarily oversimplified and incomplete, but it will provide an overview.

A comparison of administration and reorganisation requires a familiarity with each, at least in broad outline. I will start with a brief summary of Chapter 11.

2.1 Basics of Chapter 11 reorganisation

All insolvency proceedings in the United States, both individual and corporate, are called "bankruptcies" and are filed in Federal Bankruptcy Court under Title 11 of the United States Code. These specialised courts are "adjuncts" to the Federal District Courts located throughout the country and they vary greatly in bankruptcy caseloads and expertise.

Current Issues in Cross-Border Insolvency and Reorganisations (E. B. Leonard, C. W. Besant, eds.; 1–85333–958–X; © International Bar Association; pub. Graham & Trotman/International Bar Association, 1994; printed in Great Britain), pp. 33–40.

A Chapter 11 bankruptcy proceeding — a "reorganisation" — is almost always begun by a voluntary petition filed by the corporate debtor ("the debtor"). The pre-petition management of the debtor will generally remain in control throughout the proceeding, although legally transformed into a quasi-trustee in bankruptcy and called the debtor in possession (DIP). There are no statutory tests or conditions upon the filing of a Chapter 11 petition — for example, no requirement of insolvency. Nevertheless, a case can be dismissed early on if filed in bad faith or without reasonable hope of success.

A successful Chapter 11 generally results in a plan of reorganisation agreed by a majority of creditors. The plan sometimes contemplates a sale of the business, but much more often provides for continuation of the business with a composition and extension of its debts. Creditors often receive equity positions in the company as part of the reorganisation, but pre-existing owners regularly retain at least a portion of the ownership. The key steps in a typical Chapter 11 after a petition is filed are as follows:

(a) Automatic stay
The filing establishes a moratorium upon any act to collect against the debtor or its property. Even a demand letter may constitute contempt of court. Any such action taken in unknowing violation of the stay is not punishable, but is generally void.

(b) Post-petition financing
The debtor often seeks new financing immediately, frequently from its pre-existing principal lender. Often the post-petition lender receives important priorities and/or liens.

(c) Stay litigation
Secured creditors and landlords, among others, will quickly go to court seeking to lift the automatic stay so as to foreclose or evict. They will succeed unless the bankruptcy court finds that the debtor has provided them with "adequate protection" of their property interests. That protection typically consists of periodic payments. It is the debtor who must initiate court action to get permission to use cash that is subject to a lien, called "cash collateral". These issues are often resolved by an agreement approved by the court.

(d) Creditors' committee
In larger cases, a committee is appointed consisting of the seven largest creditors, with adjustments as necessary for fair representation of creditors generally. The committee has important information and negotiation roles and influences court decisions, but has a few formal powers.

(e) Business reorganisation
A DIP routinely closes or sells certain divisions, lays off employees, repositions the business and re-negotiates its labour contracts. Although the DIP is entitled to run the business "in the ordinary course" without court approval, it must get approval for major decisions like substantial asset sales, and creditors have an opportunity to oppose court approval. The DIP is required to file elaborate financial schedules at or shortly after the filing of the petition and to make periodic financial reports to the court.

(f) Negotiation
The DIP will negotiate with creditors to obtain a consensual plan, usually working through the Creditors' Committee, if one has been appointed. For at least the first four to six months of the proceeding, only the DIP can propose a plan and this "exclusive period" is often extended. Thereafter, any creditor may propose a plan.

(g) Solicitation and voting
The DIP solicits creditor approval by mail in most cases, sending creditors a disclosure document that has been approved by the court after notice to creditors. Voting is by classes of creditors. These classes are created by the plan itself and the DIP has considerable, although not unlimited, flexibility in dividing creditors into classes in a way most likely to produce a favourable result. Approval requires a majority in number and two-thirds in amount of each class.

(h) "Cramdown"
Section 1129(b) details circumstances in which a plan may be approved by the court — "confirmed" — over the objection of a particular class of creditors. Generally, a secured class may be "crammed down" if it receives the value of its collateral plus interest over time, while an unsecured class may insist that the equity owners receive nothing if a plan is to be approved over its objection. But the latter rule is subject to an important "new value" exception explained in *In Re Ablers* (108 S Ct 963 (1988)).

(i) Best interests and feasibility
Objecting creditors are also protected by the "best interest" test, which requires a finding that each objecting creditor will receive at least as much under the plan as it would in liquidation; and by the "feasibility" test, which requires a finding that the debtor is reasonably likely to be able to perform the promises it has made in the plan.

(j) Discharge
Confirmation of a plan by the court discharges the debtor from all legal obligations not specified in the plan, with almost no exceptions. The discharge applies to contingent and unmatured claims of all kinds.

2.2 Principal similarities between administration and reorganisation
The Cork Report suggests that the administration procedure was inspired at least in part by Chapter 11 and the two procedures have some important principles in common.

(a) Preservation of going concern values
Both types of proceedings have as a principal *raison d'etre*, the preservation of going concern values, which are likely to be much greater than liquidation values.

(b) Moratorium
Both provide breathing room for a beleaguered business and give at least some power to delay repossessions and evictions pending a possible salvage.

(c) Buying out secured creditors
Both systems permit the liquidation of a secured creditor's position based on payment to it of the value of its collateral, at least under certain circumstances.

2.3 Principal differences between administration and reorganisation

The list of differences is considerably longer.

2.3.1 Cultural differences

While I spend less space under this heading than I did in my lecture, it is absolutely necessary to mention key cultural differences, understanding culture to embrace the commercial and business culture as well as the larger societal culture. These cultural differences provide the indispensable context for the legal rules.

(a) The role of the banks

When the principal lender to a British company is a bank that has a floating charge (or, today, a fixed and floating charge), by far the greatest difference between administration and reorganisation is in the rights of that lender and its role in the debtor's affairs. As I noted in my lecture, if an American banker is very, very good, when he dies he will go to the United Kingdom. British banks have far more control than an American secured lender could ever hope to have. Receiverships on the British model are unknown and almost unthinkable in the US. A US banker could barely imagine a banker's Valhalla in which a bank could veto a reorganisation as a UK bank may effectively veto an administration by appointing an administrative receiver.

Subject to the caveats that must attend all cultural generalisations, it seems to me that the British assume that banks will do everything possible to save a business prior to formal proceeding, while American businesses regard banks as uncertain and fickle business allies at best. There are a number of related cultural and historical factors I would mention on another occasion, including an abiding populism in US, but the result is that banks, and other secured lenders, have far less power in a reorganisation than in a proposed administration.

(b) The role of the debtor

In the US a variety of factors, including a deep emotional commitment to the entrepreneurial ethic, make the owners of the corporation central to a salvage proceeding. In the UK, the prevailing view seems to be that the prior owners were the ones whose venality or incompetence created the problem and their interests virtually disappear from moral or legal consideration once a formal proceeding has begun. Americans are much more willing to believe that financial difficulty is the result of external forces and that preservation of the company, not just the business, is a crucial social concern.

(c) Sale versus composition

United Kingdom administrations have almost always resulted in sale of the company. Sale of the business is the central goal in the minds of most experts in UK insolvency practice. United States reorganisations sometimes result in sale of the company to a third party, but they far more often result in an agreed composition between the company and its creditors, with the old equity owners retaining at least some ownership and management being the same as before or in appointed succession from old management and old equity. A US reorganisation expert expects an agreed composition as the routine result of a reorganisation. Because it is hard to believe that any economic factor would make the markets for troubled companies grossly different in the two countries, it seems likely that cultural differences are the explanation for this profound difference in mental set.

(d) Decentralisation
Britons are accustomed to insolvency proceedings supervised by a very sophisticated Company Court and administered by highly expert accountants and lawyers, often from the heights of the City. As with so many other things, bankruptcy in the US is a largely local phenomenon, a proposition only somewhat tempered by the concentration of many really large cases in the southern district of New York (Manhattan).

(e) Lawyers versus accountants
Insolvency in the US is dominated by lawyers, like so much else in US business life. Accountants play an important role in US bankruptcies, but have nothing like the central position they enjoy in the UK.

(f) Sanctity of contract versus third party protection
The insolvency laws of the two countries, liquidation as well as salvage, have different conceptual bedrocks. The UK lawyer and judge start with the sanctity of contracts and consider what exceptions might arise in insolvency. The US lawyer and judge start with protection of the parties collectively, and of the parties' reliance interests in the marketplace, and tend to regard contract rights as relatively weak as against collective rights and marketplace expectations. US law is far more protective of property rights than of contract rights, but still less protective than UK law.

(g) Commercial versus company law
United States bankruptcy law finds its intellectual origins and contemporary academic residence in commercial law, while corporate insolvency in the UK is very much a part of company law. There is much food for thought in considering the possible effects of these differences and I have not begun to digest them fully. But one consequence, I believe, is the US tendency in bankruptcy matters to think first of third party and marketplace expectations and rights.

2.3.2 Legal differences

In general

(a) The power of secured lenders
A secured lender in a reorganisation has considerable leverage, because of its right to adequate protection, especially for cash collateral, and its frequent role as a post-petition lender, but its position is far less powerful than in the UK.

(b) The role of the pre-existing management and owners
Just as the role of the banks is the most startling feature of UK law for an American, the role of the debtor in possession (DIP) is almost incomprehensible to a British citizen. The DIP has the power to run the business with no more than general court supervision and has great leverage in controlling the outcome of the case. In the UK, the key points to keep in mind about the DIP are these:

(a) the DIP is pre-existing management, not equity ownership, although in a closely held company they may be the same;

(b) the DIP will feel an obligation to negotiate for equity holders, but that commitment is frequently weaker in a large, publicly held company;

(c) the DIP is most often new management appointed after the company's serious financial troubles began, especially in large companies;

(d) increasingly the DIP is a team of corporate-salvage experts employed pre-petition specifically to reorganise the company;

(e) the DIP has virtually the same legal position as a trustee in bankruptcy (TIB), including powers such as the power to avoid a preference, and duties including fiduciary duties to creditors of disclosure and fair dealing; and

(f) United States law has not even begun to resolve the conflicts of interest created by the DIP's duties to adversary parties.

(Oddly enough, the DIP's central role arose largely from the lobbying of the banks, an interesting historical story worth telling on another occasion.)

(c) Court supervision

Administration is almost entirely conducted outside court supervision, while Chapter 11 involves many requirements for court approval upon notice and a hearing to creditors and other interested parties. At least in part this must result from the difference in central goals, sale versus composition, as noted above. A sale of the business as a going concern requires above all, speed and flexibility while an agreed-composition result requires consensus and disclosure. Conversely, an independent administrator means little court control is needed in administration, while DIP control and the possibility of "cramdown" necessitate considerable court protection for creditors in reorganisation. These comparisons are filled with contradiction and paradox, the analysis of which is beyond the scope of this chapter, but they represent crucial differences between administration and reorganisation.

(d) Finality and comprehensiveness

Because of the broad definition of "claim" in section 101(4) of the Bankruptcy Code, and the nearly unlimited discharge given by Chapter 11, a reorganisation represents a complete "fresh start" for a corporate debtor. As the *Manville* (asbestosis) and *Robbins* (Dalkon shield) cases demonstrate, even unliquidated and *unaccrued* liabilities can be restructured and constrained in Chapter 11. Administration permits far more types of claims to remain unaffected by a voluntary arrangement. The US approach makes possible a degree of financial predictability that permits salvage in circumstances where it might be very difficult under UK law both to save the business and to protect future claimants. But the broad relief afforded by Chapter 11 also raises very serious and unresolved questions of due process and of the limits of financial forecasting, both questions being reflected in the current difficulties of the Manville trust.

2.3.3 Specific differences

When we descend from the general to the particular, there are so many differences between the two procedures that it would take a much longer paper to detail them all. It is therefore most useful to touch upon the difference in the process of approval of an arrangement (administration) and a plan (reorganisation).

(a) Approval procedure

A UK voluntary arrangement is approved at one or more meetings, while a US Chapter 11 plan is typically voted upon by mail. There are a number of related procedural differences, including the fact that a creditor's right to vote is determined in the first instance by the chair of the meeting in the UK and by the court under Chapter 11.

(b) Solicitation/notice

Both procedures require that interested parties receive a description of the company's position, financial and otherwise, and an explanation of the proposed agreement.

(c) Majorities required

A UK voluntary arrangement must be approved by two classes, members and unsecured creditors. The required majority for members is one half; for creditors, it is three-quarters in number and one half in amount. Secured and priority creditors cannot be bound without their consent. (In administration, it may be necessary for the arrangement to receive a preliminary approval as part of the administrator's proposal, at which stage only a majority in value of creditors is required). In Chapter 11 there may be many classes, including stockholders and secured creditors. The majority required for each class is more than one-half in number and two-thirds in amount. Acceptance by the requisite majority of a class binds all the members of the class. The exception is priority creditors, who are not bound by class votes and have the special rights set forth in section 1129(a)(9), which ensure they will be paid in full, often before other creditors.

In addition to the binding of a dissenting minority of a class, there are circumstances in Chapter 11 in which a whole class of creditors can be "crammed down", ie, bound by a plan even though the class rejected it. Because there is no division of creditors into classes in UK voluntary arrangements, there is nothing comparable to "cramdown".

(d) Court approval

Every Chapter 11 plan must be "confirmed" by the court as conforming to the detailed requirements of section 1129 of the Code. A voluntary arrangement does not require affirmative action by the court, although it can be challenged by application to the court. Of particular interest is the fact that a Chapter 11 plan must be approved by the court as feasible; a voluntary arrangement does not require this sort of judicial scrutiny. These differences are part and parcel of the larger truth that the US system is closely regulated by the bankruptcy court, while administration relies much more heavily on the discretion of the administrator and the agreement of the creditors.

With respect to the specific problem of protecting minority creditors, a voluntary arrangement may be challenged as "prejudicial to creditors". Under Chapter 11, the principal protection for minority creditors is the "best interests" test, which requires that each objecting creditor gets at least as much through the plain of reorganisation as it would have received in a liquidation.

(e) Post-agreement operations

Following a Chapter 11, the company's management ordinarily continues to run the reorganised entity, although sometimes a creditors' plan provides for outside control of some or all matters. In a voluntary arrangement, a supervisor is in charge of the company.

(f) Finality

Both procedures contemplate a final and complete settlement of outstanding claims. Because of the extraordinarily broad definition of "claims" in section 101 of the Code, the Chapter 11 discharge is virtually absolute; the UK settlement may be somewhat less global, primarily because of claims that may not be provable and creditors who were not given notice.

2.4 Conclusion

Any comparative study of law is enormously helpful on several levels. It is reassuring to know that other countries are struggling with similar problems. The differences in solutions have the salutary effect of forcing upon us a new perspective, one that must make us understand the problem, and the weaknesses of our own solutions, more clearly. Above all, mutual understanding is essential if we are to progress toward the goal of a co-ordination of liquidation and insolvency proceedings of multinational companies and groups.

Notes

US sources: The authoritative multivolume bankruptcy treatise in the US is *Collier on Bankruptcy* (1979). There is a serious lack of single volume scholarly treatises that are up to date. The best one volume summary description of US bankruptcy law is Triester *et al*, *Fundamentals of Bankruptcy Law* (2nd ed., 1988). For a quick, clear, very simplified description of US debtor-creditor law generally, see Epstein, *Debtor-Creditor in a Nutshell* (3rd ed., 1990). With appropriate blushes, I venture also to recommend the Chapter 11 plan section of Warren and Westbrook, *The Law of Debtors and Creditors* (1986) (with supplement, second edition forthcoming). The best way to be current on legislative developments in the field is by membership in the American Bankruptcy Institute, 510 C Street NE, Washington DC 20002.

3

Maxwell Communication Corporation plc: The Importance of Comity and Co-operation in Resolving International Insolvencies

Evan D. Flaschen
Ronald J. Silverman[1]
Hebb & Gitlin, Hartford, Connecticut, USA

3.1 Introduction

The international economy continues to expand, spreading the reach of multinational companies across the globe. Inevitably, some of these same multinational entities become multinational debtors requiring bankruptcy protection. This was the scenario that ensnared Maxwell Communication Corporation plc (MCC) in the autumn and winter of 1991. MCC is an English holding company with more than 400 subsidiaries worldwide primarily engaged in information services and electronic publishing, language instruction and general and consumer publishing. After defaulting under its loan documents with a $2 billion plus banking syndicate, MCC became concerned that the banks might seek the commencement of insolvency proceedings in England, which would effectively displace operating management. In response, MCC, whose United States subsidiaries comprise approximately 75% of the book value of the MCC corporate group, filed a voluntary petition under Chapter 11 of the United States Bankruptcy Code (the "Bankruptcy Code") in the Bankruptcy Court for the Southern District of New York (the "Bankruptcy Court") on 16 December 1991. According to pleadings filed in connection with the Chapter 11 case, MCC's board hoped that the more pro-reorganisation bent of US insolvency law would afford MCC and its management a greater chance of emerging from the process intact. On the following day, MCC obtained an order from the High Court in London (the "High Court"), putting the company into administration under the UK Insolvency Act 1986

[1]Mr Flashen is a member of the Hartford, Conneticut law firm of Hebb & Gitlin and is serving as lead counsel to the Examiner in the Maxwell Communication Corporation plc Chapter 11 proceedings. Mr Silverman is an associate at Hebb & Gitlin .

Current Issues in Cross-Border Insolvency and Reorganisations (E. B. Leonard, C. W. Besant, eds.; 1–85333–958–X, © International Bar Association; pub. Graham & Trotman/International Bar Association, 1994; printed in Great Britain), pp. 41–57.

(the "Insolvency Act"), in order to protect the company from creditors in the UK. At that point, the company was simultaneously engaged in two *primary* bankruptcy proceedings, and thus directly subject to the independent orders of two separate sovereigns.

As far as anyone could determine, this constituted the first instance where a UK company in administration was also engaged in a Chapter 11 case. The opportunities for confusion, chaos and paralysis were self-evident. Indeed, progress in the MCC insolvencies has required the resolution of a multitude of international legal issues, including: co-ordination of simultaneous primary insolvency proceedings, jurisdiction, comity, extraterritoriality and choice of law.

3.2 Co-ordination of simultaneous primary insolvency proceedings

On 20 December 1991, Mark Homan, Colin Bird and Jonathan Phillips of Price Waterhouse (UK) were appointed as joint administrators (the "Joint Administrators") in the administration proceedings by Mr Justice Hoffmann of the High Court. On that same day, in order to reconcile the potential for conflict that existed as a result of the dual proceedings and to facilitate and expedite the reorganisation of MCC, US Bankruptcy Judge Tina L. Brozman appointed Richard A. Gitlin of Hebb & Gitlin to serve as an examiner (the "Examiner") with expanded powers[2] in the Chapter 11 case. Working together, the Joint Administrators and the Examiner searched for a mechanism that would enable the two proceedings and the two insolvency courts to co-exist in a manner that would maximise the value of MCC for parties concerned. Without such a mechanism, the road to rehabilitation of MCC could be blocked by conflicting orders issued by and actions taken in the US and UK courts.

After extensive discussions in New York and London, the Examiner and the Joint Administrators crafted an "Order and Protocol"[3] to provide a blueprint for the co-ordination and harmonisation of the US and UK proceedings. The Order and Protocol was approved and adopted by the High Court on 31 December 1991 and by the Bankruptcy Court on 15 January 1992. In general, the Order and Protocol set forth procedures to carry out their stated objective: that the Examiner and the Joint Administrators will "act to harmonise . . . the Debtor's United States Chapter 11 case and the Administration so as to maximise the Debtor's prospects for rehabilitation and reorganisation". Pursuant to that objective, the parties agreed in the Order that the Joint Administrators would be recognised as the "corporate governance" of MCC in the US and the UK, while the Examiner was charged with reviewing, facilitating and at times consenting to actions taken by the Joint Administrators as MCC's corporate governance.

The Protocol comprises the heart of the agreement between the Examiner and the Joint Administrators as to the day-to-day operation of the MCC group. The Protocol maintained current management of Macmillan Inc ("Macmillan") and Official Airline Guides Inc (OAG) (MCC's most significant subsidiaries), and confirmed that management will, subject to further review, continue to have day-to-day responsibility for overseeing management of Macmillan, OAG and their

---

[2]See ss 1104 and 1106 of the Bankruptcy Code.
[3]Included here as Annex 1.

subsidiaries and affiliates (the "M&O Group"). In addition, the Protocol provides mechanisms whereby the Joint Administrators and the Examiner may select new, independent boards of directors for Macmillan and OAG and may further retain, on a joint basis, an investment banker. The Protocol also recognises the possible need for intermediate holding companies between MCC and the M&O Group to be placed in parallel insolvency proceedings in England and the United States.

The Protocol then addresses various potential transactions of significance respectively involving MCC, the M&O Group and other subsidiaries and affiliates of MCC that are not members of the M&O Group (the "Other Subsidiaries"). With regard to MCC, the Protocol requires the Joint Administrators to make a good faith effort to obtain the Examiner's prior consent and, failing such consent, approval of the Bankruptcy Court when incurring debt or liens, or concerning a proposed conversion to Chapter 7 of the Bankruptcy Code, or for filing a plan of reorganisation within the Bankruptcy Code, section 1121 "exclusivity period". With regard to the M&O Group, the Joint Administrators and MCC must also seek the Examiner's prior consent in connection with such actions.

With regard to the Other Subsidiaries, the Protocol provides substantially different treatment from that provided with respect to MCC or the M&O Group and, depending on the transaction involved, different treatment from that normally required under the Bankruptcy Code. Generally, the Joint Administrators have more discretion over the Other Subsidiaries inasmuch as the Other Subsidiaries are located outside the US and are likely to be sold, and the Joint Administrators asserted that, under English law, they would enjoy such discretion with only very few restrictions.

The Protocol provides, with regard to the Other Subsidiaries, that for bankruptcy filings and for borrowings or asset dispositions of more than £25 million, the Joint Administrators are required both to seek the Examiner's consent and to obtain approval of the Bankruptcy Court. For the exercise of stock voting rights, for commencement of material legal proceedings and for borrowings or asset dispositions between £7 million and £25 million, the Joint Administrators are required to give prior notice to the Examiner, which will enable the Examiner to seek relief in the Bankruptcy Court should the Examiner be opposed to the proposed transaction. The Protocol "pre-authorises" the Joint Administrators to sell assets or incur debt of less than £7 million, so that additional Bankruptcy Court authorisation is not contemplated. For management changes, for financial investigations, and for borrowings or asset dispositions of less than £7 million, the Joint Administrators are merely required to report to the Examiner the details of such transactions on a periodic basis. Finally, the Joint Administrators are required to obtain either prior consent from the Examiner or approval from the Bankruptcy Court before filing a plan of reorganisation for any of the Other Subsidiaries (if they are in Chapter 11) during the relevant exclusivity period.

As contemplated by the Order and Protocol, an indirect subsidiary of MCC, Tendclass Limited ("Tendclass"), the majority owner of Macmillan, did voluntarily file a petition under Chapter 11 of the Bankruptcy Code and was placed into concurrent English administration proceedings. However, disruption in MCC's reorganisation proceedings was avoided as the parties in interest utilised the provisions of the Order and Protocol to enter in the Bankruptcy Court a new order extending the Order and Protocol to Tendclass and further providing (as did Tendclass' UK

Administration Order) that the Examiner and the Joint Administrators would continue their duties as Examiner and Joint Administrators of Tendclass as well.

The Order and Protocol also confers upon the Examiner, beyond certain investigatory and reporting duties, the duty to harmonise, for the benefit of all parties in interest, MCC's Chapter 11 case and administration. In furtherance of those duties, the Examiner is authorised to mediate in disputes over MCC's rehabilitation efforts, as well as being accorded the right, as mentioned above, to be consulted and given the opportunity to respond to certain actions that the Joint Administrators may propose to take in their capacity as MCC's corporate governance (eg material borrowings, material asset pledges or sales, and replacement of directors). In support of such duties and powers, the Order and Protocol affords the Examiner the following general duties and powers:

(a) the status of a "party in interest" for purposes of MCC's Chapter 11 case;
(b) the ability to retain professionals; and
(c) the right to facilitate the process of preparing a plan of reorganisation for MCC.

Perhaps most importantly, the Examiner and the Joint Administrators confirmed in the Protocol that their objective is "for [MCC's] Chapter 11 plan and the Joint Administrators' proposals in the Administration to provide for essentially similar arrangements with respect to MCC and its main subsidiaries". In essence, the Order and Protocol proposed by the Joint Administrators and Examiner and approved by the two courts constitutes something of a bilateral treaty on the international insolvency of MCC.

3.3 Jurisdiction, comity, extraterritoriality and choice of law

In addition to co-ordinating the US and UK insolvency proceedings in order to provide a framework for progress, the Examiner and the Joint Administrators were required to address and resolve legal issues concerning jurisdiction, comity, extraterritoriality and choice of law as the proceedings developed. In one instance, these multiple issues arose together in the context of the pursuit of a potential preferential transfer to one of MCC's largest creditors, Barclays Bank plc ("Barclays").

MCC had entered into a foreign exchange contract with Barclays. On 15 July 1991, MCC defaulted on the foreign exchange contract. When Robert Maxwell died at sea under mysterious circumstances on 5 November 1991, a concerned Barclays attempted to reduce its overall exposure to MCC, which also existed in the form of an overdraft facility with a Barclays branch in London. By October 1991, the facility was overdrawn by US$30 million. Barclays pressured MCC to repay the US$30 million and after several serious letters between Barclays and Kevin Maxwell (one of MCC's directors), MCC repaid the US$30 million to Barclays on 26 November 1991, less than one month before MCC filed its Chapter 11 petition. The monies used to repay the overdraft originated from the sale of Que, the US computer publishing division of Macmillan. The monies were paid to Barclays' branch in New York, which then credited them to MCC's overdrawn account in London.

During the first several months of MCC's insolvency, the Joint Administrators, in consultation with the Examiner, analysed and investigated pre-petition MCC transfers that could be potentially preferential under either the Bankruptcy Code or the Insolvency Act. The transfer to Barclays was readily identified as a potential preference. However, as a pre-emptive strike, Barclays filed for and was granted an *ex parte* injunction in the High Court enjoining MCC and the Joint Administrators from bringing any avoidance action in the United States. In the same action, Barclays also sought to make permanent the injunction and to receive a declaration in the High Court that the US$30 million payment did not constitute a preferential transfer under UK law. In response to this injunction against MCC and the Joint Administrators, the Examiner applied to the Bankruptcy Court for expanded authority to bring preference actions against Barclays if warranted in the event that the injunction was upheld upon due hearing in the High Court. Additionally, the Joint Administrators moved the High Court to dismiss Barclays' application to make the injunction permanent.

The Barclays injunction raised various issues; including: what law should be applied to the preference issue, what forum would be proper; how should the US and UK courts treat decisions and assertions of jurisdiction by the other; and how broad was the scope and reach of US and UK avoidance laws, respectively. These issues were resolved when the High Court issued its decision dismissing the injunction.[4] In so doing, the High Court stressed that the same principles of co-operation, deference and comity behind the Order and Protocol should continue to be emphasised while addressing litigation related international legal issues.

The High Court noted that both US and UK insolvency law asserted extraterritorial, worldwide jurisdiction. Noting the American source (the sale of Que) of the potential preferential transfer, the High Court determined that it would not be unjust or unconscionable for the US court to assert jurisdiction over an avoidance action against Barclays. Accordingly, it should not act to hinder the proceedings of a foreign court. Mr Justice Hoffmann summarised:

> In other words, the normal assumption is that the foreign judge is the best person to decide whether an action in his own court should proceed. Comity requires a policy of non-intervention not only for the same reason that appellate courts are reluctant to interfere with the exercise of a discretion, namely that in the weighing of the various factors, different judges may legitimately arrive at different answers. It is also required because the foreign court is entitled, without thereby necessarily occasioning a breach of international law or manifest injustice, to give effect to the policies of its own legislation.[5]
>
> An English court has no superiority over a foreign court in deciding what justice between the parties requires and in particular, that both comity and common sense suggest that the foreign judge is usually the best person to decide whether in his own court he should accept or decline jurisdiction, stay proceedings or allow them to continue.[6]

The High Court may also have been guided in part by a recognition that the US court could authorise the Examiner to bring the preference action regardless of any English injunction. Indeed, the High Court stated that the injunction "could serve no purpose except to antagonise the US court and prejudice the co-operation which has thus far prevailed between the Chapter 11 and the English Administration".[7]

---

[4]*Barclays Bank plc v Homan, et al (In re Maxwell Communicaton Corp plc)*, slip op., No. 0014001 of 1991 (Ch 28, July 1992).
[5]*Ibid* at pp. 13–14.
[6]*Ibid* at p. 8.
[7]*Ibid* at pp. 15–6.

Barclays appealed the High Court's dismissal of the injunction to the UK Court of Appeal. The Court of Appeal affirmed the High Court's decision,[8] and declared that:

> If the only issue is whether an English or a foreign court is the more appropriate forum for the trial of an action, that question should normally be decided by the foreign court on the principle of forum non conveniens, and the English court should not seek to interfere with that decision [unless pursuit of the action would be vexatious and oppressive. Yet even then] . . . account must be taken of the possible injustice to the defendant if the injunction be not granted, and the possible injustice to the plaintiff if it is. In other words, the English court must seek to strike a balance.[9]

In issuing their decisions, the High Court and the Court of Appeal firmly stressed the importance of promoting harmony between the two insolvency proceedings, even if that harmony required deference to the Bankruptcy Court.

On the American side of the Atlantic, in connection with proceedings related to but independent of the MCC case, Judge Brozman similarly underscored the importance of comity and judicial co-operation in the resolution of multinational insolvencies. Prior to MCC's filing, Headington Investments Ltd ("Headington"), the parent company of the chain of companies privately controlled by the Maxwell family, filed for administration in the UK, and on 5 December 1991 administrators were appointed in the Headington case. The Headington administrators filed a section 304 petition[10] in the Bankruptcy Court in order to conduct discovery regarding the location of Headington property in the United States and stay certain lawsuits against Headington pending in New York State Court.

In a written decision,[11] Judge Brozman for the most part permitted the relief requested by the section 304 petition. Emphasising the importance of comity in international insolvencies, Judge Brozman pointed to the co-operation of the High Court in the matter of Barclays' application:

> Lurking in all transnational bankruptcies is the potential for chaos if the courts involved ignore the importance of comity. As anyone who has made even a brief excursion into this area of insolvency practice will report, there is little to guide practitioners or the judiciary in dealing with the unique problems posed by such bankruptcies. Yet it is critical to harmonise the proceedings in the different courts lest decrees at war with one another result.
>
> In this spirit of comity and to the essential end of co-ordinating the American and British cases, Judge Hoffmann and I have approved in the MCC case a protocol pursuant to which among other things I have recognised as corporate governance of MCC the joint administrators whom he appointed and he has granted standing to the examiner with expanded powers whom I appointed. Only a day or two ago, Judge Hoffmann reaffirmed the need for the two courts to respect one another when he vacated an injunction obtained *ex parte* by a creditor of MCC.[12]

---

[8]*Ibid* (CA 8 October 1992).

[9]*Ibid* at p. 13.

[10]s 304 of the Bankruptcy Code allows a foreign representative such as an English administrator to file a petition in a US Bankruptcy Court for relief ancillary to a foreign insolvency-type proceeding.

[11]*In re Brierly,* 145 BR 151 (Bankr. SDNY 1992).

[12]*Ibid* at p. 164.

3.4 Conclusion

There is little doubt that, as Mr Justice Hoffmann put it, "the only satisfactory solution to the possibility of jurisdictional conflicts in cross-border insolvencies would be an international convention. In the absence of such a convention, the only way forward is by the discretionary exercise of jurisdictional self-restraint".[13] In MCC's case, the courts and the parties in interest have sought to create rules that require co-operation in the absence of any such convention. The Order and Protocol, crafted to fill the void, seems to function quite well when tested. Furthermore, in recognising the need for co-operation, the courts involved have striven to avoid conflict so that the reorganisation and rehabilitation of MCC may proceed unhindered. While it may be too early to predict the ultimate course that the MCC insolvency proceedings will take, it is safe to say that a better environment for rehabilitation and maximisation of asset value has been fostered.

---

[13]*Barclays Bank plc v Homan, et al,* slip op. at p. 14, No. 0014001 of 1991 (Ch 28, July 1992).

Annex 1

United States Bankruptcy Court Southern District of New York

In re	**: Chapter 11**
Maxwell	**: Case No. 91 B 15741(Tlb)**
Communication	**:**
Corporation plc,	**:**
	:
Debtor.	**:**
	:

Final supplemental order appointing examiner and approving agreement between examiner and joint administrators

This Court having heretofore, on 20 December 1991, entered its Order Appointing Examiner (the "Examiner Order") authorising and directing the appointment of an examiner for Maxwell Communication Corporation plc (the "Debtor") in the within proceedings, and on 3 January 1992, entered its Interim Supplemental Order Appointing Examiner and Approving Agreement Between Examiner and Joint Administrators (the "Interim Order"), and Richard A. Gitlin having been appointed as examiner (the "Examiner"), and Andrew Mark Homan, Colin Graham Bird and Jonathan Guy Anthony Phillips having been appointed joint administrators (the "Joint Administrators") of the Debtor pursuant to the Order for Joint Administrators (Exhibit A hereto) of the English High Court of Justice, Chancery Division, Companies Court (Hoffman J.) (the "High Court") in the English administration proceeding (the "Administration") involving the Debtor, and it appearing that there is a desire by this Court, the High Court, the Examiner, the Joint Administrators and the Debtor (i) to harmonise the within proceedings with the Administration and (ii) to facilitate a rehabilitation and reorganisation of the Debtor, and upon the Application of Richard A. Gitlin, Examiner, for Entry of Final Supplemental Order Appointing Examiner and Approving Agreement Between Examiner and Joint Administrators (the "Application"), and upon the findings of fact in the Examiner Order (without making any other determination or finding as to the allegations made in the Motion for Appointment of Examiner), and the High Court having ordered (Exhibit B hereto) that, subject to the approval of this Court, the Joint Administrators be authorised to consent to the making of an Order in substantially these terms, and upon a hearing (the "Hearing") on the Application in this Court on 15 January 1992, and due and sufficient notice of the Hearing having been given, and after due deliberation and sufficient cause appearing therefor, It is hereby ORDERED that:

A. The appointment of the Examiner is hereby confirmed as of the date of his acceptance of such appointment and the remaining provisions of the Examiner Order and the Interim Order are superseded in their entirety by this Order.

B. The Joint Administrators and the Examiner shall be recognised as "parties in interest" in this case within the contemplation of Bankruptcy Code, section 1109(b), and the Joint Administrators will support an application by the Examiner for leave to be heard in the High Court in respect of the Administration.

C. The Examiner shall:

(a) investigate the assets, liabilities and financial condition of the Debtor, the operation of the Debtor's business and the desirability of the continuance of such business, and any other matter relevant to this case or to the formulation of a plan of reorganisation and report the results of such investigation as provided in Bankruptcy Code, section 1106(a)(4). In order to reduce duplication of effort and the needless incurrence of expense, the Examiner may, in his discretion, defer to the Joint Administrators with respect to matters being investigated by them (other than investigations relevant to the formulation of a plan of reorganisation) unless the Examiner believes that an independent or supplemental investigation by the Examiner is appropriate under the circumstances, such as where there may be a potential conflict of interest. In deciding whether to exercise his discretion to conduct an independent or supplemental investigation, the Examiner shall be mindful of, and give serious consideration to, the additional costs and expenses that would be involved in conducting such investigation. In order to facilitate the full and co-operative exchange of information, the Joint Administrators and the Examiner (including their respective professionals) are authorised and directed to hold in confidence and not disclose, except to this Court or to the High Court under such circumstances so that the confidential nature of such information will be protected or as otherwise required by applicable law, to third parties without the consent of the other any information designated as confidential provided by one to the other in connection with the investigations described in this paragraph;

(b) act to harmonise, for the benefit of all of the Debtor's creditors and stockholders and other parties in interest, the Debtor's United States Chapter 11 case and the Administration so as to maximise the Debtor's prospects for rehabilitation and reorganisation;

(c) canvas, determine and identify the issues and impediments that must be resolved to facilitate a reorganisation of the Debtor;

(d) with the Joint Administrators, the *ad hoc* bank committee (as described on Schedule 2 of the Protocol annexed hereto as Exhibit C) (the "Bank Committee") and any official committee appointed in this case, inquire of major parties in interest in the Debtor's case concerning their respective positions as to the resolution of any issues and impediments to the formulation of a plan of reorganisation;

(e) mediate any differences in respect of the positions of the various parties in interest *vis-à-vis* any issues and impediments identified or arising with respect to a plan of reorganisation;

(f) promote a consensus among all parties in interest so that a consensual plan of re-organisation may be proposed, confirmed and consummated consistent with the Bankruptcy Code; and

(g) act as a facilitator in respect of all of the foregoing matters.

D. The Examiner be and the same hereby is authorised, subject to this Court's approval, to appoint or employ pursuant to Bankruptcy Code, section 327, account-ants, attorneys and/or other agents or representatives to assist him in the performance of his duties and the exercise of his powers hereunder, and the Examiner may seek compensation for his services and reimbursement of his costs and expenses in accordance with Bankruptcy Code, sections 330 and 331.

E. The Joint Administrators be and the same hereby are recognised as the corporate governance of the Debtor subject to the terms of this Order.

F. The Protocol between the Examiner and the Administrators, annexed hereto as Exhibit C, including without limitation paragraph G.5(c) and (d) thereof authorising without further notice and a hearing, pursuant to sections 363 and 364 of the Bankruptcy Code, the transactions provided for therein, is hereby approved and the Examiner and the Joint Administrators shall exercise their powers and authority in accordance with the Protocol.

G. The Joint Administrators, the Debtor under the supervision of the Joint Adminis-trators as corporate governance, David Shaffer ("Shaffer"), and the Examiner shall take such steps as are necessary in good faith in order to effectuate the provisions, spirit and intent of this Order.

H. Pursuant to section 105 of the Bankruptcy Code and subject to the limits of this Court's jurisdiction, each member of the M&O Group and their respective directors and officers shall not direct, cause or cause another entity to consent to the following, without the consent of the Examiner and the Joint Administrators (with concurrent notice to US counsel for the Bank Committee) or approval of the Court in accordance with this Order:

(a) the filing of proceedings under the bankruptcy or insolvency law of any jurisdic-tion with respect to any member of the M&O Group; or

(b) any sale or other disposition of any member of the M&O Group, or any material assets of any of the foregoing.

I. Nothing contained herein shall:

(a) be construed to affect, diminish or increase in any way the jurisdiction provided to this Court under United States law with respect to the within proceedings or the jurisdiction provided under English law to the High Court with respect to the Administration;

(b) require the Joint Administrators to do anything or refrain from doing anything which would or would be likely to result in their being in breach of any duty imposed on them by any applicable law;

(c) authorise the taking of any action herein or in the Protocol which requires notice and a hearing or court authorisation under the Bankruptcy Code, unless (a) the requirement of notice and a hearing or court authorisation has been met or (b) the action is taken pursuant to paragraphs G.5(c) or G.5(d) of the Protocol; or

(d) preclude any party in interest from seeking further relief from this Court (whether by way of modification of this Order, expansion or reduction of the Examiner's powers, obtaining injunctive or mandatory relief or otherwise).

J. The Joint Administrators shall concurrently with delivery to the Examiner provide to (i) US counsel for the Bank Committee, and (ii) the US counsel for any official committee appointed in this case, copies of all notices or requests for consent or approval (including copies of all materials provided to justify such consent or approval) sent or furnished by the Joint Administrators to the Examiner pursuant to the Protocol (subject to appropriate confidentiality restrictions), provided that the Joint Administrators shall have leave to seek relief from this Court from the provisions of this paragraph J if the Joint Administrators determine in good faith that such disclosure in any individual case could be prejudicial to the interests of the Debtor's estate. Nothing contained herein shall preclude any other party in interest from applying to this Court to receive the same copies of notices or requests for consent or approval as are to be provided to US counsel for the Bank Committee or US counsel for any official committee appointed in this case.

K. The Joint Administrators shall not incur personal liability for failure to give any notices required herein or in the Protocol.

Dated : 15 January 1992
    New York, New York

/s/ Tina L. Brozman
The Honorable Tina L. Brozman
UNITED STATES BANKRUPTCY JUDGE

Protocol

The Examiner and the Joint Administrators hereby agree, subject to entry by the Bankruptcy Court of the Final Supplemental Order Appointing Examiner and Approving Agreement Between Examiner and Joint Administrators (the "Proposed Order") to which this Protocol is an exhibit, as follows:

A. Annexed hereto as Schedule 1 is a list of entities that are integral parts of the businesses of Macmillan Inc ("Macmillan") and Official Airline Guides Inc ("OAG"), whether subsidiaries or affiliates thereof (as identified on Schedule 1 hereto, the "M&O Group" as may be varied from time to time by further agreement between the Examiner and the Joint Administrators subject to the approval, or further order, of the Bankruptcy Court).

B. With respect to those members of the M&O Group that are identified with an asterisk on Schedule 1 hereto (the "M&O Affiliates"), the Joint Administrators have expressed the need to analyse their duties and responsibilities under English or other applicable law concerning the potential rights of the shareholders and creditors of the M&O Affiliates and the Joint Administrators and the Examiner agree to work together in good faith to effectuate the current desire and intent for David Shaffer ("Shaffer") to continue overseeing the M&O Group, as provided in paragraph C hereof, without causing the Joint Administrators to be in breach of their duties and responsibilities under English or other applicable law, with the Joint Administrators and the Examiner reserving the right to seek relief from the Bankruptcy Court in the event the foregoing cannot be accomplished.

C. Subject to paragraph G.3(i) hereof, Shaffer shall (i) remain the Chairman, President and Chief Executive Officer of Macmillan Inc, (ii) remain the Chairman of Official Airline Guides Inc ("OAG"), (iii) be paid by OAG and Macmillan, and (iv) be employed by the Debtor but without the Joint Administrators adopting or the Debtor assuming his contract of employment, it being the current desire and intent (subject to paragraph G.3(i) hereof) that his management role include overseeing management of the M&O Group.

D. The Joint Administrators and the Examiner shall consult and together agree as to the appropriate composition of the boards of directors of Macmillan and OAG. The Debtor under the direction of the Joint Administrators, in its capacity as the ultimate parent company of the M&O Group, shall procure the appointment of new boards of directors for Macmillan and OAG, provided that subject to paragraph G.3(i) hereof (i) Shaffer shall be a member of both boards, (ii) the Joint Administrators shall consult with Shaffer as to whether it may be appropriate to appoint one or more members of operating management of Macmillan or OAG to their respective boards, (iii) the remaining members of the respective boards shall be independent, outside directors of distinction, and (iv) the Joint Administrators and the Examiner shall have consented to each proposed appointment.

E. Should the Joint Administrators consider it appropriate to commence insolvency or other similar proceedings in respect of all or any of the intermediate holding companies between the Debtor and the M&O Group, they may commence such proceedings subject to giving such prior notice as is reasonable in all the circumstances of the commencement of such proceedings to the Examiner, and in that event they shall, or they shall cause the Debtor to, subject to prior consultation with the Examiner, commence parallel proceedings under Chapter 11 in the United States with respect to such intermediate holding companies in which event the Joint Administrators and the Examiner shall apply to the Bankruptcy Court for an Order in relation to such companies appointing the Examiner to serve in such cases and otherwise in substantially the same terms as the terms of the Proposed Order insofar as they may be relevant.

F. The Debtor and the Examiner may retain on a joint basis (subject to approval by the Bankruptcy Court of the specific joint retention application) an investment banker of national and international reputation selected by the Joint Administrators and the Examiner.

G. The Joint Administrators and the Examiner shall exercise their powers and authority in accordance with the following:

1. With respect to the Debtor, the Joint Administrators and the Debtor at the direction of the Joint Administrators shall:

(a) except as provided in this Protocol and the Proposed Order, attempt, in good faith, to obtain the prior approval of the Examiner and shall obtain the approval of the Bankruptcy Court to borrow funds or pledge or charge any assets of the Debtor;

(b) in good faith attempt to obtain the consent of the Examiner prior to seeking to convert the Debtor's case to a case under Chapter 7 of the Bankruptcy Code and shall obtain the approval of the Bankruptcy Court to any such conversion;

(c) obtain the prior consent of the Examiner or, having first attempted in good faith to obtain such consent, approval of this Court prior to filing a plan of reorganisation for the Debtor during the period in which the Debtor has the exclusive right to file a plan of reorganisation ("Plan") and seek acceptance of such a Plan as provided in section 1121 of the Bankruptcy Code.

2. With respect to the M&O Group, and regardless of whether authorisation to take such action is otherwise required form this Court or the English High Court, the Joint Administrators and the Debtor under the direction of the Joint Administrators shall, in good faith, attempt to obtain the consent of the Examiner and shall obtain the approval of the Bankruptcy Court prior to:

(a) commencing, or causing to be commenced or consented to, bankruptcy or insolvency proceedings (whether in the United States or elsewhere) with respect to any member of the M&O Group;

(b) in any Chapter 11 case involving any member of the M&O Group, acting to convert or seek to convert such case to a case under Chapter 7 of the Bankruptcy Code;

(c) causing any member of the M&O Group to borrow funds;

(d) causing any member of the M&O Group to pledge or charge any assets;

(e) causing any member of the M&O Group to sell or dispose of any shares or other assets outside the ordinary course of business.

3. The Joint Administrators and the Debtor under the direction of the Joint Administrators shall attempt in good faith to obtain the prior consent of the Examiner and, if such consent is not given, shall obtain the approval of the Bankruptcy Court prior to:

(a) replacing, firing, or materially reducing the operating responsibilities of Shaffer (without otherwise detracting from the Joint Administrators' powers and authority as corporate governance of the Debtor);
(b) exercising the voting rights of the Debtor or the M&O Group with respect to stock of any member of the M&O Group, except that such consent or approval shall not be required to exercise the voting rights of stock of M&O Affiliates to the extent:
    (i) the Joint Administrators have first consulted with the Examiner concerning such exercise; and
    (ii) such voting rights are not exercised in a manner inconsistent with the provisions, spirit or intent of this Order;
(c) filing a plan of reorganisation under Chapter 11 for any member of the M&O Group (to the extent that any of them is the subject of a Chapter 11 case) during the period in which such member has the exclusive right to file a plan of reorganisation and seek acceptance of such plan as provided in section 1121 of the Bankruptcy Code;
(d) causing any member of the M&O Group to commence material legal proceedings;
(e) except as provided in paragraph D, procuring the appointment of any director of any member of the M&O Group;
(f) causing the Debtor or any of its subsidiaries to take any action which is intended to or the reasonably anticipated consequences of which would have a material adverse impact on any significant member of the M&O Group.

4. The Joint Administrators may, without the prior consent of the Examiner and without giving prior notice to him, carry out investigations into the financial dealings of the members of the M&O Group provided that the Joint Administrators shall report on the details of such matters to the Examiner at weekly or such other intervals as may be agreed between the Joint Administrators and the Examiner.

5. With respect to the subsidiaries and affiliates of the Debtor that are not members of the M&O Group (the "Other Subsidiaries") or any other assets outside the M&O Group,

(a) The Joint Administrators and the Debtor under the direction of the Joint Administrators shall, in good faith, attempt to obtain the prior consent of the Examiner and shall obtain the approval of the Bankruptcy Court prior to:
    (i) disposing of shares in any of the Other Subsidiaries or any other assets outside the M&O Group or cause any of the Other Subsidiaries to dispose of any assets, for a consideration, in any one case, in excess of £25,000,000;
    (ii) causing any of the Other Subsidiaries to borrow funds or pledge or charge any of its assets to secure indebtedness (if the aggregate of all such

borrowings, pledges and charges for any single Other Subsidiary is in an amount exceeding £25,000,000 at any one time) or lend money to Other Subsidiaries (if the aggregate amount so loaned by any single Other Subsidiary shall exceed £25,000,000 at any one time); or

(iii) causing any Other Subsidiary to commence a case under the Bankruptcy Code or file a petition for relief under section 304 of the Bankruptcy Code.

(b) The Joint Administrators and the Debtor under the direction of the Joint Administrators shall, in good faith attempt to obtain the prior consent of the Examiner and, if such consent is not given, shall obtain the approval of the Bankruptcy Court, prior to fling a plan of reorganisation under Chapter 11 for any of the Other Subsidiaries (to the extent that any of them is the subject of a Chapter 11 case) during the period in which the relevant company has the exclusive right to file a plan of reorganisation and to seek acceptance of such a plan as provided in section 1121 of the Bankruptcy Code.

(c) The Joint Administrators and the Debtor under the direction of the Joint Administrators may, subject to prior notification to the Examiner:

(i) exercise the voting rights of the relevant company with respect to stock of any of the Other Subsidiaries other than to effect matters covered by Clause (d) below;

(ii) dispose of shares in any of the Other Subsidiaries or any other assets outside the M&O Group, or cause any of the Other Subsidiaries to dispose of any assets, for a consideration, in any one case, in excess of £7,000,000 but not exceeding £25,000,000;

(iii) cause any of the Other Subsidiaries to borrow funds or pledge or charge any of its assets to secure indebtedness (if the aggregate of all such borrowings, pledges and charges for any single Other Subsidiary is in an amount exceeding £7,000,000 but not exceeding £25,000,000 at any one time) or lend money to Other Subsidiaries (if the aggregate amount so loaned by any single Other Subsidiary is in an amount exceeding £7,000,000 but not exceeding £25,000,000 at any one time);

(iv) cause any of the Other Subsidiaries to commence material legal proceedings;

(v) commence, cause to be commenced or consented to, bankruptcy or insolvency proceedings with regard to any of the Other Subsidiaries.

(d) The Joint Administrators and the Debtor under the direction of the Joint Administrators may without the prior consent of the Examiner and without giving prior notice to him:

(i) cause any of the Other Subsidiaries to borrow funds or pledge or charge any of its assets to secure indebtedness (if the aggregate of all such borrowings, pledges and charges for any single Other Subsidiary is in an amount not exceeding £7,000,000 at any one time) or lend money to Other Subsidiaries (if the aggregate amount so loaned by any single Other Subsidiary is in an amount not exceeding £7,000,000 at any one time);

(ii) dispose of shares in any of the Other Subsidiaries or any other assets outside the M&O Group, or cause any of the Other Subsidiaries to dispose of assets, for a consideration, in any one case, not exceeding £7,000,000;

(iii) cause any of the Other Subsidiaries to replace, fire or materially reduce the operating responsibilities of any executive officer; and

(iv) carry out investigations into the financial dealings of any of the Other Subsidiaries; provided that, with respect to each of the matters described in this paragraph G.5(d), the Joint Administrators shall report on the details of such matters to the Examiner at weekly or such other intervals as may be agreed between the Joint Administrators and the Examiner.

(e) For the purposes of this Clause G.5, "consideration" in relation to the sale of shares means the consideration for the shares plus the amount of inter-company debt repaid.

6. The Joint Administrators and the Examiner confirm that (i) the objective of the parties is for the Debtor's Chapter 11 plan and the Joint Administrators' proposals in the Administration to provide for essentially similar arrangements with respect to the M&O Group, (ii) during the period specified in paragraph G.1(iii), the Examiner will be consulted with respect to and be involved in the formulation and negotiation of any plan of reorganisation in Chapter 11 that the Debtor under the direction of the Joint Administrators or the Joint Administrators propose to file at any time and after such period the Joint Administrators will keep the Examiner informed of any plan and will consult with the Examiner with respect to the formulation thereof, and (iii) Shaffer (subject to paragraph G.3(i) hereof) will also be consulted with, and his views will be considered, with respect to any such plan.

Dated : 15 January 1992
New York, New York

———————————————— : /s/ Richard Gitlin
Richard Gitlin, Examiner

———————————————— : /s/ Andrew Mark Homan
The Joint Administrators
by Andrew Mark Homan

Schedule 1 The M&O Group

Macmillan Inc

Official Airline Guides Inc

All subsidiaries or sub-subsidiaries of the above, except as noted below with respect to Berlitz International Inc

- Molecular Design (UK) Limited
- Maxwell Macmillan Publishing Singapore
- Maxwell Macmillan Publishing Australia
- Maxwell Macmillan International Europe Limited
- OAG (Tonbridge)
- Ivory Crest
- Ivory Crest Holdings
- BRS Software Products Scandinavia A/S
- BRS Information Technologies

- BRS Europe
- Information on Demand
- Maxwell Dictionaries
- Caxton and English Education Programmes International
- MLL Holdings

Macmillan/McGraw-Hill School Publishing Company

The Examiner and the Joint Administrators have agreed to delete Berlitz International Inc ("Berlitz") from this Schedule 1 for reasons of their own convenience. Such deletion is without prejudice to reinstatement of Berlitz on this Schedule 1 (after notice to Berlitz and an opportunity for a hearing) and without prejudice to any claim, assertion or position that Maxwell Communication Corporation plc or any of its subsidiaries and sub-subsidiaries, including Macmillan Inc (and its subsidiaries and sub-subsidiaries), may have or take regarding ownership of shares issued or to be issued by Berlitz and any other matter concerning Berlitz.

Schedule 2 members of the bank committee[*]

Bank of America N.T. & S.A.

Bank of Nova Scotia

Barclays Bank plc

- The Chase Manhattan Bank, N.A.
- Credit Lyonnais
- The Fuji Bank Ltd
- Mellon Bank, NA.
- Union Bank of Switzerland
- Westpac Banking Corporation

[*]Schedule 2 is subject to modification or supplementation from time to time on written notice filed with the Bankruptcy Court by counsel for the Bank Committee and served upon the Joint Administrators, the Examiner, the United States Trustee and any official committee formed in this case (as and when formed).

4
Dynamics of a Cross-Border Work-out

Steven Sharpe
Davies, Ward & Beck, Toronto, Canada

4.1 Introduction

As is all too well-known, the rapid disintegration of one of the world's great property developers, Olympia & York Developments, and the struggle to reorganise its affairs focused the attention of hundreds of banks and lending institutions, squads of lawyers and accountants and a number of governments on the advantages and shortcomings of non-integrated statutory schemes for corporate and debt restructurings which were never intended to deal with such complex matters.

Both the Canadian Companies' Creditors' Arrangement Act (CCAA) and Chapter 11 of Title 11 of the United States Code (the "US Bankruptcy Code") were pushed, pulled, tugged and stretched to their limits in order to accommodate the needs of a restructuring of this size and complexity. Ultimately, it was the willingness of the assigned judges, Mr Justice Robert Blair of the Ontario Court (General Division) and the Honorable James L. Garrity Jr. United States Bankruptcy Judge, to remain flexible in their approach and open-minded about their roles that allowed so much to be accomplished in such a short time.

The Canadian restructuring was conducted under the CCAA, a 20-section–long statute which was first enacted in the 1930s and has fallen in and out of vogue over the ensuing 60 years. Despite a major revamping of Canadian bankruptcy legislation in 1992, the CCAA was left in place by the Federal Parliament; its utility as a statutory tool for complex reorganisations is precisely its lack of mandated procedures and requirements. Ultimately, the statute relies upon the involvement of the court to supervise a bargaining process between the debtor company, its shareholders and creditors with a view to achieving a consensual arrangement.

What follows, therefore, is not an enlightening articulation of the legal principles that were invoked by the court during the Olympia & York restructuring. Rather, the court's involvement in the process throughout more than 100 court appearances was as referee, relying upon its broad equitable jurisdiction to ensure that the remedial purpose of the legislation was not frustrated.

Current Issues in Cross-Border Insolvency and Reorganisations (E. B. Leonard, C. W. Besant, eds.; 1–85333–958–X; © International Bar Association; pub. Graham & Trotman/International Bar Association, 1994; printed in Great Britain), pp. 59–68.

Because of the nature of Olympia & York's operations — ie the management and development of real estate in the US, Canada and the UK — and because so much of the debt was primarily secured on that real estate, Davies, Ward & Beck, as counsel to O&Y, concluded that it was unnecessary and counterproductive to attempt an integrated cross-border restructuring of the assets. In addition, given each country's natural predisposition to apply its own law to its own real estate, the effort beginning in the spring of 1992 was directed towards facilitation and co-ordination of separate restructurings in each of the jurisdictions, notwithstanding a substantial geographic overlap of lenders and the fact that much of the primary debt in the US and the UK was guaranteed by the Canadian parent company.

Unlike a liquidation, in which it might very well be necessary or appropriate to marshall the debtor's assets so as to distribute them equitably in accordance with accepted priorities, a real estate work-out is one which by its very nature is rooted to the ground. The collateral is stuck there, and so are the lenders.

This analysis led to the conclusion that there is a set of expectations on the part of the participants as to how level the playing field really needs to be and the proper role of the court in refereeing the process. In the United States, the focus is clearly said to be on rehabilitation of the debtor, and the elaborate Chapter 11 scheme enhances those prospects. In Canada, the legislative focus is more on maintaining and protecting the integrity of the collateral and hence the secured creditor. In the UK, administration is said to be a rehabilitative mechanism. To those who practise in the former colonies, however, the supplanting of management by professional insolvency practitioners, particularly in the absence of any suggestion of misfeasance, appears to do little if anything to maintain going concern value.

4.2 Size of the group

To gain a sense of the size of the enterprise which was attempting to be reconfigured, the following statistics will assist:

(a) Debt

- the O&Y Group worldwide had aggregate indebtedness to third parties of approximately $13.5 billion (Canadian dollars used throughout);
- the total direct indebtedness of the 29 Canadian companies which applied for CCAA protection, exclusive of guarantees, was approximately $8.6 billion;
- of the $8.6 billion, $8.3 billion was secured, or at least intended to be;
- Olympia & York Developments Limited (the ultimate parent company) was contingently liable as guarantor for another $2.7 billion, more than half of which related to loans associated with the Canary Wharf development in London, UK;
- the public debt issues, including commercial paper programmes, totalled $3 billion;
- the Canadian restructuring alone involved more than 90 lenders or lender groups.

(b) Assets

- more than 100 real estate development projects worldwide;
- more than 40 office buildings in North America — approximately 43 million square feet of space;

- major US projects in New York City, Los Angeles, Hartford, Portland, Chicago, Dallas, Boston, Springfield, and Orlando;
- major Canadian buildings in Toronto, Calgary, Edmonton and Ottawa;
- O&Y's investment in Canary Wharf was approximately $3.8 billion;
- directly or indirectly, O&Y had shareholdings in the following public companies:
  - — it shared control of Trizec Corporation Ltd.
  - — 75% interest in Gulf Canada Resources Limited
  - — 82% interest in Abitibi-Price Inc.
  - — 89% interest in GW Utilities Limited
  - — 15% interest in Catellus Development Corporation
  - — 15% interest in Santa Fe Pacific Corporation
  - — 15% interest in Santa Fe Energy Resources Inc.
  - — 33% interest in Stanhope Properties plc
  - — 10% interest in Rosehaugh Properties plc.

4.3 The events leading up to 14 May 1992

The move towards protective filings for the O&Y companies began early in 1992 and was accelerated by two sets of events and the public perception of the significance of those events. The first related to Olympia & York's commercial paper programmes, the second to O&Y's apparent inability to finance the acquisition of the Morgan Stanley building at Canary Wharf.

In early 1992, O&Y had two commercial paper programmes outstanding. Both programmes were secured, one by a real estate project in downtown Toronto, the other by a basket of marketable securities. Between the two programmes, more than $800 million was outstanding. In early 1992, the markets became nervous as word spread that O&Y was not rolling over its commercial paper until very late in the day. Investors do not see that as good news. Then, on 13 February, one of the Canadian bond rating agencies downgraded O&Y's commercial paper programmes. O&Y was left to scramble either to wind down the programmes or to support them in some fashion. Much of February, March and April was spent, along with a large amount of cash, in doing exactly that.

The Morgan Stanley situation was far different. Although the events did not have an immediate cost to O&Y, the timing of the news of the UK litigation between Morgan Stanley Properties and Olympia & York could not have been worse. Because the financial press misunderstood the legal issues involved, it was reported that O&Y had reneged on its agreement to purchase Morgan Stanley's building at Canary Wharf.

What the press failed to appreciate was that the entire situation — the timing and the agenda — was created by Morgan Stanley. Morgan Stanley had not only agreed to sell its building to O&Y, it had also agreed to locate the financing on O&Y's behalf and had been unable to do so. Morgan Stanley then chose to trigger O&Y's obligation to buy its building at Canary Wharf and to sue in the UK for specific performance of that obligation. What the Morgan Stanley situation demonstrated was the extent of a global problem. There was an absolute lack of real estate financing available anywhere in the world, no matter what the quality of the collateral. In the case of the Morgan Stanley building, the quality of the security related directly to Morgan Stanley's creditworthiness as the long-term lessee of the building, and not simply the quality of the real estate development. However, worldwide, real property values were continuing to drop as vacancy rates and rental rates moved in the wrong directions and financing simply could not be found.

By mid-May, the situation in Canada was critical. A number of serious defaults had occurred under various loan agreements. Hundreds of millions of dollars in available resources and stand-by lines had been used in an effort to retire the commercial paper programmes on an efficient and orderly basis. Ultimately, Olympia & York simply ran out of time. The public bondholders of First Canadian Place, O&Y's flagship building in Toronto, were in a position on 15 May to seize their security and appoint a receiver. As a result, 29 of the Canadian companies filed for CCAA protection on 14 May 1992.

For O&Y, the most pressing and urgent need was to stabilise the Canadian situation. There were a number of difficult issues for management to wrestle with:

(a) the perceived loss of control and enforced public scrutiny of their finances and operations;
(b) the need for collaboration and creditor co-operation in the spending of money; *and*
(c) the need to consult on items traditionally viewed as being within O&Y's expertise — building management, leasing, tenant inducements — those elements of the operation which were viewed as the basis for its "franchise" value.

There is a distinct difference in the psychological dynamic that is played out in a Canadian restructuring as opposed to a US work-out. The Chapter 11 scheme is elaborate, well developed and clearly articulated. Because of that vast accumulated experience and well-defined set of rules, the view was that O&Y's US companies could look after themselves. The effort was therefore made by O&Y to isolate the US operations from the Canadian proceedings.

The Canadian landscape, if not bleaker, was certainly more of a legal frontier. The CCAA was the only viable restructuring vehicle available in Canada for slowing down secured creditors long enough to undertake a restructuring.

One of the anachronistic conditions precedent to the invocation of the CCAA is that the company must have issued debt obligations pursuant to a trust indenture. There is no requirement as to the amount of debt, how long it has been outstanding or even the reasons for the issuance of those debt instruments. What has evolved over the last few years, not surprisingly, is the phenomenon of instant trust deeds. Debt instruments are issued solely to permit access to the statute with minimal debt incurred to non-arm's length lenders.

The other condition precedent to CCAA protection is that the company must be insolvent.

However, under the CCAA, the imposition of the stay of proceedings against creditors is judicial rather than administrative. O&Y would not take the risk of not obtaining an immediate stay of proceedings and thereby losing a building like First Canadian Place. Because Ontario Commercial Court judges invariably refuse to proceed in such matters on an *ex parte* basis, the decision was taken to proceed with filings in New York under Chapter 11, so as to obtain the benefit of the automatic stay of proceedings contemporaneous with the Canadian filings under the CCAA.

It appeared that the Chapter 11 automatic stay would slow down Canadian creditors (almost all of whom had a US connection) long enough that the CCAA applications could be argued later that day before Mr Justice Blair.

Only five Canadian entities, namely Olympia & York Developments (the ultimate parent) and four others, filed for Chapter 11 protection. Three of those companies can be described as "straddle" companies in the sense that they straddle the 49th parallel. Their shareholders were Canadian but their assets were American. The only other entity to file for Chapter 11 protection was Olympia & York SF Holdings, a subsidiary of one of the straddle companies which held O&Y's major shareholding in Santa Fe Pacific, Catellus Development and Santa Fe Energy which are all US listed stocks.

The decision strategically to file these entities under Chapter 11 was premised upon the view that the US real estate assets could best be restructured as a separate unit, without being involved in the CCAA process. As such, the Chapter 11 filings for the straddle companies acted as a kind of "fire wall". Creditors could not easily or quickly move north through the O&Y partnership structures nor could the Canadian creditors gain immediate control of the US restructuring process.

From the Canadian perspective, what was attempted was to borrow, whenever appropriate, from the vast experience and practice within the Chapter 11 context. What had to be grasped in the Canadian work-out were issues that, although fought out on the basis of first principles in the CCAA context, are old hat for American practices.

4.4 Creditors' committees

Very few Canadian restructurings have utilised formalised creditors' committees. However, with 91 lenders and a statutory requirement under Chapter 11 for at least one creditors' committee in the US proceedings, it made perfect sense for O&Y to seek the establishment of creditors' committees. What was proposed was that lenders be grouped by "commonality of interest" rather than identity of borrower. As such, one of the committees was composed of the "project lenders", ie mortgagees in the traditional sense (although the mortgagors were not necessarily the same O&Y entities), three committees of marketable securities lenders being those lenders whose loans were secured by pledges of marketable securities, and finally an unsecured/undersecured creditors' committee.

At the time that O&Y proposed, on 14 May, that creditors' committees be constituted, there was a huge negative reaction from the lenders. They were concerned that this proposal was the thin edge of the wedge in terms of chiselling in stone the constituencies of the voting classes for ultimate CCAA Plan approval. Unlike Chapter 11, the CCAA does not permit the cramming down of an entire class of creditors. Only a very limited concept of "cramdown" is available in Canada. Each class of creditors is entitled to vote on the plan, but a double majority of 50% in number, 75% in value, is all that is required for the plan in respect of that class to be approved. As a result, far more ingenuity is called for in the design of the creditor classes. The project lenders and others were concerned that they would be stuffed into the same class, notwithstanding that they were lenders to different corporate entities, and that O&Y could utilise this "mini cramdown" to deal with unco-operative lenders.

4.5 Creation of a cash management system

Historically, Olympia & York Developments acted as internal banker to the entire group and operated cash concentration accounts. As a result of the CCAA filing, O&Y was forced to revise its entire treasury and accounting operation onto an asset-specific system in which cash and expenses could be tracked on any asset-by-asset basis. Ultimately, a mechanism was negotiated with the lenders whereby management fees and assessments against the cash flows of specific assets were levied and used to fund Head Office general and administrative expenses as well as the restructuring costs. The balance in each asset account was dammed up and distributed to the appropriate secured lenders monthly. Unlike Chapter 11, there is no concept of super priority, debtor-in-possession financing available. As a result, no new money was available to fund the ongoing operations.

4.6 Timing

Canadian debtors are forced to move at lightning speed in propounding a plan of compromise and arrangement. The CCAA does not provide for an automatic 120 or 180-day stay period and, as a result, the process moved forward very quickly. There was, of course, an internal incentive to do so. Without the concept of debtor-in-possession financing, a Canadian debtor may run out of money before it finalises its plan.

In addition, the court simply will not permit creditors to be frozen out of their contractual rights forever. There is a point at which the debtor's right to restructure its debt will give way because of the continuing prejudice to the creditors. It was possible to obtain extensions of the stay of proceedings to eight and a half months, in part because creditors had not been kept entirely out of the fruits of their collateral and partially, it is submitted, because of the sheer size of the work-out and the number of lenders involved.

Unlike some of the other major multinational restructurings, like Maxwell Communications and BCCI, we ultimately concluded that there was no need to put in place a general operating protocol between the Canadian and US courts in order to regularise or co-ordinate the proceedings. Rather, the situation was dealt with on an issue-by-issue basis.

4.7 Bankruptcy petitions

After the CCAA Order was made and the Chapter 11 cases were filed, one of the first applications brought in both Canada and the US by a number of very large undersecured lenders was for relief from the stay long enough to allow those lenders to issue bankruptcy petitions against the 29 Canadian companies that had filed for CCAA protection. The purpose for issuing the petition was to stop the 90-day preference period under the Canadian Bankruptcy Act from running out, thereby preserving the lenders' ability to attack certain transactions in the event that the restructuring failed and the companies were left in bankruptcy. Unlike the US Bankruptcy Code, a filing under the CCAA does not toll the Bankruptcy Act preference period.

The major difficulty faced by these lenders was that they were not in a position to commence bankruptcy proceedings against most of the Canadian entities because they were not creditors of most of the CCAA applicants.

Although Mr Justice Blair and Judge Garrity gave the lenders leave to commence bankruptcy proceedings against *their* debtors without difficulty, the lenders were forced to find a creative basis for initiating proceedings against the other O&Y entities.

What was ultimately devised was this scheme. The banks proposed to lend $1,100 to each of the relevant entities on a demand basis. The loans would then be called and not repaid; an act of bankruptcy there committed.

When this procedure was raised in Canada before Mr Justice Blair, he concluded that it represented a method of allowing technical compliance with the bankruptcy statute. In this age of instant trust deeds, why not instant debt and instant acts of bankruptcy? There was, interestingly, one bank that objected to this proposal as a matter of principle. Its counsel asked to be given notice of the demands on the O&Y companies so that his bank could make good on the loans on behalf of the O&Y companies and thereby prevent the bankruptcies.

While Mr Justice Blair was prepared to sanction this scheme, Judge Garrity was far less sanguine. When the lenders brought their parallel motion before the US Bankruptcy Court, Judge Garrity, who was being asked to do some admittedly strange things — to order the O&Y entities to borrow money and then not repay it — was not certain he would have granted the order if Mr Justice Blair had not already done so.

Judge Garrity ultimately made the order. He recognised the inevitability of conflicts between US and Canadian practice and law in a case of this complexity, but made it clear that the relief sought was novel and would have not been allowed but for the purpose for which it was being sought; namely, the Canadian proceedings.

Judge Garrity also made the point that notions of comity would not push him blindly to follow the lead of the Canadian court, but that given the unique situation, he was prepared to make the order. What was clear in his judgment was a warning to all parties: the US court would not be a mere rubber stamp on what was being done in Canada.

As the months passed and the negotiations amongst the creditors and O&Y continued, there were a great number of motions, many involving the sale of O&Y assets and other procedural matters, which required the approval of both the Canadian and US courts. In all instances, whether based upon pragmatism, comity or natural respect, Mr Justice Blair and Judge Garrity displayed tremendous flexibility and understanding of each other's court, jurisdiction and need to maintain control of the process.

4.8 The Joint Plan

The O&Y Plan of Arrangement and Compromise, which dealt with all of the Canadian entities, including the five that had filed for Chapter 11 protection, was filed as a Joint Plan with the Canadian court on 27 October 1992. It was intended to constitute a plan both for Canadian CCAA purposes and for US Chapter 11 purposes. The necessity for concurrent sanctioning of the Plan by both the Canadian court and the US Bankruptcy Court was dictated by the inclusion in the Plan of a very delicate corporate reorganisation of the O&Y group of companies, and the transformation of Olympia & York Realty Corporation (one of the straddle companies that had also filed under Chapter 11) from a subsidiary of Olympia & York Developments into a sister company. No one believed that such a corporate manoeuvre could be safely undertaken without the simultaneous blessings of both courts.

What was encountered, though, in attempting to mesh the two procedures for obtaining formal creditor support, was a technical morass through which it was only possible to move extremely slowly. The procedures in the two jurisdictions differ in one fundamental way, which triggered this problem. In Canada, unlike the US, much of the negotiation takes place *after* the plan is filed with the court. Indeed, the negotiations frequently continued right up to the holding of the votes. As the procedure under Chapter 11 was understood, any substantive change made to the Plan after the court approval of the Disclosure Statement necessitated the drafting of an amendment to the Disclosure Statement and a restarting of the 40-day clock for approval of the Amended Statement before acceptances could be solicited from creditors. This apparently simple difference in the timing of allowable negotiation made it impossible to undertake the two procedures in tandem.

What was proposed, therefore, was to start the processes at the same time, by the filing of a Joint Plan, but not to file a motion in New York for approval of the companies' Disclosure Statement until the Canadian Information Circular (which does not require court approval) had been mailed to creditors and the meetings of the 35 classes of creditors had been held. At the conclusion of the series of creditors' meetings, there would then be a finally negotiated Plan suitable for the purposes of preparing a Chapter 11 Disclosure Statement. The US clock could then be set running, approval for the distribution of the Disclosure Statement could be obtained and acceptances from the very same creditors who had already voted on the Plan could then be solicited. It was recognised (although not relished) that the Canadian voting profile would not match precisely the Chapter 11 acceptances. Ultimately, it was contemplated that confirmation of the Chapter 11 Plan and sanctioning of the CCAA Plan should be sought at the same time.

After the Canadian Information Circular had been mailed to creditors, but just before the votes of the various classes of creditors were scheduled to be held, it became apparent that in at least some of the key classes, the companies would not garner sufficient support for the Plan to be accepted. Major structural revisions were required, including the abandonment of the Realty Corporation transmogrification and, happily, the need for concurrent rather than consecutive court approvals.

4.9 Split plenary jurisdiction

What was also required, though, was more time — for the companies, their counsel and the lenders — to work out the structure and the detail of a new set of plans. Negotiating an extension of the CCAA stay period with a number of lenders who perceived themselves to be well secured and therefore disinterested in the ultimate restructuring proved to be difficult, particularly because these lenders believed that their rights of enforcement were impaired by both the Canadian and US stays of proceedings. In the lenders' view, O&Y had no justification whatsoever for filing the five Canadian entities for Chapter 11 protection, and the lenders' ability to enforce their security would continue to be impeded, even if the CCAA stay of proceedings was lifted by the Canadian court, because of the continued existence of the Chapter 11 stay.

In order to allay that fear, and as part of the agreement whereby those lenders agreed to a further extension of the CCAA stay, O&Y negotiated the terms of a Stipulation and Interim Order with those lenders. The Stipulation, which was approved by Judge Garrity on 24 November 1992, provided that the US Bankruptcy Court would refrain from exercising jurisdiction over any of the real estate situate in Canada and any of the marketable securities pledged by O&Y, all enforcement rights with respect to that property would be determined as if the O&Y entities were not debtors under the US Bankruptcy Code and the automatic stay under section 362 of the Bankruptcy Code with respect to enforcement rights against the property was vacated. In essence, the US Bankruptcy Court retained jurisdiction in respect of the non-specified aspects of the debtors' estates, as well as their US assets.

So far as could be determined, this Stipulation and Interim Order represented the first time that the US Bankruptcy Court had declined jurisdiction, in a plenary case, in respect of a portion of a debtor's estate.

4.10 The Revised Plans of compromise and arrangement

On 16 December 1992, the O&Y companies mailed the Revised CCAA Plan to their creditors. The Plan was a radical departure from the earlier one and was the product of intensive negotiations with the major creditors and representatives of all the Creditors' Committees. It did not represent, though, a complete consensus and the ensuing weeks were spent negotiating literally hundreds of compromises, most of which were inter-creditor issues.

One such inter-creditor issue almost pushed the judicial comity between the two courts to the limit. On 4 January 1993, barely a week before the creditors' meetings were scheduled to begin, one of the major banks served motion papers, returnable the following afternoon before Judge Garrity in New York, seeking a preliminary injunction restraining O&Y from convening the Canadian creditors' meetings that Mr Justice Blair had ordered or from taking any steps to further or facilitate the adoption of the CCAA Plan. The bank also sought the appointment of an Examiner, under section 1104(b)(2) of the US Bankruptcy Code, to moderate negotiations of certain provisions of the CCAA Plan.

This unique cross-border distress call was prompted by the fact that the bank believed that a number of its fellow creditors had agreed to a provision in the CCAA Plan which would impair Realty Corporation's ability to utilise approximately $900 million of net operating loss carry-overs for US federal income tax purposes. Having been unable to persuade the other lenders in the boardroom that this was a serious tax risk, the bank decided to try the courtroom. Ultimately, the motion was withdrawn and the spectacle of the US Bankruptcy Court being urged to restrain actions which had been directed to be taken by the Canadian court was avoided.

In the end, that issue, along with a host of others, was resolved, and 27 of the 35 creditor classes approved the CCAA Plan which was sanctioned and implemented by Mr Justice Blair on 5 February 1993.

The CCAA Plan sanctioned in respect of Olympia & York Developments did not require dual sanctioning in order to provide the creditors with adequate protection. The need for Canadian and US plans remained a moving target throughout the process, in terms of ensuring enforceability of plan provisions beyond the jurisdictional reach of each court, the availability of certain tax advantages under the US Bankruptcy Code and the co-ordination of the parent company Chapter 11 case with those of the ultimate debtors. In the final analysis, however, the creditors and the company concluded that the best course was to seek the dismissal of the parent company Chapter 11 case, and Judge Garrity did so on 12 March 1993.

While the completion of the Canadian debt restructuring has resolved the bulk of the outstanding debt, billions of dollars of loans remain to be restructured, both in the US and the UK. Indications of a recovering economy may do much to improve the odds of a successful work-out of O&Y's US operation; this result would benefit both the lenders to those entities and the Canadian creditors who hold, through their economic interest in the Canadian parent company, an 80% equity interest in the US operation.

In the UK, the prospects for a continued interest of the Canadian creditors in the Canary Wharf project are limited. However, recent negotiations between groups of lenders to the Canary Wharf project and the Canadian creditors may prove beneficial. If the proposed loan transactions can be consummated, the Canadian unsecured creditors may see a diminution in the size of the guarantee claims asserted by the Canary Wharf lenders against the Canadian companies by an amount in excess of $1 billion. The result, of course, would be to increase dramatically the proportionate interest of the Canadian creditors in ultimate returns from the Canadian operation.

What is clear, however, as this is written, less than 12 months after the initial filings, is that many more years will pass before the Olympia & York restructuring is completed, and as Mr Justice Blair observed when he sanctioned the CCAA Plan:

> "with a reorganisation and corporate restructuring of this dimension, it may simply not be realistic to expect that the world of the secured creditor, which became not-so-perfect with the onslaught of the Applicants' financial difficulties, and even less so with the commencement of the CCAA proceedings, will ever be perfect again."

5

Treatment of International Insolvency Issues in Japan

Koji Takeuchi

Sakura Kyodo Law Offices, Tokyo, Japan

5.1 Introduction

The first modern Japanese law of insolvency was modelled after French law and created by a German scholar, whose ideas drew upon mercantilist and suspension of payment doctrines in bankruptcy.[1] Thereafter, bankruptcy (*Tosan* or *Hasan*) and composition with creditors (*Wagi*) laws were effected under the primary influence of the German legal system.[2] Originally provisions concerning liquidation and reorganisation were included within the corporate law sections[3] of the Commercial Code. The synthesis of various laws of reorganisation culminated, after the Second World War, in the reception of the American law governing corporate reorganisation (*Kaisha Kosei*).[4] Consequently, there is an enormous variety of proceedings, means and

---

*The following abbreviations are used in the footnotes to this chapter:
Hasanho — Bankruptcy Law — Bankr. Law;
Shoho — Commercial Code — Comm. C.;
Kaisha Koseiho — Corporate Reorganisation Law — Corp. Reorg. Law;
Wagiho — Composition Law — Comp. Law;
Saibanshoho — Judicial Law — Jud. Law.

[1] Comm. C., Part 3, Law No. 32, 1890 (*Meiji* 23); Draftsman, Herman Roesler; M. Kato, *Hasanho Yoron* [*Digest of the Law of Bankruptcy*], (1934) 22.
[2] Bankr. Law, Law No. 71, 1922 (*Taisho* 11).
Comp. Law, Law No. 72,1922 (*Taisho* 11).
[3] Liquidation is regulated both under Law No. 32, Comm. C. 1890 (*Meiji* 23), and under Law No. 48, Comm. C. 1899, (*Meiji* 32). Neither arrangement nor special liquidation were modelled after foreign legal systems, and both were created based upon the revision of the Commercial Code in 1938 (*Showa* 13).
[4] Corporate reorganisation is governed by the Corp. Reorg. Law, Law No. 172, 1952 (*Showa* 27). For its legislative history, see Ministry of Legal Affairs, the History of the Enactment of the Corporate Reorganisation Law, and the amendments to the Bankr. Law and Comp. Law (1) or (10). For scholars, see A. Mikazuki, *Kaisha Koseiho Kenkyu* [*Studies in the Corporate Reorganisation Law*] (1970) pp. 167, 169, 174.

Current Issues in Cross-Border Insolvency and Reorganisations (E. B. Leonard, C. W. Besant, eds.; 1–85333–958–X; © International Bar Association; pub. Graham & Trotman/International Bar Association, 1994; printed in Great Britain), pp. 69-102.

potential parties involved in Japanese insolvency proceedings, and the modern Japanese law of insolvency is unique among legal systems in that a synthesis of several substantively different legislative enactments has been created. The present situation of noticeable gaps in the rights and remedies available under such enactments, depending on which law is invoked, has been accepted without much question, and is regarded as the result of Japan's choice to integrate differing laws into one civil code system. Under the Japanese system, the highest position among the various sources of the law is accorded to statutes, containing principles representing the nation's general will, and which are to be applied using deductive reasoning, it being understood that they carry greater weight than judicial precedent (although the precedent has a great significance within the body of law).[5]

The jurisdictional foundation of Japanese international insolvency is its strict territorialist principles, which are set out in the aforementioned statutes. As will be seen later in this chapter, various inherent contradictions between these statutes and economic realities in international insolvency may well be the price of legal stability under the doctrine of statutory pre-eminence. As to the relationship between the law of insolvency and the Japanese economy, even if one were confidently to acknowledge Japan's economic success in the world's economy, many of the former weaknesses of the Japanese economy stand uncorrected, and business failures continue to occur for structural or managerial reasons. While free market principles function, conservation of capital and work place entitlements has also been effected simultaneously through the exercise of social and industrial policies. The Japanese insolvency system may have been constructed in a piecemeal fashion, but it currently provides support for many of the societal, economic and industrial expectations of the Japanese. Consequently, despite the legendary antipathy towards litigation felt by the Japanese people, there is, compared to general litigation, a relatively high level of interest in bankruptcy-related court proceedings, occasioned by the ample opportunities for participation. International bankruptcy is an area to which this general interest has been directed; it has also occasioned some official comment.[6]

5.2 General domestic proceedings

5.2.1 Insolvency remedies available

Should a Japanese *Kabushiki Kaisha* (limited company) plan to reorganise in Japan, provided it is cognizant that the rights of stockholders are completely subordinated to ordinary claims, and that the right to administer assets and management thereof is completely transferred to a third party (the trustee or, prior to the decision or

---

[5]Jud. Law, Chapter 4: "The judgment of an upper court is binding upon a lower court concerning the very same case." Relating to statutes and case law as sources of Japanese law, see generally T. Kawashima, *Minpo Sosoku [General Provisions of Civil Law]* (1965) pp. 26 *et seq* (1965). Japanese statutes probably belong to the first category described in R. Pound, "Common Law and Legislation", 21 *Harv. L Rev.* 383,385 (1908). See also, Schuster, *German Civil Law*, p. 17, cited by Pound at p. 388.

[6]In the form of a pronouncement from a judge of the Tokyo District Court, see M. Aoyama, "*Kokusai Tosan Jidai Ni Sonaeta Hosei No Seibi*" ["*Legislative Preparation for the Age of International Insolvency*"], in 65 *Minjiho Joho [Civil Law Information]*, 1(1992).

Representing the administrative agency, Kokusai Ogata Tosan, "*Kankeiho Seibi e*" ["Towards Preparation of Related Laws in Large Scale International Insolvency"], Nihon Keizai Shinbun, Morning issue, 1 June 1992, information from the Finance Ministry.

judgment, the administrator for the preservation of the estate, subject to selection by the court), it could take advantage of the corporate reorganisation procedures established by the Corporate Reorganisation Law ("Corporate Reorganisation") as the most appropriate procedure for business reorganisation. If management seeks to preserve the rights of stockholders and management's rights to administer corporate property, and if there is adequate capital and profitability to justify the holding of those rights, it may utilise the procedures for corporate arrangements established by the Commercial Code ("Commercial Code arrangement"), or composition under the Law of Composition ("composition") (note that under these procedures, the secured creditors' right to proceed against the collateral will not be impaired). On the other hand, if the dismantling of the *kabushiki kaisha* is inevitable, bankruptcy procedures under the Bankruptcy Code ("bankruptcy") and winding-up under the Commercial Code ("winding-up") are available. Winding-up will be converted to special winding-up proceedings where the debtor is shown to be insolvent or the reasons for conversion exist ("special winding-up"). A foreign company, ceasing to do business, has the option of utilising special winding-up procedures. There is no obligation to petition for bankruptcy adjudication unless one is found to be insolvent in winding-up procedures. Out of court workouts are available for purposes of both liquidation and debtor rehabilitation (although there is little of case law on this).

The following discussion will only deal with corporate reorganisation and bankruptcy proceedings for a *kabushiki kaisha*. Under corporate reorganisation, creditors holding not less than 10% of capital as well as stockholders owning not less than 10% of the total number of issued shares in the *kabushiki kaisha* have petition rights.[7] Under bankruptcy, creditors (regardless of the number and the amount owed), the *kabushiki kaisha* and its managing director all have petition rights.[8]

5.2.2 Effects of an insolvency petition upon actions by individual creditor

Under corporate reorganisation and bankruptcy, insolvency proceedings do not open automatically upon the submission of a petition. Rather, the insolvency proceedings commence only after a hearing and upon an order to open such proceedings. In addition, the prohibition of individual remedies is the result of the order which commences the proceeding (the "order"). The period from the submission of a petition until the order is made may be brief, but may, depending on each case, also take from three to six months. During this period, the prohibition against individual creditor remedies can be raised by the court's own motion, or by a petition by a party in interest with respect to a specific individual action.[9] Collection in fact and non-legal actions are not generally addressed by such orders.[10] Even were a creditor to

---

[7]Corp. Reorg. Law, s 30.

[8]Bankr. Law, ss 132, 133 and 134.

[9]Corp. Reorg. Law, s 37. Generally speaking, an affirmative effort is being made towards issuing orders to prohibit generally the exercise of individual rights. However, the majority who have influence lean towards a negative view of this trend. See *Jou* [1] A. Mikazuki, M. Takeshita, K. Kirishima, Y. Maeda, J. Tamura, and Y. Aoyama, *Jokai Kaisha Koseiho* 331 (H. Kaneko, 1973), cited hereinafter simply as "Kaneko, *Jokai Kaisha Koseiho*".

[10]An order prohibiting payment by debtors may be issued, the forceful result being that debtor's incentive to refuse to make payments is created. However, this order is not addressed to the debtor. Corp. Reorg. Law, s 39.

undertake individual remedies, to the extent not expressly forbidden by law or by specific order, the court does not have the power to restrain or sanction such creditors for contempt.

5.3 Extraterritorial effects of Japanese insolvency proceedings

5.3.1 Fundamental rules relating to insolvency jurisdiction in Japan

The following discussion refers only to corporate reorganisation and bankruptcy.

There are specific rules referring to jurisdiction within the Japanese statutes. In bankruptcy, the court may take jurisdiction over the bankrupt when the debtor's principal place of business or its major business location is in its territorial jurisdiction[11] or, if the debtor has its principal place of business or its major business location outside Japan,[12] when the debtor's major business location in Japan or the debtors' assets are located in its jurisdiction[13] (subject-matter jurisdiction always lies in the District Court[14]). Generally, these statutory provisions are those relating to determination of venue rather than that of international bankruptcy jurisdiction, modelled on similar statutory provisions in the Civil Procedure Law. Consequently, in view of this general concept concerning jurisdiction over civil litigation and its admitted reference to international civil litigation, it could be assumed that Japanese international bankruptcy jurisdiction lies whenever bankruptcy jurisdiction is acknowledged under those venue provisions by one of the domestic courts.[15] Thus, parallel international bankruptcies involving Japanese concerns were anticipated by Japanese legislators. However, a growing minority of legal commentators now argue that the courts of the jurisdiction where the centre of the debtor's business is located should have exclusive bankruptcy jurisdiction on the basis that factors such as efficiency of proceedings and equity should determine jurisdiction, not simply the text of statutory provisions.[16]

5.3.2 Treatment of foreign creditors in Japanese insolvency proceedings

The standing of foreign creditors under corporate reorganisation is premised on complete equality, while in bankruptcy, equality of treatment is accorded on the principle of mutuality.[17] The weight of authority is that the provisions in the bankruptcy law calling for mutuality[18] are to be construed as a formulaic mutuality (ie that a Japanese creditor should be treated the same as local creditors in the foreign jurisdiction),[19] or

[11]Bankr. Law, s 105; Corp. Reorg. Law, s 6.

[12]*Ibid.*

[13]Bankr. Law, s 107.

[14]Jud. Law, s 25.

[15]Judgment of 16 October 1981 (*Showa* 56), Supreme Court of Japan, No. 2, Small Court, 35 *Saihan Minshu* No. 7, 1224, employing inference theory in relation to international civil jurisdiction. See M. Takeshita, "*Wagakuni ni okeru Kokusai Tosanho no Genjo*" ["The Present State of International Bankruptcy Law in Japan"] in Takeshita, *Kokusai Tosanho*, 3, 13 (1991), for an application of the inference principles of international insolvency jurisdiction from those of international civil procedure, cited simply hereafter as "Takeshita, *Kokusai Tosanho no Genjo*".

[16]K. Takeuchi, "*Kokusai Hasan e no Shiron*" ["Proposal for International Insolvency"], 76 *Hoganku Shirin* 45,98 (1978), cited hereinafter simply as "Takeuchi, *Shiron*".

[17]Corp. Reorg. Law, s 3.

[18]Bankr. Law, s 2.

[19]Y. Taniguchi, *Tosan Shoriho* [*The Law of Dispositions in Insolvency*], (1st ed.) pp. 413, 414 (1976).

that such provisions should be disregarded in practice.[20] Indeed, in actual practice, foreign creditors are sometimes accorded better treatment than their Japanese counterparts, as in the cases of *Sapporo Toyopet* and *Osaka Shoken Shinyo* (1981).[21]

5.3.3 Effects of Japanese insolvency proceedings upon the property of the insolvency estate in a foreign country

(a) Statutory considerations

Japan's statutory insolvency law is based upon the so-called territorial principle in its purest form (ie in both domestic and foreign application).[22] Both Korea and Taiwan seem to rely upon the same principle.[23] There is ample documentation for the proposition that the legislators in Japan intended to adopt this territorial principle.[24] As a result, traditional case law and theory reflect and realise this principle of territorialism. One clear outcome is that the Japanese trustee receives no authority to litigate in a foreign country, having neither the power to dispose of assets located in the foreign country, nor to impede the exercise of individual rights by Japanese or foreign creditors in the foreign country against assets located there.[25] At best, as against the debtor (or its representative), the trustee has the power to order that assets located in a foreign country be removed to Japan, to require that a responsible employee delegate to the trustee the power of disposition over such assets, and to assert authority over assets transferred from the foreign country to Japan after insolvency proceedings have been initiated.[26] The remarkable economic achievements made by Japan, the flow of its capital into foreign countries, the growing amount of foreign capital entering into the Japanese market and the increasing number of corporate insolvencies have all emphasised this inequity when compared to similarly-situated creditors — ie the void in the law of insolvency that results from this approach to jurisdiction — and the wisdom of territorialism has been called into question. A view in favour of

[20]Y. Aoyama, *"Tosan Tetsuzuki ni okeru Gaikokujin no Chii"* ["The Status of Foreign Nationals Under Insolvency Proceedings"], 7 *Shin Jitsumu Minji Sosho Koza [Lectures on the New Practice of Civil Litigation]* pp. 267, 279 (1982).

[21]H. Kobayashi, *Kokusai Torihiki Funso [International Transactional Disputes]*, p. 216 (1987), cited hereinafter simply as "Kobayashi, *Kokusai Torihiki*".

[22]Bankr. Law, Art 3 (Principle of Territoriality):

1. A bankruptcy adjudged in Japan shall be effective only with respect to the bankrupt's properties which exist in Japan.
2. A bankruptcy adjudged in a foreign country shall not be effective with respect to properties existing in Japan.
3. Obligations, of which demand may be made by way of judicial proceedings under the Code of Civil Procedure, shall be deemed to exist in Japan.

[23]Korean Bankruptcy Code (*Kankoku Hasanho*), s 3 (1962). Republic of China Bankruptcy Code (*Chuka Minkoku Hasanho*), s 4 (1934).

[24]K. Ume, *"Hasanho Gaisetsu"* ["*Summary of Insolvency Law*"] in *Hogaku Kyokai Zasshi (Gogai) [Legal Studies Association Magazine* (Special Ed.)], February 1903 (*Meiji* 36). See also M. Kato, 6 *Hasanho Kenkyu [Studies in Insolvency Law]*, Vol. 6,455 (Transcripts of a 1922 lecture).

[25]Y. Aoyama, *"Tosan Tetsuzuki ni okeru Zokuchishugi no Saikento"* ["Critical Re-examination of Universalism within the Insolvency Procedural Law"], 25 *Minji Sosho Zasshi* 131 (1979), cited hereinafter simply as "Aoyama, *Zokuchishugi Saikento*".

[26]See eg, Motobayashi, *"Hasan Kaisha ya sono Kogaisha no Zaigai Zaisan to Hasan Zaidan"* ["The Foreign Assets and the Bankruptcy Estates of An Insolvent Corporation and its Subsidiaries"] in *Tosan Kaisha v Saikensha [Debtors v Creditors]* 62 (1978).

limited construction, and even of revision and amendment of the territorialist statutes, has become conspicuous in case law, academic opinion and practice in the courts. This revisionist movement has made significant progress, and seems to have reached a point where it is accepted as a fixed theory of interpretation of such jurisdictional provisions.

(b) Case law

In one case ("Case I"), a Japanese court permitted a foreign trustee (Swiss) to litigate the rights of a foreign debtor (a Swiss corporation) in Japan as against the attachment of its Japanese trademark by a Japanese creditor, holding that the trustee was entitled to exercise in Japan on behalf of the debtor all of the debtor's rights of which vested in the trustee under the law of the foreign jurisdiction.[27] This has recently been followed in a case in which a foreign representative as a shareholder successfully petitioned the court for revocation of certain shareholders' resolutions at a meeting called in contravention of the Commercial Code ("Case II-A").[28] It is not unreasonable to draw inferences from the foregoing as to the likely interpretation in Japan of the effects of Japanese insolvency proceedings upon foreign assets of the debtor.

(c) Academic opinions

Academic opinions advocating dynamic construction of the territorial principle have flourished since 1975, and the scope of suggested amendment and the grounds therefor naturally vary from implicit acceptance of territorialism to approaches which would lead to wholesale revision of the principle. They may be summarised as follows:

(a) One view, which inclines strongly towards the doctrine of the universality of bankruptcy proceedings, argues that a Japanese insolvency judgment, including its comprehensive power of execution (including the rights to manage assets and to prohibit individual remedies) in foreign countries, should be given effect by means of an executory judgment, or even effected without any formality, where such judgment is ordered by a Japanese court exercising jurisdiction over the centre of the debtor's business.[29]

(b) A second view, which allows for concurrent bankruptcies, presumes that Japanese insolvency judgment would affect foreign assets located in foreign jurisdictions which recognise such effects.[30]

(c) A third approach contends that the right to manage foreign assets should be recognised, but only to the extent that this does not impede the individual remedies taken by foreign creditors not participating in Japanese proceedings.[31]

(d) A fourth opinion advocates that the rights to manage assets be recognised without the right to prohibit remedies, subject to the limitation that individual remedies

---

[27]Decision of 30 January 1981 (*Showa* 56), Tokyo Kosei, 994 *Hanrei Jiho* 53 (1981).

[28]Decision of 26 September 1991 (*Heisei* 3), Tokyo Chisai, 897 *Kinyu Shoji Hanrei* 30 (1992).

[29]Takeuchi, *Shiron*, p. 100; Aoyama, *Zokuchishugi Saikento*, pp. 125, 155; and Y. Kaise, *Kokusai Tosanho Josetsu [An Introduction to International Insolvency Law]*, p. 487 (1989), cited hereafter simply as "Kaise, *Josetsu*".

[30]Kobayashi, *Kokusai Torihiki*, p. 223.

[31]K. Ishiguro, *Kokusai Shiho to Kokusai Minji Soshoho to no Kosaku, [The Antagonism between Private International Law and the Law of International Civil Litigation]*, p. 249, n. 557 (1988), cited hereinafter simply as "Ishiguro, *Kosaku*".

taken in conflict with such rights over assets should not result in any unlawful enrichment (although a question of fraudulent conveyance or preference may arise, subjecting the creditor to the hotchpot rule which denies distribution to that creditor within the jurisdiction until other creditors become entitled to the same rate of distribution).[32]

(e) A fifth opinion would recognise the trustee's rights to recover assets from abroad, including the right to require co-operation from the debtor, and would deem any advantage resulting from any individual remedy taken by a Japanese creditor to be an unjust enrichment.[33]

If an attempt is made to analyse the common factors of each of the above opinions, the current view would appear to be that the trustee's direct or indirect (through the debtor) powers of administration and disposal over assets held overseas be recognised, that the comprehensive power of execution be negated to the extent that it prohibits individual execution against assets held overseas (except for cases where such effects are acknowledged by foreign courts), and that individual remedies taken by domestic creditors shall be readjusted through the application of preference, unjust enrichment and hotchpot rules.

However, this conclusion is only a synthesis of common factors in academic positions. Whether the administration of an insolvency estate faced with imminent threat of piecemeal execution will actually be accomplished in accordance with these views — ie whether fairness, equity and successful reorganisation are to be attained — remains to be seen.

Nevertheless, a draft revision of the essential points in statutes relating to Japanese international insolvency ("revision outline") has recently been presented by a group of scholars based on the notion of universalism.[34] The revision outline comprises the following points:

(a) Domestic insolvency proceedings should have extraterritorial effects, and both the trustee's power of administration and the comprehensive power of execution over foreign assets shall extend to assets abroad, provided that the proceedings are based upon the jurisdiction (principal jurisdiction) over the centre of the debtor's business.

(b) The trustee should have the responsibility of administration and/or disposal of the foreign assets.

(c) Co-operation may be requested from foreign courts.

(d) A creditor, having taken individual remedies in contravention of the above, should be subject to disgorgement of the benefit as an unjust enrichment.

---

[32]Takeshita, *Kokusai Tosanho no Genjo*, p. 47; see also M. Ito, *Hasanho [Bankruptcy Law]* (New ed.), p. 116 (1991).

[33]Y. Taniguchi, *"Tosan Tetsuzuki to Zaigai Zaisan no Sashiosae"* ["Attachment of Assets Abroad and Insolvency Procedure"] in Yoshikawa Tsuito (in dedication to Professor Yoshikawa): *Tetsuzukiho no Riron to Jissen [Procedural Practice and Theory]*, pp. 578, 587 (1981), hereinafter cited simply as "Taniguchi, *Zaisan Sashiosae*". See also M. Takeshita, *Kokusai Tosanho no Genjo*, pp. 15 *et seq.*

[34]See M. Takeshita(ed.), *Kokusai Tosanho [International Insolvency Law]*, pp. 417 *et seq* (1991), including commentary by M. Ito, pp. 381 *et seq.* Cited hereinafter simply as "Takeshita, *Kokusai Tosanho*". The Revision Outline is set in Amex 1.

The revision outline makes clear that certain effects of insolvency proceedings filed in Japan involving *kabushiki kaisha* would automatically extend to foreign countries. Consequently, neither an individual execution taken by creditors in Japan or in a foreign country against foreign assets owned by the *kabushiki kaisha*, nor against the rights of the *kabushiki kaisha*, would be permitted.

(d) Legal practice

Practitioners, comprised of judges and trustees (usually attorneys), are more actively pursuing and effecting the goals of universalist doctrine. Efforts to weaken the territoriality principle made by those practitioners have become increasingly obvious since 1975. Reflection on the progress of such "law as practice" enables several different evolutionary stages to be discerned. Stage I involved the trustee's self-constrained administration and disposal of foreign assets, all the while having to endure and defend against attacks against the foreign assets initiated by advantageously-placed creditors (both domestic and foreign). This process usually ended by the trustees settling for a negotiated solution. Stage II involved the debtor's request for assistance from foreign courts and then its attempt to defend and if necessary obtain protection for foreign assets. These requests extended to enjoining all creditor actions. Stage III — the current situation — is characterised by highly sophisticated efforts to recover and preserve foreign assets, utilising to the fullest extent available, foreign bankruptcy systems to effect the goals of the Japanese trustee.

Examples of large-scale international insolvency cases belonging to Stage I are: *Koyama Kaiun* (1975),[35] *Terukuni Kaiun* (1975),[36] *Eiko Business Machine* (1975),[37] *Petri Camera* (1977),[38] and *Issei Kisen* (1978).[39] Belonging to Stage II are *Osawa*

[35]Tokyo District Court, (*Hu*) No. 115, (1975 [*Showa* 50]), Bankruptcy. In this case, the Hong Kong liquidation (of a Hong Kong subsidiary) was initiated by the parents' Japanese bankruptcy trustee. The Hong Kong liquidator sued its parent, Koyama Kaiun (Koyama Shipping Enterprise), pursuant to its duties as liquidator. Thereafter, the Japanese trustee submitted a bankruptcy petition against Koyama Kaiun's Hong Kong branch office. The case was settled in a closing consultation between both trustees and liquidator as described in Kobayashi, *Kokusai Torihiki*, p. 215. Many thanks to T. Nomiya for his guidance concerning this case.

[36]Tokyo District Court, (*Mi*) No. 19, (1975 [*Showa* 50]), Corporate Reorganisation.

[37]Tokyo District Court, (*Mi*) No. 15, (1975 [*Showa* 50]), Corporate Reorganisation. See also a report related to this case in Takeuchi, *Shiron*, p. 104, n. 12.

[38]Tokyo District Court, (*Hu*) No. 220 (1977 [*Showa* 52]), Bankruptcy. A report related to this international bankruptcy case is in Takeuchi, *Kokusai Hasan e no Shiron*, p. 104, n. 11.

[39]Kobe District Court, (*Mi*) No.] (1978 [*Showa* 53]), Corporate Reorganisation: this case triggered a major incident involving a petition to foreclose based on a vessel mortgage by Japanese creditor, and an arrest of vessels owned by debtors in Canada. The initial arrest was cancelled but was later revived. In the end, it turned out to be a full foreclosure and sale action, during which Japanese scholars and attorneys testified as to the state of Japanese law. The Canadian Federal Court, Trial Division, permitted claims in this case (as well as a foreclosure) on the premise of Japanese principles of territorialism. There is a detailed report on this case in Y. Masuda, "*Kaiun Kosei Kaisha Shoyu Senpaku no Gaikoku ni okeru Sashiosae*" ["The Foreign Attachment of the Vessel Owned by An Ocean Carrier"], 73 *Kaijiho Kenkyukaishi* [*Admiralty Law Magazine*] 1(1986). See also M. Takeshita, *Kokusai Tosanho no Genjo* p. 1. Cf. regarding the Canadian judgment, *Orient Leasing Company Ltd v The "Kosei Maru"* (1979) 94 DLR(3d) 658 (Fed. TD).

Shokai (1984),[40] *Riccar* (1984),[41] *Sobu Tsusho* (1985),[42] and *Sanko Kisen* (1986).[43] Belonging to Stage III are *Maruko* (1991),[44] *Urban* (1991),[45] *SAC* (1991),[46] and *Ken International* (1992).[47] During Stage I, the bankruptcy or reorganisation estate in Japan

[40]Tokyo District Court, (*Mi*) No.1 (1984 [*Showa* 59]), Corporate Reorganisation. For a report related to this case, see S. Miyake Osawa Shokai, "*Kaisha Kosei ni miru Kokusai Tosan to sono Taio*", Pts. (1), (2), (3) ["Viewing International Insolvency Through the Corporate Reorganisation of Osawa Trading Company and its Response"], 2 *Debt Administration*, 4 (1987), 3 *Debt Administration* 10 (1987), and 4 *Debt Administration* 8 (1988), which mainly deal with trustees' foreign strategy, insolvency proceedings by foreign subsidiaries (US and France), and the handling of the parent companies' debts; hereinafter cited simply as "S. Miyake, *Osawa Shokai (Part 1), (Part 2),* or *(Part 3)*".

[41]Tokyo District Court, (*Mi*) NO. 7 (1984) [*Showa* 59], Corporate Reorganisation. It involved cases of liquidations of foreign subsidiaries, such as German enterprises, and foreign creditors.

[42]Tokyo District Court, (*Hu*) No. 511 (1985 [*Showa* 60]), Bankruptcy, involving the disposal of shares of stock issued by foreign subsidiaries. A report regarding this case is in Miyake, *Osawa Shokai (Part 1)*, p. 7 and *Osawa Shokai (Part 2)* p. 15.

[43]Tokyo District Court, (*Mi*) No. 6 (1985 [*Showa* 60]) Corporate Reorganisation: a notable case in that the trustee filed a proceeding under US Federal Bankruptcy Code, s 304, and was granted a stay against Sanko Kisen's (a foreign creditor) action against Sanko's assets. *In re Sanko Steam Ship Co Ltd*, No. 86 B10291 (SDNY decided 30 July 1986). See K. Takeuchi, "*Kokusai Tosan Shori no Genjo to Kadai*" ["The Present Status and Task of International Insolvency Administration"], 39 *Jiyu to Seigi* 45,50, in co-operation with K. Tezuka (1988). The US Federal District Court's order is given in K. Takeuchi, "*Jitsurei kara Mita Kokusai Tosan no Hoteki Sho Mondai (1)*" ["Problems of International Bankruptcy Viewed from Actual Cases (Part 1)"], 7 *Debt Administration* 4, 10 n. 8.

[44]Tokyo District Court, (*Mi*) No. 1, (1991 [*Heisei* 3]), Corporate Reorganisation: this case is noteworthy in that the Japanese trustee applied for domestic US bankruptcy administration under s 303 of Chapter 11 of the US Federal Bankruptcy Code, *In re Maruko Inc* (No. SD91-12303-LM11), which aimed at a full-scale reorganisation, instead of s 304 ancillary proceedings, since the estate involved considerable US real estate. Cf. the Chapter 11 petitions of the two subsidiaries under Federal Bankruptcy Regulations R1015: *In re Maruko, Guam Inc*, (No., SD91-12546-LM), and *In re Maruko New York Inc*, (No. SD91-13398). Many thanks to H. Sakai.

[45]Nagoya District Court, (*Hu*) No. 87 (1991 [*Heisei* 3]), Bankruptcy. This case involved substantial real estate and works of art located in several foreign countries. It is remarkable that the court appointed two trustees, dividing their responsibilities between domestic and foreign administration. In addition, the foreign trustee's *exequatur* petition was acknowledged in France (Jugement rendu le 11 Juillet 1991, Tribunal de Grande Instance de Paris). My thanks to K. Narita for his assistance on this case.

[46]Nagoya District Court, (*Hu*) No. 91(1991, [*Heisei* 3]), Bankruptcy. This case is remarkable for three reasons: (1) as with *Urban*, the court appointed an additional trustee for a purpose of administration and disposal of foreign assets; (2) its petition for the execution of judgment was acknowledged (Jugement rendu le 26 Septembre 1991, Tribunal de Grande Instance d'Argentan); and (3) workouts of French grandchild companies (which own a great number of golf courses) were supervised by the Japanese courts in the course of a liquidation of the subsidiary Japanese corporation. Many thanks to T. Kosugi and T. Ikeda concerning this case.

[47]Tokyo District Court, (*Hu*) No. 1594, (1991 [*Heisei* 3]), Bankruptcy. This case is related to the Ibaraki Country Club scandal. It is worth mentioning that the petition for reorganisation procedures was filed under Chapter 11 (not Chapter 7) and based upon s 303 instead of s 304 requesting recognition of the Japanese insolvency proceedings. Presumably the trustee recognised some procedural advantage such as the ability to utilise US discovery procedure to search for concealed outflow of capital and avoid preferences under provisions more advantageous than those available under Japanese law. For the US, it is an *Axona* version of foreign insolvency proceedings. Cf. *In re Axona International Credit & Commerce Ltd*, 88 BR 597 (Bkrtcy. SDNY 1988), in which a petition for Chapter 7 based on US Federal Bankruptcy Code s 303 was made by a Hong Kong company, achieving an avoidance. Upon recovering its assets, the trustee petitioned for suspension of Chapter 7 proceedings and for turnover of the domestic US assets to a Hong Kong trustee, which petition was granted under the conditions that administrative expenses and US priority creditors would be paid first and the trustee conduct the distribution in Hong Kong within 72 hours after the assets had been transferred to Hong Kong. My thanks to K. Ohashi concerning Tokyo District Court (*Hu*) No. 1594.

suffered attacks, such as attachments filed in various regions against vessels used by shipping companies. However, the attaching creditors were usually domestic creditors or their foreign affiliates. This stage can be said to represent a period in which economic realities continuously projected legal questions to be solved. Stage II was notable for vigorous activities in foreign countries by Japanese trustees, who won various approvals of power from the court, such as having administrative expenses allowed by the court from the estate, and also for the successful results therefrom. One noteworthy occurrence was the petition and order given to the *Sanko Kisen* trustee authorising ancillary proceedings under the US Federal Bankruptcy Code.

During Stage III, some radical changes have taken place, which include the following:

(a) appointments of additional trustees solely for the purpose of administering and disposing of foreign assets;

(b) successful petitions for *exequatur* for the recognition of a bankruptcy judgment in foreign countries;

(c) a high degree of legal techniques of corporate reorganisation utilising, for example, parallel petitions under full Chapter 11 (US) reorganisation together with its joint administration of US subsidiaries; and

(d) a sophisticated application of law of foreign countries in aid of Japanese liquidation bankruptcy which utilised parallel petitions under full Chapter 11 reorganisation, aiming at an advantageous application of the US preference and discovery provisions.[48]

It can be seen from Stage III cases, therefore, that the basis of Japanese insolvency jurisdiction, although predicated on territoriality in theory, has essentially shifted to universalism in practice.

5.3.4 The theoretical basis of the foreign impact of Japanese insolvency proceedings

The foreign impact of Japanese insolvency proceedings is based on the propositions that a foreign judgment is entitled to full recognition, and that insolvency proceedings can be viewed as one judgment (or at least as analogous to a judgment) or as a series of judgments to carry out the inherent purposes of such proceedings.[49] A minority view is that an insolvency proceeding is merely an execution, but this view tends to result in territorialist conceptions.[50] The Anglo–American concept of assignment is not widely accepted in Japan.[51] An explanation deriving from personal

---

[48]In addition to the aforementioned cases, the writer refers the reader to a report of study of international bankruptcies (prior to March, 1987) based upon the records of Japanese courts: M. Ito and M. Wagatsuma, "*Kokusai Tosan Jitsumu ni arawareta Mondai-Kokusai Tosan Jittai Chosa Hokoku*" ["Publication of the Results of a Study of Problems in Actual International Bankruptcies"], in Takeshita, *Kokusai Tosanho*, pp. 57 *et seq.*

[49]T. Mitsui, "*Kokusai Hasan*" ["International Bankruptcy"], in *Shogai Hanrei Hyakusen*, 188 (1967); Takeuchi, *Shiron*, p. 92; Aoyama, *Zokuchishugi Saikento*, p. 154; Kaise, *Josetsu*, pp. 477 *et seq*; Takeshita, *Kokusai Tosanho Genjo*, pp. 40 *et seq.*

[50]M. Kato, "*Hasan Senkoku no Kokusaiteki Koryoku*" ["International Co-operation in Bankruptcy Judgments"], in *Hasanho Kenkyu* [*The Study of Bankruptcy Law*], Vol. 1 (5th ed.), p. 310 (1924).

[51]Along the same lines, see K. Takeuchi, "*Hasan to Torimodoshi-ken*" ["Bankruptcy and the Right of Recovery"], in *Hasanho Jitsumu To Riron No Mondaiten* [*Insolvency Practice and Theoretical Issues*] (new ed.), p. 218 (1990).

jurisdiction and *in rem* jurisdiction is similarly only accepted by a minority.[52] Japanese private international law theory selects the law of the jurisdiction of incorporation of a company to govern such matters as incorporation, organisation, management and dissolution. Based upon this theory, there are also reasons to support the conclusion that effects arising from Japanese corporate law should be recognised in other forms.[53]

5.4 The domestic effect of foreign proceedings

5.4.1 Effects of foreign proceedings upon individual creditor actions in Japan

(a) Case law

Case I (*see* **5.3.3(b)**) is of importance in that it represented a major shift in the approach of the Japanese courts to territorialism. However, the real issue in that case was not whether individual creditor remedies should be disallowed, but rather whether a foreign insolvency representative's power over Japanese assets was to be recognised. The court answered in the affirmative. With respect to another issue, whether an execution judgment on a foreign insolvency adjudication should be obtained, Case I's holding presupposed that such judgment was not required (it is still not clear whether such an execution judgment is statutorily recognised within Japanese procedural law, or whether it is an invention derived from academic opinions or case law). This analysis also applies to Case I–A, another case that touched upon the power of a foreign insolvency representative in Japan. An apparent conflict with these two cases is Case II, which actually occurred between Case I and Case I–A, and which took the somewhat traditional approach to the law of international bankruptcy. In that case, an individual of Indian nationality was declared bankrupt in Hong Kong.[54] His banking creditor filed a complaint against the debtor in Japan on overdrafted accounts both in Hong Kong and in Japan. The court there held that the debtor, notwithstanding the bankruptcy, had the capacity to defend the case because of the Japanese territorial principle (the banking creditor seems to have known of the Hong Kong representative, but may have sought to avoid the trustee's interference; from the judgment itself it is not clear whether the debtor's centre of business was located in India or Hong Kong).

(b) Academic opinions

Logical consistency requires that the academic approach to the effect of foreign insolvencies on proceedings and remedies in Japan should be the converse of their

---

[52]Taniguchi, *Zaigai Sashiosae*, p. 589 and Ishiguro, *Kosaku*, p. 250, follow up on this concept.

[53]T. Kawakami, *"Kaisha"* ["The Company"], 3 *"Kokusai Shiho Kosa [Private International Law]* 739 (1964); J. Tsubota, *"Kigyo Tosan o Meguru Kokusai Mondai"* ["International Problems Involving Business Bankruptcies"], in 3 *Kokusai Torihiki Jitsumu Kosa [Lectures on International Transactional Practice]* 757, (1979). See also K. Ishiguro, *Kokusai Shiho* (new ed.), p. 255 (1990), cited simply hereinafter as "Ishiguro, *Kokusai Shiho*" and Ishiguro, *Kosaku*, pp. 171, 198, which view an insolvency proceeding from the perspective of judicial or administrative action as creating private legal relationships (*Gestaltung*). It is argued that we take an international civil actions approach (cf. factors mentioned with s 200 of the Law of Civil Procedure) rather than a private law approach which applies as the *lex causae* to the formalities and validity.

[54]Judgment of 30 September 1983 (*Showa* 58), Osaka District Court, 516 *Hanrei Times* 139.

answer to the question of what effect is to be given to Japanese insolvency proceedings upon creditor actions in foreign countries. As already noted, synthesis of the common elements of the foregoing academic opinions leads to the conclusion that a foreign trustee appointed in the court of the principal jurisdiction will have the right to manage foreign assets in Japan. Similarly, a creditor's action, foreign or domestic, shall not be impeded, except that those creditors who have strong contacts with the foreign proceedings may be subject to adjustments or prohibition under the proceedings afforded to the foreign insolvency representative.[55]

Academic commentators are divided in their review of Case II. One opinion holds the result in Case II to be correct, in that the bankruptcy court was sitting in Hong Kong and not in India, which was merely a non-principal jurisdiction for the debtor.[56] Another opinion also considers Case II to be justifiable due to the heavy burden placed upon the creditor to show evidence that the requirements of section 200 of the Civil Procedure Code were satisfied.[57] However, the author of this second opinion reserved his decision with respect to whether the debtor's business in Japan was distinct from the business in Hong Kong, and whether a proof of claim had been filed in the Hong Kong court. The author of the second opinion recognises, as a matter of general theory, the right of the foreign representative to sue. However, it would appear from a view of the Case II decision that the debtor conducted business both in Hong Kong and in Japan to a similar extent, although its bank accounts were slightly more overdrawn in Hong Kong than in Japan. It would also seem that the location of the debtor's centre of business, as well as the identity of the chosen trustee for the debtor in Hong Kong, must have been clear to the creditor and that Case II seems to have neglected to clarify these points. This lack of precision resulted in the court reverting to a formalistic construction of the territorial principle.

If we look at the revision outline, we see that it suggests that a foreign bankruptcy granted in the principal jurisdiction of the debtor be recognised in Japan, including both the trustee's right to manage assets automatically and the right to enforce the comprehensive power of execution upon an order recognising foreign bankruptcy. Therefore, where a foreign law prohibits a creditor's individual remedies, any such remedial actions taken by both domestic and foreign creditors in Japan would be prohibited as against the assets of the foreign debtor or against the foreign debtor after the recognition order had been entered. In a case similar to Case II under the revision outline, the outcome would depend upon whether the foreign insolvency jurisdiction had been based upon the location of the debtor's centre of business.

(c) Legal practice

Heretofore, we have seen that Japanese practice (or the law of practice) has essentially abandoned territorialism with respect to insolvency proceedings commenced in Japan. The question remains as to whether the law in practice will result in the same co-operative attitude upon the receipt of a request for co-operation in relation to a

---

[55]One can conclude that the stronger the tendency towards universalism, the more likely to prohibit the execution of individual creditors' (both domestic and foreign) rights in Japan (Country B), as we can see in Takeuchi, *Shiron*, p. 100, and Aoyama, *ZokuchiShugi Saikento*, p. 158, describing prohibition of such rights following the execution judgment; or in Kaise, *Josetsu*, p. 518, describing prohibition without such execution judgment.

[56]Takeshita, *Kokusai Tosanho no Genjo*, p. 47.

[57]Ishiguro, *Kokusai Shiho*, p. 277.

foreign insolvency proceeding. It seems likely that the Japanese courts will not self-ishly pursue their own interests in view of the long passage to the present practical interpretations. However, it is still possible that such co-operation might be denied under the pretext of the lack of law or the protection of domestic creditors, thus pro-voking criticism from friendly nations. Fortunately, there has not been any instance in which a Japanese court has received a request deriving from a foreign proceeding to recognise the comprehensive power of execution in order to prohibit an individual creditor's actions in Japan; thus, so far, the law in practice appears seamless.

In the future, should a Japanese court receive a request from a foreign court or trus-tee to provide assistance by refusing to sustain a creditor's individual action, whether domestic or foreign (eg a request for an execution judgment based upon a foreign insolvency adjudication; a request for an execution judgment to Japanese insolvency court; a request to stay execution on judgment or enforcement on a secured claim, litigation, or preservative provisional remedies; or a request for avoidance of prefer-ences); it would be preferable for the court to make its disposition in light of the five following considerations.

First, any posture effectively refusing to co-operate would be regarded as disre-garding the norms of international good faith, considering the present evolution of Japanese practice. Second, from a closer analysis of both Case I and Case I–A (the wording adopted in Case I is that the foreign trustee is recognised in respect of its rights to exercise the bankrupt's rights in Japan on its behalf, although that wording is excessively technical and in essence is the same as having directly recognised the trustee's full power to manage the property and to sue in Japan), and the synthesis of academic opinion given herein, it becomes clear that the impact of the Japanese judi-cial recognition of the foreign trustee's power to manage assets is far greater than it may appear at first glance. Given that a literal reading of the statute, which states that foreign insolvency proceedings shall have no effect upon property or assets in Japan, would lead to the conclusion that the administration of the Japanese assets would be entrusted only to the Japanese trustee, it is clear how far case law and academic opin-ion have progressed. Furthermore, it should be noted that precedent and academic opinion make a clear distinction between the concepts of the trustee's authority to manage assets and its comprehensive power of execution. These arguments are prem-ised upon creating separate and independent concepts. Thus criticism that such separation is not proper alone would not engender much support. It will, however, be admitted that under the law of insolvency in Japan, it is expected that the comprehensive power of execution is enforced immediately upon the rendering of the judgment, which marks the commencement of insolvency proceedings. In addi-tion, the trustee (the choice of whom is legally required to be made concurrent with the adjudication of bankruptcy) is expected to take possession of all of the debtor's properties,[58] to close the debtor's books of account[59] and to require a sheriff to levy execution based upon the adjudication of bankruptcy. The court, on the other hand, gives orders to the debtor's account debtors and holders of debtor's assets prohibiting them from paying or making delivery to the bankrupt.[60] These orders are both served upon creditors and published. Regardless of whether this enforcement of the compre-

---

[58]For a bankruptcy example, see Bankr. Law, s 142, Clause 1 and s 185.

[59]Bankr. Law, s 186 and 187.

[60]Bankr. Law, s 143, Clause 1, No.4, Clause 2.

hensive power of execution is regarded as a comprehensive levy or a general assignment to the trustee, it is clear that the prohibition of a creditor's individual remedies takes effect immediately upon the statutory commencement of the insolvency proceeding. Therefore, to be precise, the appointment of the trustee and his rights to manage the property arise once the comprehensive power of execution is exercised, while at the same moment effecting the prohibition of individual remedies.

If the foregoing reasoning is accepted, only a small step of logic and consistency remains towards recognition of a foreign trustee's comprehensive power to manage assets, and the acknowledgement that the prohibition of individual creditor action is a part of the same comprehensive power of execution, once such trustee's power to manage assets has been recognised. To borrow a phrase, the question of whether to afford recognition only to the extent of the right to manage property, or whether to accept prohibition of individual remedies, seems to be akin to the absurdity of the person retreating 50 steps ridiculing the person who retreats 100 steps. While the difficulty of providing protection to local creditors is a serious matter, such protection would be futile where there are insufficient assets within the jurisdiction to satisfy fully all local creditors on their claims (there has been no reported incident in which local creditors have locally obtained complete satisfaction of their claims). Rather, it would seem more vital to the protection of the interests of local creditors that their priority within the local order of law be preserved in the foreign proceedings, and that appropriate accommodations be provided such that local creditors do not incur unnecessary expense or inconvenience in filing their proofs of claim, and that they be notified and given the opportunity to speak or object in a hearing for an execution judgment or other bankruptcy administration matters, thus satisfying the requisites of due process.

A third consideration is that the argument utilising *in personam* jurisdiction theory from a foreign system to justify the denial of individual remedy taken by a creditor who has sufficient contact with a foreign country fails to refer to such foreign system's *in rem* jurisdiction, which extends the coverage of the foreign proceedings to the property within foreign countries. In other words, those who argue only by borrowing concepts of *in personam* jurisdiction will face difficulty in justifying their denial of a foreign court's request to protect the property of the forum.

Fourthly, the dynamic concept of due process, as applied to the exercise of jurisdiction by courts in the countries which gave birth to that principle, deals with particular issues involving the level of contacts and whether certain means of effecting jurisdiction upon those having such contacts should be permissible. Due process does not simply exclude purely local creditors merely by the fact of their status as such. It should be noted that there has never been any serious argument that section 304 of the US Bankruptcy Code is in violation of the federal due process clause.

Finally, if it is sensible to view a foreign insolvency proceeding as a species of foreign judgment, then, in terms of the statutes, the civil execution law provides a special proceeding only for a foreign monetary judgment. The means of recognising other kinds of foreign judgments embraced by section 200 of the Civil Procedure Code rests with the discretion of the Japanese court. Subject to the local Japanese creditors' exercise of rights being protected by way of summons, hearings, objection rights, petitions for adequate protection and so forth, it is quite possible that a Japanese court taking jurisdiction under Japanese insolvency law (being the court of the centre of the debtor's business in Japan) could recognise the foreign judgment opening the foreign bankruptcy proceedings upon the motion of the foreign court or the foreign representative. Based upon this recognition judgment, the Japanese court could exercise and act upon its power to prohibit individual creditor's remedies upon such conditions as are deemed appropriate under the circumstances. The Japanese execution system anticipates that another court would intervene to stop execution proceedings.

From a different perspective, the rendition of assistance by the Japanese insolvency court could be seen as co-operation between courts in terms of the fair distribution of a court's responsibility. Such co-operation by the Japanese court with other courts would be deemed to be required under the Law relating to the Reciprocal Judicial Aid given at the request of Foreign Courts (the "Judicial Aid Law") and the Law of the Judiciary in its section on mutual assistance or the insolvency law (eg Bankruptcy Law, section 109). Therefore, as international co-operation grows, it is probable that Japanese courts would assist foreign proceedings by entering execution judgments in the court where the debtor's business is located in Japan, or where the debtor's assets are located. Japan will show that, as a matter of procedural policy, it intends to follow international co-operation, as shown in section 200 of the Civil Procedure Law (section 200 can possibly, by the exercise of logic, be treated as a part of Bankruptcy Law through its section 108 and likewise as a part of the Law of Corporate Reorganisation through its section 8). The practice of law, centering upon case law, has the capacity to create law and creatively to "find" law in this field through the resolution of specific legal issues. However, the foregoing is mere speculation; the gulf separating these proposals from current reality may well never be bridged.

(d) Major relevant insolvency cases

Two cases, *US Lines Inc* (1987)[61] and *Bank of Commerce and Credit International SA* (*"BCCI"*) (1991),[62] have contributed a great deal to current discussion. In *US Lines*,

---

[61]Tokyo District Court, (*Hu*) No. 216 (1987 [*Showa* 62]), Bankruptcy. A US corporation filed a petition under Chapter 11 for reorganisation in November of 1986 in the US A petition for bankruptcy in Japan in May 1987 concerning its branch in Japan, by the debtor-in-possession. My thanks to H. Yamakawa on this issue.

As a reference, US Lines filed for protective orders around the world. Upon filing the US petition, US Lines sought to extend the effect of the US automatic stay against those who executed a *Mareva* injunction in the UK after the petition for Chapter 11. However, the petition was denied in the UK, due to the fact that the reorganisation targeted only North America (however, this decision has clearly indicated that the *Mareva* injunction creditors should have been treated equally in the UK regarding liquidation), *Felixstowe Dock and Railway Co v US Lines Inc* [1989] 2 All ER 77, QB. See also, Smart, *Cross-Border Insolvency*, p. 147 (1991), regarding the effects of domestic provisional attachments and foreign insolvency proceedings in relation to the above case.

[62]Tokyo District Court, (*Hi*) No. 2012, (1991 [*Heisei* 3]), Special Liquidation: a petition for a special liquidation was filed by the Minister of Finance as an interested party (Commercial Code, s 485, Clause 1) on the basis that the debtor's business location had been discontinued (under s 485, Clause 3) and a judgment of commencement was granted. As neither the debtor nor the creditor filed a petition it is a notable liquidation case, and there is apprehension why independent autonomy in the framework of disciplines of the private law failed to function. Of course, the Minister of Finance would assert that authority under s 51, Clause 1 of the Banking Law [*Ginkoho*], and that the same provision under the Commercial Code was thereby invoked by operation of Clauses 2 and 3 of the same section of the Banking Law. Legally, both liquidation and special liquidation are available. But Okamoto, 13 *Annotated Corporate Law*, pp. 544 *et seq* (1990), argues only for special liquidation, the rationale being a reference in s 485, Clause 2 to ss 431 through 456. If BCCI was insolvent, then either BCCI was left with either special proceeding of liquidation bankruptcy by mixture of ss 485, 430, and 24 of the Comm. Code. and Section of the Comm. Code. It is unclear whether there was any preference in this case. My thanks to Mr. Kugisama for his assistance in considering this case.

the debtor-in-possession under Chapter 11 of the US Bankruptcy Code successfully petitioned for Japanese bankruptcy adjudication with respect to its Japanese branch, and it is to be noted that the rights of the debtor to sue in Japan, where there is no court-appointed trustee, were recognised. The *BCCI* matter, although in actuality a bankruptcy, is being processed under special liquidation proceedings following the close of the debtor's business. As a colossal case involving concurrent bankruptcies, it will be quite interesting to observe the kinds of co-operation which will be achieved among the different courts administering liquidation proceedings in the various countries.[63]

5.4.2 *Effect of foreign insolvency proceedings upon concurrent bankruptcy petition in Japan*

A debtor in Japan who has a main business office in a foreign country is subject to Japanese insolvency jurisdiction, so long as it maintains a place of business in Japan. Based upon this, there is adequate statutory groundwork for the court to commence insolvency proceedings in Japan against a foreign debtor along with the insolvency proceedings overseas. As a matter of interpretation, whether petitions for insolvency proceedings filed in Japan by creditors can be dismissed or whether the proceedings can be stayed in Japan, depends, ultimately, upon the application of precedents, academic opinions and law in practice. While academic opinions leaning strongly towards universalism may support these results, there are likely to be more negative responses from the common elements in the academic world generally. However, the aforementioned revision outline is clear that it supports the approach based on universality. It is not apparent how insolvency distributions which come from two proceedings should be adjusted where concurrent insolvencies are administered, but it is possible that those who have received distributions in a foreign country are not entitled to distributions in Japan until other creditors have received the same rate of distribution in Japan.

---

[63]For a report on the degree of progressive co-operation between the liquidators of BCCI, see, "*BCCI Jiken no Sono Ato*" ["BCCI and its Aftermath"], 499 *NBL* 4 (1992). This type of co-operation and consultation between insolvency representatives will hereafter be an important theme in international bankruptcy, whether we call it "Universalist + Ancillary Procedure" or "Concurrent Insolvency". According to the new Anglo-American case of a English company, *Maxwell Communication Corporation plc* (English High Court, No. 0014001 of 1991), simultaneous administration is occurring in England, under s 8 of the Administrative Proceeding (Insolvency) Act 1986 and in the US under Chapter 11, *In re Maxwell Communication Corporation plc* (No. 91 B15741 (SDNY 1991)).

The representatives in the two proceedings, an Examiner appointed under 11 USC s 1104(b) in the US, and in England an Administrator pursuant to s 13 of the Insolvency Act of 1986, reached an accord termed the "Order and Protocol", designed effectively to delineate a common scheme. This operational plan has been approved both by the High Court of Justice, Chancery Division, Companies Court and the US Bankruptcy Court for the Southern District of New York. Proceedings have only recently commenced under this management plan so there are few results to investigate, however, if we examine the concrete decision relating to management, the Protocol confirms that: (i) court permission and consent of the US Examiner is required for any transfer, lease or collateralisation of assets within the set group administered by the British Administrator; (ii) any other disposal shall require consultation with the US Examiner; (iii) modification in management issues requires the consent of the US Examiner; (iv) any auditing plans made by the British Administrator will require the consent of the US Examiner; and (v) the bankruptcy plans of the two proceedings shall be consistent in substance.

Incidentally, it is abundantly clear that a petition for insolvency proceedings against a foreign debtor filed by a representative of the foreign insolvency proceedings in Japan will now be recognised (cf *US Lines*).

5.4.3 Extent of assistance to foreign insolvency proceedings

Recognition of a representative of a foreign insolvency proceeding will be definitely given as to the power of administration and disposal over Japanese assets. As to requests for service of process in relation to insolvency proceedings from overseas, it is conceivable that Japan may be able to offer co-operation under the Judicial Aid Law. However, this law is said to be applicable exclusively to "litigation", and thus there is apprehension that the said law might not be applicable to insolvency proceedings. At the same time, however, the term "litigation" may be too narrowly defined when contrasted with the corresponding expression of "case law on civil or criminal matters" in the original English text of the Law, and the relevant provisions in the Convention of Civil Procedure (1954, the "Civil Procedure Convention") and the Convention on the Service Abroad of Judicial and Extra-judicial Documents in Civil or Commercial Matters (1965). Nonetheless, co-operation in examining evidence for foreign insolvency proceedings can be provided either under the Judicial Aid Law, where the word "litigation" may be broadly interpreted, or under the Civil Procedure Convention where there is no qualification other than "civil or commercial matters". Japan is not a signatory to the Hague Convention on the Taking of Evidence Abroad (1970). (*See* **5.4.1** for discussion on recognition and co-operation; eg prohibitions on individual execution and the petition for concurrent insolvency).

5.5 Private international law

5.5.1 Priorities, fraudulent conveyance set-offs and executory contracts: governing law in Japanese proceedings

(a) Introduction
What would be the effect if Japan's insolvency proceedings extended to foreign countries? To begin, choice of law rules from the perspective of private international law are not clear, due to the lack of precedents resulting from the past dominance of the principle of territorialism. And frankly, at present, arguments on the subject are not particularly sufficient in number or extent . Certainly what is described below is more a product of theory, although some generalisations can be made.

As a starting point, the purely procedural rules for the purpose of achieving the final objective of the insolvency procedure of a Japanese *kabushiki kaisha* — ie its reorganisation or liquidation — are, of course, those of Japan. Generally speaking, the principle of *lex fori* as to proceedings is also applicable in Japan.[64] Consequently, Japanese procedural rules now extend to issues such as general priority creditors, secured creditors, recipients of fraudulent conveyances, those entitled to set-offs, and parties to bilateral executory contracts in a foreign country.

---

[64]Takeshita, Kokusai, *Tosanho no Genjo*, p. 26; Ito, *Hasanho [Bankruptcy]*, p. 115; K. Yamato, *"Hasan"* 3 *Kokusai Shiho Koza [Lectures on Private International Law]*, pp. 882, 893 (1964), hereinafter cited simply as "Yamato, *Hasan*".

(b) General priority (preferred) claims

Under Japanese insolvency procedures, general priority given to a labour claim, for example, is determined theoretically, first, as a premise, by applying the law of the contract as to its creation (or the non-existence thereof) and its priority and preferential range, which law shall be chosen according to principles of private international law.[65] However, this is then subject to review according to the local labour laws of the place where the labour is to be furnished, which review proceeds from the vantage point of societal strategy.[66] Thereafter, priority claims are re-evaluated under Japanese insolvency proceedings for the purpose of a determination as to its status in that country's insolvency law system, taking into consideration other preferences as well as their standing in relation to general claims.[67]

The revision outline, published as a proposed summary of amended text relating to international insolvency law, is reproduced in Amex 1. This outline is being made public simultaneously with the Draft Model Provisions of Bilateral Treaties.[68] According to the Draft Bilateral Treaty ("Model Treaty"), full recognition of the effect of insolvency procedures begun in the jurisdiction in which the debtor's business is centred shall be afforded by the other contracting state. Thus it will be quite informative to refer to the Model Treaty in dealing with the disposition of foreign countries' general priority claims in Japan. According to the provisions of the Model Treaty, the existence of general priority claims, their scope and their standing shall be determined in relation to the substantive law of the claim (labour claims being determined according to the laws of the place where labour is furnished), and the standing for purposes of bankruptcy law shall be determined according to insolvency procedural law.

A foreign country's general principles regarding rights of taxation — ie the rejection of a foreign government's exercise of its taxation rights — have been introduced by scholars.[69] Consequently, although it is possible that their priority rights will not be recognised since we have inserted a premise that the Japanese insolvency procedure shall be effective in a foreign country, tax priority claims will probably be recognised as to standing and scope, in alignment with the Japanese insolvency procedural system (although when the limits of scope and standing in the foreign country are more restrictive than in Japan, then the tax creditor is subject to such restrictions.[70]

(c) Secured claims

The traditional view is that determination as to the creation (the existence or non-existence thereof) of the secured claims is to be made by applying the governing law for the secured claims, which is chosen, first according to general principles of pri-

---

[65]*Horei* [Choice of Law], s 7; Yamato, *Hasan*, p. 897.

[66]R. Yamada, *Kokusai Shiho*, pp. 282 *et seq* (1989); Judgment of 26 April 1965 [*Showa* 40], Tokyo Chisai 16 *Rominshu* 308.; S. Kuwada, "*Tojisha Jiji no Gensoku*" ["Principle of Self-autonomy"], in *Shogai Hanrei Hyakusen*, 76 (1967); M. Jikkata, *Kakushu no Keiyaku* ["Various Contracts"], in 2 *Kokusai Shiho Koza* 460 (1955).

[67]Yamato, *Hasan*, p. 897.

[68]Takeshita, *Kokusai Tosanho*, p. 422 including Nishizawa's commentary at p. 397. Cf., the text of the Model Bilateral Treaty reproduced in Amex 2.

[69]K. Ishiguro, *Gendai Kokusai Shiho Jou (Part 1)*, p. 473(1986).

[70]This concept is similar to that underlying the Model Treaty.

vate international law.[71] Thereafter, the creation, existence and effect of property rights are to be determined according to the laws of the place where the property is located (for movable property such as ships and airplanes, the law is that of the property's place of registration, rather than the location of the property).[72] On the other hand, as opposed to those espousing the theory that secured claims arising by statute are to be considered in the same way as those arising by contract (by aggregation of the laws governing the secured claims and the laws governing collateral where the property is located), the view that the only law to be considered is that governing the secured claim is also strong.[73] Incidentally, the status and standing of such claims under Japanese insolvency procedure would probably be decided (solely) under Japanese procedural laws.[74]

(d) Fraudulent conveyances, set-offs and executory contracts

Fraudulent conveyances, set-offs and bilateral executory contracts present problems of considerable difficulty. Japanese theory first considers the law governing claims to evaluate the creation of a claim, and the law governing contracts for the formation and the validity of a contract.[75] Thereafter, the requisites and effects of fraudulent transfers (avoidance powers), the requisites for authorisation of set-offs (although the effect of set-off is determined either from the aggregate application of laws governing mutual claims or the laws governing passive claims), and the definition, refusal and performance under bilateral executory contracts — resolutions of which all function to maintain equality and impartiality between creditors — are to be finally determined in accordance with the law of the country where the insolvency proceedings are opened.[76] (As a minority view, it is possible that the governing law would be that of the location where the transaction in question took place, or where the set-off is to be performed.)[77]

5.5.2 Priorities, secured claims, preferences, set-offs and executory contracts: governing law in recognised foreign proceedings in Japan

The present state of Japanese theory is basically that explained in **5.5.1**. As to general priority claims and secured claims, one would think that the theory could be applied by reversing that analysis. There may be, however, a strong inclination to protect the rights of Japanese domestic creditors with respect to the avoidance of fraudulent conveyances, set-offs and bilateral executory contracts, and it is possible that the court will emphasise the application of Japanese insolvency procedural law to the extent it feels is appropriate (in particular in cases where Japanese creditors are all local and

---

[71]Yamato, *Hasan*, p. 903; Takeshita, *Kokusai Tosan no Genjo*, p. 26.

[72]H. Tanigawa, "*Tampo Bukken*" ["Collateral Rights"], in *Kokusai Shiho* [*International Private Law*] 60 (1973), cited hereafter "Tanigawa, *Tampo Bukken*"; S. Hayashida, "*Gaikoku Tampoken no Jikko*" ["Execution of Security Rights Abroad"], in *Kokusai Minji Soshoho no Riron* [*Theories of International Civil Litigation*], pp. 437 *et seq* (1987).

[73]Tanigawa, *Tampo Bukken*, p. 63.

[74]Takeshita, *Kokusai Tosan no Genjo*, p. 26; K Takeuchi, "*Kokusai Tosan Shori*" ["International Insolvency Disposition"], in *Gendai Tosanho Nyumon* [*Introduction To Modern Insolvency Law*], p. 298 (1987).

[75]Yamato, *Hasan*, p. 901.

[76]T. Terao, *Kokusai Shiho* [*International Private Law*] (1898); Yamato, *Hasan*, pp. 896, 901, 903; Takeshita, *Kokusai Tosanho no Genjo*, p. 26.

[77]Kaise, *Josetsu*, p. 516.

have no connection to the foreign country). However, in these cases there is no doubt that the foreign trustee's competence as plaintiff is fully acknowledged and that, therefore, while using the avoidance regulations under an insolvency procedure commenced in a foreign country seems to be supportable (particularly given that there is no Japanese adjudication that would trigger Japanese bankruptcy law provisions), there should be pause for thought before asserting the use of avoidance regulations under Japanese bankruptcy law. As discussed already, concerning the recognition of foreign insolvency proceedings, it is submitted that a better understanding of the law would require an execution judgment for a foreign adjudication by a Japanese court and an application of the avoidance law provisions of the applicable foreign jurisdiction.

5.6 Combined enterprises

5.6.1 Treatment of a foreign wholly-owned subsidiary of a Japanese parent company in Japanese insolvency proceedings in Japan

(a) Background

Some background is useful in understanding the Japanese disposition of an insolvent combined enterprise.[78] First, one notices that there are considerable differences between corporate reorganisation and bankruptcy. Under corporate reorganisation, if a parent corporation becomes insolvent, then usually the subsidiary is also considered to be insolvent, and the parent corporation and the subsidiary petitions are submitted as part of the same insolvency procedure. The bankruptcy court receives the parent and subsidiary petitions, assigning separate case numbers to each based upon the status of each as a legal entity, but appointing the same person as representative (trustee) for both. The procedural progression in which, for example, creditors meet will also be consolidated. Documentation that must be effected by the trustee, including reports and plans for the parent and subsidiary, are also presented in one document. Then there is the issue of possible inequality between creditors arising from such matters as the merits and demerits of the condition of the various assets of the parent and subsidiary, or opaque transactions between the two, and the complications from multiple or secondary obligations (and such additional issues as the protection of the exception of the contractual party who relied upon one rather than the other). When necessary, these issues are settled according to the plan dealing with the merger of the parent and subsidiary, the result being that only one claim remains, which is more beneficial to a creditor. (Furthermore, there is also the method of providing for the same rate of distribution without a merger as to both the parent and the subsidiary.)

On the other hand, in bankruptcy there is usually no automatic linkage of the bankruptcy petitions of the parent and subsidiary. Even should both submit bankruptcy petitions, the procedural representative (trustee) will be different for each, and proceedings will progress separately under the separate administration of each of the estates. However, in practice it is common for the creditors meeting to convene in the same place at the same time, or to have other limited joint administration.

[78]Dispositions of combined enterprises under Japanese insolvency procedure are taken from the vantage point of procedural law and developed into the concept of procedural consolidation. M. Ito, *Saimusha Kosei Tetsuzuki no Kenkyu* (*Debtor Rehabilitation Procedure*, pp. 277,321(1984).

Obligations between the parent and subsidiary, and guarantee obligations on behalf of another party, and other obligations, following general principles, are to be separately settled (given the premise of separately established legal entities, but subject to a piercing of the corporate veil). This type of clear distinction between corporate reorganisation and bankruptcy arises from the economic need that the operation and preservation of a subsidiary's assets must be maintained for the benefit of the continuing operation and reconstruction of the parent corporation. Thus, one must separate this inquiry into two cases: (i) that in which a Japanese parent debtor intends to reorganise (for the success of the reorganisation, the foreign subsidiary is considered here to be indispensable); and (ii) that in which the debtor is to be liquidated.

(b) Reorganisation of Japanese parent company

Assuming that the foreign subsidiary (either registered in the foreign country or having a principal office, as set forth in the articles of incorporation, in the foreign country) is vital to the successful reorganisation of the parent debtor, management of a wholly-owned subsidiary will ordinarily be based in Japan. For the purpose of jurisdiction, it will usually suffice that there is at least an operational office in Japan (and, if there is more than one such office, that one of them is principal). If this is the case, then section 6 of the Corporate Reorganisation Law establishes the Japanese District Court's jurisdiction over the foreign subsidiary. In this case, no obstacle is presented by the fact that the subsidiary is a company organised according to the corporation law of a foreign and not a Japanese corporation.[79] Thus, in theory, corporate reorganisation procedures of the parent as well as its subsidiary can proceed jointly in Japan.

From this perspective, a Japanese parent and its foreign subsidiaries may benefit from consolidated, unified procedures for reorganisation. In the alternative, the trustee may draft proposals maintaining the independence of the corporate personality of the parent and its subsidiary in the foreign country (claiming, for example, that problems of multiple filing creditors can be resolved by altering the payout ratio).

Moreover, it is not inconceivable that the jointly proposed plan may contain a provision for a bold international merger between the parent and the subsidiary.[80] If such

---

[79]Corp. Reorg. Law, s 1; Kaneko, *Jokai Kaisha Koseiho*, p. 133.

[80]For introduction of the International Law Association, at their 1960 Hamburg Convention, T. Kawakami, "*Kaisha*" ["Corporations"], in 3 *Kokusai Shiho Koza (International Private Law* 727 (1964). s 4, paragraph 4 of the Treaty Relating to the Acknowledgment of the Corporate Character of Foreign Company, Affiliations and Corporate Associations, adopted at the Seventh Hague International Private Law Convention: Mergers between a company, association (*Die Verein*), or estate (*Die Stiftung*) chartered as a legal entity in a contracting state with another company, association or estate chartered as a legal entity, the legal entity in another contracting state shall be recognised by all contracting states, provided that such merger is permitted within each of the relevant states.

In Japan, prior to the Seventh Hague Convention, a response to the questionnaire published relating to affiliated countries was returned by the Tokyo University Property Law Research Association, as follows: "The establishment of provisions concerning mergers between corporations incorporated in one of the contracting countries and another such corporation established in another contracting country is desirable. However, for such a purpose, it is necessary that the merger be recognised according to the incorporation law governing each company." Furthermore, T. Suzuki and T. Yazawa prepared the "Opinion on the Treaty Concerning Corporation", according to which, since "Japanese law lacks such legislation," the envisaged international mergers would not be recognised. See 340 *Homushiryo [Materials Concerning Legal Affairs]*, No. 340: *Shusengo ni Okero Kokusai Shiho ni Kansuru Hague Joyakuan (3)*, [Post-War Treaty Provisions of the Hague Convention Relating to International Private Law], pp. 152, 653, 674 (1956).

a merger can be seen as an actual investment in kind, then the difficulty of having two corporations' laws governing both companies would cease to be a problem. In any event, under the Corporate Reorganisation Law, there are widespread exceptions to mergers pursuant to the Commercial Code. Furthermore, the merger of a domestic corporation and foreign company must be approved under the corporate and other laws of the foreign legal system.[81] However, whether the foreign country recognises the corporate reorganisation procedure in Japan, and whether the legal entity resulting from the international merger will be recognised, are separate problems. Further, the above discussion describes what is possible in theory, but as yet there have been no test cases using these arrangements.

If the methods described in **5.6.1(a)** are seen to be unusual techniques in the foreign country, then after having followed separate reorganisation procedures following the laws of the country, the foreign court could still select the Japanese reorganisation representative as the procedural representative of the subsidiary. Whether this choice is made or not, the second step must be to create a common plan which maintains equality among creditors, while adequately protecting creditors who have relied upon the legal distribution between the parent and subsidiary companion, all in an equitable and impartial manner.

At that time, creditors of the subsidiary may attempt to employ various devices, such as piercing the corporate veil, confidential/fiduciary relationships, and tort theories[82] in filing their proofs of claim, or in litigating against the Japanese parent debtor. Conversely, the creditors of the debtor in Japan may also use various theories to attempt to assert their claims against the assets of the foreign subsidiary. When these types of issues arise, the decision of how to conduct the disposition will probably be made by providing in each of the plan(s) with a balancing device, whereby their claims are treated as much as possible in the same way as they would be in a consolidated or jointly processed proceeding.

(c) Bankruptcy of the Japanese parent company

When the parent debtor undertakes bankruptcy instead of corporate reorganisation, a major concern is to gain direct access to the foreign subsidiary, in other words, to its assets and liabilities. Of course, it should not be forgotten that reasonable steps to preserve assets for the employees of the subsidiary resident in the foreign country are also necessary. Thereafter, as seen from corporate reorganisation described theoretically in **5.6.1(b)** (as also in the instance of an insolvency at the Japanese court where the bankruptcy procedure of the parent debtor was commenced), there are grounds for the court assuming bankruptcy jurisdiction over the foreign subsidiary if the activities of the foreign wholly-owned subsidiary operations are controlled from Japan, or if not, if the Japanese principal office is ascertainable.

Theoretically, it is conceivable that there would be no harm in the same person undertaking the responsibilities of the trustee for both parent and subsidiary, and indeed many benefits could be derived. However, conflicts of interest arising from the debt and credit obligations between the parent and subsidiary, and instances where the parent's misman-

---

[81]Business Corporation Law, s 907 (New York).
[82]S. Ochiai, "*Takokuseki Kigyo ni okeru Kogaisha no Saikensha Hogo*" ["Protection of Creditors of the Subsidiaries of Multi-National Enterprises"], in *Takokuseki Kigyo to Kokusai Torihiki* [*Multinational Enterprises and International Transactions*], pp. 381 *et seq* (1987).

agement extends to the subsidiary, would have to be carefully considered, and would probably result in the appointment of a different bankruptcy trustee. Amongst the innovations for maintaining impartiality and equality between creditors, a merger would, unfortunately, probably be rejected as lacking substance, and partiality or inequality would be settled according to general principles. In particular, various balancing means should be employed to achieve equality and fairness, whether it be a so-called hotchpot style adjustment, a disallowance of the debts and obligations between the parent and subsidiary, or a negation of a claim (ie the treatment as stock) or subordination.[83] Furthermore, all this is based upon the premise that the bankruptcy in Japan as against the foreign subsidiary will be acknowledged in the foreign country (or, at least that objections will not be voiced or a duplicate procedure will not be commenced).

On the other hand, the trustee may employ the strategy of entrusting the bankruptcy procedure to the courts of the foreign country, and only exercising its stockholder's rights (including the right to initiate liquidation, or to cause a legal representative to petition for bankruptcy). At that time, one should yield to the foreign country's procedures, thereafter seeking adjustments of many of the legal relationships including those discussed above with the foreign subsidiary's procedural representative (the Japanese trustee and its designee or some unrelated party).

Cases are reported in which the trustee of the Japanese parent concluded the disposition of its subsidiary in a foreign country by making sales abroad, including in the foreign country itself, of the stock of the subsidiary. There are others in which the trustee effected the liquidation of its foreign subsidiary following the laws of the foreign country, to be followed by a bankruptcy petition filed due to a deteriorated situation concerning the liquidation. And there are other known situations in which the trustee, while designating the responsible management of the foreign country, effected an out of court workout with local creditors in the foreign country.

5.6.2 Effect of foreign parent insolvency proceedings upon its Japanese subsidiary

(a) Effect where there are foreign proceedings against the Japanese subsidiary
Japan's basic policy is as previously described. The case to be described here first is one in which Japanese courts have received requests for co-operation from a foreign country, when bankruptcy proceedings were commenced there involving a Japanese subsidiary. If the centre of the Japanese subsidiary's operations, notwithstanding that its registered office is in Japan, is in the foreign country and the foreign insolvency proceedings are based upon principal jurisdiction over the subsidiary, the effect of such proceedings will more likely than not be recognised in Japan, and the courts will be greatly inclined to provide the requested co-operation.

When there are bankruptcy petitions from Japanese creditors against the Japanese subsidiary, whether the court may halt their petitions (given that the court has recognised the effect of the bankruptcy procedure of the Japanese subsidiary commenced in the foreign country) and dismiss such claims in its discretion is a difficult problem. Essentially, this is particularly the same kind of problem as that posed with respect to the effect of the foreign insolvency procedures concerning a foreign debtor: whether

---

[83]Y. Tashiro, *Oyako Kaisha no Horitsu* [*The Law of Parent and Subsidiary Companies*], pp. 52 *et seq* (1968).

the creditor's petition against the foreign debtor in Japan is subject to discretionary dismissal. In that particular case if one can conclude that individual creditor actions may be prevented in the domestic setting, then with the same argument it could also be concluded that the petition for bankruptcy against the foreign debtor in Japan may be dismissed. If such is the case, then it is also conceivable that the court should be able to stop the bankruptcy procedures against the Japanese subsidiary petitioned by creditors in Japan under the rationale that bankruptcy procedures of the Japanese subsidiary in the parent's country have already been commenced, and dismiss them under its discretion. However, it is safe to predict that parallel bankruptcy procedures would be initiated in Japan because of a strong notion among Japanese jurists that the subsidiary is incorporated under the corporate laws of Japan, and the home office of the company is registered in Japan.

(b) Effect where there are no foreign insolvency proceedings against the Japanese subsidiary

If no insolvency proceedings have commenced in a foreign country with respect to the subsidiary in Japan, then proceedings initiated by its parent debtor as the stockholder of the Japanese subsidiary based upon its ownership will be processed as a domestic Japanese proceeding. If the procedure undertaken in Japan is essentially extra-judicial (eg winding-up or even special winding-up), the appointment of the representative of the parent debtor in the foreign proceedings as the local representative of the subsidiary in Japan would be respected, but one might be safer predicting a negative attitude in Japanese judicial proceedings. However, it is submitted that this type of co-operation would not be inappropriate. Under Japanese domestic procedure, the repayment plan, even where such plan is presented by the foreign representative and contains a provision for maintaining equality among domestic and foreign creditors, will be subjected to majority rule, and the majority may fairly authorise it.

Aside from the case in which Japanese bankruptcy procedure for the subsidiary has been opened in Japan, the exercise of individual rights by creditors of either the foreign country or Japan against the subsidiary in Japan or its assets there will probably be permitted, since it is taken as a premise that bankruptcy proceedings are not pending in the foreign country against the Japanese subsidiary.

5.7 Bilateral and multilateral treaties

5.7.1 Bankruptcy treaties to which Japan is a signatory

Japan is not a signatory to any such treaty, except the previously described Model Treaty which has been published.

5.8 Legislation

5.8.1 New bankruptcy legislation or any preparation in process

There is no such relevant domestic legislation in preparation, although the published revised outline has already been mentioned. However, demands for legislation from scholars, as well as from the business community, have been quite strong. It is anticipated that the development of the law through future cases and business practice will increase these demands.

Annex 1
Preliminary Draft of the
International Bankruptcy Related Provisions
in the Japanese Insolvency Proceedings

Section 1 Purpose of this preliminary draft

The purpose of this preliminary draft is fairly to satisfy the rights of local and foreign creditors by establishing and/or revising statutory provisions related to international insolvency cases with respect to insolvency proceedings in Japan such as bankruptcy, corporate reorganisation, composition, arrangement, and special liquidation.

Section 2 International jurisdiction of insolvency cases

(1) Ordinary jurisdiction

(i) Japanese courts have jurisdiction over insolvency proceedings for debtors who have their principal office or centre of business in Japan.

(ii) It is presumed that Japanese persons and legal persons established under Japanese laws have their principal office or center of business in Japan.

(2) Complementary jurisdiction

Even if a debtor has his principal office or centre of business in a foreign country, if such debtor has property in Japan, the Japanese courts will have jurisdiction. However, if a petition for the commencement of insolvency proceedings is made on the ground that nominal property exists in Japan, the court has the discretion to dismiss the petition.

Section 3 Extraterritorial effect of Japanese insolvency proceedings

(1) Extraterritorial effect of insolvency proceedings based upon ordinary jurisdiction

If Japanese courts commence bankruptcy proceedings based upon ordinary jurisdiction as specified in section 2(1), the effect thereof shall extend to property which the debtor owns in foreign countries.

(2) Extraterritorial effect of insolvency proceedings based on complementary jurisdiction

Alternative I. If Japanese courts commence proceedings based on complementary jurisdiction as specified in section 2(2), the effect thereof shall not extend to property of the debtor in foreign countries.

Alternative II. If Japanese courts commence proceedings based on complementary jurisdiction specified in section 2(2), provided that foreign courts have not commenced proceedings based upon ordinary jurisdiction, the effect of the proceedings in Japan shall extend to property of the debtor in foreign countries.

(3) Trustee's responsibility for administration and disposal of property in foreign countries

A trustee shall be responsible with due diligence and care for the administration of property in foreign countries to which the effect of proceedings in Japan extend, provided, however, that, in accordance with Article 197, section 12 of the Bankruptcy Law and Article 54, section 7 of the Corporate Reorganisation Law, the trustee may waive the right of administration and disposal of such property in foreign countries if the administration and disposal of such property is difficult.

(4) Request of co-operation of foreign courts

(i) If there is the necessity for the administration of property to which the extraterritorial effect extends, the trustee may request a foreign court's co-operation in taking any appropriate measures therefor.

(ii) In case of the request of cooperation specified in i) above, the trustee shall obtain the approval of courts in accordance with Article 197 of the Bankruptcy Law, Article 54 of the Corporate Reorganisation Law, and others.

(5) Authorisation of preservation administrator

A preservation administrator appointed by a court based on preservative measure: prior to commencement of insolvency proceedings shall have the same rights as the trustee with respect to property in foreign countries.

Section 4 The intraterritorial effect of foreign insolvency proceedings

(1) Intra-territorial effect

If a foreign court commences insolvency proceedings based on ordinary jurisdiction and a Japanese court recognises such proceedings based on a petition by the trustee in accordance with section 4(3), the effect of the foreign proceedings shall extend to the property of the debtor in Japan. However, before such recognition is made, the foreign trustee can exercise rights as to the property in Japan in place of the debtor.

(2) Variation of foreign proceedings

Even if a debtor, instead of the trustee, has a right to administer and dispose of his property under foreign insolvency proceedings, Japanese courts may recognise the intra-territorial effect thereof based on a petition of the debtor.

(3) Application for recognition of intra-territorial effect

(i) A foreign trustee may petition Japanese courts to recognise foreign proceedings.

(ii) If a petition in accordance with section 4(3)(i) is made, the court may examine persons interested.

(4) Court of recognition

A petition for acknowledgment of foreign insolvency proceedings shall be made to the court which has jurisdiction over the recognition proceedings.

(5) Order for preservation

The court which accepts the petition for recognition may issue an order for preservation based on the petition until such court makes a judgment regarding the recognition.

(6) Requirements for the recognition

The courts shall rule to recognise foreign insolvency proceedings only if it is determined that the foreign insolvency proceedings have been commenced under ordinary jurisdiction and that none of the following occur:

(A) there is a possibility that the rights of all persons interested as to debtors may not be treated fairly;
(B) there is a possibility that the interests of local creditors may be unduly harmed;
(C) there is a substantial discrepancy between the applicable foreign laws and the Japanese proceedings with respect to the priorities of the rights of the persons interested; or
(D) the foreign insolvency proceedings violate Japanese public policy.

(7) Petition of protest

A person interested may make an immediate complaint against the decision on the petition for recognition.

(8) Effect of recognition

(i) In case a court makes a decision approving recognition, the court shall make an official request for registration of the bankruptcy with respect to the corporation registration and real estate registration and issue an official notice of such decision, and notices to all creditors known to the court.
(ii) In case a court makes a recognition decision, the foreign proceedings shall become effective in Japan retrospectively as of the date of the decision to commence the proceedings in the foreign country.
(iii) The effect of foreign proceedings recognised by Japanese court shall be decided in accordance with the laws of the place where the insolvency proceedings are commenced. The effect shall be specified in the recognition decision, provided, however, that if as a result of the effectiveness of the recognition, any creditors of priority, such as creditors of tax claims or labour claims, are prohibited from exercising their claims and the disadvantages to the creditors caused by the prohibition is substantial, the court may withdraw the prohibition of the exercise of such claims.

(9) Supervision of foreign trustee

(i) In case a recognition decision is made, supervision of a foreign trustee is determined by foreign insolvency proceedings, provided however that the court of recognition may order that a foreign trustee report the execution of his duties to the court or to a representative of the local creditors.

(ii) In case the execution of the duties of the foreign trustee substantially harms the interests of the local creditors the court of recognition may revoke all or part of the recognition decision.

(10) Co-operation in foreign proceedings

In case of necessity, the court of recognition may take measures, including appointment of an assistance trustee to the foreign trustee.

Section 5 Concurrent insolvencies

(1) Equalisation of distribution

When insolvency proceedings are pending simultaneously in Japan and a foreign country with respect to a certain debtor and a certain creditor files claims in both proceedings, a court shall deem any distribution which the creditor received or is expected to receive in the foreign proceedings as a distribution which the creditor receives in the Japanese proceedings.

(2) Suspension of concurrent insolvency proceedings

If an insolvency proceeding is commenced with respect to a certain debtor in a Japanese court under complementary jurisdiction, thereafter an insolvency proceeding is commenced with respect to the debtor in a foreign court under ordinary jurisdiction, and the foreign proceeding is recognised under section 4(3) above, the Japanese court which commenced the Japanese insolvency proceeding shall suspend the Japanese insolvency proceedings.

(3) Concurrent insolvencies based upon petition of foreign trustee

A foreign trustee may petition a Japanese court to commence insolvency proceedings for a debtor against whom insolvency proceedings have already been commenced in a foreign country.

Section 6 Position of foreigners in insolvency proceedings

Foreigners or foreign corporations shall have the same position as Japanese and Japanese corporations with respect to insolvency proceedings.

Section 7 Discharge

(1) Recognition of the foreign discharge

If discharge is granted to a debtor under a foreign insolvency proceeding, and if a foreign trustee or the debtor petitions the recognition of the foreign insolvency proceeding in the Japanese courts under section 4(3) and obtains a recognition decision, the discharge shall become effective in Japan.

(2) Recognition of Japanese discharge

If a debtor obtains a decision of discharge under Japanese insolvency proceedings, the decision shall be effective in foreign countries.

The International Bankruptcy Research Group which developed the draft was comprised of: M. Takeshita, M. Ito, K. Takeuchi, M. Nishizawa, T. Uehara, J. Yokoyama, H. Nomura, and Y. Hasebe. (The above translation is a reproduction of the same in Takeshita, KOKUSAI TOSANHO 428.)

Annex 2
International Bilateral Treaty

Japan and _____ make the following treaty with respect to their respective insolvency laws:

1 The scope of the treaty

(1) This Treaty shall apply to the following proceedings in a contracting State.

1 "Bankruptcy", "Composition", "Arrangement", "Special Liquidation", and "Corporate Reorganisation" under Japanese Law.

2 ————, ————, under the laws of ————————.

(2) Under this treaty, the proceedings in the preceding subsection shall be called "insolvency proceedings".

2 Jurisdiction

(1) The court having jurisdiction over the insolvency proceedings is that of the state where the debtor has its principal office or its centre of business.

(2) If the court given jurisdiction in accordance with the preceding subsection is prevented from commencing insolvency proceedings by domestic law, and if the debtor has a place of business or property in the other state's territory, this territory's court shall have jurisdiction. In this case, the insolvency proceedings shall have effect only within the territory of the state where proceedings are commenced.

3 Universality

(1) The effect of insolvency proceedings which are commenced in one contracting state according to this treaty shall extend to the other, except in the case of the second sentence of 2(2). The same is true of the effect of preservative measures, where the laws providing for the insolvency proceedings allow this before the commencement of the insolvency proceedings.

(2) Insolvency proceedings commenced in one contracting state shall take effect in the other contracting state at the time the proceeding is to take effect according to the laws of the commencing state.

4 Unity

(1) When a court in one of the contracting states commences insolvency proceedings, as long as proceedings continue, a court in the other state cannot commence insolvency proceedings with respect to the same debtor. Where the latter has already taken some preservative measures, these measures shall be deemed to have been taken by the former.

(2) When a court in one of the contracting states dismisses a petition to commence insolvency proceedings on the ground that a court in the other state has jurisdiction,

and the decision is final and binding, the court in the latter state cannot dismiss the petition to commence insolvency proceedings on the ground that a court tn the former state has jurisdiction.

(3) When insolvency proceedings are commenced in a court in one of the contracting states, the court has jurisdiction over the litigation to allow creditor's claim and the litigation concerning propriety of the trustee's administration, except in the following situations:

1. Where the litigation concerns an employment contract, under which the work is or should be performed in the other state.
2. Where the litigation concerns taxes or a similar claim based on public law.

5 Applicable law

The laws of the state where insolvency proceedings are commenced shall be applicable.

6 Proclamation and notice

When a court in one of the contracting states commences insolvency proceedings, the court can make official requests in the following matters to the previously appointed authorities of the other state, provided that the debtor has either a place of business or property in the other state, or that any obligees lives there.

1. Proclamation of those matters requiring notification according to the law of the state where the insolvency proceedings take place.
2. Notice of the above matters to known obligees.
3. Entry in public records, such as registers, where commencement of insolvency proceedings must be so entered in accordance with the law of the state where the proceedings take place.

7 Trustee's power

(1) Powers vested in a trustee by the law of the contracting state commencing insolvency proceedings shall extend to the territory of the other state.

(2) The court commencing insolvency proceedings can request the court of the other state to appoint a co-trustee.

8 Executory contract

When, at the commencement of insolvency proceedings, a contract has not been completely performed on both sides, the law of the contracting state commencing the insolvency proceedings shall determine the validity of the contract, except the following cases:

1. The effect of insolvency proceedings on an ongoing employment contract shall be determined according to the law of the state where the work is or should be performed.
2. The effect of an insolvency proceeding on a contract to lease real estate shall be determined according to the law of the state where the real estate lies.

9 Continuing litigation or execution

When any litigation or execution by an individual creditor is pending at the commencement of insolvency proceedings in one of the contracting states, the law of the contracting states commencing the insolvency proceedings shall determine the effect of the insolvency proceedings on the litigation or execution.

10 Claims and priority claims

The law of the contracting state commencing insolvency proceedings shall be applicable in determining the allowance of claims and priority claims.

11 Preferential claims and securities (draft I)

(1) The validity, extent, and priority of preferential claims for the entire insolvency estate (except as provided at (6)) shall be determined according to the law applicable to the claims, and the status of such preferential claims under insolvency proceedings shall be determined according to the law of the state commencing such proceedings.

(2) The validity, extent, and priority of preferential claims for specific movables that are situated in one of the contracting states at the commencement of insolvency proceedings shall be determined according to the law of that state, and the status of such preferential claims under insolvency proceedings shall be determined according to the law of the state commencing such proceedings.

(3) The validity, extent, and priority of preferential claims for specific real estate that is situated in one of the contracting states at the commencement of insolvency proceedings shall be determined according to the law of that state, and the status of such preferential claims under insolvency proceedings shall be determined according to the law of the state commencing such proceedings.

(4) The validity, extent, and priority of preferential claims for specific ships and airplanes that are registered in one of the contracting states at the commencement of insolvency proceedings shall be determined according to the law of that state and the law applicable to the preferential claims, and the status of such preferential claims under insolvency proceedings shall be determined according to the law of the state commencing such proceedings.

(5) The validity, extent, and priority of preferential claims for specific claims that are situated in one of the contracting states at the commencement of insolvency proceedings shall be determined according to the law of that state, and the status of such preferential claims under insolvency proceedings shall be determined according to the law of the state commencing such proceedings.

(6) The validity, extent, and priority of preferential claims for the entire insolvency estate based on employment relations for the work that is or should be performed in one of the contracting states shall be determined according to the law of that state, and the status of such preferential claims under insolvency proceedings shall be determined according to the law of the state commencing such proceedings.

(7) The validity, extent, and priority of preferential claims for the entire insolvency estate concerning taxes or social security in one of the contracting states shall be determined according to the law of that state, and the status of such preferential

claims under insolvency proceedings shall be determined according to the law of the state commencing such proceedings.

11 Preferential claims and securities (draft II)

(1) The same as draft I.

(2) The validity, extent, and priority of preferential claims for specific movables that are situated in one of the contracting states at the commencement of insolvency proceedings, and the status of such preferential claims under insolvency proceedings, shall be determined according to the law of that state.

(3) The validity, extent, and priority of preferential claims for specific real estate that is situated in one of the contracting states at the commencement of insolvency proceedings, and the status of such preferential claims under insolvency proceedings, shall be determined according to the law of that state.

(4) The validity, extent, and priority of preferential claims for specific ships and airplanes that are registered in one of the contracting states at the commencement of the insolvency proceedings and the status of such preferential claims under insolvency proceedings, shall be determined according to the law of that state.

(5) The validity, extent, and priority of preferential claims for specific claims that are situated in one of the contracting states at the commencement of insolvency proceedings, shall be determined according to the law of that state.

(6) The validity, extent, and priority of preferential claims for the entire insolvency estate based on the employment relations for the work that is or should be performed in one of the contracting states, and the status of such preferential claims under insolvency proceedings, shall be determined according to the law of that state. As to property in the other contracting state, this privilege is subordinate to preferential claims for the entire insolvency estate based on employment relations for the work that is or should be performed in the other state.

(7) The validity, extent, and priority of preferential claims for the entire insolvency estate concerning taxes or social security in one of the contracting states, and the status of such preferential claims under insolvency proceedings, shall be determined according to the law of that state. As to property in the other contracting state, this privilege is subordinate to preferential claims for the entire insolvency estate concerning taxes or social security in the other country.

12 Filing, hearing and allowance of claims

(1) The proceedings relating to the filing, hearing, and allowance of claims by interested persons shall be governed according to the law of the state where insolvency proceedings are commenced.

(2) The court may grant an extension of time for the filing of claims for the sake of interested persons living in the other contracting state.

13 Disqualification and so on

Whether or not and to what extent the commenced proceedings take effect for purpose of disqualification etc in the other state as against the insolvent debtor is determined according to the law of the other state.

14 Respect for other treaties

No provision in this treaty shall violate the provisions of other insolvency proceedings treaties that one of the contracting states has concluded or will conclude.

15 Disputes in administration of this treaty

Disputes between the contracting states regarding the interpretation or application of this treaty shall be resolved in a diplomatic manner.

The International Bankruptcy Research Group which developed the Draft was comprised of: M. Takeshita, M. Ito, K. Takeuchi, M. Nishizawa, T. Uehara, J. Yokoyama, H. Nomura, and Y. Hasebe. (The above translation is a reproduction of the same in Takeshita, KOKUSAI TOSANHO.)

6

New Frontiers in Canadian Cross-Border Insolvencies

E. Bruce Leonard and Christopher W. Besant

Cassels Brock & Blackwell, Toronto, Ontario, Canada

6.1 Introduction

Reorganisations of multinational corporations have occupied an increasingly greater role in the Canadian insolvency experience, particularly in the last 24 months. As the trend toward continentalisation in North America and globalisation worldwide continues, lenders and credit-grantors and their professional advisers are being confronted more and more frequently with restructurings and reorganisations of businesses that have multinational dimensions. In the same way that courts have structured innovative and flexible solutions to domestic restructurings, a comparable approach seems to be emerging in restructurings that have cross-border aspects. In the cross-border context, however, the application of non-traditional solutions to conventional financial problems can sometimes result in unusual or surprising consequences.

The scope and extent of this new approach to cross-border restructurings is best illustrated by the recent series of unprecedented orders made by the Ontario Court of Justice in supervising the cross-border reorganisation of the Bramalea Limited Group of companies (the "Bramalea Group"). The *Bramalea* restructuring has dramatic implications for restructuring planning, as well as for cross-border lending practices. For lenders, *Bramalea* carries with it the potential to undo the benefit of lending arrangements made to stable subsidiaries of unstable corporate groups. Internationally, it also suggests that lending arrangements outside Canada concerning assets located outside Canada may be vulnerable to renegotiation by the borrower with the assistance of a Canadian court.

At first glance, the *Bramalea* reorganisation may appear to indicate the development of protectionist sentiment in the handling by Canadian courts of international insolvency cases. When closely examined, however, it is in fact not a nationalist exer-

Current Issues in Cross-Border Insolvency and Reorganisations (E. B. Leonard, C. W. Besant, eds.; 1–85333–958–X; © International Bar Association; pub. Graham & Trotman/International Bar Association, 1994; printed in Great Britain), pp. 103-117.

cise but rather more of a landmark on the path towards a cross-border reorganisational policy. It is significant, moreover, that the development of a cross-border reorganisational policy should emanate from the judicial arena — a reflection on the obvious absence of legislative or treaty solutions to multinational insolvencies and reorganisations.

6.2   The reorganisational context

Reorganisational statutes have been part of international legal landscape for decades but they are now becoming an integral feature of commercial life in all the major industrialised countries. The implications of this development are still being worked out, but it is clear that the very nature of the insolvency process has been altered and that the balance of power between lenders and their borrowers has been shifting toward the borrowers.

All insolvency processes seek to resolve the tension between the legal and economic structures of an organisation. Bankruptcy has traditionally achieved such a resolution by terminating contractual overcommitments and punishing the errant promisor by the distribution of its assets to creditors. While bankruptcy is not supposed to be punitive, the subtle references in the process to the "rehabilitation of the debtor" betray the nineteenth century origins of modern bankruptcy statutes. In other words, bankruptcy, in its origins, could be seen as the result of commercially inappropriate behaviour by a debtor and, perhaps, even as evidence of moral deficiencies as well. Indeed, the stigma of bankruptcy persisted as a deterrent to the use of the process until the dawn of the "workout" philosophy of recent times.

With the shift to a reorganisational emphasis in the insolvency process, the core problem of insolvency is no longer the immoral debtor, but poor risk management by all of the affected parties, including creditors. Consequently, the emphasis in the process is no longer on asset distribution and the natural outcome of the process is no longer a full liquidation. Rather, the thrust of the process is negotiation and problem-solving, and both the debtor on the one hand and its creditors on the other must participate because they are all responsible in some degree for their common plight. To encourage such negotiations, the debtor has been given certain remedies to forestall the liquidation process and force a renegotiation to take place.

Although the focus of the reorganisation process is on negotiation, reorganisational statutes also recognise the limits of contractual solutions for complex problems. In any restructuring negotiation, there is always a potential for inconclusive results, particularly where a large number of stakeholders is involved. Reorganisational statutes therefore inevitably provide for court supervision of the negotiation process, and allow the creditors democratically to resolve those issues that cannot be solved to everyone's satisfaction through negotiation. The nature of the court-supervised negotiating framework imposed by a reorganisational statute influences the negotiations that occur and dramatically shapes the outcome of that process. There was a monumental contrast between the outcomes of the largely unsuccessful *Olympia & York* restructuring and the *Bramalea* reorganisation. Both processes took place under the same statute, and although the difference in outcomes was due to a host of factors, it is clear that the judicial role in defining the outcome of a restructuring looms large.

The structure of the *Bramalea* reorganisation addressed a further tension between the economic and legal organisation of business activities which has not been dealt with adequately in traditional insolvency processes. Generally, a single business is often carried on by a range of different legal entities, ie, corporations and various subsidiaries, and even partnerships and joint ventures. To restructure such a business in accordance with traditional principles requires a series of reorganisational processes to be established in parallel, each of which must reach a successful conclusion. If the entity is multinational in scope, it becomes virtually certain that more than one court will be involved in the process, and that more than one reorganisational scheme will be applicable to various parts of what is in reality the same business. Restructuring can easily become virtually impossible in such an environment. The disintegration of the *Olympia & York* restructuring was in part due to this phenomenon.

The traditional approach ignores the reality of the organisation of a business in which various legal entities are assembled in a hierarchy which only loosely parallels the economic structure of the overall business. It also overlooks the fact that a multinational business has a centre of gravity where its senior management is usually located and from which a number of centralised banking and other business arrangements are arranged and operated. It does not adequately reflect the fact that lenders regard their exposure as being to the corporate group generally, as well as to the particular legal entity to which they have lent. And it ignores the fact that there are cross-default clauses in the debt instruments of the various legal entities in the group which effectively merge their respective financial fates.

Consequently, fragmented reorganisational processes, particularly those that are also jurisdictionally fragmented, are ultimately self-defeating. The object of the process should be to facilitate all of the stakeholders of a business renegotiating their claims in a manner compatible with the financial realities of the business in which they have invested. The fact that a reorganisation filing has been made is recognition that the process cannot be concluded consensually, ie without the structure and compulsion provided by a reorganisational statute. Fragmented reorganisation processes are much less likely to lead to a solution for the business as a whole, and, if part of the business fails, the rest is much more likely to collapse. This might be called the "O & Y problem".

The *Bramalea* restructuring was a reaction to the O & Y problem. It created a single process for the restructuring of multiple, multi-jurisdictional entities that together arguably constituted a single business. However, in adopting an essentially economic rather than legalistic approach to restructuring that was macro-economically rational, it by-passed a number of the traditional legal and micro-economic issues involved in the process. While the costs of the failure of the business as a whole were thereby successfully avoided, the process dealt less adequately with the question of how the costs of saving the business were to be allocated among the creditors involved. This issue is not simply one of legal fairness but it also has serious ramifications for financing practices: the issue of who wins and who loses in a restructuring affects risk assessment and the pricing and legal structure of future loans. The ripples from the *Bramalea* restructuring have already begun to affect financial ratings of corporate groups that contain unstable members.

6.3 The CCAA: Chapter 11 without rules

To appreciate the context in which the *Olympia & York* and *Bramalea* restructurings proceeded, an understanding of the reorganisational parameters of the Companies' Creditors Arrangements Act (the "CCAA") will be of assistance. The CCAA is probably the most unusual piece of reorganisational legislation in the world. It is only 20 sections long and, in its origins in the depths of the Depression of the 1930s, it was intended to facilitate the reorganisation of major public companies with complicated public debt structures. Instead, 60 year later, it has turned out to provide the most effective framework for financial restructurings that Canada has ever had.

Canada's old (pre-30 November 1992) Bankruptcy Act had procedures that allowed for the financial restructuring of *unsecured* debt and, while these provisions contained a form of automatic stay of proceedings by unsecured creditors, they contained only a very limited ability to deal with secured creditors. As secured credit became more and more important in Canada, the relevance of reorganisational regime that could deal only with unsecured credit became more and more questionable. The CCAA, through its ability to deal effectively with both secured and unsecured debt, has consequently emerged as an effective regime for reorganising financially-troubled businesses and has become the reorganisational vehicle of choice in large and complicated restructurings.

Virtually any business in financial difficulty is potentially eligible to use the CCAA. Where the court grants protection under the CCAA, a general stay of proceedings is imposed against both secured and unsecured creditors unless the court grants permission for the proceedings to take place. The scope and the extent of stays granted by the courts under the CCAA have become steadily broader and more comprehensive as experience with the CCAA continues such that, at present, stay orders in CCAA proceedings are routinely granted in extraordinarily comprehensive terms. The initial stay of proceedings is effective for a period of, typically, from 30 to 60 days (although initial periods of protection for up to six months have been granted on occasion) and the period of protection can usually be extended if the court is satisfied that constructive negotiations for the reorganisation are taking place.

The evolving practice under the CCAA shows the extent to which the CCAA framework can be utilised to protect reorganising debtors. The key to an appreciation of the CCAA as a reorganisational statute is the unparalled jurisdiction that it provides to the courts to supervise the reorganisational process. There are very few fixed rules within the CCAA. The time-limits within which a reorganisation must be completed are not set out in the statute and are governed by the discretion of the court. Applications for relief from the comprehensive stays imposed by CCAA orders are difficult and are usually unsuccessful. There are no specific provisions in the statute for the classification of creditors into distinct classes for purpose of voting on a CCAA plan of arrangement and thereafter participating in it. Suppliers to the reorganising business are, moreover, normally prohibited from terminating their arrangements with the business except with the court's permission and suppliers have, on occasion, been required to continue to supply goods and services under their existing agreements with the reorganising business as long as the goods and services were paid for on normal trade terms.

To be successful, a debtor's plan of arrangement under the CCAA must be accepted by all of the classes of creditors to whom it is proposed and, thereafter, it must be approved by the court. Within classes of creditors, the plan must be accepted by 50% in number of the creditors present and voting who hold at least 75% in value of the claims represented.

What has not as yet developed adequately under the CCAA are principles dealing with the means by which creditors are classified for purposes of participating in CCAA plans. This is significant because there is no cram down procedure applicable in CCAA reorganisations for dissenting creditors. There are some signs that the courts may be prepared to deal with dissenting creditors that they consider unreasonable by placing them in larger classes where their dissenting votes might be neutralised in a much larger group of creditors supporting the plan. In Canada, perhaps, dissident creditors will be "swamped" rather than "crammed down", but the result seems quite similar.

The CCAA has been developing into a rough equivalent of a US Chapter 11 proceeding. But while Chapter 11 has detailed procedures and rules which are applicable to all reorganisations, CCAA reorganisations proceed in an *ad hoc* fashion and the rules are made up as the reorganisation proceeds. Canadian courts and legislators have always been slightly suspicious and apprehensive of certain features of Chapter 11 reorganisations, primarily the potential for delay by businesses that have no hope of successfully reorganising, and the expense involved in reorganisational proceedings. On the other hand, the creditor-oriented predilections of Canada's former Bankruptcy Act were clearly not efficient in fostering workouts and rehabilitations of viable but over-committed businesses.

The CCAA provides an effective and workable solution for restructuring complex financial arrangements. There is a discretion on the part of the courts as to whether protection will or will not be granted to a reorganising debtor which tends to eliminate from the system improperly-motivated debtors whose only desire is to stall for time. The very ambiguity in the CCAA which makes it maddeningly imprecise to some may actually be its strongest virtue. Faced with the prospect of a court with a virtually unlimited range of powers available to handle a reorganisation, a reorganising business and its major creditors have a real incentive to negotiate a commercially reasonable basis for the reorganisation in order to avoid the all-or-nothing choice that is often presented by contested reorganisational proceedings.

One of the objectives of Canada's new insolvency legislation was to attempt to convert the Bankruptcy Act (now entitled the "Bankruptcy and Insolvency Act") into an effective reorganisational statute and ultimately to dispel the need for parallel legislation such as the CCAA. The CCAA, however, has achieved such a degree of popularity and frequency of utilisation that it may be difficult to repeal it unless the reorganisational provisions of the new legislation are more successful than anyone at this point can predict. It is quite clear that, with the *Bramalea* restructuring and other recent developments under the CCAA and the arrival of the Bankruptcy and Insolvency Act, reorganisational practice in Canada will never be the same again.

6.4 Canada's new reorganisational system

The reform of Canada's insolvency legislation, which became effective late in 1992, and held the attention of the insolvency community and Canada's legislators for over 25 years. The last full-scale revision of Canada's insolvency legislation prior to 1992 took place in 1949 and the first studies in connection with reforming the 1949 legislation originated in the mid-1960s with the first formal report being presented in 1970. The first of seven actual legislative attempts to pass bankruptcy legislation took place in April 1975. After six failed attempts and another formal Commission to review insolvency reform generally, the seventh attempt at achieving new legislation was successful and Canada's new insolvency regime became effective on 30 November 1992.

The new legislation attempts to strike more of a balance between the rights of creditors and debtors, particularly in the area of commercial reorganisations. Some of the creditor-orientation of the old legislation has disappeared in the new regime, reflecting an express legislative policy toward favouring the reorganisation of financially-troubled businesses. Although greater protection is given to reorganising debtors, the new Act imposes specific tests and time-frames to attempt to curtail the potential for abuse by improperly-motivated debtors. There will, moreover, be a parliamentary review of the new Act after three years in operation which should allow deficiencies experienced in the initial phase of the new legislation to be identified and corrected.

The new legislation is not a complete revision and replacement of the old Bankruptcy Act, but it does offer far-ranging changes in some of the most significant areas of Canadian insolvency law and practice. Major changes have been enacted to facilitate commercial reorganisations and to enhance the rights of unpaid suppliers to recover their goods. There are new provisions dealing with realisations by secured creditors on their security and extensive amendments have been introduced to encourage consumer debtors to work out their financial difficulties in preference to simply declaring bankruptcy. New provisions were also introduced to reduce the preferential treatment currently given to government claims in reorganisations.

The primary focus of the new legislation, however, is on providing financially-troubled businesses greater opportunities to reorganise successfully. The old Bankruptcy Act was seen as being overly deferential to the rights of secured creditors. Because, in practice, it could effectively deal only with reorganisations of unsecured debt, it was in danger of losing its relevance as a reorganisational system. The new Bankruptcy and Insolvency Act has improved the opportunities for reorganising businesses to deal successfully with their creditors.

The most significant change in reorganisational practice under the new Bankruptcy and Insolvency Act is the availability of an automatic stay against proceedings by both secured and unsecured creditors. Upon the commencement of a reorganisation, there is an automatic stay for an initial period of 30 days in which the debtor is expected to file its plan of reorganisation. Subsequent to the plan filing, the stay continues until the meeting of creditors held to consider it which provides an additional stay period of 21 days. The stay of proceedings can be extended to permit the reorganising business additional time within which to file its plan. Extensions can be granted by the court up to a maximum period of six months although extensions can only be granted for 45 days at a time. As a counterbalance, the new legislation provides opportunities for secured creditors to challenge the stays of proceedings on the grounds of "material prejudice" or other equitable grounds. In an early case under the new legislation, moreover, an opposing majority of *unsecured* creditors were able to persuade the court to terminate the protection granted to the reorganising business even prior to the meeting of creditors scheduled to consider the debtor's plan.

Consequently, while the advantages of the new Bankruptcy and Insolvency Act for the reorganisation of smaller and medium-sized business are fairly clear, there is still some doubt that it provides the most flexible means to restructure a large or complicated commercial organisation. For the most part, large reorganisations have, even after the inception of the Bankruptcy and Insolvency Act, proceeded under the familiar and flexible provisions of the CCAA, and the *Bramalea* restructuring was no exception to this general rule.

6.5 Background to the *Bramalea* restructuring

Bramalea Limited was the ultimate parent company of a range of over 30 Canadian and American subsidiaries which were involved in various aspects of real estate development, investment and management. Some of these subsidiaries were incorporated in Canada, while others were incorporated in various US states. Some of the subsidiaries carried on business and owned investments primarily in Canada; others were incorporated, carried on business and owned investments solely in the United States. Some of the subsidiaries were solvent; some of them were insolvent. The liabilities of the corporate group were in excess of $4.5 billion.

This empire posed a difficult problem for the company's planners, confronting them with an international insolvency involving corporations and properties in a variety of financial conditions. The situation was further complicated in that a number of Bramalea subsidiaries owned limited partnerships and occasionally general partnership interests in various partnerships, as well as interests in joint ventures where insolvency filings could be expected to give rise to a wide variety of legal complexities and difficulties.

Bramalea dealt with the issues facing it by making a single court application in Ontario under the CCAA on behalf of the ultimate parent company, Bramalea Limited, and a large number of its Canadian and American subsidiaries and affiliates. The Bramalea application claimed that all of these subsidiaries and affiliates were insolvent and had assets in and/or carried on business in Canada. The application also suggested that the affairs of all of the companies were interwoven, that they shared a common management administration and that they banked using a centralised cash management system which concentrated their liquid assets back into the Toronto-based bank accounts of the ultimate parent company.

6.6. "Whatever it takes to make it work"

The order made by the Ontario court in the *Bramalea* restructuring set some startling new precedents and established new frontiers in Canadian reorganisational practice. The court accepted Bramalea's contention that it was, by and large, a single integrated business and made a single order which imposed a global stay of proceedings not only over Bramalea Limited itself but also over some 30 to 40 separate Bramalea affiliates and even over entities that were not applicants for court protection. In granting CCAA protection, the Ontario court also accepted an unprecedented geographical jurisdiction. In some instances, the court order was broad enough to include single-purpose limited partnerships whose principal assets were real estate developments in the United States. This is even more striking in the context of the CCAA which, strictly speaking, is available only for the protection of corporate borrowers with property or assets in Canada.

The order made by the Ontario court also dealt with a number of significant issues of consolidation of corporate entities and liabilities in an unprecedented fashion. There were in fact five levels of consolidation involved in the Bramalea filing:

(a) procedural consolidation under which the administration of several dozen separate entities took place in a single proceeding;
(b) substantive consolidation of the financial affairs of various of the Bramalea companies;
(c) substantive consolidation of creditor classes;
(d) substantive consolidation of non-corporate and corporate entities; and
(e) cross-border consolidation of assets and liabilities within the corporate group.

Each of these aspects of the consolidated filing contributed to a process whereby the Ontario court was able to carry out a reorganisation of a multi-billion dollar company in a single proceeding in three months. While it is frequently noted that reorganisation processes tend to proceed more rapidly in Canada than in the United States, this was a record for brevity even for Canadian reorganisations. Examining the various aspects of consolidation involved in this extraordinary reorganisation will shed light on the mechanisms of its success, the potential perils of proceeding in this manner and the lessons it may hold for the future.

It is important to note that the initial court order permitting the consolidated filing by Bramalea was not the subject of any formal adjudication. No formal reasons or opinions were delivered by the court. The affidavit material on which the order was granted claimed that the criteria for the applicability of the CCAA had been met by each of the Bramalea applicants, but this was never effectively tested in cross-examination. While jurisdictional challenges to the Bramalea filing were launched by certain US and other creditors, the final version of the plan of arrangement simply noted that certain of the Bramalea Group's applicants and assets, which had been the subject of such challenges, had been excluded from the plan before it was put to the creditor classes for a vote. In other words, most dissident creditors obtained concessions in return for dropping their challenges. Thus the key aspects of the Bramalea plan which adopted the "centre of gravity" approach to reorganisation, ie consolidation of the creditors and assets of the corporate group and cross-border consolidation of its affiliates, were not subject to judicial consideration in an adversarial context. As such it is premature to conclude with certainty that a similar order could be obtained in future, or, if obtained, that it could not be successfully challenged before another court, either on appeal in Ontario, or in another jurisdiction. Bramalea won its battle to reorganise, but the war over control of cross-border reorganisational activity is far from over.

6.7 *Bramalea*'s cross-border consolidation

When the cross-border aspects of the Bramalea CCAA reorganisation are examined, its impact is even more surprising. In some very clear instances, loans by US lenders to US single-purpose Bramalea subsidiaries owning only US real estate projects and carrying on business only in the United States, became subject to being rewritten in a Canadian reorganisation. This extraordinarily broad approach would seem clearly to undermine the basis of US lenders' loans to single-purpose entities in the United States. In making such loans, lenders would usually have assumed that they had successfully insulated themselves from the risk of any financial decay that might occur higher up in the *Bramalea* empire at its head office in Canada. The CCAA, as it was used in *Bramalea*, was clearly not comparable to the operation of Chapter 11 reorganisations in the United States which could be expected to proceed on a company-by-company basis. The *Bramalea* reorganisation could be (and was) perceived to involve an unprecedented exercise of extraterritorial jurisdiction by the Canadian court.

It is important to analyse the basis on which Bramalea claimed that the Canadian courts could assume jurisdiction over the reorganisation of its US affiliates. The CCAA only permits companies to resort to the statute if they are incorporated in Canada, have assets in Canada or carry on business in Canada, ie the statute itself recognises that there must be a sufficient nexus between the debtor and the jurisdiction supervising the reorganisation. While few, if any, of its US affiliates were incorporated in Canada, Bramalea claimed that its US affiliates both had assets in and carried on business in Canada. The basis for these claims proved controversial.

Bramalea's application for CCAA protection suggested that the US affiliates had assets in Canada, relying on a combination of rather thin, self-constructed evidence and evidence of existing management administrative practices. For example, a number of the affiliates had opened up $100 bank accounts in the Canadian branch of Bramalea's main bankers in Toronto, thereby establishing an "asset" in Canada. In addition, the main banker to the Bramalea Group operated the Group's accounts in such a way that all funds in the accounts of the various affiliates across North America were concentrated back daily into the parent company's main Toronto account. As a result, various of the affiliates which, prior to the concentration sweep, had positive balances in their accounts, were either creditors of the parent company in respect of this amount, or claimed an equitable interest in the concentrated amount in the parent's Toronto bank account. Bramalea also contended that it maintained various assets for the Group as a whole in Canada, such as insurance policies stored in Canada in which various of its US affiliates and their properties were named as insureds.

Although the opening of a $100 bank account may technically create an asset in Canada, it does not seem to constitute a sufficiently material asset to confer jurisdiction under the CCAA. In the international sense, a court should hesitate to assume jurisdiction over a company that does not have a substantial connection with the forum. If a court purports to assume jurisdiction on the basis of an "instant" bank account, orders issued by that court (eg granting a stay of proceedings or approving a reorganisation) may be afforded little recognition in jurisdictions where the company and its real assets are located. Canadian courts are, hopefully, likely to be circumspect in dealing with filings predicted on instant bank accounts and similar considerations should be applicable to attempts to rely on the existence of various types of "common Group assets" which Bramalea offered as a basis for assumption of jurisdiction by the Ontario court.

Bramalea also claimed that various of its single-asset US affiliates were in fact carrying on business in Canada. The basis for this claim seemed to be that certain officers of the US affiliates were physically located in Canada at Bramalea's head office. It seems unlikely that a court would find the mere presence in Canada of an executive officer of a US affiliate would be sufficient to constitute the conduct of business in Canada by the US entity. On the other hand, there was some practical realism to Bramalea's position. Many of the creditors that had loaned to single-purpose US subsidiaries had in fact negotiated their loans with officers of the parent company in Toronto and negotiating sessions had taken place in Toronto. Further, many of those loans were in fact supported by the parent company's guarantee. While the rental markets for US properties owned by the US affiliates were local, and while their day-to-day operations were carried out and managed locally, large strategic decisions were probably dealt with in Toronto. As usual, the question of where a corporation resides or carries on business is a slippery concept, offering ample flexibility to a result-oriented court.

6.8 Consolidation with a vengeance

The *Bramalea* filing lifted the corporate veil: the filing ignored the separate corporate existence of the parent company and its various affiliates. In essence, the filing was made on behalf of the empire as a whole, not on behalf of the entities of which it was comprised. This was achieved by treating all of the assets of the corporations as being in a single pool and classifying them by type rather than by owner. Creditors were then classified in turn by asset category and by the nature of their security, if any. By this process, six mega-classes of the Bramalea Group's creditors were constructed. Creditors were assigned to these classes without reference to the particular subsidiary or affiliate against which they held their claim.

Proceeding in this way offered substantial advantages to Bramalea. Bramalea had negotiated with its major creditors over a long period of time before filing its plan. By consolidating the Group's creditors and assets, Bramalea was able to place key creditors with which it had achieved an understanding in positions where they could influence various of the creditor groups. This virtually assured that Bramalea would obtain the necessary support in terms of creditor approval once the CCAA plan of arrangement was put to a vote.

At the best of times the possibility of structuring creditor classes in order to ensure creditor approval is a difficult matter for the court to control. Typically the debtor will present an ostensible rationale for the classification. In a plan with a high degree of consolidation, ostensible rationales for a particular creditor classification scheme are easier to come by and Bramalea's major bank lenders were well represented in most of the classes proposed by Bramalea. Various challenges were launched against the classification of creditors in the *Bramalea* filing, but none of these met with success. The plan was ultimately sanctioned by the court after the creditors' vote.

Quite apart from a result-oriented creditor class structuring, substantive consolidation of creditors and assets of different affiliates of a corporate group creates other difficulties. Most significantly, this strategy undermines the benefits of protections typically negotiated by lenders and upon which they usually rely in their relationships with their loan customers. By structuring its corporate group such that various specific entities carried on various specific operations, Bramalea had isolated various of its assets and creditors into discrete legal groupings. It may often have been that lenders had demanded these arrangements: they would not assume an exposure to the

Group as a whole, but would only lend against a specific property and to a specific entity with a known and defined set of liabilities.

It is fundamental that those who seek the benefit of limited liability must bear the costs of such a privilege. Bramalea obtained funds from its various lenders on the basis of the way in which its empire was structured into various legal entities. When Bramalea filed a plan that substantively consolidated its creditors and assets, it eliminated the boundaries between its subsidiaries and affiliates. Lenders with exposures to subsidiaries that had particular balance sheets occasionally found themselves with exposures to the Bramalea Group as a whole. In short, the limited liability of the subsidiaries which protected them against exposure to the remainder of the Bramalea Group's liabilities was erased. Substantive consolidation is the inversion of the ultimate creditors' weapon — the corporate veil is lifted by the incorporator instead of by its creditors. Traditionally, the lifting of the corporate veil is a remedy for fraudulent or inequitable conduct, not a means by which the obligations and responsibilities of a company are rewritten.

Seen from afar, it would seem that larger creditors who had poor loans to the wider Bramalea Group as a whole may have used their leverage to force Bramalea into filing a consolidated plan for the Group which diminished the value of the security held by lenders to various isolated subsidiaries who had less bargaining power. Those lenders who had made and stipulated for the protection of an exposure to an isolated and more stable subsidiary, were, through the substantive consolidation process, worse off than those who had made less secure loans to the Group as a whole and who were thereby undersecured. The result would seem to undermine the environment in which the assessment of credit risk, loan pricing and the monitoring of the financial status of borrowers takes place.

The implications of a *Bramalea*-type substantive consolidation are very far-reaching and, conceivably, loans to corporate subsidiaries may have to be viewed by lenders as exposures to the corporate group as a whole for purpose of risk and credit assessment, loan pricing and loan monitoring. Various standard loan and security covenants might have to be re-examined in light of the *Bramalea* experience to determine what protections against *Bramalea*-type orders can be built into loan documentation. In fact, there has been some early post- *Bramalea* experience which suggests that credits and exposures are now much more susceptible to group-wide assessment than was the case prior to *Bramalea*.

The initial court order which permitted the *Bramalea* consolidated filing extended the scope of the CCAA in another way as well. Unlike a Chapter 11 filing in the United States, a filing under the CCAA does not create an automatic stay of all proceedings and enforcement actions against the debtor. However, the CCAA empowers the court to grant a broad range of protection at the time it makes an order permitting the initial filing. In practice, if the filing is allowed, a general stay of proceedings against the debtor is granted as a matter of course. Because the granting of protection is discretionary, the court can define the scope of the protection to be granted and the initial part of the CCAA process is often consumed in "carve out" applications to the court brought by particular creditors seeking to extricate themselves from the effect of the protection granted to the debtor.

Bramalea exploited the CCAA's flexibility to a new purpose. The CCAA order extended the scope of the court's protection to prevent enforcement actions being taken against any partnerships in which Bramalea companies participated as general or limited partners, or in which they otherwise had an interest (whether directly or indirectly). This is, of course, an extension of the CCAA because the CCAA does not apply on its face to partnerships but only to corporations. Furthermore, where a Bramalea affiliate was the general partner of a partnership, the reorganisational proceedings purported to restructure its indebtedness as well. This approach would seem to go well beyond any of the words in the CCAA statutory text, which makes it clear that only the debt of corporations can be restructured, and is indicative of the extent to which the Canadian court was willing to be creative in order to deal with all aspects of the reorganisation of the global Bramalea operation. Had it not done so, a number of creditors which had financed single-purposed partnerships (and there were several large assets financed through US partnership structures) would have been able to wait out the protection period and take enforcement proceedings immediately once the restructuring was completed in Canada and the stay was lifted.

6.9 The special problems of insolvencies of corporate groups

Upsetting what was achieved in *Bramalea* may not really produce a better reorganisation process. As section 304 of the US Bankruptcy Code indicates, the objective of the courts in reorganisation is to design a process which "will best assure an economical and expeditious administration". The *Bramalea* approach offered a single forum and an expedient administration for a troubled Group and all of its creditors, and provided certainty as to their position within a very short period of time. In that sense, it was consistent with universalist principles of international law in allocating jurisdiction over multinational insolvencies of single legal entities. Foreign courts should be loathe to interfere with a process that offers this type of result, as long as it has a rational justification and is seen to be fair.

A "centre of gravity" approach to a restructuring can be seen to have a rational basis. It recognises the practicalities of how corporate groups and their financiers operate. Groups do several things in common. They prepare consolidated financial information. They use common banking arrangements. They purchase certain assets in common. They adopt certain strategic policies in common. They share common good will and trade marks. This is not to say, however, that corporate distinctions between the various affiliates of a multinational corporate group should be ignored.

Bramalea highlighted the problems of group restructurings. Unless the whole group is dealt with, it is difficult to restructure the parts. Otherwise, creditors whose claims remain uncompromised will continue to press and divert cash flow from the restructured parts of the empire. Morevoer, holdouts tend to be rewarded because the debtor can afford to be more generous when it has a smaller scale problems left to resolve. Thus, there is no incentive to compromise with the debtor. Clearly, it is advantageous not only to have a degree of procedural consolidation of both domestic and international claims, but also to have a way of driving the whole process to a conclusion at once.

The central concern of a financial restructuring is to preserve an operating business, both because of the costs of liquidation and because the whole is usually greater than the sum of the parts. Behind the latter concern is a concern to protect employment, and to control the spin-off effects of a bankruptcy on creditors with significant investments in the company. All of these motivations naturally weigh heavily on a court and, in a multinational reorganisation, these factors become important issues.

In the jurisdiction where the centre of gravity, investment and employment is located, a court supervising the process is more likely to take account of the macro-economic impact of a financial failure. Courts of other jurisdictions are more likely to be sympathetic to creditors' interests rather than these macro-economic externalities. Foreign creditors are always sensitive to these realities and usually consider how they might "repatriate" the portion of the restructuring process in which they are involved to their own jurisdiction. Fragmented reorganisational processes facilitate such tactics.

6.10 Options in multinational restructurings

Faced with a multinational insolvency of a single corporation, there are really three approaches that the courts of the participating jurisdictions can adopt:

(a) parallel filings of primary proceedings in both jurisdictions;
(b) a primary filing in one jurisdiction recognised by a secondary "recognition filing" in the other jurisdiction; and
(c) a filing solely in the jurisdiction of the centre of gravity of the case, recognised if necessary by a "recognition order" in other jurisdictions.

In parallel insolvency filing, the company can make a "primary filing" in both the jurisdiction of its central management and control and in the other jurisdictions where key assets are located. *Olympia & York* followed this approach, ending up with a CCAA filing in Ontario, various Chapter 11 filings in the United States and a later administration in England. A key advantage of parallel filings from the debtor's perspective, apart from fragmenting creditor opposition, is that such an approach might avoid the application of certain laws in the home jurisdiction, including those relating to avoidable preferences. From the creditors' perspective, this approach increases the likelihood that the corporate veil of the particular subsidiary to which it has advanced funds will be respected. As well, access to favourable preference and avoidance laws where the particular asset or subsidiary is located can be obtained. The obvious disadvantage is that the approach of the courts to the matter needs to evolve as the case proceeds and there are no clear ground rules for resolving conflicts or for ensuring co-operation and co-ordination between the jurisdictions involved.

In a secondary recognition filing, a filing in the primary jurisdiction where the debtor's key head office operations are located would be followed by or occur simultaneously with a recognition filing in other jurisdiction, thereby subjecting those assets to the foreign insolvency proceeding and, to some degree, to the influence or control of the foreign trustee or administrator. The advantages are that, to a larger extent, the law of the primary jurisdiction controls the affairs of the debtor. For example, an application for recognition under section 304 of the US Bankruptcy Code does not permit a foreign trustee or administrator access to US avoidance powers and avoidance issues are left to the law of the primary jurisdiction. This can be a disadvantage or an advantage to various parties depending on the debtor's pre-filing activities and which laws are applicable.

From a systemic perspective, if the primary court relies on the co-operation of the foreign court to implement its control over foreign assets, it may well be in for an unfortunate surprise, as even courts with liberal recognition rules often find excuses to permit the institution of competing parallel proceedings. Secondly, even in a situation of primary and secondary proceedings, there will be two courts involved, which may create conflicts and situations in which the administrations proceed at different speeds. A conflict over an asset under a secondary filing might, for example, hold up the restructuring in the primary proceeding.

A centre of gravity filing, unlike a secondary filing, contemplates a single reorganisation of all of the assets of the debtor by a single court in the forum where the centre of gravity of the debtor's operations is located. In a case like *Maxwell Communication*, the centre of gravity would have been England, and, in the case of *Olympia & York*, it would have been Ontario. Where necessary, recognition orders would be sought in other jurisdictions to give effect to the decisions of the court of the primary filing.

The advantage of a centre of gravity filing is that it prevents fragmentation. The disadvantage is that it requires a court to exercise a very long-arm jurisdiction without domestic bias, creating a serious issue of jurisdiction under most foreign laws and under international law as well. Secondly, the court in the centre of gravity jurisdiction may well be called upon to decide difficult questions of foreign law, including foreign priorities.

Courts in all countries, however, continue to be influenced by the interests of domestic creditors and experience has shown that courts of one country are generally reluctant to yield authority to the courts of another. Consequently, neither of the three major options applicable to multinational restructurings had achieved a consistent judicial following. While the "centre of gravity" filing would seem to be the most logical and equitable of the three approaches, it is, perhaps, the least likely to be accepted by courts of different countries. The unsuccessful draft Canada-United States Bankruptcy Treaty was developed along lines of the centre of gravity theory and may have foundered because of mutual misgivings as to the deficiencies in the system.

Recent experience in international restructurings, however, shows that there is an ability for the courts and the professional advisers involved in international cases to improve the current situation. Parallel filings as in *Olympia & York* and *Maxwell* show that orderly administrations of portions of business entities in different countries can be successfully carried out. The parallel filing theory recognises, perhaps, the reality of a situation in which courts of one jurisdiction are reluctant to yield their jurisdiction to the courts of another but wish to co-ordinate their administrations with a view to improving the final result for all affected stakeholders. In the absence of multinational treaties involving insolvency, perhaps the best that can be expected in the short to medium term is an increased level of co-ordination and co-operation between courts of various jurisdictions in dealing with the difficult and complex problems of multinational commercial insolvencies.

6.11 Conclusion

The *Bramalea* restructuring was a successful reorganisation of a major real estate-related enterprise carried out on a "global enterprise" basis. The restructuring could probably not have been accommodated in any other reorganisational statute than the Canadian CCAA. It is, however, not surprising that a major corporate group reorganisation along such non-traditional lines should produce some surprising results. In the post-*Bramalea* scheme of things, lenders will have to be cognizant of the fact that reorganisational plans may be able to impact them in some hitherto unexpected ways. While it is probably clear that less violence was done to the interests of stakeholders through the non-traditional solutions reached in the *Bramalea* restructuring than would have been the case in a more traditional liquidation of the entities in the Bramalea Group, this may not be of much comfort to lenders who structured their loan arrangements along more traditional lines.

In the same way that nature abhors a vacuum, the lending and credit industry feels very uncomfortable in a situation where the rules of the game are either unknown or are generated on an *ad hoc* basis. If the *Bramalea* reorganisation had taken place in the context of an international structure based either on reciprocal statutory regimes or on a protocol-derived system of co-ordination between courts, the result would have been the same and the elements of unpredictability would have been dramatically lower. In that sense, *Bramalea* points out the advantages of having a more co-ordinated international approach, whether by statute or by judicial co-ordination, to multinational restructurings. Because legislatures seemed unconcerned with the area, the area is ripe for credit grantors and their professional advisers, in conjunction with the courts, to build up co-ordinating systems that would improve the prospects for efficient and effective international reorganisations. It is an area where, in particular, Committee J and the legal profession can make their marks and, conceivably, lead the way to significant improvements in a major area of international commercial activity.

7

The Revision of International Insolvency Law in Germany*

Hans-Jochem Lüer
Lüer & Görg, Cologne, Germany

7.1 Introduction

When the Act to Reform Private International Law was promulgated on 25 July 1986,[1] and became effective shortly afterwards,[2] a process of legislation finally came to an end which had lasted for more than three decades. The German Council for Private International Law had been founded in 1954, and under its President, Professor Kegel, it was now extremely gratified to discover that the legislature had profited greatly from its comprehensive pioneer efforts and publications, which — in their turn — had given rise to a wide variety of publications.[3] Even if the amendments implemented by the Act were only restricted to such central fields as international law of civil status, family law and the law of succession on the one hand, and to international law of contracts on the other, the 1986 Private International Law Act must still

---

*This article discusses the preliminary draft of the reform of international insolvency law of 1989 (the "draft"). The draft bill recently published by the German government follows the basic principles of this preliminary draft.

[1]BGBl. I 1142.

[2]According to Art 7, para 2 of the Act of 25 July 1986, being effective since 1 September 1986 (Private International Law Act).

[3]The reform proposals of the German Council for Private International Law (*"Deutscher Rat für Internationales Privatrecht"*) are published in: *Vorschläge und Gutachten zur Reform des Deutschen Internationalen Eherechts* (1962); *Vorschläge und Gutachten zur Reform des Deutschen Internationalen Kindschafts-, Vormundschafts- und Pflegeschaftsrechts* (1966); *Vorschläge und Gutachten zur Reform des Internationalen Erbrechts* (1969); *Vorschläge und Gutachten zur Reform des Deutschen Internationalen Personen- und Sachenrechts* (1972); *Vorschläge und Gutachten zur Reform des Deutschen Internationalen Personen-, Familienund Erbrechts* (1981). As to the history of the Private International Law Act see Bohmer, *"Das Deutsche Gesetz zur Neuregelung des internationalen Privatrechts von 1986"*, *Rabelsz SO* (1986), pp. 646–662 (646–655). As to references of comments on the reform see: Kegel, *Internationales Privatrecht* (6th ed. 1987), pp. 136–138.

Current Issues in Cross-Border Insolvency and Reorganisations (E. B. Leonard, C. W. Besant, eds.; 1–85333–958–X; © International Bar Association; pub. Graham & Trotman/International Bar Association, 1994; printed in Great Britain), pp. 119-151.

be regarded as being a major step forward.[4] Most commentators holding this view generally support their argument primarily by referring to the general shift towards universal rules and standards governing the conflict of laws proposed under the Acts;[5] with these rules and standards, they associate an evaluation in terms of legal policy of the fundamentally equal status of domestic and foreign private international law and an opening-up in the direction of universal validity in respect of the conflict of laws,[6] this latter principle coming closest to the ideal of an international legal community.[7]

Traditional international insolvency law in Germany is different from the universality principle in the conflict of laws.[8] Bound up for decades in its policy of territorial isolationism against everything from outside,[9] this area of law has concentrated blindly on regulating the legal relationships in existence at home; the consequences in terms of legal policy would appear to be extremely questionable.

One example for this is to be found in the fundamental contradiction in valuation developed in terms of defining the debtor's estate, a contradiction that has still not been resolved to this day. With reference to section 237 of the German Bankruptcy Act (*Konkursordnung* — "KO"), it has for many years been considered standard practice to withhold assets located in Germany from any bankruptcy proceeding abroad. The Supreme Court of the German Reich (*Reichsgericht*) ruled in this context that"... a bankruptcy proceeding instituted abroad shall only take account of the assets of the debtor held abroad, not of those held in Germany".[10] At the same time, however, it was assumed from section 1 KO that all assets of the bankrupt located abroad were to form part of the supposed estate for the purposes of any domestic bankruptcy proceeding.[11] From the standpoint of the conflict of laws, it is clearly apparent from this that the laws governing bankruptcy in Germany and abroad are not at all being afforded "equal" treatment and that there is a lack of any universal standard in conflict of laws granting the power to determine what forms part of the estate to the law of the state governing the respective bankruptcy proceeding. The *principle of territoriality* on which the *Reichsgericht* based its decision above was obviously being

---

[4]See Ferid, *Internationales Privatrecht* (3d ed. 1986), n. E-2; Lüderitz, "*Fortschritte im deutschen internationalen Privatrecht*", in *Festschrift der Rechtswissenschaftlichen Fakultät zur 600-Jahr-Feier der Universität zu Köln* (1989), pp. 271–292.

[5]Lüderitz (*see* n. 4), p. 273.

[6]Kegel (see n. 3), p. 194; Neuhaus, *Die Grundbegriffe des Internationalen Privatrechts* (2d ed. 1976), p. 43; Raape/Sturm, *Internationales Privatrecht I* (6th ed. 1977), p. 95.

[7]Kegel (*see* n. 3), p. 86; Neuhaus (*see* n. 6), pp. 49–63; see also Savigny, *System des heutigen römischen Rechts VIII* (1849, reprint 1974), pp. 27, 129.

[8]See Hanisch, "*Auslandsvermögen des Schuldners im Inlandsinsolvenzverfahren und vice versa*", in *Festschrift Einhundert Jahre Konkursordnung 1877-1977* (1977), pp. 139–167 (140–153); Lüer, *Einzelzwangsvollstreckung im Ausland bei inländischen Insolvenzverfahren* (KTS 1978), pp. 200–215 and (KTS 1979) pp. 12–29; Pielorz, *Auslandskonkurs aud Disposition uber das inländischen* (1977), pp. 15–22.

[9]As to references of court decisions since 1884 see: Pielorz (*see* n. 8), pp. 15–18.

[10]RG, 21 October 1920, RGZ 100, 241 (242).

[11]RG, 23 March 1903, RGZ 54, 193; complete reprint in: *Zeitschrift fur Internationales Privat- und Strafrecht* (1903), pp. 431–433 (but see as to this decision n. 47); Jaeger(-Weber), *Konkursordnung* (8th ed. I 1958), para 1 KO n. 71; see also as to recent comments: Ness/Kropshofer, *Ko~entar zur Konkursordnung* (3d ed. 1989), s 1 KO n. 2; Kilger, *Honkursordnung* (15th ed. 1987), s 1 n. 1 B a; Kuhn/Uhlenbruck, *Konkursordnung* (10th ed. 1986), s 1 KO n. 3 a; Kuhn/Uhlenbruck(-Lüer) (this note), ss 237, 238 KO n. 57.

employed for the purposes of preventing the application of foreign law,[12] for which section 237, paragraph 1 KO could have been cited in legal support.[13] The above provision is still valid today, more than 110 years after becoming effective, although it would long since appear to be false in terms of legal policy.[14] It not only runs contrary to the principle of universality in the conflict of laws, it also symbolises the dualist approach to dealing with the conflict between the statutes governing insolvency proceedings at home and abroad which is the hallmark of the legislation heretofore in force.

In the meantime, legal commentaries and decisions taken by the Supreme Court have unmasked this intolerable situation for what it is, and have recommended suitable action. Since the important contribution made by Muller-Freienfels in 1963,[15] a large number of commentators have subjected the principle of territoriality, its foundation and consequences, to critical analysis, and have prepared the way for a shift in direction towards a principle of universality in the conflict of laws.[16] The far-reaching comments given by Jahr in the Jaeger Commentary dating from 1973[17] are particularly worthy of note in this context. Courts were able to profit from this work when a fundamental reorientation of international insolvency law in Germany was initiated several years ago.[18] The way to this development was paved by two decisions of the Federal Court of Justice (*Bundezgerichtzhof*) in 1976 (recognition of the right of action of a domestic receiver to conduct proceedings in respect of assets located abroad)[19] and in 1983 ("Savings bank case"),[20] which gave added support to the extraterritorial application of the German bankruptcy law (section 1, paragraph 1, section 117, paragraph 1 KO). The real breakthrough[21] finally came with the decision of the

---

[12]Lüer (*see* n. 8) HTS 1979, pp. 14 *et seq.*

[13]But see: BGH, 4 February 1960, NJW 1960, 774; BGH, 12 December 1961, WM 1962, 263 (266); BGH, 30 May 1962, NJW 1962, 1511; BGH, 2 April 1970, NJW 1970, 1187; BGH, 23 September 1975, GRUR 1976, 204 as well as the court decisions of the "Reichsgericht" cited in: Pielorz (*see* n. 8), p. 16 n. 9.

[14]See the fundamental comment of Thieme, *"Inlandsvollstreckung und Auslandskonkurs"*, in *Rabelsz* 37 (1973) 682-718 (691-696); see also Ebenroth, *Die Inlandswirkungen der ausländischen lex fori concursus bei Insolvenz einer Gesellschaft* (ZZP 101 1988), pp. 121-151 (131-136); Hanisch (*see* n. 8), pp. 151 *et seq* 165; Xuhn/Uhlenbruck(-Lüer) (*see* n. 11), ss 237, 238 KO n. 80; Liner, *Trberlegungen zu einem kunftigen deutschen Internationalen Insolvenzrecht* (HTS 1990), pp. 377–402 (392); Hers, *Probleme bei Insolvenzverfahren im internationalen Rechtsverkehr* (ZIP 1983), pp. 136–140 (138); Pielors (*see* n. 8), pp. 57 *et seq*; Jurgen Schmidt, *System des deutschen internationalen Honkursrechts* (1972), pp. 148 *et seq.*

[15]Müller-Freienfels, *"Auslandskonkurs und Inlandsfolgen"* in *Festschrift Dölle II* (1963), pp. 359–398.

[16]See the list of references reprinted in the recently republished doctoral theses in the field of international insolvency law: Aderhold, *Auslandskonkurs im Inland* (1992); Favoccia, *Vertragliche Mobiliarsicherheiten im internationalen Insolvenzrecht* (1991); Riegel, *Grenuberschreitende Konkurswirkungen zwischen der Bundesrepublik Deutschland, Belgien und den Niederlanden* (1991); Summ, *Anerkennung auslilndischer Konkurse in der Bundesrepublik Deutschland* (1992).

[17]Jaeger(-Jahr), *Konkursordnung* (8th ed. 11/2 1973), ss 237, 238 KO.

[18]See particularly Hanisch, *Deutsches Internationales Insolvenzrecht in Bewegung* (ZIP 1983), pp. 1289–1301; Hanisch, *Die Wende im deutschen internationalen Insolvenzrecht* (ZIP 1985), pp. 1233–1243; Luke, *Zu neueren Entwicklungen im deutschen internationalen Konkursrecht* (KTS 1986), pp. 1–19; Hers (*see* n. 14), pp. 136–140; Luke, *Probleme des internationalen Konkursrechts im Verhaltnis zu der Bundesrepublik Deutschland und Italien, Jahrbuch fur italienisches Recht I* (1988), pp. 3–10; Pielorz, *Wende im deutschen internationalen Insolvenzrecht* (IPRax 1984), pp. 241–244.

[19]BGH, 10 December 1976, BGHZ 68, 16 (18).

[20]BGH, 13 July 1983, BGHZ 88, 147–157.

[21]Hanisch (*see* n. 18) (ZIP 1985), pp. 1233 *et seq.*

IXth Division for Civil Matters of the *Bundesgerichtshof* dating from 11 July 1985, in which universality in the conflict of laws was recognised as a valid principle under international insolvency law in Germany.[22] This carefully prepared ruling, in which the *Bundesgerichtshof* granted a Belgian receiver a right of action to conduct proceedings in Germany on the basis of the foreign bankruptcy law, goes far beyond the actual material content of the decision reached.[23] It represents an act of legislation by a court in which previously valid rules of law were repealed and new ones prescribed instead. However welcome this brave step by the IXth Division for Civil Matters may have been to all those to whom the conventional phraseology of territorial isolationism had long since been a bone of contention,[24] it cannot be denied that this "judicial *tour de force*" has nevertheless become a source of some considerable legal uncertainty. For not only do the provisions of section 237, paragraph 1 and section 238 KO continue to be valid as prevailing law, traditional forms of thinking and argument have also not disappeared overnight. Among the latter are such phrases as respect for foreign sovereignty,[25] the equal status afforded in argumentation to bankruptcy and expropriation,[26] and the affirmation of territorial self-limitation of single rules of the insolvency laws applied;[27] all these phrases pursue the sole aim of sustaining basic concepts of territorial delimitation. To what great extent this sense of legal uncertainty is currently felt in international bankruptcy law in Germany may clearly be seen in the decision of the Ist Division in Civil Matters of the *Bundesgerichtshof* of 7 July 1988, which found that a case of bankruptcy occurring abroad was to have no interruptive effect on legal proceedings in Germany within the meaning of section 240 of the German Code of Civil Procedure (*ZivilprozeBordnung* — "ZPO").[28] The explanation given and the consequences of this decision show a blatant lack of regard and understanding for what had been the intention behind the ruling of the special

---

[22]BGH, 13 July 1985, BGHZ 95, 256 (263 *et seq*); as to recent judgments of the *Bundesgerichtshof* confirming this decision see BGH, 9 December 1987, ZIP 1988, 247; BGH, 11 January 1990, ZIP 1990, 246; BGH, 11 July 1991, ZIP 1991, 1014; BGH, 30 April 1992, ZIP 1992, 781.

[23]Flessner, *Entwicklungen im internationalen Konkursrecht, besonders im Verhaltnis Deutschland–Frankreich* (ZIP 1989), 749–757 (753); Hanisch (*see* n. 18) (ZIP 1985), pp. 1233.

[24]According to Baur/Sturner, *Zwangsvollstreckungs-, Konkursund Vergleichsrecht* (12th ed., Vol. II, Insolvens–recht 1990), n. 37.25; Ebenroth in *Munchener Kommentar* (2d ed., BGB 1990), nach Art 10 EGBGB n. 352; Geimer, *Internationales Zivilprozeflrecht* (1987), n. 2365; Kilger (*see* n. 11), s 237 n. 5; Leipold, *"Wege zu einem funktionsfahigen internationalen Konkursrecht"*, in *Festschrift sum 3OjShrigen JubilSum des Instituts fur Rechtsvergleichung der Waseda Universitat* (1988), pp. 787–820; Riesenfeld, *Das neue Gesicht des deutschen Internationalen Konkursrechts aus ausländischer Sicht, Festschrift Merz* (1992), p. 497. See also Hanisch, *Die Wende im deutschen internationalen Insolvenzrecht* (ZIP 1985), p. 1233 (1235); Lüderitz (JZ 1986), pp. 96 *et seq* as to certain exceptions.

[25]OLG Köln, 31 January 1989, ZIP 1989, 321; Hanisch, EWiR, s 812 BGB 2/89, 349 (350); Hanisch, *Erlöse aus der Teilnahme an einem auslandischen ParallelInsolvenzverfahren — Ablieferung an die inllindische Konkursmasse oder Anrechnung auf die Inlandsdividen* (ZIP 1989), pp. 273–279 (276). But see Kegel (*see* n. 3), p. 194; Raape/Sturm (*see* n. 6), p. 95: in the conflict of laws field sovereignity interests should not be considered; according to Ackmann/Wenner, *Inlandswirkung des Auslandskonkurses: Verlustscheine und Restschuldbefreiungen* (IPRax 1990), p. 209 n. 12.

[26]Kuhn, Note, BGH, 4 February 1960, MDR 1960, 579. Contra BGH, 2 April 1959, NJW 1959, 1085; see also Pielorz (*see* n. 8), p. 50; Soergel(-Kegel), *Burgerliches Gesetzbuch* (11th ed. VIII 1983) n. 692 vor Art 7 and additional references at n. 4.

[27]Hanisch (*see* n. 25) (ZIP 1989), p. 276.

[28]BGH, 7 July 1988, NJW 1988, 3096 *et seq*.

division responsible for such matters on 11 July 1985,[29] with its shift towards universality in the conflict of laws in international insolvency law in Germany.[30]

The Federal Ministry of Justice correctly concludes that in the foreseeable future courts and legal commentators will no longer be in a position, on the basis of the decisions cited above, to develop a new international insolvency law in Germany, capable not only of implementing the principle of universality but also of representing a reliable, translucent and easily applicable system of rules, without the aid of legislation.[31] Particularly from the practical standpoint, it would certainly prove intolerable in the long run for such a complex area of law as that of international insolvency law, characterised as it is by bitterly conflicting interests, to have no standards or rules available to ensure a certain degree of predictability in future court decisions. For this reason alone, it is to be welcomed that the Federal Ministry of Justice has now taken the initiative in reforming and recodifying German international insolvency law. Any action at all by legislators on the law currently valid for bankruptcy and composition proceedings would be desirable, even if it is scarcely to be expected; such action would appear more than necessary in the context of the planned major reform of insolvency law. As early as August 1988, the Federal Ministry of Justice published its draft version of an Act for the Reform of Insolvency Law ("EInsO") for this purpose, although this draft does not as yet take account of international insolvency law.[32] This was only to be expected, once the reform commission had admitted the necessity for reform in its First Report[33] but had refrained from passing any comment on it in its Second Report.[34]

The Federal Ministry of Justice is also correct in recognising that a reform of international insolvency law in Germany by legislation cannot content itself merely to prescribe a number of rules on international jurisdiction and on the choice of law applicable; there is also a pressing need for additional substantive law rules to govern cases with a foreign element. This may be seen not least in the fact that there is frequently no guaranteed opportunity of enforcing the legal rules to be applied under German conflict of laws abroad, or this opportunity is at times simply impossible. For examples such as these, only substantive law rules of German insolvency law are capable of providing solutions that would appear appropriate from the national

[29]BGHZ 95, 256.

[30]See Ackmann/Wenner, *Auslandskonkurs und Inlandsprozefl: Rechtssicherheit kontra Universalitat im Deutschen Internationalen Konkursrecht* (IP Rax 1989), pp. 144–148, also with references as to the positions expressed by commentators; Koch, *Auslandskonkurs und Unterbrechung des Inlandsprozesses* (NJW 1989), pp. 3072 *et seq*; Leipold (*see* n. 24), pp. 787, 799; Aiegel, *Prozeflunterbrechung nach § 240 ZPO im Fall auslandischer Konkurserdffnung,* (RIW 1990), pp. 546, 549 *et seq*; Trunk, *Auslandskonkurs und inlSndische Zivilprozesse* (ZIP 1989), pp. 279–286; Zoller/Stephan, *ZPO* (17th ed. 1991), s 240 n. 1; contra Flessner (*see* n. 23), p. 753 arguing that alleged jurisdictional interests conflict with this principle. However, there is no such interest of creditors requiring that the proceeding be continued against the bankrupt himself. See Ackmann/Wenner (this note), pp. 146 *et seq*; OLG Karlsruhe, 21 February 1992, RIW 1992, 940.

[31]Explanation [at pp. 36 *et seq*].

[32]Published in: "Discussion Draft on the Insolvency Law Reform, Draft of an Insolvency Act (EIns0)", German Ministry of Justice (*Bundesministerium der Justiz*) (1988).

[33]First report by the Commission on Insolvency Law, published by the German Ministry of Justice (1985), p. 23.

[34]Second report by the Commission on Insolvency Law, published by the German Ministry of Justice (1986), pp. 14 *et seq*.

viewpoint in terms of legal policy. The previously valid obligation to provide compensation under sections 50, 55 and 56 KO is an example of rules that will need to be supplemented by further substantive law rules. The intention of the Federal Ministry of Justice to establish an overriding concept in conjunction with the reform is thus in full harmony with the logical objectives of legal policy.

7.2 Practical need for revision

7.2.1 Explanation of preliminary draft

Even though the sense of legal uncertainty outlined above should be sufficient grounds in itself for quick legislative action, a closer look at the concrete need for such action in practice is nevertheless recommended. The Federal Ministry of Justice prefaces the legislative history to its preliminary draft with a number of considerations which are certainly correct. The previous reticence among law-making authorities, which have so far only provided legal rules for elements relating to matters abroad on a piecemeal basis within the framework of prevailing law (cf. sections 5, 50, 56, 237 and 238 KO and section 37 of the Composition Act (*Vergleichsordnung* — "Vg10")), is certainly no longer justified in an environment of international integration in which insolvencies transcending national borders are becoming more and more regular occurrences, particularly in the industrial sector. The prevailing sense of insecurity on the extraterritorial claim for application of substantive law rules in case of bankruptcy proceedings instituted in Germany[35] definitely requires clarification by legislative means; the same is true for the consequences arising in Germany from the non-recognition of the claim for application abroad. The ruling given by the *Bundesgerichtshof* in the "savings bank case"[36] only covers an extremely restricted set of circumstances; indeed, it is very doubtful how far the assumed obligation to surrender assets to the domestic receiver can be justified in other cases.[37] The movement taken towards a principle of universality in the conflict of laws by accepting a basic and universal rule under German international insolvency law to determine the respective substantive law governing insolvency,[38] presupposes a closer definition of its scope of application and a delimitation with respect to conflicting substantive laws.[39] Finally, the previous lack of progress in reaching international harmonisation by way of multilateral treaties[40] also provides sufficient justification for a new national system of codification aimed at satisfying these changing circumstances.

Even if the more theoretical considerations outlined above should provide adequate grounds for assuming a need for regulation, it is nevertheless also useful to

---

[35]*See* **7.3.2**.
[36]BGH, 13 July 1983, BGHZ 88, 147.
[37]*See* **7.3.2(b)**.
[38]Jaeger(-Jahr) (*see* n. 17), ss 237, 238 KO n. 253, 256; Kuhn/Uhlenbruck(-Lüer) (*see* n. 1l) ss 237, 238 KO n. 42.
[39]Kuhn/Uhlenbruck(-Lüer) (*see* n. 11), ss 237, 238 KO n. 45.
[40]As to the draft of an EC-Insolvency Convention of 1980 (with 1984 amendments) see Thieme, *"Der revidierte Entwurf eines EG-Honkursubereinkommens von 1984"*, in *Vorschlage und Gutachten sum Entwurf eines EGHonkursubereinkommens* (Kegel 1988), pp. 465–490 (474–477); as to an overview with regard to various possibilities of conventions in the field of international insolvency law see Stummel, *Honkurs und Integration +(1991). Recently, the work on an EC Insolvency Convention has been continued, a revised draft has been prepared which, however, has not been published yet.*

give, at the same time, more detailed consideration to the worries and uncertainties prevailing in practice, thereby revealing the conflicting and extremely complex interests arising in cases of transborder insolvencies.

7.2.2 Legal and practical difficulties

The various practical difficulties occurring regularly in the event of cross-border insolvencies apply in like fashion to both domestic and foreign proceedings, although their effect is felt inversely and depends on the difference between the conflicting legal systems in each case. As it has become common practice to treat questions arising in domestic insolvency proceedings separately from those arising in Germany from foreign insolvency proceedings, the same distinction will be made below.

(a) Domestic bankruptcy

(i) The starting point for our considerations will initially be the simple case in which a German bankruptcy court institutes a bankruptcy proceeding against the assets of a German businessman located not only in Germany, but also in Switzerland, the US, the UK and Canada. Contracts for work and services are pending and have only been partly performed. The assets of the bankrupt without special privileges located in Germany are not sufficient to satisfy priority claims against the estate, in particular tax claims. The assets located abroad are not exhausted by the liabilities of the debtor at the state of *situs* in each case.

Once the German receiver is in possession of the adjudication order (section 108 KO) and the certificate of appointment (section 81, paragraph 2 KO) in the above case, the battle for the estate has generally long since begun. Once the receiver leaves court to present himself at the debtor's offices, he may well find that the latter is already on the way abroad to take care of the assets located there in his own fashion. What the receiver did not learn as sequestrator may no longer be revealed to him by the debtor in spite of section 100 KO, and it will subsequently then be too late for a statutory declaration in accordance with section 125 KO. If the receiver follows the view of the *Bundesgerichtshof* with respect to section l, paragraph 1 and section 117, paragraph 1 KO, it is also his duty "to take custody of and realize the debtor's assets abroad",[41] which may possibly also have been made clear by the bankruptcy court in its adjudication order.[42] Once the receiver has then duly made his way abroad to fulfil his legal duty in the foreign countries concerned, he will encounter the following typical difficulties arising from such a constellation.

While the receiver is struggling to obtain recognition of his authority, the debtor will be busy appealing against such recognition. He will nurture doubts about the validity of recognising the receiver by arguing that the insolvency proceeding in Germany only has restricted extraterritorial application,[43] which the foreign court

---

[41]BGH, 10 February 1976, BGHZ 68, 16 (17).

[42]See AG Holn, 24 January 1986, confirmed by LG Küln, 17February 1986 and OLG Köln, 28 April 1986, ZIP 1986, pp. 658 *et seq*. As to the constitutional complaint filed unsuccessfully — BVerfG,28 April 1986, ZIP 1986, pp. 1336 *et seq*. The judgments of the first and the second instance are reported in the statement of facts of the judgment of OLG Küln, 3 March 1986, ZIP 1986, 384 (385).

[43]The prevailing view until some years ago has been that s 14 of the German Bankruptcy Code only applies to property located in Germany, see RG, 28 March 1903, RGZ 54, 193 (194); BayObLG, 17 February 1908, column 550–553; OLG Hamm, 14 July 1982, ZIP 1982, 1343 (1345); OLG Holn, 9 March 1978, HTS 1978, 249 (252); Jaeger(-Jahr) (*see* n. 17), ss 237, 238 KO n. 225–230; Jurgen Schmidt (*see* n. 14), p. 160; for a detailed comment see Lüer (*see* n. 8) (HTS 1978), pp. 200–208 with additional references.

may see confirmed by the fact that German law grants the receiver no recourse to legal prosecution proceedings against the debtor abroad.[44] The debtor in the afore-mentioned example will also find sympathy for his argument that the German receiver is indirectly pursuing the tax claims of priority creditors as defined under section 60, paragraph 1, no. 2 KO, which may not be enforced by way of individual enforcement proceedings in the foreign states of *situs* (eg US, Canada) because of lack of international treaties on enforcement and execution.[45] Should the German receiver demand from a foreign principal that the contractual partner surrender equipment and machinery following the refusal to perform the contract, he will be informed that these have been initially "taken into custody" in the interests of the company in question, which frequently means that the assets are lost forever to the debtor's estate; enormous claims for compensation against the list of creditors' claims are the result. If, however, the German receiver opts to determine what enforceable legal power he has at his disposal abroad under the German bankruptcy law, while all the other parties affected by the bankruptcy strive to keep the "damage" caused to themselves to a minimum, he will encounter difficulties in the areas described now.

(ii) In contrast to the bankrupt, the German receiver will discover that on the basis of the adjudication order he is able to enforce the surrender of a debtor's personal property in accordance with section 794, paragraph 1, no. 3 and section 883, paragraph 1 ZPO in Germany,[46] but not abroad.

Wherever the Federal Republic of Germany is a signatory to international treaties on enforcement and execution, rulings in respect of insolvency law are regularly excluded.[47] Even in cases in which the transfer of power to administer and dispose of property as defined in section 6, paragraph 2 KO may be recognised in principle, the adjudication order does not include any concrete statements capable of enforcement abroad. Even though the bankruptcy court may rule in its adjudication order that the bankrupt is to issue the receiver the appropriate authority over his assets abroad in order to facilitate their attachment,[48] this in itself is of no use if the bankrupt does not obey this ruling. Such measures as administrative fines or coercive detention provided under section 101, paragraph 2 KO are not executable or enforceable abroad. As the adjudication order — unlike a judgment to make a declaration of intention — does not therefore result in any *res judicata* effect, which thus precludes it from being an effective substitute for a declaration of authority defined under section 894 ZPO,[49] it has no significance on the assets of the bankrupt located abroad in cases in which he refuses to comply with the order to give such co-operation. If the

[44]*See* **7.3.2(c)**.
[45]Hanisch (*see* n. 25) (ZIP 1989), pp. 276, 279.
[46]See BGH, 26 February 1954, BGHZ 12, 380 (389); BGH, 23May 1962, NJW 1962, 1392; Jaeger (-Henkel), *Honkursordnung* (9th ed. 1977), s 1 KO n. 148; Kuhn/Uhlenbruck (*see* n. 11), s 117 n. 6–6d.
[47]Geimer/Schrntze, *Internationale Urteilsanerkennung 1/2* (1984), p. 1451 with references; see also Art 1 II No. 2 Gw.
[48]See AG Köln, 24 January 1986, reprinted in the statement of facts of OLG Köln, 3 March 1986, ZIP 1986, 384 (385) (as to this proceeding *see* n. 42); see also Hanisch, *Pflicht des Gemeinschuldners zur Vollmachterteilung bezuglich seines Auslandsvermtigens* (ZIP 1980), pp. 170–172; contra OLG Hoblenz, 15 May 1979, HTS 1980, pp. 68 *et seq*; see also LG Memmingen, 20 January 1983, ZIP 1983, pp. 204 *et seq*: warrant of arrest against the bankrupt impeding the sale of real property located abroad.
[49]See Wieczorek, *ZivilprozeBordnung* (2d ed. IV 1981), § 894 A II b 1.

German receiver discovers that the bankrupt has transferred or assigned objects of property from his estate abroad to third parties, he could possibly seek redress by requesting a protective stay through the bankruptcy court in accordance with section 108, paragraph 1, section 110, paragraph 1 and section 118 KO. However, he will then find himself advised by a number of legal commentators that a protective stay of action is only applicable to debtors in Germany.[50] Conversely, third party debtors who make payments to the bankrupt abroad once bankruptcy proceedings have been instituted are regularly freed of their liabilities; appeal is generally made in this context to section 8, paragraph 3 KO, where the important factor is knowledge on the part of the third party debtor following official proclamation of the institution of bankruptcy proceedings, which is generally not given abroad.

These short references to German bankruptcy law will have already revealed how little support prevailing law gives the German receiver in his efforts to enforce attachment of bankrupt's estate abroad; to supplement these references, it is also possible to cite conceivable rights not developed as such under German law. Thus, for example, it is the prevailing opinion that no material claim to surrender property may be considered against a bankrupt who offers resistance, which would be capable of enforcement by legal action before a court of law and, in the event of such action being successful, of execution according to the general rules of individual enforcement prevailing abroad.[51] Similarly, German bankruptcy law provides for no claim for damages against a bankrupt who withholds part of his foreign assets from the receiver or the estate which the receiver could also enforce in a civil court in Germany and pursue abroad according to the generally held rules of individual enforcement or execution of title to render payment.[52] No consideration is even given to whether the receiver might be entitled to seek an injunction — as is the case under English law[53] — which would bind the bankrupt to refrain from hindering the receiver in his duties. Similarly, German procedural law knows of no form of temporary legal redress against the bankrupt, such as an action for protective stay or temporary injunction, because such a claim to stay or disposal is already lacking in substantive law.[54] German law has so far also not recognised any form of legal representation of creditors by the receiver, even in cases in which their claims have been registered, which might allow the receiver to claim against the bankrupt abroad.

It is not surprising, in view of the unsatisfactory terms of reference afforded the receiver in Germany, that he has even more difficulties than the bankrupt if he wishes to obtain attachment of the latter's assets located abroad. These must be located in a country particularly willing to recognise his authority if he is in any way to press the claim imposed upon him by the German substantive law governing bankruptcy. In

---

[50]Jaeger(-Weber), *Honkursordnung* (8th ed. II 1973), s 118 KO n. 7; Mentzel/Kuhn/Uhlenbruck, *Honkursordnung* (9th ed. 1979), s 118 n. 4; but see now Kuhn/Uhlenbruck (*see* n. 11), s 118 KO n. 4.

[51]The reason therefore is that, according to the prevailing view, all legal powers pass over to the receiver by statute and that the receiver may directly start execution proceedings because of the adjudication order.

[52]eg in the US according to the Uniform Foreign Country Money Judgments Recognition Act, reprinted at: Geimer/Schlltze (*see* n. 47), pp. 1914 *et seq* n. 2.

[53]Because of the comprehensive jurisdiction of English bankruptcy courts this is enforced by court orders, which are rendered upon the request of the receiver, see Berry/Bailey, *Bankruptcy: Law and Practice* (1987), p. 273.

[54]This, too, follows from the prevailing view that safeguard measures are to be rendered by the bankruptcy court, *see* 106 KO.

Switzerland, in the meantime, he may be granted recognition in principle under recent legislation,[55] but he may not enforce attachment of the bankrupt's estate.[56] In the UK, he is allowed to obtain direct attachment in respect of movables, provided they have not already been disposed of otherwise, but he may only exert his influence over real property assets through the assistance of the courts.[57] In the US, under the US Bankruptcy Code in force since 1978, the receiver has to consider whether he wishes to institute general bankruptcy proceedings[58] or to apply for an "ancillary proceeding" under section 304.[59] Should the competent US Bankruptcy Court decide not to avail itself of its competence, which is one of the possible courses of action left to the discretion of a Bankruptcy Court (under section 305), the receiver is then left with no alternative cause of action. The legal power of the German receiver is not recognised in Canada, because the principle of territoriality prevails there to this day; consequently, a German receiver can bring no action whatsoever against a bankrupt in that country.[60] In contrast to the US, a German receiver cannot even file a petition of bankruptcy in his own name against the person adjudicated bankrupt in Germany, as his legal power to do so is not recognised; the receiver is also not permitted to appear as representative of German creditors. In such cases, commentators recommend the receiver to negotiate with an understanding creditor for the latter to pursue claims against the bankrupt in favour of the estate on the receiver's behalf.[61] This possibility is discussed below.[62]

It is not the object of these considerations to list the difficulties of recognising the authority of a receiver under foreign systems of law from the standpoint of comparative law; the factors quoted are merely intended to indicate the weakness of German substantive law governing bankruptcy in equipping the receiver with legal forms of redress against the bankrupt. Prevailing substantive insolvency law in Germany is basically not geared to supporting any action at all by the receiver abroad. Similarly, prevailing law does not concern itself with elements, which through substantive law rules would at least create the necessary requirements ensuring that the claim defined under section 1

---

[55]Arts 166–175 of the Swiss Private International Law Act of 18 December 1987; see also Breitenstein, *Internationales Insolvenzrecht der Schweiz und der Vereinigten Staaten* (1990); Hanisch, *Wirkungen deutscher Insolvenzverfahren auf in der Schweiz befindliches Schuldnervermogen* (JZ 1988), pp. 737–744; Nussbaum, *Das Schweizerische internationale Insolvenzrecht gemäß dem Bundesgesetz vom 18.12.1987 uber das internationale Privatrecht und sein Umfeld in Europa* (1989).
[56]See Dilger, *Die Zugriffsrechte des deutschen Honkursverwalters an Massevermogen in der Schweiz* (WH 1988), pp. 849–852 (852).
[57]See Cheshire/North, *Private International Law* (12th ed. 1992), pp. 912, 914; Dicey/Morris, *The Conflict of Laws* (11th ed. II 1987), pp. 1121 *et seq.*
[58]11 USC § 303 (b) (4); and see Hay, *"Auslandskonkurs und Inlandsfolgen aus amerikanischer Sicht"*, in *Festschrift Muller-Freienfels* (1986), pp. 247–269 (250).
[59]See Breitenstein (*see* n. 55), pp. 83–109; Hay (*see* n. 58), pp. 251–254, 257–269; Riesenfeld, *"Probleme des internationalen Insolvenzrechts aus der Sicht des neuen Honkursreformgesetzes der Vereinigten Staaten"*, in *Probleme des internationalen Insolvenzrechts* (v. Marschall 1982), pp. 39–49 (44–49); Aiesenfeld, "Transnational Bankruptcy Law: Recent Developments in Argentinia and the United States", in *Festschrift Hegel* (1987), pp. 483–504 (489–504).
[60]See eg Quebec Court of Appeal, 8 February 1988, *Re Karen* (1988), 47 DLR (4th) 626-632; see as to details Grace, "Law of liquidations: The recognition and enforcement of foreign liquidation orders in Canada and Australia — A critical comparison", *Int.Comp.L.Q.* 35 (1986), pp. 664–703 (665–682).
[61]See Hanisch (*see* n. 18) (ZIP 1983), p. 1295; see also Hers (*see* n. 14), p. 140; see also the critical comments of Westermann, *"Auslandsvollstreckung wahrend eines inllindischen Vergleichsverfahrens?"*, in *Festschrift Werner* (1984), pp. 989–1013 (1007).
[62]*See* **7.3.2 (c) (ii)**.

(paragraph 1), 6 (paragraph 2) and 117 (paragraph 1) KO may be enforced to an economic end in cases in which the receiver is refused recognition of his authority abroad.

(iii) The weakness of the receiver gives the creditors their real opportunity. The more successful the adjudicated bankrupt proves to be in withholding those of his assets located abroad from attachment by the receiver, the more possibilities there are for creditors to seek satisfaction outside of bankruptcy proceedings in Germany. As their rights derive from legal relationships not associated with the bankruptcy itself, they can follow the standard route to prosecution abroad. Where German law governing insolvency is not observed in the foreign country concerned, they are not basically encumbered by the provisions of sections 12 and 14 KO, and 47 Vg10. This may result in temporary injunctions to secure assets, to initiate legal proceedings and to execute individual enforcement measures abroad, or even in the institution of a foreign insolvency proceeding. Of course, the bankrupt will maintain that sections 12 and 14 KO should also take effect abroad,[63] whereas the creditors will claim that such provisions are without extraterritorial application.[64] Thus, for example, a German bankrupt recently attempted in the course of a Canadian bankruptcy petition proceeding to oppose the petition in respect of bankruptcy filed by a German bank by appealing to sections 12 and 14 KO, while at the same time insisting that the authority of the German receiver was not to be recognised on account of the prevailing principle of territoriality under Canadian law. After hearing expert witnesses, the Canadian bankruptcy court saw through the equivocal nature of such argument, and instituted a separate Canadian bankruptcy proceeding alongside the German proceeding already in existence.[65]

(iv) The success of creditors to the detriment of the assets of the bankrupt, which form part of the estate in accordance with section 1, paragraph 1 KO and which, contrary to section 117, paragraph 1 KO, cannot be appropriated by the domestic receiver, must have consequences in Germany. It is known that the Bankruptcy Act and the Composition Act are silent on this question, which resulted in the frequently cited Kozmos decision of the *Reichsgericht* at the beginning of this century.[66] After many years of discussion about different solutions and interpretations,[67] the *Bundesgerichtshof* at least partially put an end to speculation in the "savings bank case" of 1983.[68]

In this case a creditor, who successfully pursues abroad individual enforcement against the assets of a bankrupt, is obliged to surrender the net proceeds to the receiver under the provisions governing unjust enrichment. Even if choice of the statute governing enrichment as legal grounds for such a ruling may seem unfortunate,[69] the decision in essence nevertheless leads to the formulation of a substantive law rule in German bankruptcy law providing economic redress in Germany for the fact that

---

[63]See Westermann (*see* n. 61), p. 993.
[64]See OLG Hamm, 17 July 1982, ZIP 1982, 1343 (1345) being the previous instance of BGH, 13 July 1983, BGHZ 88, 147, see also the prevailing view until recently (for references *see* n. 43).
[65]Quebec Court of Appeal, 8 February 1988, *Re Karen* (1988), 47 DLR (4th) 626–632.
[66]RG, 28 March 1903, RGZ 54, 193 (*see* n. 11).
[67]See Canaris, *Die Auswirkungen eines im Ausland ausgebrachten Arrests im inländishen Konkurs und Vergleich* (ZIP 1983), pp. 647–651 (648–651); Hanisch (*see* n. 8), pp. 154–158; Liner (*see* n. 8) (HTS 1979), pp. 21–28.
[68]BGH, 13 July 1983, BGHZ 88, 147 (153–156)
[69]Canaris (*see* n. 67), p. 651; Hanisch (*see* n. 18) (ZIP 1983), p. 1291; Kuhn/Uhlenbruck(-Lüer) (*see* n. 11), ss 237, 238 KO n. 62; Westermann (*see* n. 61), pp. 1002–1007.

the debtor's assets are supposed to be assigned to the estate under section 1, paragraph 1 KO, even though their attachment has been successfully enforced abroad.[70] It still remains to be clarified, however, whether this is also to apply in cases in which a creditor gains full or partial satisfaction abroad by any other means. It will no doubt be possible to take account of voluntary payments rendered by the debtor abroad under the provisions for avoiding such actions defined in sections 29 *et seq* KO. Whether this also applies to cases in which a bankrupt's creditors are successful in a foreign insolvency proceeding subsequently instituted would appear doubtful. In a recent commentary on the still pending *Kaussen* case, Hanisch[71] forcefully argues that the creditors are under no obligation to surrender such assets.[72] He bases his view on the assumption that the foreign assets of the bankrupt would "also not be counted as belonging to the German estate if a parallel, equivalent insolvency proceeding were to take place on the basis of jurisdiction capable of being recognised".[73] The same would then apply if domestic creditors were successful in participating in a US probate proceeding, ie a proceeding in which the estate is subject to administration.[74] It is patently obvious that this view drastically restricts the extraterritorial application of sections 1 (paragraph 1), 6 (paragraph 2), and 117 (paragraph 1) KO. Whether this view is correct on the basis of prevailing law is immaterial. It will at least require careful examination *de lege ferenda* as to whether such a ruling can be thought at all desirable in terms of legal policy; much careful consideration will need to be given to this question in the context of Article 22 of the Draft. The main task for the law-making authorities is at least clear: namely, to end the prevailing legal uncertainty.[75]

(v) To summarise, from the practical standpoint there are two concrete reasons for the need for revision: On the one hand it would appear very necessary to equip the future receiver in cases of insolvency with sufficient legal power to permit him to include foreign assets in a domestic proceeding more effectively than at present. On the other hand, there is a need for legal clarification of the circumstances and legal consequences under which the future receiver in insolvency matters is to be able to counteract the effects of non-recognition abroad by compensatory claims at home. Both areas are not to be regulated in German insolvency law by conflict of laws rules, rather by substantive law rules.

(b) Foreign bankruptcy [76,77]
As far as treatment of foreign bankruptcies in Germany is concerned, the fact that sections 237 (paragraph 1) and 238 KO largely preclude the recognition of foreign

[70]Kuhn/Uhlenbruck(-Lüer) (*see* n. 11) ss 237, 238 KO n. 62.
[71]Hanisch (*see* n. 25) (ZIP 1989), pp. 273–279; Hanisch, *EWiR*, s 812 BGB 2/89, pp. 349 *et seq.*
[72]As to the same result see OLG Köln, 31 January 1989, ZIP 1989, 321; according to Baur/Stürner (*see* n. 24), n. 37.17; Flessner (*see* n. 23), p. 752; Grasmann, *Inlandswirkungen des Auslandskonkurses ilber das Ver mogen eines im Konkurseröffnungsstaat ansassigen Gemeinschuldners* (HTS 1990), pp. 157, 159 n. 8.
[73]Hanisch (*see* n. 25) (ZIP 1989), p. 277; contra eg Wenner, *Ausländisches Sanierungsverfahren, Inlandsarrest und § 238 KO* (HTS 1990), pp. 429–436 (435).
[74]Eg recently Professor Hanisch, being appointed as an expert witness in a s 304 proceeding in Atlanta applying the concept of "collective proceedings".
[75]*See* **7.3.2 (b)**.
[76]Ebenroth, *Neuere Entwicklungen im deutschen internationalen Gesellschaftsrecht Part I* (JZ 1988), pp. 18–30 (28).
[77]BGH, 11 July 1985, BGHZ 95, 256 (267 *et seq*).

insolvency law would appear to constitute sufficient grounds in itself for the need for legislation. A description of the "loophole in bankruptcy law" under which it is possible for foreign proceedings to be recognised at all, similar to the description given by the *Bundesgerichtshof* of the range of situations not covered by section 238, paragraph 1 KO in which it is not possible to institute a proceeding due to the lack of any international competence in Germany similar to the provisions outlined in section 71, paragraph 1 KO, leaves a wide field in theory. In reality, however, this is considerably reduced by the alternative provisions contained under section 237, paragraph 1 KO; for if proceedings are not instituted in accordance with section 238 KO, then section 237, paragraph 1 KO precludes the recognition of foreign insolvency law for further cases. Thus the only area still open for the recognition and application of foreign insolvency law in respect of the bankrupt's assets located in Germany is that range of cases not covered either by individual enforcement or by domestic bankruptcy. Furthermore, depending on the circumstances of the case, questions may arise concerning the application of foreign insolvency law rules which:

- provide for any restrictions in offsetting to the detriment of third party debtors in Germany;
- regard the removal of assets within Germany as being avoidable;
- lay partial or full claim to any real property security interests created in Germany prior to the institution of proceedings;
- regulate any intervention caused by the process of instituting foreign proceedings in legal relationships pending with domestic citizens (contractual and security interests);
- link special consequences with the conclusion of proceedings, to the detriment of domestic creditors (decree effect); *or*
- may assume importance within the framework of domestic regulations for clarifying subsidiary questions (section 240 ZPO).

In essence, the scope within which the question of recognising foreign insolvency proceedings under prevailing law may in practice become urgent now proves to be extremely restricted ("scope of recognition"). It is thus also not surprising that the recognition of foreign proceedings in legal rulings in Germany has most frequently been considered within the context of section 240 ZPO.[78] If the fact that there is thus a severe lack of pertinent rules in prevailing law does not in itself constitute sufficient grounds for the need for action by the legislators, then the need for such action must surely follow from the ruling of the *Bundesgerichtshof* in 1985.[79] For hand-in-glove with the shift towards the principle of universality in the conflict of laws goes the question of the extent to which claims for the application of foreign insolvency law should be met within the scope of recognition indicated. Two problem areas spring to mind in which action by the legislators would appear necessary. First, there is the question of when a foreign receiver may take legal action in Germany, ie his legitimation, proof of his legal authority and execution and enforcement of decisions and orders relating to insolvency law which have been passed abroad. There is a lack of any legal provision in Germany capable of defining what formal or substantive

---

[78]See recently OLG Harlsruhe, 21 February 1992, RIW 1992, 940.
[79]BGH, 11 July 1985, BGHZ 95, 256.

conditions are necessary for the foreign receiver to assert his claims in Germany. In those cases in which he has so far been permitted to do so,[80] proof of his legal authority in the pending proceeding has always been sufficient until now. Only in some cases have there been any indications of also granting the foreign receiver security interests under German bankruptcy law, such as entries in the land register in accordance with section 113, paragraph 1 KO.[81] Associated with this is the general question of whether to give serious recognition to the foreign receiver by creating formal recognition proceedings on his behalf in Germany, which would consequently permit him to obtain the same measures from a German bankruptcy court as are available to a German receiver to safeguard the bankrupt's estate.

Secondly, there would appear to be a need to regulate the extent to which German citizens need to be protected from the effects of the foreign substantive bankruptcy law rules which seem intolerable in Germany. The obstacle of public policy is surely not sufficient, as the conditions under which it may apply are extremely severe. The question that really needs to be asked is in what cases should the business interests in Germany preclude the application of foreign bankruptcy law rules. It would also be desirable for the legislators to make up their minds to develop concrete rules to this end; it would then no longer be necessary for these to be deduced in practice from general principles.

7.3 Basic positions in preliminary draft

If we examine the existing draft submitted by the Federal Ministry of Justice in the light of dramatic changes in the law due to recent court decisions and against the background of multitudes of theoretical commentaries over the last three decades, unsuccessful attempts at international harmonisation and widespread legal uncertainty in practice, then it would be wrong to maintain that it is too global in outlook at its current stage of development or to criticise it for its proposed solutions to detailed questions. Its extremely liberal attempt to develop rules and standards for the normal elements relating to both sides of insolvencies transcending national boundaries, while turning its back on the principle of territorial isolationism, is clearly apparent. It is also obvious that the draft strives to achieve a balanced delimitation of opposing interests with a view to pacifying all sides to the best of its ability. Whether the tendency to favour parallel bankruptcy proceedings against portions of the insolvent debtor's estate is a particularly suitable approach will, however, no doubt require careful analysis. Several matters already seen as needing regulation remain without mention in the draft, but can no doubt be added to it at a later date. It is important to stress at this stage, however, that the draft provides a basis for discussion on the reform of international insolvency law in Germany. It reveals a number of basic positions that require careful consideration. Without distorting the draft too drastically, these basic positions may be summarised in three fundamental principles which deserve closer analysis.

[80]eg BGH, 11 July 1985, BGHZ 95, 256 (261).
[81]Lau, *Zur Anderung der Rechtsprechung des Bundesgerichtshofs uber die Wirkung des Auslandskonkurses im Inland* (BB 1986), pp. 1450–1453; see now OLG Zweibrucken, 17 April 1989, NJW 1990, 648, 649 with Note, *Gottwald, Auslandskonkurs und Registereintragung im Inland* (IPRax 1991), pp. 168–172.

7.3.1 Principle of universality in the conflict of laws

(a) Preliminary draft

According to the draft, insolvency proceedings and their effects are legally prescribed in future as being subject to the law of the state initiating proceedings (Article 2). This is already a basic rule recognised under prevailing law in German international bankruptcy law.[82] However, referral to the law of the state instituting proceedings is subject to the general proviso of international jurisdiction under the provisions of German law.[83] As international jurisdiction may be assumed to exist when insolvency proceedings are instituted in Germany, the draft formulates this provison only in the context of recognition of the institution of proceedings abroad (Article 9, paragraph 1). However, the draft does not define what is to be understood by "insolvency proceedings" within the understanding of a general rule on the conflict of laws. The Explanation states that these must be proceedings which:

> "... largely serve to fulfil the purposes described as the task of German insolvency law under section 1 of the Insolvency Act: the best possible settlement for all the creditors as a whole, the best possible winding up of the debtor's assets and the best possible adjustment of the debtor's liabilities." [at pp. 39 *et seq*]

The draft also refrains from providing a general definition of the scope of application of the insolvency law to be applied; in the Explanation, there is merely a reference to "indicators" which are supposed to follow from Articles 3 to 7. Under these provisions, avoidance in insolvency law (Article 4, paragraph 1) and the effects of instituting insolvency proceedings on pending, ie non-performed or not yet completely performed reciprocal contracts (Article 6, paragraph 1) are always subject to the law of the state governing insolvency. It is possible to deduce from Article 25 that consideration of special privileges and restrictions in the possibility of off-setting will also be subject in principle to the law of the state governing insolvency. However, this insolvency law is to have no effect on the execution of *ad rem* property rights (ie security collateral) located abroad at the time proceedings are instituted (*lex rei sitae*). Furthermore, the effects of insolvency proceedings are to be applied separately in the case of rental and lease agreements, in the latter case to the state of situs and in the case of service contracts to the law of the state in which services are generally to be rendered (Article 7, paragraph 1).

(b) Evaluation from the standpoint of legal policy

The starting point of the draft, namely the establishment in law of the principle of universality in the conflict of laws, meets the demands made by what has become the general consensus of opinion, and by what the IXth Division for Civil Matters of the *Bundesgerichtshof* ruled to be prevailing law in recognising a Belgian receiver in Germany.[84] It is also in keeping with the fundamental principle on which the 1980 EC Agreement is based;[85] the Council of Europe draft contains an almost identical

---

[82]Jaeger(-Jahr) (*see* n. 17), ss 237, 238 KO n. 253, 256; Kuhn/Uhlenbruck(-Lüer) (*see* n. 11), ss 237, 238 KO n. 42.
[83]Kuhn/Uhlenbruck(-Lüer) (*see* n. 11), ss 237, 238 KO n. 43.
[84]BGH, 11 July 1985, BGHZ 95, 256 (263).
[85]See Arts 2, 17, 34; see Hanisch, *"Anwendbares Recht und Honkurswirkungen"*, in *VorschlSge und Gutachten (see* n. 40), pp. 319–339; Liner, *"Allgemeine Wirkungen des Honkurses"*, in *Vorschlage und Gutachten (see* n. 40), pp. 341–356; Thieme (*see* n. 40), pp. 213 *et seq.*

provision. Furthermore, the draft thus also follows trends in those foreign legal systems in which statutory reforms reveal signs of a movement towards the principle of universality, such as the US Bankruptcy Code of 1978[86] and the Swiss Private International Law Act (IPRG).[87] The proposed general rule on international insolvency law in Germany is thus to be welcomed in this context.

The approach taken by the draft is not fully understandable in that it dispenses completely with any material delimitation of the type of insolvency proceedings for which the choice of law clause is to apply. Sufficient grounds to make such a delimitation were given according to the Explanation ([at p. 39], [at p. 40]), because it was the aim to provide against "unrestricted recognition" of the effects of foreign proceedings on insolvency law. Mention of this was already made by Muller-Freienfels;[88] constant warnings have been raised since then on the unwelcome consequences of the principle of universality in the conflict of laws.[89] These reservations would appear only partially justified:

Although the decision of the *Bundesgerichtshof* in 1985 points out that the process of recognising foreign bankruptcy in Germany is subject to restrictions, such considerations must be seen against the background the *Bundesgerichtshof* itself cites. It explains that recognition of the law of the foreign state governing insolvency must be "incorporated in the overall structure of German provisions and legal principles governing bankruptcy law".[90] The *Bundesgerichtshof* saw such restrictions to exist particularly in the provisions specified in sections 237 (paragraph 1), 238 and 71 (paragraph 1) KO. The *Bundesgerichtshof* was no doubt correct in its view, in so far as it did not want to ignore statutory prescribed rules and standards. Such restrictions would appear to be superfluous in a process of new legislation, however, as the object it sets out to regulate may be adapted to the principle of universality now being pursued. Moreover, the only additional restriction cited by the *Bundesgerichtshof* is the proviso of German public policy, which follows the generally held view[91] and would appear completely justified. It only remains to examine how the scope of recognition will be organised in future between permissible individual execution and enforcement (currently section 237, paragraph 1 KO) and parallel bankruptcy proceedings in Germany (currently section 238 KO).

The reservations raised in the Explanation to the draft that unsuitable foreign insolvency proceedings might fall under the proposed general rule are justified; however, legislation could obviate this risk by defining at least in the form of a general clause what German international insolvency law intends to understand under the term "insolvency proceedings". Accordingly, consideration should be given to inserting an additional clause containing the major criteria necessary to qualify as "insolvency proceedings" as the second paragraph to the provision outlined under Article 2. Reference could be made here to substantive insolvency law. Until now, the concepts

[86]Riesenfeld (*see* n. 59) in *Festschrift Hegel*, p. 500.
[87]Hanisch (*see* n. 55), p. 738.
[88]Müller-Freienfels (*see* n. 15), pp. 382–388.
[89]Ebenroth (*see* n. 14), pp. 138–141; Flessner (*see* n. 23), pp. 752–754; Hanisch (*see* n. 18) (ZIP 1985), pp. 1297 *et seq*; Lüderitz, comment, BGH, 11 July 1985, JZ 1986, 96 *et seq*; Lüke (*see* n. 18), p. 17–19.
[90]BGH, 11 July 1985, BGHZ 95, 256 (269 *et seq*).
[91]BGH, 11 July 1985, BGHZ 95, 256 (270); Hanisch (*see* n. 18) (ZIP 1983), pp. 1297 *et seq*; Kilger (*see* n. 11), s 237 KO n. 6; Kuhn/Uhlenbruck (-Lüer) (*see* n. 11), ss 237, 238 KO n. 39; Pielorz (*see* n. 8), pp. 74 *et seq*; as to additional references see Aderhold (*see* n. 16), p. 202.

of uniform settlement of debt and of equitable treatment of all creditors have always been principles central to German bankruptcy and composition law.[92] For the new Insolvency Act, this principle of unity and uniformity of insolvency proceedings should be given even more prominence than it has hitherto enjoyed.[93] This is not only expressed by the fact that there is to be no distinction in future between bankruptcy and composition law, but also by the circumstances whereby the circle of those involved in insolvency proceedings is to be extended to include those creditors previously not participating in proceedings at all or only with a portion of their claims.[94] The principle of creditors participating as justly as possible in the debtor's estate could well be included in such a statutory definition, even if the insolvency proceedings appealed to provide for different standards of distribution from what German law has prescribed until now.

The additional reservations outlined in the draft that the universally formulated general rule for German international insolvency law might lead to recognition of foreign proceedings that provide not for a uniform settlement of debts incorporating the entire estate, but for a continuation of business activities for reasons not primarily lying in the best interest of creditors, would also appear justified in principle. However, in so far as the draft refrains from providing for this eventuality in a supplement to the general rule, this is in accordance with its tendency to refuse to give concrete formulation to the object and contents of such a general rule, and thus to the scope of the substantive insolvency law to be applied. Consequently, the draft restricts itself in Article 15 to prescribing "defensively" the conditions under which foreign insolvency proceedings are to be recognised in Germany. The doubtful nature of this formulation lies in the fact that the question of extraterritorial claim for application could possibly be deduced conversely from Article 15 for insolvency proceedings in Germany. Thus, for example, it might be concluded from Article 15, paragraph 3 that a German insolvency compensation scheme does not apply to an involved party from abroad who has appealed against the scheme at German insolvency proceedings, resulting in his being in a worse situation than he would have been without such a scheme. The ruling proposed under Article 15 of the draft will no doubt require careful study. The aim of the above considerations is to emphasise that the future organisation of German international insolvency law should not include without important grounds provisions intended to protect against foreign law and which turn out to incorporate an unnecessary self-restriction of the German substantive insolvency law.

(c) Restriction of scope
Those cases within the framework of its General Provisions in which the draft refrains from providing a positive restriction in the scope of the substantive insolvency law applicable do not appear convincing for a number of reasons. First, legislators should define as accurately as possible what they intend to regulate in principle, before proceeding to list a catalogue of exceptions to an extremely generalised central principle. Secondly, the broad range of what the substantive insolvency law

[92]Jaeger(-Lent), *Honkursordnung* (8th ed. vol. I 1958), preliminary remarks, n. III; as to details see Lüer (*see* n. 8) (HTS 1978), pp. 210–213 with references.
[93]See "General Explanation", in *Discussion Draft* (*see* n. 32), A 31 *et seq.*
[94]"General Explanation", in *Discussion Draft* (*see* n. 32), A 20 *et seq.*

applicable regularly includes should be classified under the conflict of laws to allow those addressed by the standard to refer to concrete elements, and not to have to deduce features of such elements themselves from abstract concepts and principles when they are searching for the legal consequences applicable to a specific case. Thirdly, the clearer the description of the scope of the insolvency law as a general rule of the governing law, the easier it is to define the boundaries separating this statute from elements that it does not encompass in terms of the conflict of laws. Finally, it should not be forgotten that future international insolvency law in its legislative form must also appear comprehensible and applicable to those persons not wishing to have to undergo a course of specialist training in order to be able to follow the object of the legal provisions it contains. This applies not only to courts and practitioners at home, but particularly also to foreigners seeking information on German law in cases of insolvencies transcending national boundaries.

In contrast to the current version of the draft, consideration should also be given to supplementary specification of the basic standard contained under Article 2 on the basis of the major areas regulating domestic insolvency law by including additional, and by all means broadly formulated, subordinate provisions, as has already been proposed for prevailing law.[95] Thus, for example, it should not prove too difficult to formulate a conflict of laws rule providing that procedural law in insolvency proceedings be subject to the law of the place where the proceedings are instituted; special restrictions would then need to be defined for whether and in what cases procedural rules valid in the foreign country in which proceedings are instituted can be applicable in Germany. Three subordinate areas may be distinguished to characterise the principle of uniform debt settlement in the sector of *substantive insolvency law*.[96] Thus, for example, according to the Insolvency Act, future substantive law will also strive to achieve the *unity* of a *debtor's assets*, their *administration* and *distribution* in a uniform proceeding. From the standpoint of the conflict of laws, this automatically results in the substantive laws applicable to *regulations governing assets, regulations governing administration and regulations governing distribution*. Even if this standpoint has been criticised for its "lack of clarity",[97] it nevertheless recommends itself because it creates clearly definable categories for the systematisation, classification and delimitation of individual elements. The subordinate regulations resulting from the criteria mentioned above within the scope of the insolvency law applicable from the standpoint of the conflict of laws may be formulated as follows:

(a) The law of the state in which insolvency is instituted shall determine the assets of the debtor going to make up the bankrupt's estate; all legal relationships relating to the assessment, protection and establishment of the estate shall follow from this rule (law governing insolvency assets).

Such a definition of the law governing insolvency assets would make it clear that not only *assessment of the estate*, but also the *obligations of the debtor to disclose information and to co-operate* in establishing which objects go to make

---

[95]Kuhn/Uhlenbruck(-Lüer) (*see* n. 11), ss 237, 238 KO n. 52 *et seq*, 70 *et seq*; Liner (*see* n. 14) (HTS 1990), pp. 398 *et seq*.
[96]Kuhn/Uhlenbruck(-Lüer) (*see* n. 11), ss 237, 238 KO n. 52.
[97]Hanisch (*see* n. 25) (ZIP 1989), p. 276 and n. 34.

up the estate, avoidance of *insolvency and restriction of possibilities for off-setting* basically lie within the concern of the law governing insolvency itself. The same applies to those substantive law rules developed by this applicable law to provide sanctions with the objective of establishing or recovering the estate, in cases in which actual registration of individual items of property has been prevented. This would apply, for example, to the claims for damages currently deduced from sections 50, 55 and 56 KO, or to claims for the surrender of assets, in so far as the statute will also encompass substantive law in future in accordance with the savings bank case of the *Bundesgerichtshof*.[98]

(b) The law of the state in which insolvency is instituted shall determine the legal power which the receiver is entitled to exercise for the purposes of seizing property, administering and realising items of property and rights against the estate, and organising and arranging all legal relationships forming part of the insolvency proceedings (law governing insolvency administration).

On the basis of these subordinate regulations, the law governing insolvency would cover the equipping of the receiver of the estate with appropriate rights in respect of items of property, *claims for the surrender of property* against the bankrupt and third parties, *administrative authorities* and the rights and obligations to *realise property* on behalf of the creditors. This applicable law could also cover the effects resulting from instituting proceedings in respect of any legal transactions pending and on the formative possibilities of the receiver, such as those provisions currently contained in sections 17 *et seq* KO. The law governing insolvency administration should cover all factors related to *liquidation of assets and settlement of pending legal transactions*.

(c) The law of the state in which insolvency is instituted shall determine the use to which the estate is put in the interests of the creditors (law governing insolvency distribution).

This provision would make it clear that the law governing insolvency is uniformly responsible for regulating settlement of assets within the framework of the insolvency proceedings, either by their immediate utilisation within the scope of liquidation or in the form of their assignment in the form of an insolvency compensation scheme in cases in which business activities are continued.

This *proposal* to give positive definition in legislation to the scope of the law governing insolvency by way of universally formulated rules for the conflict of laws in German international insolvency law has the recognisable aim of not only postulating the principle of universality in abstract terms, but also of converting it into concrete rules for the conflict of laws, promoting their practical application and implementation. Such a proposal gives rise to the question of whether those elements not covered by the law governing insolvency should not also be defined in the form of universally formulated rules for the conflict of laws.

A special problem in the conflict of laws arises in the context of claims for damages on the termination of contracts resulting from instituting insolvency proceedings, such as those cited in prevailing law under section 26, clause 2 KO. In German bankruptcy law, it is generally assumed that such a claim constitutes a contractual

98BGH, 13 July 1983, BGHZ 88, 147 (156).

claim[99] which must arise from the law applicable to contracts. In contrast, it has also been argued that the claim to damages originates specifically in bankruptcy law itself;[100] for this reason, when it comes to the conflict of laws, this should be covered by the law governing insolvency. The difference in qualification under the divergent standards establishing the damages incurred can be of practical significance. Much is to be said in favour of continuing to allow the legal consequences of a breach in the contract caused by insolvency to be covered by the law applicable to contracts; the legislator should take the opportunity to provide for clarification here.

7.3.2 Principle of restricted extraterritoriality

(a) Preliminary draft

The existing draft is based on the fundamental principle of *restricted extraterritorial claim to application* of the German law governing insolvency. This conclusion would appear to be contradicted by the fact that under Article 20 the draft equates domestic and foreign creditors (previously regulated by sections 5 KO and 37 VglO), and under Article 21, by supplementing section 39 EInsO, it clearly states that the assets of the debtor located abroad also form part of the estate for German insolvency proceedings. This conclusion is confirmed, however, by the proposed provisions formulated under Articles 22 to 24, which only to a limited extent oblige creditors to surrender in favour of the estate to the receiver what they have received abroad to the detriment of the self-same estate defined under Article 21. Article 22, paragraph 1 admittedly provides for a claim by the receiver against creditors who have successfully pursued *individual enforcement proceedings* abroad, or who have achieved satisfaction by means of payments by the debtor, by a third party or in some other fashion abroad to the detriment of the estate, to surrender the assets or property so received. This claim to surrender property will not exist, however, against creditors who have received part or full satisfaction in *foreign insolvency proceedings*. This important restriction is apparently based upon the view that the German law governing insolvency does not lay claim to foreign assets of the debtor whenever such assets become the object of separate insolvency proceedings abroad. The restriction becomes all the more important, because the draft itself seeks to promote the conducting of parallel insolvency proceedings at home and abroad, as may be deduced from its reintroduction of the concept of international jurisdiction according to the situs of the bankrupt's assets (Articles 1 (paragraph 2) and 26 (paragraph 2)). It is also of vital importance, because it is generally left to the discretion of the *creditors* whether to seek satisfaction abroad by way of individual or joint enforcement. Equipped with the privilege of being permitted to retain what they have obtained in foreign insolvency proceedings, the creditors have been granted the option of interpreting the extraterritorial claim to application of the domestic law governing insolvency to their own advantage.

At the same time, however, the draft refrains from including in the domestic law governing insolvency such provisions which could make it easier for the German

[99]RG, 1 February 1932, RGZ 135, 167 (170); BGH, 30 May 1963, NJW 1963, 1869 (1870); Kuhn/ Uhlenbruck (*see* n. 11), s 17 KO n. 37, s 26 KO n. 9; Frusielak, *Die Erfullungsablehung des Honkursverwalters. Zur Auslegung des § 17 Abs. 1 der Honkursordnung, AcP 179* (1979), pp. 189–213 (203) with references.
[100]Jaeger(-Henckel), *Honkursordnung* (9th ed. 2d supplement), ss 10–l8 KO (1980), s 17 KO n. 171.

receiver — in contrast to prevailing law — to incorporate the bankrupt's foreign assets in the domestic estate for proceedings. If Article 22, paragraph 2 were to become law in its present form, without providing the German receiver with better possibilities to seize foreign assets, the same disastrous conflict would be perpetuated between the abstract extraterritorial claim to application and its planned suspension, which is the hallmark of prevailing law. The planned off-setting clause under Article 23 is only apparently of assistance here. For in all those cases in which creditors have received more abroad than they are entitled to receive in domestic proceedings, this will result in a reinforcement of the inequitable treatment of creditors and so in an incomprehensible contradiction to the objectives of domestic insolvency law.

(b) Evaluation from the standpoint of legal policy

The evaluation from the standpoint of legal policy, on which the regular restriction of claims for application across national boundaries for the law governing insolvency is based, would appear dubious on several counts, and is ultimately not justified. The draft makes it clear that it has not overcome the past, ie the idea of supposed territorial self-limitation by domestic insolvency law,[101] any more than it has mastered the route shown by the *Bundesgerichtshof* in the "savings bank case"[102] and later in recognising a foreign receiver.[103] The draft endeavours to reinforce the rule of law propounded by the *Bundesgerichtshof* in the savings bank case, while simultaneously regulating differently on its extension to cases of participation in foreign insolvency proceedings. In so doing, the draft follows proposals made in prevailing law,[104] which will not be commented on here. From the standpoint of legal policy, the draft offers a dubious picture for future constitutive legislation, as the following considerations illustrate.

(i)   In so far as the German substantive law governing insolvency seeks to marshal the entire assets of the debtor, one might assume that the legislating body would also show an interest in implementing such a ruling for cases in which the receiver is not successful in his attempt to seize the bankrupt's assets located abroad. Should it instead prove possible for creditors participating in domestic proceedings successfully to appropriate these assets abroad, then they are obviously interfering in the process of assigning such items of property to the estate as specified under section 39 EInsO and Article 21 of the draft. This assignment of foreign assets to the estate, and thus to the group of creditors participating in domestic proceedings, provides the sole reason why the condition of attachment (for lack of any other foundation to such a claim) has been chosen to be added under prevailing law (sections 1 (paragraph 1) and 117 (paragraph 1) KO), in order to furnish grounds for surrendering the proceeds from individual enforcement to the receiver.[105] This obligation of assignment is not restricted or revoked by the fact that the foreign legal system at the *situs* ignores German insolvency law or tolerates the enforced attachment by individual creditors. Even if the foreign legal system also allows them to avail themselves of its machinery

[101]*See* nn. 10 and 43.
[102]BGH, 13 July 1983, BGHZ 88, 147.
[103]BGH, 11 July 1985, BGHZ 95, 256.
[104]Hanisch (*see* n. 25) (ZIP 1989), pp. 275–278; Flessner (*see* n. 23), pp. 752–754.
[105]BGH, 13 July 1983, BGHZ 88, 147 (155 *et seq.*); Canaris (*see* n. 67), p. 650.

for individual or joint enforcement, this also constitutes lawful behaviour according to the law governing such enforcement and/or insolvency.

However, individual enforcement measures abroad and joint enforcement in insolvency proceedings are not suitable actions to exert a different influence on the obligation to attach foreign assets for the domestic estate under German law. For there is no qualitative difference whether the prohibition of execution under domestic insolvency law is ignored, or whether international jurisdiction is assumed to apply, which from the domestic standpoint is not the case in Germany, at least not for the case in which proceedings have been instituted beforehand. Canaris is perfectly correct when he indicates that the claim to surrender property does not constitute an attack on the legality and conformity of the change of law under foreign procedural rules, but that it merely aims to reinstate the assignment of assets principle in accordance with the law governing insolvency in Germany by way of an *in personam* claim.[106] This specific principle of *restitution under bankruptcy law* must always intervene in all cases of enforced attachment by creditors abroad, not least in order to give credence to the seriousness of the claim to comprehensive settlement of assets and debt.

(ii) If the obligation to surrender assets is precluded in future for creditors participating in foreign insolvency proceedings, this would appear blatantly anti-social from two standpoints. It has been shown in practice that large institutional creditors generally have the economic means and sufficient contacts at their disposal to pursue their rights even abroad.[107] Small creditors, such as tradesmen and employees, are usually not in a position to exert their rights in the same way, even if they agree to co-operate. Experience reveals only too clearly the difficulties that arise when attempting to instruct small domestic creditors even on how to register their claims correctly in a French-speaking country, not to mention the costs for legal counsel which are frequently unattainable. If the proposals made here become law, these small creditors will in future have to look on while large creditors exploit their advantage abroad which they are then ultimately also permitted to retain. This will be all the more intolerable in cases in which practically nothing can be achieved at home, but full satisfaction gained abroad because the debtor had removed his assets outside the borders of Germany prior to proceedings being instituted; for in such cases, the off-setting clause under Article 23 will obviously then no longer apply. The regulation proposed would also appear inappropriate on account of section 131, paragraph 2 EInsO. Since under this provision, future claims under a social compensation scheme will not be permitted to exceed a quarter of the total estate available to creditors. If a business collapses in Germany with a large workforce but only small resources at its disposal to form the estate, even though it has considerable assets located abroad, it is simply not conceivable why recipients of payments under the social compensation scheme should be prevented from exploiting to the full the legally prescribed dividend when the assets abroad form the object of foreign insolvency proceedings not subject to restitution.

---

[106]Canaris (*see* n. 67), p. 651.
[107]Ebenroth (*see* n. 14), pp. 134 *et seq*; Grasmann, *System des internationalen Gesellschaftsrechts* (1970), n. 1131; Pielors (*see* n. 8), p. 57; Jurgen Schmidt (*see* n. 14), pp. 148 *et seq*.

(iii)   The regulation proposed in the Draft would also appear unjustified from the standpoint of legal policy because it would lead to the systematic discrimination of those creditors not able to pursue their claims abroad for legal reasons. If a German debtor possesses few assets in Germany, but at the same time leaves a high tax debt coupled with assets abroad which are then placed at the disposal of private creditors within the framework of an insolvency proceeding to which German tax authorities are not admitted as creditor,[108] the question raised is what interest the German legislator can possibly have in voluntarily abandoning the obligation to surrender property contained under section 29 EInsO and Article 21 of the draft to the disadvantage of German authorities. However justified the termination of tax privileges may seem within the scope of future regulations governing distribution, it is nevertheless beyond comprehension why German tax authorities should systematically be excluded as creditors from participating in the foreign assets of a debtor simply because the creditor has successfully removed his assets abroad and creditors are able to bring about institution of insolvency proceedings there.[109] This is even less justified for two further reasons: on the one hand, it is generally institutional creditors who manage to insure against losses by way of securities, which tax creditors are unable to do; on the other hand, the tax liabilities remaining are often extremely high when the debtor has been able to deceive the tax authorities.

(iv)   If, in contrast, it is argued — as has recently been the case — that separate treatment of the proceeds from individual enforcement and insolvency proceedings is to be preferred out of respect for foreign sovereignty and the idea of comity,[110] it must be countered that there is no cogent basis for this in legal policy. Canaris has correctly emphasised that even the legality of individual enforcement under the foreign law governing such enforcement or execution does not prevent German substantive law from creating the obligation of attachment provided for under sections 1 (paragraph 1) and 117 (paragraph 2) KO by way of restitution.[111] Lawful intervention by enforcement abroad where German insolvency law is ignored also ultimately does not constitute grounds for removal of assets.[112] The same is true for intervention by enforcement in the form of foreign insolvency proceedings; for it is difficult to comprehend how a foreign legal system can claim that the removal of assets contrary to German law should be economically final, although this system does not even recognise German insolvency proceedings. Restitution in bankruptcy under German insolvency law does not impinge on foreign sovereignty as long as foreign insolvency proceedings may continue to be held without interference. This aspect was recognised extremely clearly by the judge at the Canadian Bankruptcy Court in the *Kauflen* probate bankruptcy case from Cologne. With the support of the domestic receiver, a large German creditor had pursued institution of a bankruptcy proceeding because the German receiver and the

---

[108]eg in the US.
[109]This is the constellation of the *Haussen* case, even as this case concerns the administration of a deceased's estate; as to this proceeding see AG Köln, 24 January 1986, LG Köln, 17 February 1986 (both laid down in the statement of facts of OLG Köln, 3 March 1986, ZIP 1986, 384 [385]) and OLG Köln, 28 April 1986, ZIP 1986, 658 *et seq*.
[110]Hanisch (*see* n. 25) (ZIP 1989), p. 276; Hanisch, *EWiR*, s 812 BGB 2/89, 349 (350); contra Ackmann/Wenner (*see* n. 25) (IPRax 1990), p. 209 n. 12; Wenner (*see* n. 73) (HTS 1990), p. 435.
[111]Canaris (*see* n. 67), p. 651.
[112]See also BGH, 13 July 1983, BGHZ 88, 147 (156).

express assignment of Canadian assets to the German estate were not recognised in Canada. On institution of the bankruptcy proceeding, the German receiver had stated categorically that — on the basis of recent rulings of the *Bundesgerichtshof* — he considered the German creditors bound to surrender the proceeds from the bankruptcy proceeding in Canada to him, and that he would demand this of them. The objection raised by counsel on behalf of the debtor, which bitterly opposed institution of the proceeding, that such a demand would constitute breach of Canadian sovereignty because it led to a different financial distribution than the one proposed in the Canadian proceeding, was expressly denied by the judge at the Canadian Bankruptcy Court: it would in no way affect Canadian sovereignty if German bankruptcy law knew of claims by the receiver which aimed at establishing a counter-balance for non-recognition in Canada.[113] This view deserves unreserved support.

(v) It should of course not be ignored that the obligation to surrender assets will be difficult to explain to local creditors and may possibly prove to be unenforceable. This is at least true for the creditors listed under Article 22, paragraph 2, if these creditors do not file their claims at the German proceeding and the foreign law governing enforcement does not recognise the German bankruptcy proceeding. On the other hand there is no conceivable reason why the creditors listed here should not be subject to the obligation to surrender assets, at least when they file their claims at the German insolvency proceeding. As this possibility is at least open to all foreign creditors whose claims arise from legal relationships under private law, Article 22, paragraph 2 should only exclude the obligation to surrender assets for those groups of creditors listed in (ii) and (iii) above if they stay away from the German insolvency proceeding. With this restriction, the proposed exemption provision would appear justified. The same must apply in principle to claims by foreign creditors resulting from legal relationships under public law, insofar as they participate in proceedings. It is surely false to assume that particularly foreign tax claims are not entitled in principle to participate in proceedings in Germany. On the contrary, tax claims by the appropriate foreign authorities should be considered in German proceedings in all those cases in which the Federal Republic is bound by international enforcement and execution agreements to furnish legal assistance,[114] and such claims are to be treated without priority, as is expressly stated, for example, in the agreement with Finland.[115]

---

[113]Quebec Superior Court [In Bankruptcy], 26 September 1986, *Re Kauflen Estate* (1987), 64 CBR 97 at 98: "The bankruptcy in Germany did not take away, in and of itself, the right of the petitioner to file a bankruptcy petition. Although German bankruptcy law appears to deny to any creditor the right to pursue a recourse for recovery of its claim elsewhere than in Germany, the sanction for doing so is not a declaration of illegality of the foreign proceeding (which a German domestic court does not, in any event, have the power to do) but rather a right in favour of the German trustee to recover from the creditor in question, in Germany, whatever that creditor has recovered abroad, so that the proceeds of this recovery may be equitably distributed amongst all of the creditors.

Canadian law is not offended by the prospect of a concurrent bankruptcy in another jurisdiction. The fate of bankruptcy proceedings initiated in Canada must be determined in accordance with the laws of Canada and not in accordance with the laws of another country, even where there has been a bankruptcy of the same debtor in that other country."

[114]See the references at Tipke/Kruse, *Abgabenordnung* (13th ed., loose-leaf edition as of 1988), s 250 AO n. 11.

[115]See Final Protocol (No. 7) of the Convention between Germany and Finland as to "Rechtsschutz und Rechtshilfe in Steuersachen" of 25 September 1935 (RGBl. II 37), reprinted at Korn/Pebatin, *Doppelbesteuerung II* (loose-leaf edition as of 1989), sub Finland, p. 25.

If a foreign public authority then pursues its claim in a German insolvency proceeding by availing itself of German legal assistance, there is no apparent reason why this should not be linked to the obligation to surrender what it has successfully enforced on its own sovereign territory after the proceeding has been instituted in Germany. If it is not prepared to do so, it should not be given consideration in the course of German proceedings in cases in which the German dividend does not exceed the foreign proceeds.

(vi) To summarise, it may be concluded that the absence of an obligation to transfer proceeds from foreign insolvency proceedings proposed under Article 22, paragraph 2 of the draft is not justifiable for reasons of legal policy. It is also not justified on the part of the groups of creditors listed under Article 22, paragraph 2, in so far as they participate in filing their claims in German insolvency proceedings. The proposal made in the draft should therefore be carefully reconsidered.

(c) Additional proposals

It was indicated at the outset that prevailing bankruptcy law ill equips the receiver with legal powers in order to fulfil his assigned task under sections 1 (paragraph 1) and 117 (paragraph 1) KO; the future Insolvency Act should not perpetuate such shortcomings. Additional case rules and standards should be included in the future Act in advance of the proposed regulation governing restitution in bankruptcy, in order to provide the receiver with better legal grounds for seizing the assets of the debtor held abroad. These could then eradicate the basic fault contained in prevailing law. Three suggestions may be made:

(a) First, the future Act should prescribe a substantive claim on the part of the receiver against the debtor to surrender assets, extending to all of his assets at home and abroad subject to execution and enforcement, and providing the opportunity to demand damages in favour of the estate before a German court in the event of non-performance. This could provide the German receiver with grounds to proceed against the debtor in certain cases in which the latter succeeds in avoiding direct attachment of his foreign assets by the receiver due to non-recognition of German insolvency proceedings abroad.

(b) Secondly, the future insolvency law should grant the receiver legal authority to be able to proceed against the debtor abroad in the name of creditors and on behalf of the claims they have filed in German proceedings. This naturally only makes sense if it is linked with the legal authority to seize assets in favour of the estate in Germany, irrespective of whether the German receiver pursues individual enforcement of such claims abroad or participates in foreign insolvency proceedings. The proposal under prevailing bankruptcy law that the receiver should have the creditors issue him authority on a voluntary basis[116] is in practice not only difficult to implement, but also without any purpose if the obligation to surrender assets on participating in foreign insolvency proceedings is simultaneously negated, and the risk of the expenses incurred by pursuing legal action abroad is to remain with the estate.

(c) Finally, the future insolvency law should expressly grant the receiver the right of forbearance over those creditors who have filed claims at a German proceeding,

[116]Merz (see n. 14), p. 140.

to prevent them from appropriating the assets of the debtor held abroad with the self- same claims or otherwise interfering with the process of attachment by the German receiver. Breach of this obligation should also incur a claim for damages which can be pursued by the German receiver in Germany. Such claims may possibly even arise under prevailing law if, according to Canaris, sections 12 and 14 KO are also regarded as protective laws within the understanding of section 823, paragraph 2 of the German Civil Code ("BGB").[117] Moreover, reference can also be made to English law here for the purposes of comparison.[118]

7.3.3 Principle of restricted recognition

(a) Preliminary draft

The section of the draft referring to the domestic effects of foreign proceedings is preceded under Article 9, paragraph 1 by the *principle of recognition* valid for cases in which international jurisdiction may be seen to apply according to German criteria at the state of *situs* at which proceedings are instituted. The draft may be seen to advocate a principle of *restricted recognition*; this interpretation is based on the fact that the proposed system of regulation contained in the following provisions considerably narrows the actual scope of such recognition. In spite of the sections assuming recognition of the foreign law governing insolvency, the overriding impression remaining is that the principle of universality in the conflict of laws, such as was postulated in general form under Article 2 of the draft, is subsequently being undermined. An examination of the relevant provisions contained in the draft clearly shows that the scope of recognition is restricted from three sides. The definition of recognition thus differs considerably from prevailing law and is worth examining with particular care.

(i) First, recognition of the foreign law governing insolvency is precluded because German law allows for *individual enforcement* or *execution* in spite of foreign insolvency proceedings. Seen from this viewpoint, the scope of recognition would appear to be widened in contrast to prevailing law, since Article 17 of the draft provides for a reduction in the number of possibilities for individual enforcement in Germany listed under section 237, paragraph 1 KO. Admittedly, the draft does not go so far as to follow the proposal to exclude individual enforcement altogether in Germany, as has been suggested by commentators wishing to delete section 237, paragraph 1 KO completely.[119] And yet the draft does adopt the suggestions advanced by Thieme on prevailing law to limit individual enforcement measures in Germany to German creditors.[120] Consequently, individual enforcement measures are to be admissible in future on claims that are of a *public law nature*, are based on services in Germany or stem from *business relationships* with German subsidiaries of a foreign debtor; the same is to apply to claims which are *not entitled to participate* in foreign proceedings. The draft is thus striving to achieve the opposite effect from Article 22, paragraph 3. In dropping the requirement of title, which according to general opinion has come to

---

[117]Canaris (*see* n. 67), p. 650.
[118]See Dicey/Morris (*see* n. 57), pp. 1109 *et seq.*
[119]Ebenroth (*see* n. 14), p. 135. The draft bill recently published by the German Government now precludes any domestic individual enforcement during the continuance of a bankruptcy proceeding abroad.
[120]Thieme (*see* n. 14), p. 712.

be generally required as a curb on section 237, paragraph 1 KO,[121] the draft is following legal reality, since neither tax claims nor claims arising from current business
operations or employees' claims are generally awarded a title at the point of instituting proceedings. Limitation of the number of possibilities for individual enforcement
in Germany only makes sense if access to the courts of law is simultaneously upheld.
It is in keeping with the system of the draft, however, that it also provides for admissible individual enforcement measures in Germany to result in the final distribution
of assets among creditors, even if the foreign law governing insolvency stipulates an
obligation for them to be assigned to the estate. Under Article 17, paragraph 3, the
draft admittedly only excludes the possibility of appeal; however, what this means is
the prevention of any kind of restitution in favour of the foreign estate. The right to
be able to postpone temporarily an individual enforcement granted to the foreign
receiver, as stipulated under Article 17, paragraph 2, may be seen in conjunction with
a process of reorganisation under foreign law,[122] which makes immediate liquidation
of German assets seem inappropriate. It may thus be concluded from Article 17 that
the draft does indeed intend the scope of individual enforcement measures to be
narrower than in prevailing law.

(ii) In addition, the draft is also extremely cautious in only restricting the scope of
the claim of application of foreign insolvency law where this affects protection of
German third party debtors and continued existence of the insolvency claims of
German creditors. Thus, for example, Article 11 grants German third party debtors
special protection when making payments to the foreign debtor in ignorance of the
institution of foreign proceedings. Freedom from residual debt under foreign law,
which is apparently seen with an eye to the effects of Anglo-Saxon "discharge",[123] is
not recognisable under Article 16, paragraph 2 on the part of creditors who are unable
to participate in foreign proceedings or are unfairly obstructed or otherwise at a disadvantage there. These reservations come very close in essence to the restrictions of
public policy. A similar interpretation may be made of recognition of foreign insolvency compensation schemes; according to Article 15, paragraph 2, these schemes
are not recognisable for creditors unable to participate in foreign proceedings or restricted from co-operating in the compensation scheme for legal reasons, or if they
are unfairly obstructed or otherwise at a disadvantage in relationship to other creditors. In addition, the foreign insolvency compensation scheme is not to take effect in
Germany whenever a creditor has appealed against it and is worse off under the
scheme than he would be without it. The exemptive ruling whereby German legal
proceedings may only be postponed on request of the foreign receiver is of less importance in this context. Overall, it may be concluded that the regulations proposed
only very cautiously resist the scope of application of foreign insolvency law.

[121]OLG Dusseldorf, 17 August 1982, ZIP 1982, 1341 (1342) (in favour of EC); OLG Harlsruhe, 9 July
1987 NJW-RR 1987, 1407 with note Pilger, RIW 1988, 225 et seq; Ebenroth (see n. 14), p. 123; Hanisch
(see n. 8), p. 142; Grasmann (see n. 72) (HTS 1990), p. 157; Jayme, "Sanierung vom Großunternehmen
und internationales Honkursrecht", in Festschrift Riesenfeld (1983), pp. 117–128; Kuhn/Uhlenbruck
(-Lller) (see n. 11), ss 237, 238 KO n. 72; Leipold, (see n. 24), pp. 798 et seq; Luke (see n. 18), p. 13;
Pielorz (see n. 8), 91–94; Wenner (see n. 73) (HTS 1990), p. 432; see also BGH, 11 July 1985, BGHZ 95,
256 (267, 270); BGH, 11 January 1990, ZIP 1990, 246, 247 (obiter).
[122]eg US Bankruptcy Code 1978, Chapter 11.
[123]As to US law see eg 11 USC s 727; as to English law see Berry/Bailey (see n. 53), pp. 117 et seq.

(iii) By contrast, the extension of international jurisdiction to include the situs of a debtor's assets subjects the future scope of recognition to very serious restrictions, the consequences of which cannot be stressed too much. For with the institution of German insolvency proceedings limited geographically to the debtor's assets located within national boundaries, the scope of recognition pales into insignificance.

Examination of the whole series of regulations contained in the draft concerned with the execution of insolvency proceedings against a restricted range of items of property in Germany, in which international jurisdiction is based solely on the *situs* of any of the debtor's assets, leaves us with the impression that the main aim of the draft is to promote *a system of parallel insolvency proceedings*. Such a system would render the application and observance of foreign insolvency law in Germany under the principle of the conflict of laws largely obsolete.

Article 9, paragraph 2 rules that recognition of foreign insolvency proceedings does not preclude the institution of German insolvency proceedings against assets located in Germany. Article 13 deals in detail with the question of how to settle legal disputes in cases of parallel insolvency proceedings. Articles 26 to 34 concern themselves exclusively with the organisation of an insolvency proceeding restricted to assets located in Germany. Unlike section 238 KO, this legislative extravagance is given real foundation in Article 1, paragraph 2 of the draft: here, the courts of any country "in which the debtor has a subsidiary business or any other assets" is to have jurisdiction over instituting an insolvency proceeding "encompassing only those assets of the debtor located in the country in question". In effect, this means nothing less than the possibility of instituting territorially restricted insolvency proceedings in Germany irrespective of the general venue for a debtor or the centre of his self-employed economic activities, provided at least one item of the debtor's property is located in Germany. In this way, the draft would appear to pursue a concept of territorially restricted parallel insolvencies, frustrating all efforts to achieve universality in the conflict of laws. The "loophole in bankruptcy law" to which it is still possible to have recourse under prevailing law,[124] is restricted in respect of the debtor's assets located in Germany, with due consideration given to Article 26, paragraph 2, to the case in which the value of such assets is "out of all proportion" to the expenses of German insolvency proceedings. If Article 29, paragraph 2 is considered, which rules that in foreign bankruptcy proceedings grounds for insolvency in Germany are no longer required in order to institute proceedings, the mechanism that will prevent the majority of regulations discussed so far from ever assuming practical importance in the event of bankruptcy occurring abroad becomes apparent. The scope of recognition, which would appear to be widened in contrast to prevailing law under the revised Article 17, is completely absorbed by the insolvency proceedings held in Germany against restricted assets.

(b) Evaluation from the standpoint of legal policy

An evaluation of the regulation proposed in the draft from the standpoint of legal policy is extremely difficult. On the one hand, it shows that efforts have been taken to expand the scope of recognition by reducing the previous range of application of section 237, paragraph 1 KO, thus promoting the application and/or observance of foreign insolvency law. The same applies to the cautious resistance to foreign

[124]*See* **7.2.2 (b)**.

insolvency law in cases in which protection would appear necessary in Germany for reasons that cannot be dismissed lightly; the concern for protection of business interests justifies protecting third party debtors in Germany who have made payments to the debtor in ignorance of the institution of foreign insolvency proceedings; the discriminatory treatment of domestic creditors in a foreign proceeding justifies protecting continuance of the claim. It would thus seem impossible to oppose differentiation from the law governing foreign insolvency from the point of view of legal policy. It only remains to give careful examination to whether Article 17 of the draft can indeed fulfil what the legislator intends it to fulfil.

On the other hand, Article 1, paragraph 2 clearly contradicts the aim of expanding the scope of recognition. The concept of parallel, geographically restricted German bankruptcies on the basis of a pure site of *situs* jurisdiction requires careful analysis.

(i)   The proposed revision of Article 17 as replacement for section 237, paragraph 1 KO is a clear compromise, with the objective of permitting three groups of German creditors to pursue priority enforced attachment. First, the aim of this section is apparently to grant German tax creditors the possibility of execution and enforcement which they do not have if agreements on enforcement and execution proceedings have not been concluded with foreign countries abroad. Secondly, employees are to be granted easier attachment and to be spared the effort of pursuing their rights abroad for social reasons. Lastly, German partners in the German subsidiary of a foreign debtor are also to be given the opportunity to achieve priority satisfaction from the standpoint of protecting their business interests.

Without wishing to resume the far-reaching discussion on the reason and purpose behind section 237, paragraph 1 KO,[125] it must unreservedly be acknowledged that the groups of creditors specified are indeed in need of special protection in Germany. Nevertheless, it is doubtful whether the path of individual enforcement is suited to achieving this form of protection in the best manner possible. If we accept the Explanation of the preliminary draft that those creditors requiring protection are not in possession of an enforceable title at the stage at which proceedings are instituted, and that it is also the aim of the proposed ruling to grant them the possibility of temporary legal protection in the form of attachment of assets (Explanation [at p. 45]) to which they were previously not entitled,[126] then we can expect Article 17 to trigger off a race for priority seizure and attachment of assets. It is not difficult to forecast that this will generally tend to result in chance priority rankings, especially in view of the fact that the priority of attachment liens is determined according to the date on which the attachment order has been served on the the third party debtor. If separate proceedings are not subsequently instituted in Germany as a result of the restriction of reversal stipulated under section 94 EInsO or by avoidance on the part of the representative in insolvency (cf. Explanation [at p. 46]), priority rankings will be determined according to the general regulations governing enforcement, which would appear dubious in terms of their fortuitousness not only from the standpoint of legal policy. Even if the system of priority in individual enforcement is normally

[125]Recently, some authors, as opposed to those mentioned in n. 14, have commented in a more positive way as to s 237 KO; See Lllderitz (*see* n. 89), p. 97 and Flessner (*see* n. 23), p. 752 *et seq.*
[126]OLG Dusseldorf, 17 August 1982, ZIP 1982, 1341 (1342); Kilger (*see* n. 11), s 237 KO n. 7; Pielorz (*see* n. 8), pp. 94 *et seq*; Thieme (*see* n. 14).

considered to be justified, this does not apply to the flood of creditors caused by the economic collapse of the debtor, as prevailing law indicates.[127] Furthermore, it may be deduced from the new insolvency law that priority claims will soon be a thing of the past. This leads to an initial conclusion that it would be far more in keeping with German insolvency law for those creditors requiring protection listed under Article 17 of the draft to be treated equitably, along the lines of equal priority lienholders in the course of Swiss collocation proceedings.[128] Other possibilities offered by procedural law should also be considered from this aspect, in order to ensure the required protection in Germany.

(ii)   The crucial question raised in terms of legal policy in those cases in which neither the general place of venue for the insolvent debtor nor the centre of his economic activities are located in Germany, aims to provide justification for *linking international jurisdiction* in Germany solely to the *situs* of assets, such as it is proposed to become law under Article 1, paragraph 2 of the draft. Answers to this question may be sought in different ways. It is a known fact that in itself the concept of site of *situs* jurisdiction, as it is defined for general procedural law under section 23 ZPO, offers sufficient opportunity to develop widely differing views and theories.[129] But apart from such considerations, in the sector of international insolvency procedural law, the assumed consequences of such a jurisdiction are themselves grounds enough to deduce that it cannot in any way be deemed desirable. Three aspects are worthy of note here:

(a)   The principle of situs jurisdiction in insolvency procedural law makes it necessary to institute *parallel insolvencies* based on the principle of national isolation from the outside world, thus realising the principle of territoriality in the conflict of laws.

In the past, parallel insolvencies have been particularly recommended because they appeared well equipped to mitigating the damaging effects of the outdated principle of territoriality.[130] In theory, insolvency proceedings conducted in parallel and encompassing the widely disseminated assets of the debtor, in which all the respective creditors are allowed to participate, should lead to their all being satisfied to the same degree, as in unitary proceedings.[131] These proceedings represent the model for a perfect implementation of the principle of territoriality. In practice, however, precisely the opposite occurs: parallel insolvency proceedings regularly lead to a systematic preferential treatment of large creditors, and consequently to discrimination against small creditors. Particular interests overshadow provisions aimed at encompassing the assets of the debtor,

---

[127]See s 47, 48 VglO. Under bankruptcy law rules, enforcement measures may be subject to avoidance under general provisions, see Kuhn/Uhlenbruck (*see* n. 11), s 29 KO n. 16.

[128]See Art 110, paras 1, 114, 146, 219, 281 SchHG.

[129]See only Schack, *Vermdgensbelegenheit als Zustandigkeitsgrund* (ZZP 97 1984), pp. 46–68; Jochen Schroder, *Internationale Zustandigkeit* (1971), pp. 374 *et seq*; Schumann, *Aktuelle Fragen und Probleme des Vermögensge- richtsstandes (§ 23 ZPO)* (ZZP 93 1980), pp. 408–443 and a recent judgment limiting the application of s 23 ZPO in international cases, BGH, 2 July 1991, NJW 1991, 3092.

[130]Hanisch (*see* n. 18) (ZIP 1985), p. 1237; Hanisch, *"Parallelinsolvenzen und Hooperation im internationalen Insolvenzfall"*, in *Festschrift Bosch* (1976), pp. 381–392 (384 *et seq*).

[131]However, because security rights of creditors and avoidance by the receiver are treated differently in the various legal systems, this appears to be practically impossible.

his business undertaking and his liabilities as a whole; the uniform purpose behind overall settlement is systematically obstructed; global solutions for the business enterprise within the framework of reorganisation are prevented.

(b) Independent *parallel insolvencies* concentrating on assets in Germany weaken the extraterritorial claim to jurisdiction raised by the set of German regulations governing insolvency if the venue for the debtor or the centre of his economic activity is situated in Germany.

The Higher Regional Court in Dusseldorf (*Oberlandesgericht*) and the *Bundesgerichtshof* have correctly indicated in recent years that it is not possible to claim jurisdiction abroad under one's own law without being prepared to grant the same at home.[132] Whoever supports parallel insolvencies in Germany systematically combats the application of foreign law. Whenever a German receiver endeavours to institute an "ancillary proceeding" in the US according to section 304 of the US Bankruptcy Code of 1978, he will encounter opposition even from domestic creditors that section 238 KO is the best proof of not being able to advance claims of comity because German law conversely does not have to recognise the US receiver.[133] How much stronger will this defensive argument become in future if domestic debtors and creditors are allowed to demonstrate to a US Bankruptcy Court that the *situs* of an item of property belonging to a US debtor is sufficient in itself to justify international jurisdiction in Germany for the institution of insolvency proceedings which are not subordinated to the US proceeding. Where reciprocity is otherwise deemed necessary abroad in order to recognise the German receiver, the proposed provision contained under Article 1, paragraph 2 would be the best evidence for its lack of existence.

(c) *Situs* jurisdiction for parallel insolvencies in respect of restricted assets destroys the protection Article 17 of the draft seeks to confer upon groups of German creditors requiring it.

The simple *situs* jurisdiction provokes the *Herstatt syndrome*.[134] When in 1974 a number of large international banks sought to seize the US dollar currency account held by the former Herstatt Bank at a large bank in New York by way of attachment, the other creditors who were threatened with losing priority had no choice but to institute bankruptcy proceedings; as a result, 56 banks argued before two different courts — namely the Court of Enforcement and the Bankruptcy Court — about who was to receive the pot of more than 150 million which had been discovered more or less by chance. In the case of priority of domestic insolvency proceedings before individual enforcement measures, it is clearly apparent that the group of creditors protected under Article 17, paragraph 1 will always come off second best.

The arguments raised above to oppose the proposed expansion of international jurisdiction contained in Article 1, paragraph 2 can easily be further supported by citing the large number of difficulties these procedural variety will automatically engender.

---

[132]OLG Düsseldorf, 17 August 1982, ZIP 1982, 1341 (1342). BGH, 11 July 1985 BGHZ 95, 256 (264).

[133]However, this was the argument pleaded recently in a US s 304 proceeding by a German creditor against a domestic receiver.

[134]See Spennemann, *Insolvenzverfahren in Deutschland — Vermbgen in Amerika: Das Beispiel Herstatt* (1981), pp. 13–16.

Such major catchwords as duplication of filing procedures with the obligation to submit documents in the language of the court, observance of foreign rules of procedure, the need to obtain legal counsel repeatedly at home and abroad, and considerably higher overall costs for organisation of proceedings, should suffice in this context. Particularly serious, however, is the fact that the proposed statutory provision runs completely contrary to the trend observed abroad to move even closer to the principle of universality in the conflict of laws. Reference may here be made again to the "ancillary proceeding" contained in the U.S. Bankruptcy Code of 1978, to the Swiss solution outlined in the Private International Law Act of 1987 and to the position taken under English law which is extremely pro-recognition. Against this background, the route via expansion of international jurisdiction to parallel bankruptcies would hardly appear a progressive one.

In spite of the numerous reasons it is possible to cite against creating the possibility of insolvency proceedings with restricted assets in Germany, it cannot be denied that it does meet a practical need — even in the case of insolvency abroad — to have a proceeding available at home leading to the ordered settlement of those assets of the foreign bankrupt located within national boundaries. It is self-explanatory, of course, that such a proceeding must not be allowed to compete with the possibilities for enforcement that Article 17 seeks to regulate. On the contrary, it is more advantageous to combine protection of vulnerable domestic creditors with an interest in the ordered settlement of a debtor's assets located at home and to deal with them in a unified proceeding. This proceeding should not however be organised as a parallel full proceeding, but as an ancillary proceeding to the insolvency proceeding held abroad. It is in keeping with the principle of universality to accept this subordination of one proceeding over the other.

(c) Different solutions

Before the German legislative body decides to proclaim the submitted draft as prevailing law, alternative possibilities for a solution need to be considered. From the standpoint of comparative law, both the US and the Swiss solution offer possibilities. In addition, reference is drawn here to the fact that Committee J of the International Bar Association, which is concerned with creditors' rights, reorganisations and insolvencies, has developed a Model International Insolvency Co-operation Act (MIICA) containing principles based on US law defining how insolvencies transcending national boundaries can be conducted as uniformly as possible under direction of that proceeding which is to count as the full proceeding. In mid 1992, the Council of the Section of Business Law within the International Bar Association recommended discussing this Model Act as a proposal in those countries currently preparing a revision of their international insolvency law. The text and an abbreviated version of the Explanation are appended to this commentary (*see* **Appendix 1**) for the purposes of information and discussion.

7.4 Conclusions

The proposed legal revision of international insolvency law in Germany is formally being pursued by the legislative body separately from that of recodification of domestic insolvency law, even if it is to come into force together with the new Insolvency Act. This approach involves the inherent danger of affording regulations on the conflict of laws considerably less attention than they deserve. If it is also considered that the scope of future legal provisions on German international insolvency law will continue to be curtailed in international agreements, as for example in the Austro-German Agreement on Bankruptcy and Enforcement of 25 May 1979[135] or in the Treaty which is to come into force on the initiative of the Council of Europe, then this increases the fear that international insolvency law could be treated as a relatively insignificant part of the revisions to be made in German insolvency law.

On the other hand, the dogmatic argument on the principles of universality and territoriality, the turning away in legal decisions from what previously were clearly defined legal positions, and the apparent lack of any governing provisions indicate that the resulting sense of legal uncertainty can only be combatted by decisive action taken by the legislating bodies.

The preliminary draft that has been submitted goes a long way towards satisfying this need. It provides for legislation on a whole series of elements which the legislature has previously omitted to regulate and whose solution has frequently been in dispute. Basic positions that the preliminary draft adopts for this purpose deserve to be evaluated differently and circumspectly. The movement towards a *principle of universality in the conflict of laws* deserves unreserved support. However, further legislative organisation of this basic principle would appear necessary to provide legal clarity and to facilitate its application. An explanatory legal definition of the law governing assets, their administration and distribution in the course of insolvency should therefore be added. The principle of *restricted extraterritoriality* on which the preliminary draft is based unfortunately cuts back on the scope and implementation of German substantive insolvency law to a degree that is not justifiable in terms of legal policy. It would therefore seem appropriate to reinforce further the domestic statute governing bankruptcy whenever it is applied in the context of the conflict of laws. The principle of *restricted recognition* of the effects of foreign proceedings at home is neither necessary nor appropriate. The idea of promoting defence against foreign insolvency law by the institution of domestic proceedings runs completely contrary to the value set in terms of legal policy on the principle of universality, and does not constitute sufficient grounds for its introduction. Previous theoretical discussion has already shown that nothing is more suited to shaking the principle of universality in the conflict of laws to its foundations than a system of parallel insolvency proceedings; for it is precisely the institution of domestic insolvency proceedings once proceedings against the assets of the self-same debtor are already under way abroad which incorporates so perfectly the much criticised principle of territoriality.

On the basis of the above comments, the legislative bodies would be well advised to reconsider whether their intentions could not be achieved more clearly and cogently by including additional provisions. Similarly, further consideration needs to be given to the question of whether the apparent goal of parallel insolvency proceedings does not effectively prevent by force what it is essential to promote against the background the fundamental principle of universality in the conflict of laws.

[135]BGBl. 1985 II 410.

8

Cross-Border Insolvencies:
An Australian Perspective

Richard Fisher
Blake Dawson Waldron, Sydney, Australia

8.1 Introduction

"This (the existence of property of an insolvent in a number of jurisdictions) is an emerging and important area of insolvency law because of the growth in international trade and commerce, the use of national and international forms of business organisation, resort to overseas borrowing and, to a lesser extent, the apparent ease with which an insolvent debtor (or persons closely associated with an insolvent debtor — such as directors of an insolvent company) can transfer some forms of property from one jurisdiction to another."[1]

That necessarily anonymous observation by the Law Reform Commission highlights the increasing significance of cross-border recognition of insolvency administrations.

Within Australia the problems associated with cross-border insolvencies have been exacerbated, at least in relation to corporate insolvency. That stems from Australia being a federation of formerly independent States. The federation of those States was effected through the Australian Constitution[2] by which a number of specific powers were conferred upon the Australian Parliament with each of the States retaining the balance of their powers. Amongst the powers conferred upon the Australian Parliament were the powers to make laws with respect to both "bankruptcy and insolvency" (section 51 (xvii) of the Constitution), and "foreign corporations, and trading and financial corporations formed within the limits of the Commonwealth" (section 51(xx) of the Constitution).

Whilst the Australian Parliament has exercised the power to make laws in relation to bankruptcy for the purpose of enacting a law regulating the insolvency of natural persons — the Bankruptcy Act 1966 (C[th]) — corporate insolvency law has remained

---

[1] Australian Law Reform Commission, General Insolvency Inquiry Discussion Paper No. 32; August 1987, para 654.
[2] Commonwealth of Australia Constitution Act 1900 (being an enactment of the UK Parliament).

Current Issues in Cross-Border Insolvency and Reorganisations (E. B. Leonard, C. W. Besant, eds.; 1–85333–958–X; © International Bar Association; pub. Graham & Trotman/International Bar Association, 1994; printed in Great Britain), pp. 153-173.

within the domain of Australia's companies legislation. In 1990, the Australian Parliament enacted a law of general application to companies that provided for their formation or incorporation, conduct, liquidation and dissolution. The High Court of Australia, however, held that the power of that Parliament to make laws with respect to companies is not a plenary power and as a result some parts of the legislation were held to be invalid.[3] The political consequence of the decision in *New South Wales v The Commonwealth* was that, by an agreement between the Commonwealth and the various States, co-operative legislation has been enacted which provides for a uniform companies law throughout Australia; the Corporations Law, which will be referred to as the "Law". Moreover, under that agreement, the administration of the Law as well as its reform and amendment are now within the exclusive power of the Australian Parliament. That agreement and the co-operative legislation that followed it represent the latest stage in an evolutionary process for Australian corporate regulation, which has progressed over at least the last 30 years towards a completely uniform legislative environment for corporations operating within Australia. The process began with the enactment in the early 1960s by each of the States of companies legislation generally called the Uniform Companies Acts and was followed in 1981 by the Australian Parliament and the various State legislatures adopting uniform legislation which was referred to as the Companies Code. For the Code to be amended or reformed, there had to be agreement between the Commonwealth and the States and the regulation of corporate behaviour was undertaken by what was, in effect, a joint venture between them. As has been observed, the latest stage in this process has been the enactment of the Law and the effective consolidation of legislative and regulatory power in the Australian Parliament.

It has been within this legislative framework that the problems associated with cross-border corporate insolvencies, both within Australia as well as between Australia and other countries, have been addressed.

Notwithstanding the movement towards national corporate regulation in Australia, one option that appears not to have been considered, at least so far as concerns insolvent companies, was for the Australian Parliament to invoke its power to make laws with respect to bankruptcy and enact a Uniform Insolvency Act dealing with both companies and natural persons. In this respect, Australia has stood out against the observable trend in other English common law countries. Indeed, the terms of reference given to the Law Reform Commission for the General Insolvency Inquiry, at least in the Commission's view of them, specifically contemplated the continuation of what might be described as the "traditional" approach to insolvency law; ie for the Bankruptcy Act to regulate the insolvency of natural persons and for corporate insolvency to come under the purview of general company law.[4]

In the context of that background, consideration will be given to the recognition of Australian corporate insolvency administration — liquidations, schemes of arrangement and voluntary administrations — within Australia, and their efficacy beyond Australia as well as the extent to which Australian courts will both exercise control over foreign companies and recognise foreign insolvency administrations. Additionally, attention will be directed to the procedures available for procuring the

---

[3]*New South Wales v The Commonwealth* (1990) 169 CLR p. 482.
[4]Australian Law Reform Commission, Report on the General Insolvency Inquiry, ALRC 45, December 1988, paras 9 to 11 (incl.).

recognition within Australia of foreign bankruptcies of natural persons and the steps which can be taken by the trustee of a natural person's bankrupt estate who was appointed under Australian law to seek assistance in another jurisdiction.

8.2 Liquidation

8.2.1 Winding-up applications in an Australian State[5] of companies incorporated outside the State

The jurisdiction of the Court[6] to wind up a company on the ground of its insolvency is conferred by section 459A of the Law. That section, however, only applies to a "company" which is defined as meaning a company incorporated under the Law of the relevant State. However, by Part 9 of the Corporations Act of each State, each of the Federal Court of Australia and the Supreme Courts of the other Australian States are also invested with jurisdiction under the Law of the relevant State, including, pertinently, the jurisdiction to make winding-up orders in respect of companies incorporated in that State.

Moreover, section 583 of the Law extends the jurisdiction of the Court so as to enable it to order the winding-up of a foreign company which is either registered under the Law or which carries on business within the State. A foreign company is one which, for present purposes, is incorporated outside Australia.

8.2.2 Winding-up a foreign company

Where a company is registered as a foreign company under the Law (Part 4.1, Division 2), it is taken, in effect, to have submitted to the jurisdiction of the Court and is amenable to a winding-up order being made against it. However, where the foreign company has not been registered, a threshold question which will arise on an application to wind it up is whether it carried on business in the State.[7]

Section 21 of the Law provides as follows in relation to "carrying on business":

"(1) : [Place of business] A body corporate that has a place of business in Australia, or in a State or Territory, carries on business in Australia, or in that State or Territory, as the case may be.
(2) : [Shares and property] A reference to a body corporate carrying on business in Australia, or in a State or Territory, includes a reference to the body:
    (a) : establishing or using a share transfer office or share registration office in Australia, or in the State or Territory, as the case may be; or
    (b) : administering, managing, or otherwise dealing with, property situated in Australia, or in the State or Territory, as the case may ·be, as an agent, legal personal representative or trustee, whether by employees or agents or otherwise.
(3) : [Exceptions] Despite subsection (2), a body corporate does not carry on business in Australia, or in a State or Territory, merely because, in Australia, or in the State or Territory, as the case may be, the body:

[5]References to States include all of the States of Australia as well as the Northern Territory and the Capital Territory but do not include the external Territories. Separate legislative provision is made for the external Territories which will not be considered in this paper.
[6]References to the Court in this and the next section of the paper are references to the Supreme Courts of the States and the Federal Court of Australia.
[7]See 59 of the Law for a definition of "Part 5.7 body".

(a) : is or becomes a party to a proceeding or effects settlement of a proceeding or of a claim or dispute;

(b) : holds meetings of its directors or shareholders or carries on other activities concerning its internal affairs;

(c) : maintains a bank account;

(d) : effects a sale through an independent contractor;

(e) : solicits or procures an order that becomes a binding contract only if the order is accepted outside Australia, or the State or Territory, as the case may be;

(f) : creates evidence of a debt, or creates a charge on property;

(g) : secures or collects any of its debts or enforces its rights in regard to any securities relating to such debts;

(h) : conducts an isolated transaction that is completed within a period of 31 days, not being one of a number of similar transactions repeated from time to time; or

(j) : invests any of its funds or holds any property."

The meaning of the phrase "carrying on business" was considered by the High Court of Australia in *Luckins v Highway Motel (Carnarvon) Pty Limited*,[8] which suggested that determining whether or not a company carried on business within a jurisdiction was substantially a question of fact. Thus, Gibbs J. (with whom Mason J. agreed) observed (at p. 178) (in holding that the relevant company carried on business) that:

"In particular, a company is not to be regarded as carrying on business within the State simply because it conducts an isolated transaction there. Subject to the limits indicated by these provisions, the question whether a company is carrying on business within the State is simply one of fact and must be decided having regard to all the circumstances of the case. In the present case Trailways would not have conducted business within Western Australia simply because travel agents within that State received requests for bookings and transmitted them to Victoria for confirmation. It is unnecessary to confirm whether the Company would have carried on business within Western Australia if the only relevant fact had been that its tours had proceeded through that State without receiving or depositing passengers and if its employees or agents had no dealings with persons within the State. That, however, was not the case. It can be inferred from the evidence that the company agreed to provide tourists, whom it conveyed through Western Australia on its buses with food and either accommodation or camping facilities, and that to fulfil its obligations it bought food, and hired accommodation or camping sites, from persons within Western Australia. It was submitted on behalf of the appellant that a motel proprietor, for example, who supplied accommodation to one of the tourists would have been carrying on his own business and not the business of Trailways, but the proper inference to be drawn is that such a motel proprietor would have been doing business with Trailways and not directly with the tourist. The evidence thus supports the conclusion that for the purposes of its business Trailways despatched bus loads of passengers through Western Australia and in the course of so doing entered into commercial transactions with various people in various parts of the State and that it did so not merely on isolated occasions but from time to time during 1973 and the early part of 1974."

Similarly, Jacobs J. (at p. 189) held:

"A disputed question of ultimate fact or of mixed fact and law is whether the company was carrying on business in Western Australia either at the time of creation of the charge or at any particular time thereafter up until the day when the bus was taken in execution. There was in my view evidence sufficient to establish that throughout this period the

8(1975) 133 CLR 164.

company was carrying on business in Western Australia. I agree with the conclusion of the Judge at first instance and of the Supreme Court of Western Australia that repeated running through Western Australia with coach tours (involving the purchase of food and accommodation for passengers in Western Australia) from time to time through 1973 and early 1974 was a carrying on of business in Western Australia over that time."

More recently in *Re Norfolk Island Shipping Line Pty Limited*[9] Young J. observed (at p. 991):

"The question (of whether the relevant company was carrying on business) is one of fact and may need to be decided on the facts as available at the final hearing. It would seem to me, however, on the facts presently before me that the company was, by its agent, carrying on more than isolated transactions in New South Wales and in all the circumstances was pursuing activities with a view to pecuniary gain in New South Wales and hence would be carrying on business in New South Wales, see *Luckins v Highway Motel (Carnarvon) Pty Ltd* (1975) 133 CLR 164 at p. 178.

In any particular case, therefore, the question of whether a company carries on business in a particular jurisdiction will be determined by reference to an analysis of the transactions which make up that business and an enquiry as to whether some or all of such transactions were effected in the ordinary course by the company in that jurisdiction."[10]

In his judgment in the *Norfolk Island Shipping* case, Young J went on to observe (at p. 991):

"Having thus concluded at least for assuring myself that the company comes within section 469 of the Code [section 582 of the Law], I must now proceed to see whether it is appropriate that the company be wound up.

There are a series of English cases commencing with *Re Compania Merabello San Nicholas SA* (1973) Ch 75 and at least for the moment concluding with *International Westminster Bank plc v Okeanos Maritime Corp* (1987) BCLC 450 (reported *sub nomine Re a Company* (1987) 3 WLR 339) which considers the factors which need to be present for an English court to wind up a company under the corresponding section of the 1948 Companies Act namely section 399. However, these cases are not complete guides because the categories of companies which may be wound up under the English section 598 do not coincide with those referred to in section 469 of our Code. Accordingly, some of the factors which in the English cases do not go to jurisdiction but go to discretion, in Australia are matters of jurisdiction. However, making allowances for this, the case is established that there must be a proper commercial connection with the jurisdiction, normally that the company has some assets within the jurisdiction and that there are people in the jurisdiction concerned with the proper distribution of the assets and that there is some reasonable possibility of benefit accruing to creditors from making a winding-up order.

There are few Australian cases in which the problems in this area of the law have been considered. In *Re Kailis Groote Eylandt Fisheries (No. 3)* (1977–1978) CLC 40-363 at pp. 29, 591; (1977) 2 ACLR 574 at p. 579, Bray CJ held that one could only wind up a foreign company if there were assets within the jurisdiction. In *Re Buildmat (Australia) Pty Limited* (1981) CLC 40-714; (1981) 5 ACLR 689, even though there were only negligible assets in the jurisdiction in a case where the company was clearly insolvent and almost all its creditors were in New South Wales Needham J. made a winding-up order.

---

[9](1988) 6 ACLC 990.
[10]See also *Saccharin Corporation Limited v Chemische Fabik von Heyden A. G.* [1911] 2 KB 516, CA.

In the present case it is clear that there are no substantial assets of the company in New South Wales, the main asset being the ship in Auckland Harbour. As appears from the judgment of Bray CJ referred to above, it is a time when the proceedings are instituted that is usually vital in this connection. The evidence as to whether there are 'negligible' assets in New South Wales is equivocal. The law as to whether assets negligible or not are absolutely required as a basis for jurisdiction is not yet certain. It may be that a judge in this court could say that so long as there is some commercial advantage in making a winding up order in New South Wales an order may be made. On the other hand, no case has gone further than the *Buildmat* case requiring 'negligible assets' in the jurisdiction."

With respect to his Honour, the cases to which he refers were decided in a quite different statutory environment to that in which he found himself and, indeed, as he acknowledged. The English authorities and Australian decisions are relevant where the jurisdiction conferred upon the Court to wind up foreign companies is expressed without limitation as, for example, was the case under the Uniform Companies Act, eg the Companies Act 1961 in New South Wales, and the English legislation to which his Honour referred. In that circumstance, the Courts have held (and with this view there can be no legitimate quarrel) that for an applicant to be able to invoke their jurisdiction it is necessary to establish some nexus between the company and the "territory" in which the Court exercises that jurisdiction.

That, however, was not the circumstance which had to be considered by Young J. Rather, it is submitted that the legislature, by the Law, has established the only test that is necessary and sufficient to found a jurisdictional nexus; namely, whether, in the case of an unregistered foreign company, it carried on business within the State. Once that connection is established, the Court may exercise the same powers and is subject to the same constraints as though it were considering an application to wind up a company incorporated or taken to be incorporated under the Law.

In that regard, section 582(1) of the Law provides:

"This Part [ie, the Part of the Law dealing with, inter alia, the winding up of foreign companies] has effect in addition to, and not in derogation of sections 342 and 350 and any provisions contained in this Law or any other law with respect to the winding up of bodies, and the liquidator or Court may exercise any powers or do any act in the case of [foreign companies] that might be exercised or done by him, her or it in the winding-up of companies."

Further, section 582(3) of the Law relevantly provides:

"[A foreign company] may be wound up under this Part notwithstanding that it has been wound up or has been dissolved or has otherwise ceased to exist as a body corporate under or by virtue of the laws of the place under which it was incorporated."

Moreover, one of the "constraints" which is imposed upon the Court on the hearing of a winding-up application in respect of a company incorporated within the State is to be found in section 467(2) of the Law which states: "The Court shall not refuse to make a winding-up merely because ... the company has no property."

Accordingly, it is argued that Young J. misdirected himself when he held that it was necessary to establish more than that a foreign company carried on business within the jurisdiction for the Court properly to exercise the power to order the winding-up of such a company. In particular, it is not appropriate for the Court to require evidence that there are assets within the jurisdiction as a prerequisite to the exercise of its power.

8.2.3 Co-operation between Australian and foreign courts in insolvent administrations

Upon the commencement of the Law, there was introduced into Australian company law a provision that facilitates the recognition of the insolvency administrations of foreign companies. The relevant part of that provision in section 581, reads:

> "(2) : In all [matters relating to the insolvency administration of a foreign company], the Court:
>
>   (a) : shall act in aid of, and be auxiliary to, the courts ... of prescribed countries, that have jurisdiction in [such] matters; and
>
>   (b) : may act in aid of, and be auxiliary to, the courts of other countries that have jurisdiction in [such] matters.
>
> (3) : Where a letter of request from a court ... of a country other than Australia, requesting aid in [such a] matter is filed in the Court, the Court may exercise such powers with respect to the matter as it could exercise if the matter had arisen within its own jurisdiction.
>
> (4) : The Court may request a court ... of a country other than Australia, that has jurisdiction in [such] matters to act in aid of, and be auxiliary to, it in [such a] matter."

The prescribed countries for the purposes of that provision are:

- Jersey;
- Canada;
- Papua New Guinea;
- Malaysia;
- New Zealand;
- Singapore;
- Switzerland;
- the UK; *and*
- the USA.

That provision, being of recent origin, has only been the subject of one reported decision — *Re Dallhold Estates (UK) Pty Ltd*.[11] However, it substantially corresponds with section 29 of the Bankruptcy Act, the operation of which is considered below.

In the *Dallhold* case, the company was incorporated in Australia and was in provisional liquidation in both Australia and England. Its only substantial asset was leasehold property in England. The Court was satisfied that, if the value of that asset was to be maintained, the company should not be wound up in England but rather should be the subject of an administration order in that country. In that circumstance it ordered that a letter of request issue to the English High Court seeking that such an order be made should that court see fit to do so. The terms of that letter of request are set out in Annex 1 as neither the Corporations Regulations nor the Rules of Court specify a form of general application.

---

[11](1992) 10 ACLC 1374.

8.2.4   *Recognition beyond a State of the liquidation of a company incorporated within a State*

(a) Recognition of "Australian liquidations" within Australia

The introduction of the Code and the co-operative scheme for the regulation of companies and related legislation resulted in a less cumbersome procedure for the liquidation of companies incorporated within Australia. Prior to the enactment of that legislation, liquidators were entitled to exercise the powers with which they were invested in States and Territories other than the jurisdiction in which they were appointed under section 352(2)(b) of the Uniform Companies Acts. However, a winding-up order in one State did not operate in another State so as to invoke, for example, the statutory injunction contained in section 230(3) of the Uniform Companies Acts which restrained the commencement or continuation of proceedings against the company or its property.

It is arguable that section 352(2)(b) of the Uniform Companies Acts merely codified the position at general law, in that it merely acknowledged the extent to which courts in common law countries would recognise a liquidator and his or her standing in any event.

In this regard, Professor Michael Pryles[12] has observed:

"Dicey & Morris state in Rule 143 that the authority of a liquidator appointed under the law of the place of incorporation is recognised in England. As a matter of principle this must surely be correct. It is clear that the capacity of a corporation, the powers and functions of its organs and officers and other matters relating to its constitution and internal affairs, are governed by the law of domicile (*Carl Zeiss Stiftung v Reyner & Keeler Ltd (No. 2)* [1967] AC 853). As the law of domicile determines various matters relating to a corporation, including the authority of its organs and officers, it must follow that a liquidator appointed by the law of the place of incorporation who is authorised to act on behalf of the company will similarly be authorised to act in other States. Consequently a liquidator who is authorised to institute actions on behalf of the foreign corporation can institute actions in the forum, suing in the company's name. He becomes the agent or organ of the company to the extent that he is so authorised under the law of the place of incorporation."

The capacity on the part of a liquidator to exercise powers in a jurisdiction must be distinguished, however, from the importation into that jurisdiction of the legislative regime that governs the liquidation of companies in the forum in which the liquidator was appointed. Mention has already been made of the consideration that, prior to the commencement of the Code and, thereafter, the Law, section 230(3) of the Uniform Companies Acts did not operate to restrain proceedings in a State in which a winding-up order had not been made against the company.

That there is a distinction between the extraterritorial exercise by a liquidator of powers and the operation of the laws governing the liquidation is well illustrated by the decision in *Primary Producers Bank of Australia Limited v Hughes*.[13] In that case, a company was incorporated in Queensland and registered as a foreign company in New South Wales. A creditor of the company instituted an action in the Supreme

---

[12]Professor Michael Pryles, "International and Interstate Aspects of Insolvency", (1987), Conference on Insolvency Law, Monash University, p. 11.
[13](1931) 32 SR (NSW) 14.

Court of New South Wales to recover a debt owing by the company to him and the company thereupon sought an injunction to restrain the plaintiff from proceeding with his action at law. The ground upon which the injunction was sought was that the company had gone into voluntary liquidation in Queensland and that liquidators had been appointed. Under the law of Queensland, it was provided that in such circumstances the property of the company was to be applied in satisfaction of the discharge of the company's liabilities to all its creditors *pari passu*.

Harvey CJ in Eq. held that the relevant provisions of the Queensland companies legislation did not apply in New South Wales and observed (at pp. 19 *et seq*):

"In my opinion it is stating the rights of the liquidator in the country of domicile too high to say that he has any title to the assets outside the jurisdiction. The Companies Act of this State is in my opinion a code for the determining the rights of the companies and their creditors in the event of liquidation, and it provides that the only form of liquidation of an unregistered company which can be recognised by this Court is compulsory liquidation. In this State the Primary Producers Bank is an unregistered company within the meaning of the Companies Act. Section 88 of the Companies Act of 1899 provides that no unregistered company shall be wound up voluntarily or subject to the supervision of the court. That is tantamount, as it appears to me, to a statutory direction that, so far as the jurisdiction of this Court is concerned, the Primary Producers Bank is not to be regarded as in liquidation, and it appears to me to follow that unless the Primary Producers Bank is in liquidation this Court has no jurisdiction to interfere with the rights of a creditor to sue the company and to carry his judgment to execution against the company.

The same conclusion may be arrived at in another way; it is not because of any special provision in the constitution of this company that when it passes a resolution to go into voluntary liquidation the assets of the company are impressed with a trust for equal division among all its creditors. That result follows from the legislation of the State of Queensland, which has enacted that if any company registered under its Companies Act does pass such a resolution that result shall follow. The trust thus imposed by the Queensland legislature does not in my opinion extend to any property except such as is in the jurisdiction of the Queensland Court. In cases where foreign creditors are for the time being subject to the jurisdiction of the Queensland Court, the Queensland Court may possibly by its jurisdiction in personam prevent such creditors from obtaining preference over other creditors out of foreign assets after the company is in liquidation. In my opinion the Queensland Court would have no jurisdiction itself to stop the present defendant from pursuing his action at law in this jurisdiction, because he is not subject to the jurisdiction of the Queensland Court."

It is to be noted that in that case it was not suggested that the liquidator did not have standing to bring proceedings in the name of the company. Moreover, in *Russian and English Bank v Baring Brothers & Co Limited*,[14] it has been specifically held by the House of Lords that a liquidator did enjoy such standing.

Whilst Sir John Harvey's remarks in the *Primary Producers Bank* case might be thought to suggest that a different result would follow if the company had been would up compulsorily, it was held in *Re Suidair International Airways Ltd*[15] that the liquidation of a company by the court in its place of domicile was not sufficient to deny a creditor the right to levy execution against the assets of the company located in another jurisdiction.

[14][1936] AC 405.
[15][1951] 1 Ch 165.

The Code contained (in section 465) what could be described as a modified scheme for the reciprocal enforcement of winding-up orders within Australia. That scheme has been continued in the Law by section 588A which provides, in effect, that an order for or in connection with the winding-up of a company in one State has effect and may be enforced in all respects in any other State as though it were an order of a court of that other State.

The relevant provision of the Code, section 465, only operated, and section 588A of the Law only operates, however, with respect to liquidations ordered by a court. Notwithstanding the provisions of section 468 of the Code and section 588B of the Law (which permit a liquidator appointed to a company in one State to perform or exercise any function or power exercisable in that State in any other State), it may be that that is not a sufficient provision to protect the position of a company which is in voluntary liquidation. Certainly that section of the Law would not be sufficient to enable a liquidator in a creditors' voluntary liquidation to invoke the statutory injunction (being the restraint on the commencement or further prosecution of civil claims against the company or its property) and other relief provided by section 500 of the Law in a State other than the State in which the company was incorporated.

(b) Recognition of "Australian liquidations" beyond Australia
Circumstances may arise, therefore, where the liquidator of an Australian company has to consider the commencement of winding-up proceedings of that company in another country or, in the case of a creditors' voluntary liquidation, in a State other than the State in which the company was incorporated. It is not appropriate here to consider legislative provisions in other jurisdictions which correspond to section 581 of the Law, although the availability of such provisions may obviate the need to consider a winding-up or like application in another country. However, there are various general law principles which have been developed in Australia and other English common law countries to which pertinent attention may be given.

Where the company is registered as a foreign company in a common law country, it will have submitted itself to the jurisdiction of the courts in that country and, in particular, will be amenable to having a winding-up order made against it. In the event that the company has not been so registered, however, it may nonetheless have assets in the jurisdiction, control of which is most conveniently assumed by having the company ordered to be wound up.

As has been noted, the Law also provides for the winding-up of foreign companies, whether registered in Australia or not, which carry on business. Similar provisions are to be found in the companies legislation of other common law countries including New Zealand,[16] Papua New Guinea,[17] Singapore,[18] Malaysia[19] and Hong Kong.[20] The UK Companies Act merely provides generally for the liquidation of unregistered foreign companies.[21] Notwithstanding that, it would be necessary to establish some nexus between the company and the jurisdiction in order to invoke the relevant court's power

---

[16]Companies Act (NZ), s 388.
[17]Companies Act (PNG), s 326.
[18]Companies Act (Singapore), s 351.
[19]Companies Act (Malaysia), s 315.
[20]Companies Ordinance (Hong Kong), s 327.
[21]Companies Act (UK), s 666.

to make a winding-up order (see *Russian and English Bank v Baring Brothers & Co Ltd*[22]) although it was held in *Banque des Marchandes de Mosco Kindersley*[23] that it was not necessary for the company to have a place of business in the jurisdiction but it was sufficient if there were assets of the company and persons claiming as creditors within the jurisdiction as being indicia of a business in some sense being carried on by the company. Moreover, in *Re Eloc Electro-Optieck and Communicatie B.V.,*[24] it was decided that even where no assets are to be found in the jurisdiction but that an order for the winding-up of the company was a necessary prerequisite to propounding a claim on the UK Employee Protection Fund that that was a sufficient ground to justify the court exercising its discretion to make a winding-up order.[25]

For the purposes of the legislation in common law countries, other than the UK, it may be necessary to establish whether the company was carrying on business if that legislation is to be successfully invoked to obtain a winding-up order against the company. The principal Australian decision as to the meaning of that phrase, *Luckins v Highway Motel (Carnarvon) Pty Limited,*[26] was considered above.

Whilst there would be a concern on the part of the liquidator to avoid creating a circumstance where there was a multiplicity of administrations, those administrations in common law countries other than the country of domicile would be regarded as being ancillary to the liquidation in the country of domicile. Thus Vaughan Williams J. observed in *Re English, Scottish, and Australian Chartered Bank Limited*[27]:

> "...in construing the statute, one must bear in mind the principle upon which liquidations are conducted, in different countries and in different courts, of one concern. One knows where there is a liquidation of one concern the general principle is — ascertain what is the domicil of the company in liquidation; let the court of the country of domicil act as a principal court to govern the liquidation; and let the other courts act as ancillary, as far as they can, to the principal liquidation. But although that is so, it has always been held that the desire to assist in the main liquidation — the desire to act as ancillary to the court where the main liquidation is going on — will not ever make the court give up the forensic rules which govern the conduct of its own liquidation."

This principle receives legislative expression in section 350 of the Law.

That is not to say that the substantive as distinct from the procedural law of a country which is foreign to the domicile in which the company is incorporated has no application. In that regard Wynn-Parry J. in *Re Suidair International Airways Limited*[28] held at p. 173 that:

> "It appears to me that the simple principle is that this court sits to administer the assets of the South African company which are within its jurisdiction, and for that purpose administers, and administers only, the relevant English law; that is, primarily, the law as stated in the Companies Act 1948, looked at in the light, where necessary, of the authorities."

[22][1936] AC 405.
[23][1951] Ch 112.
[24][1981] 2 AU ER 1111.
[25]For a useful review of the English decisions reference should be made to the decision of Young J. in *Re Norfolk Island Shipping Line Pty Limited* (1988) 6 ACLC 990.
[26](1975) 133 CLR 164.
[27][1893] Ch 385 at p. 391.
[28]*See* n. 15.

The ramifications of that decision are well illustrated by the decision in *Re Standard Insurance Company*,[29] [1968] Qd. R 118 the effect of which was summarised by Professor Pryles[30] as follows:

"There a New Zealand company carried on business in Australia. After a winding-up order was made in New Zealand, similar orders were made in each of the Australian states, including Queensland. The New Zealand liquidator had discussions with the Australian liquidators with a view to co-ordinating the winding-up of the company and orders were made in Queensland that the winding-up there should be ancillary to that taking place in New Zealand. The Queensland court ordered the Queensland liquidator to get in the assets of the company in Queensland and to settle a list of creditors whose debts were incurred in Queensland. He was then to adjudicate upon the proofs of debt in accordance with the law of Queensland and remit the balance of Queensland assets to the liquidator in New Zealand. Similar orders were made in each of the other Australian states and the Supreme Court of New Zealand made an order in conformity with the agreed scheme of winding-up.

The company owned real and personal property in Queensland. The proceeds of the real estate amounted to some $90,000 and the proceeds of the personal estate amounted to some $93,000. The debts contracted in Queensland totalled approximately $119,000. By section 339 of the Companies Act of Queensland, it was provided that in the event of the winding-up of a company registered under the Act, all land of the company within Queensland should be applied in the first instance in payment and discharge of the debts of the company contracted within Queensland in priority to any other debts of the company. It was clear, therefore, that the Queensland creditors were to receive the $90,000 representing the proceeds of the sale of the Queensland land. The question for the court was whether the remaining $29,000 of debts owing to the Queensland creditors was to be paid out of the proceeds of the personal property or whether such proceeds were to be paid to the liquidator in New Zealand. Were the latter course to be adopted, it was clear that the Queensland creditors would not be paid in full because the assets of the company were insufficient to pay all the creditors.

Lucas J. observed that when a winding-up was proceeding in different jurisdictions, the principle to be applied was that, subject to priority secured by local law, all creditors of the company were as far as possible to be treated equally wherever they were and wherever their debts were contracted. Thus his Honour concluded that the Queensland court should be careful not to give the Queensland creditors any advantage additional to that given to them by Queensland law. That law only gave the Queensland creditors priority with regard to the proceeds of the sale of the land. It followed that they were not entitled to priority in the proceeds of the personal property in Queensland. The court therefore ordered that the Queensland liquidator transmit to the New Zealand liquidator the balance of the funds of the company. To preserve the principle of equality, this was done on the condition that the Queensland creditors should receive no more than they had received in the Queensland proceedings until the other creditors had been paid to the same proportion."

It might be concluded, therefore, that where there is an ancillary liquidation the interests of creditors who enjoy some special advantage by reference, for example, to the rules governing priorities, those interests will be protected. However, beyond that, courts having supervision of an ancillary administration will seek to procure the result that all creditors proving in the liquidation will be treated equally.

[29][1968] Qd. R 118.
[30]Pryles (*see* n. 12) pp. 8 *et seq.*

8.3 Schemes of arrangement and voluntary administrations

8.3.1 Schemes of arrangement

Under section 411 of the Law, a company may propound a compromise or arrangement between itself and its members of its creditors. With regard to creditors' schemes of arrangement, these have typically, but not invariably (see, eg, *Re Asia Oils & Minerals Ltd*[31]) been employed to restructure the affairs of an insolvent company.

Prior to the enactment of the Code, a scheme of arrangement only had effect within the State in which the Court making the order approving the scheme exercised jurisdiction.[32] Accordingly, it was necessary for a company conducting business in more than one State and with creditors in each State to propound schemes under the companies legislation for each of them.[33]

However, the Code provided (in section 315(20)) and the Law now provides (in section 415A) for a scheme of arrangement approved by the Court in the State to have force and effect in all other States and binds creditors in those States as though it had been approved by the Court in those States.

Where a creditor has a claim against the company under a contract the proper law of which is the law of a jurisdiction outside Australia, a scheme of arrangement approved by the Court does not bind that creditor.[34] This has implications for so-called multi-national companies which have assets and creditors in a number of countries. It will be a question in the case of each such company as to where its assets are located and the circumstances in which judgments against the company can be enforced in the relevant jurisdiction.[35]

Moreover, the proponent of a scheme will need to give consideration in such a circumstance as to whether application needs to be made under corresponding provisions in the laws of those other jurisdictions. The general law principles considered in relation to liquidations are pertinent to that enquiry as is the possibility that reciprocity provisions akin to section 581 of the Law may be available in those jurisdictions.

8.3.2 Voluntary administrations

By the Corporate Law Reform Act 1992, the Law was amended to introduce a new regime for insolvent companies; "voluntary administration"; Part 5.3A of the Law. That amendment to the Law was a response to one of the recommendations of the Law Reform Commission which:

> "... proposed the introduction of a new voluntary procedure for insolvent companies which integrated the procedures for the voluntary winding-up of a company and for a

---

[31](1986) 5 NSWLR 42.

[32]See *New Zealand Loan & Mercantile Agency Co v Morrison* [1898] AC 349; *Re Nelson, ex parte Dave & Dolphin* [1918] 1 KB 459.

[33]See *Re Kailis Groote Eylandt Fisheries Pty Ltd* [1977] VR 511; (1977–78) CLC 40–357; 23 ACLR 510 (Victoria); *Re Kailis Groote Eylandt Fisheries Pty Ltd* (1977) 17 SASR 35; (1977–78) CLC 40–363; 2 ACLR 574 (South Australia); *Re Kailis Groote Eylandt Fisheries Pty Ltd (No. 2)* (1977–78) CLC 40–364; 2 ACLR 288 (South Australia); *DMJ Bennett, "Multi-State Schemes of Arrangement"* (1978) 52 ALJ 320.

[34]See *New Zealand Loan & Mecantile Agency Co v Morrison* (*see* n. 32); *Re Nelson, ex parte Dave & Dolphin* (*see* n. 32); and *DMJ Bennett, "Multi-State Schemes of Arrangement"* (*see* n. 33).

[35]See *Re K. G. Renwick Holdings Pty Ltd* (1979–81) CLC 40–705; 5 ACLR 461.

scheme of arrangement. The procedure proposed was designed with the aim that it would be:

- capable of swift implementation,
- as uncomplicated and inexpensive as possible, and
- flexible, providing alternative forms of dealing with the financial affairs of the company."[36]

Without exploring that regime in detail it provides, in essence, for the appointment of a voluntary administrator to an insolvent or near insolvent company (section 435A of the Law) by any of the company (section 436A), a secured creditor of the company which holds a charge over the whole or substantially the whole of the company's property (section 436C) or a liquidator of the company (section 436B). During the administration there is a moratorium on the prosecution of all claims against the company or its property (section 440D) other than claims by the company's secured creditors or the owners or lessors of property which is in the company's possession where enforcement proceedings in relation to their claims have been commenced prior to the administrator's appointment (sections 441B and 441F) in the case of a secured creditor with a charge over the whole or substantially the whole of the company's property, enforcement proceedings are commenced within the ten business days after the administrator's appointment (section 441A). The administrator is required to report to the company's creditors on the company's financial condition and recommend to creditors whether it would be in their interests:

(a) for the company to be wound up;
(b) for the administration to end; *or*
(c) for the company to execute a deed of company arrangement and, if so, its terms (section 439A).

A deed of company arrangement, in essence, will provide for the terms upon which the company will compromise the claims of its existing creditors as well as the basis upon which it will continue to trade (section 444A). However, it will not bind either secured creditors or the owners and lessors of property in the possession of the company except to the extent to which they expressly agree to be bound (section 444D).

As with a scheme of arrangement, provision is made by the Law for both an administration and a deed of company arrangement to be effective in all States (section 588AA) and for any order made by the Court in connection with a voluntary administration or a deed of company arrangement to have effect and be enforceable throughout Australia (section 588AB). However, also as with schemes of arrangement, consideration will need to be given as to what procedures may be available to protect a company's assets and business in jurisdictions other than Australia.

8.4 Bankruptcy

8.4.1 Recognition of "local" bankruptcies within Australia

The Bankruptcy Act has application throughout Australia with the result that, unlike the administration in insolvency of a company, a sequestration order (being the order

---
[36]ALRC 45, p. 29.

made by which a natural person's property is brought under the control of an insolvency administrator), is recognised throughout the Commonwealth other than in its external territories. The exclusion of those territories from the operation of the legislation has produced some curiosities as French J. remarked in *Re Clunies-Ross, ex parte Totterdell*[37] where his Honour observed (at p. 487):

> "This case discloses that the affairs of the Cocos (Keeling) Islands Territory are regulated by a system of law which is Byzantine in its complexity. It would be reasonable to expect that persons living in Australia or its territories live under a reasonably intelligible set of laws and legal framework. It is not going too far to say that the ramshackle collection of leftover colonial ordinances and territorial laws by which the Cocos (Keeling) Islands Territory is governed falls well short of that minimum requirement."

That conclusion, if no more, supports the recommendation of the Law Reform Commission that the Act apply throughout Australia's external territories.[38]

8.4.2 *Recognition of "foreign" bankruptcies within Australia*

Section 29 of the Bankruptcy Act relevantly provides:

> "(2) : In all matters of bankruptcy the Court —
> a) : shall act in aid of and be auxiliary to the courts of the external Territories, and of prescribed countries, that have jurisdiction in bankruptcy; and
> b) : may act in aid of and be auxiliary to the courts of other countries that have jurisdiction in bankruptcy.
> c) : Where a letter of request from a court of an external Territory, or of a country other than Australia, requesting aid in a matter of bankruptcy is filed in the Court, the Court may exercise such powers with respect to the matter as it could exercise if the matter had arisen within its own jurisdiction."

It is plain from that provision that where a letter of request issues to an Australian court[39] from the court of a prescribed country (being the United Kingdom, Canada, New Zealand, Jersey, Malaysia, Papua New Guinea, Singapore, Switzerland and the US as well as their colonies, overseas territories and protectorates), the Court has no discretion as to whether to grant aid even where to do so may facilitate the collection of a revenue debt in the country of the court which made the request.[40] In other cases, however, the Court does have a discretion although the matters which might affect its exercise are not addressed in the section.[41] In *Ayres v Evans*[42] McGregor J. (Fox and Northrop J. J. expressing no view) said, by way of *obiter*:

> "By the use of the word 'may' in para (b) (of section 28(2)), a discretion seems to be envisaged. I suggest that any such discretion is concerned with factors such as lack of reciprocity or use to be made of funds to be recovered (by, eg, a hostile foreign power) not to mention the particular circumstances of those who might in the Commonwealth of Australia have to yield up property to persons in another country, rather than the

---

[37](1988) 82 ALR 475.
[38]ALRC 45, para 963.
[39]s 27 of the Bankruptcy Act prescribes the courts which may exercise jurisdiction under the Act and they are collectively referred to as the "Court" in this section of the paper.
[40]*Ayres v Evans* (1981) 39 ALR 129.
[41]ALRC 45, paras 970 *et seq*.
[42]*See* n. 40.

discretion, if any, is related to heads of public policy. As to the existence of a discretion in a court as to what assistance it may give: cf. *Re Osborne, ex parte The Trustee* (1932) B & CR 189, *per* Farwell J. at p. 194. This is consistent with what I understand to be conceded, correctly in view that in subsection (3) of section 29 'may' is permissive, offering the court a selection of the remedies set out in, for example, section 30 of the Act. However, considerations other than the interpretation of section 29(2)(a) do not directly arise and call for no separate decision here."

8.4.3   Recognition of "local" bankruptcies outside Australia

In addition to providing for the recognition of "foreign" bankruptcies within Australia, section 29 of the Act also empowers the Court to request a court in another country to act in aid of an Australian bankruptcy administration:

"(4) : The Court may request a court of an external Territory, or a country other than Australia, that has jurisdiction in bankruptcy to act in aid of and be auxiliary to it in any matter of bankruptcy."

R. W. Harmer observed of the operation of that section[43]:

"It is necessary to show some sense of purpose for an order under section 29(4). It is therefore, necessary to show a fair probability that there are assets in a foreign country before an order will be made for a letter of request to the relevant court of that country. It may also be necessary to show that the law of the foreign country would permit of recognition and assistance."

Examples of an appropriate form of order under section 29(4) and letter of request are attached as Annex 2 and 3.

Section 29(4) of the Act provides a useful mechanism for seeking to exert control over assets which have already been removed from Australia as where, for example, directors of a company which is in liquidation have "fled the jurisdiction" and taken assets with them. This is particularly so if that company has significant claims against those directors (whether in debt or for breach of duty). In that circumstance the company may have sufficient evidence to found creditors' petitions relying on, as the relevant act of bankruptcy, the allegation that the directors have absented themselves from the jurisdiction with the intention of defeating or delaying their creditors (section 40(1)(c) of the Act). Having filed that petition application may then be made for the appointment of an interim receiver under section 50(1) of the Act which provides:

"(1) : If, on application by a creditor, it is shown to be necessary in the interests of the creditors, the Court may, at any time after the presentation of a creditor's petition and before sequestration, direct the Official Trustee or a specified registered trustee to take control of the property of the debtor and may make such orders in relation to that property as the Court considers just."

The relevant considerations applicable in such an environment were conveniently summarised by Mr Harmer[44] as follows:

"In the terms of section 50 this application must be made by a creditor. The petitioning creditor may make the application.

---

[43]R. W. Harmer, "Financial Failure and International Aspects of Insolvency Law", International Aspects of Bankruptcy; BLEC Seminar (Sydney 1988), pp. 22 *et seq.*
[44]*Ibid*, pp. 18 *et seq.*

It is necessary to show the appointment is 'necessary in the interests of the creditors'. Facts such that the debtor has departed from and remained out of Australia, the size of the debt and the circumstances under which it was allegedly incurred and the presence of assets outside of Australia may, in some circumstances, be sufficient to show, inferentially at least, the necessity for the appointment of an interim receiver.

Although the section does not refer to the term 'receiver', *Re Choi*, unreported, Wilcox J., 11 July 1985 is authority for the proposition that the appointment can be made in a form as a receiver of the property of the debtor (rather than as a trustee with control) with power to collect, get in and preserve and maintain the property of the debtor. The receiver should also have liberty to apply.

An interim receiver appointed pursuant to section 50 has the necessary standing to make such an application. The jurisdiction in section 29(4) is for a foreign court to act in aid 'in any matter of bankruptcy'. That phrase includes, it may be substituted, acting in aid of an appointment under section 50 since 'bankruptcy' in section 5 as mentioned includes any proceedings under the Act. If reference to additional power is necessary, section 30(1)(b) (of the Act) is also relevant."

8.5 Conclusion

The review that has been undertaken of just some of the problems that emerge where an insolvency administration involves more than one jurisdiction (even within Australia) demonstrates (if the words of French J. in the *Clunies-Ross* case[45] might be adopted) the "Byzantine complexity" which will confront the practitioner. It was that consideration which prompted the Law Reform Commission to recommend that:

"in seeking to resolve difficulties of international cross-frontier insolvency Australia should actively promote multilateral international treaties with respect to

● the adoption of common basic elements of insolvency laws; and
● the recognition of insolvency laws between nations."[46]

[45]*See* n. 37.
[46]ALRC 45, para 969.

Annex 1
Letter of Request

<u>TO</u> : Their Lordships, the Justices of Her Majesty's High Court of Justice, Chancery Division of the Supreme Court of Judicature of England

WHEREAS applications for an order for the winding-up of the Respondent are now pending in The Federal Court of Australia and in England, in The High Court of Justice, Chancery Division (proceedings No. 9287 of 1991);

AND WHEREAS the Respondent was incorporated in the State of Western Australia;

AND WHEREAS it was represented to The Federal Court of Australia by the Applicant that it was necessary for the purposes of justice and for the due determination of the matters in dispute between the parties to the said application that it is desirable to request the assistance of your Honourable Court to act in aid of and be auxiliary to this Court in these proceedings;

AND WHEREAS The Federal Court of Australia found that the only significant assets of the Respondent is a leasehold interest in an agricultural holding situated at Hertfordshire in England know [*sic*] as the Up Hall Estate (hereinafter referred to as "the leasehold");

AND WHEREAS The Federal Court of Australia reached the conclusion that it is desirable that the best possible realisation of the assets of the Respondent be achieved for the benefit of all its unsecured creditors;

AND WHEREAS The Federal Court of Australia formed the view that an administration order under Part II of the Insolvency Act 1986 (UK) offers the possibility that the value of the leasehold might be preserved and that the making of a winding-up order would not do so;

AND WHEREAS on 27 November 1991 The Federal Court of Australia declared that it is desirable to request the assistance of the English Courts to act in aid of and be auxiliary to it in proceeding NG3093 of 1991;

AND WHEREAS copies of the said declaration and orders made 27 November 1991 and entered 3 December 1991, and of the Reasons for Judgment of The Honourable Mr Justice Gummow delivered 27 November 1991 are annexed hereto and marked with the letters, "A" and "B" respectively;

NOW I, James Thomas Howard the Registrar of The Federal Court of Australia have the honour to request and do hereby request the assistance of the English Courts to act in aid of and be auxiliary to The Federal Court of Australia in this proceeding.

Dated: 3 December 1991.
Registrar.

Annex 2
Draft Form of Order for
Issue of Letter of Request

UPON the Application of the Receiver/Trustee of the property of [name of debtor or bankrupt], for an Order under section 29(4) of the Bankruptcy Act 1966, seeking aid and for a request to the [name of overseas court] to act in aid of and be auxiliary to the Federal Court of Australia in the matter of the performance of the powers of the abovenamed receiver/trustee in respect of the property of the abovenamed debtor/bankrupt:

THE COURT ORDERS THAT:

A Letter of Request issue under the hand of the Registrar requesting the [name of the foreign Court] to act in aid of and be auxiliary to the Federal Court of Australia in the following matters:

(a) by appointing the Official Receiver to the Court hereinbefore mentioned or such other private Trustee lawfully entitled to act in the administration of insolvent estates anywhere in [name of foreign country] who shall be required by the said [name of Australian receiver/trustee] to act and who shall accept that appointment (hereinafter referred to as the "[name of country] Receiver") to be the interim receiver/trustee (without security) of the property of the abovenamed debtor/bankrupt situate in [name of country] with power to do in [name of country] all things necessary or convenient to be done for or in connection with, or as incidental to, the attainment of the objective of collecting, getting in and preserving and maintaining the property of the debtor/bankrupt until further order;

(b) by permitting the [name of country] Receiver to make such applications to any Court in [name of country] having jurisdiction under the [relevant foreign legislation] as he may in relation to the matters referred to in this Order consider necessary and proper.

Annex 3
Draft Form of Letter of Request

TO The [Chief Justice of the relevant foreign court]

Whereas an Order was made [recite terms of relevant order/or legislation provision by which the receiver/trustee was appointed to property of the debtor/bankrupt].

And whereas it appears from information given to the said [name of receiver/trustee] that the debtor/bankrupt is or may be entitled to or possessed of certain property situated in [foreign country].

And whereas it has been represented to the Federal Court that it is necessary for the purpose of justice that the property should be made available to [name of receiver/ trustee], so that it may be dealt with by him under and in accordance with the [relevant order] under the Bankruptcy Act 1966.

And whereas in order that the property may be made available and dealt with his Honour [name of judge] ordered that the Registrar issue a letter to the [name of foreign court] requesting that Court to act in aid of and be auxiliary to the Federal Court of Australia in certain matters.

Now I, as Registrar in Bankruptcy for the Bankruptcy District of [name of bankruptcy district], have the honour to request, and do hereby request, that for the reasons aforesaid and for the assistance of the Federal Court of Australia you as the Justice of the [foreign court], or some one or more of you, will be pleased to appoint the [title of official] or such other private trustee lawfully entitled to act in the administration of insolvent estates anywhere in [foreign country] who shall be required by the said [receiver/trustee] to act and who shall accept that appointment (hereinafter referred to as "the [foreign country] Receiver") to be, subject always to the jurisdiction of the [foreign court], the interim receiver/trustee (without security) of the property of the abovenamed debtor/bankrupt situate in [foreign country] with power to do in [foreign country] all things necessary or convenient to be done for or in connection with, or as incidental to, the attainment of the objective of collecting, getting in and preserving and maintaining the property of the debtor/bankrupt until further order and with authority to take such steps and do all such acts and things as may be necessary and proper for the purposes of receiving such property and to permit the [foreign] Receiver to make such applications to the [foreign court], or any other Court having jurisdiction under the [relevant foreign legislation] as he may in relation to the matter herein referred to consider necessary and proper.

9

International Bankruptcy Proceedings and Claims

Dott. Proc. Giorgio Cherubini

Studio Legale Associato, Rome, Italy

9.1 Introduction

In order to understand this chapter better, it is perhaps appropriate to begin with a comparative overview of how bankruptcy proceedings are handled under both common and civil law. Specifically, it must be borne in mind what the origins and conceptions of "trust" are, this being most relevant concept in matters of equity, as they are handled in common law. As will be seen, "equity" has no equivalent in civil law.

In fact, in civil law, the natural consequence of an adjudication of bankruptcy is that the debtor loses only the capacity to dispose of his/her property, not the ownership thereof. Under common law systems, however, the "bankruptcy trustee" actually becomes the owner of the debtor's estate, taking charge of it through a form of ownership deriving from equity; as already mentioned, this type of arrangement does not exist under civil law systems.

Another characteristic that differentiates one system from the other is that under common law, particularly in North America, it is possible for an individual who is not associated with any type of entrepreneurial activity to file for bankruptcy, something that cannot be done under civil law, particularly in Italy. In Italy, bankruptcy is possible only where the debtor is a medium to large commercial entity for which it is possible to establish a lawful owner. Moreover, in the North American system, once the debtor's property has been collected and proportionally distributed to the creditors, the court may issue an order of discharge, which releases the debtor from all dischargeable obligations and liabilities which might be proved in court, and he/she may start accumulating assets once again.

Another problem to be considered is the so-called "universal" nature of the judgment of bankruptcy, whereby the debtor's entire estate is to be used in settling the creditors' claims. In fact, it is from this concept of "universality" that the doctrine of

Current Issues in Cross-Border Insolvency and Reorganisations (E. B. Leonard, C. W. Besant, eds.; 1–85333–958–X; © International Bar Association; pub. Graham & Trotman/International Bar Association, 1994; printed in Great Britain), pp.175-190.

single adjudication of bankruptcy becomes necessary. Indeed, if there were several adjudications of bankruptcy for each case, the concept of "universality" would no longer be applicable.

More specifically, the bankruptcy of a business is an economic phenomenon which may extend beyond the jurisdiction of each nation's legal system, or which perhaps cannot be remedied within such boundaries. This may occur in situations where the debtor's estate is located in several countries or where it can be recuperated through a foreign legal system. Hypothetically, in such cases, the single adjudication of bankruptcy could be enforceable by means of a declaration that the bankruptcy is to be effective anywhere, or, at least, in any place where the estate to be recuperated may be located. The economy of the world, however, is much too varied to allow such a unification, which could not take into consideration the numerous differences in legislation regarding bankruptcy.

Currently, the two most commonly debated doctrines with regard to bankruptcy are those of universality and territoriality. Under the concept of universality, the trustee with control of a bankruptcy adjudicated in one country may reclaim the debtor's estate regardless of its location in another country. Conversely, territoriality allows the enforcement of the adjudication of bankruptcy only in the country in which it is declared.

What follows is a discussion of this topic within the context of Italian jurisprudence.

9.2 Recognition of foreign proceedings

9.2.1 Necessity of legal effect in Italy for the foreign adjudication of bankruptcy — legitimation of the trustee — trends in Italian jurisprudence and precedents

A foreign company that has been adjudicated bankrupt in its own country, and which must recuperate a credit from an Italian company should present its adjudication of bankruptcy to the Italian judge. The trustees who represent the foreign business must justify their empowerment to act before the Italian judicial authorities.

Prior to 1942 Italian law provided that certain parts of the judgment issued under the national law of the foreigner regarding his/her capacity to act could be effective under Italian legislation without first being given legal effect by an Italian judge. This doctrine was applied in accordance with Article 17 of the Provisions on the Law in General of the Italian Civil Code which states:

> "The status and capacity of persons and family relations are governed by the law of the state of which they are nationals.
>
> However, if an alien takes an action in Italy for which he/she lacks capacity according to his/her national law, he/she is considered capable of such act if according to Italian law a citizen would be capable, unless the matter involves family relations, inheritances, donations, or acts of disposition of immovables situated abroad."

Under this doctrine, it ensued that the foreign adjudication of bankruptcy regarding the capacity of the debtor would automatically be recognised in the Italian legal system, without being granted legal effect beforehand, as long as the judgment itself had been issued by a judge of the national legal system of the debtor.

Before the Italian Civil Code became effective in 1942,[1] the theory of direct recognition of certain provisions of foreign judgments without legal effect being granted was based on whether these were immediately enforceable or not. Given the fact that the adjudication of bankruptcy is a decision regarding the status of an entity, and is therefore immediately enforceable, it was considered that the process of giving it legal effect was not necessary.

After the Civil Code took effect in 1942, however, precedents demonstrate that foreign adjudications of bankruptcy have almost always been given legal effect in accordance with Article 796 of the Italian Civil Procedure Code. With regard to the enforceability of foreign judgments and the capacity of foreign authorities to act, Article 796 provides:

> "…any person who wishes to obtain legal effect in Italy for a foreign judgment, must file a petition with the Court of Appeals of the place where said judgment must be enforced. The declaration of enforceability may be requested through diplomatic channels when such a procedure is authorised by international conventions or by reciprocity.
>
> In this case, if the interested party has not nominated a representative, the president of the Court of Appeals, upon the request of the prosecuting attorney, will appoint a special curator who will file the request. In any case, the action of the prosecuting attorney is always required."

Many precedents confirm this trend. A few examples are the judgments issued by the Supreme Court, (17 April 1980 (no. 2512), 9 January 1975 (no. 42) and 12 December 1966 (no. 2895)); by the Court of Appeals of Genoa (24 May 1973); and by the Court of Appeals of Milan (20 June 1967).

It can be stated, therefore, that the necessity of obtaining legal effect before a foreign trustee can act in Italy is consistently required in Italian jurisprudence. In the absence of legal effect, foreign judgments are not recognised as executable under the Italian legal system. In fact, the appointment of a trustee is considered to be a result of the adjudication of bankruptcy, and therefore can be recognised in the Italian legal system only when the judgment itself has been given legal effect.

In brief, as the nomination of the trustee is an effect of the bankruptcy, in order to legitimise his/her actions in Italy, it is not sufficient to provide documentary proof of the existence of the nomination by the foreign judge. Rather, one must obtain legal effect for the adjudication of bankruptcy. Based on this interpretation, sales in Italy by a foreign trustee of goods which were part of the debtor's estate, without previously obtaining legal effect for the foreign judgment, have been declared null and void.

Because it is to be assumed that in order to enforce a foreign adjudication of bankruptcy in Italy it is necessary to obtain legal effect in accordance with Article 796 of the Civil Procedure Code, it is worth examining the procedure involved in terms of the differences which exist between Italian legislation in this field and that of common law systems with regard to the legitimation of authority to act.

Generally, under Italian law, only the parties that were originally involved in the bankruptcy proceedings before the foreign judge, or their universal or singular

---

[1] The Bankruptcy Law, decree no. 267, came into force on 16 March 1942, almost simultaneously with the Civil Code.

successors, can request legal effect in Italy. If this principle were applied literally and inflexibly with regard to adjudications of bankruptcy, the trustee's right to request legal effect could be questioned. In reality, it can be stated more correctly that any party upon which the adjudication will have effect if approved under the Italian system can request legal effect. This is further supported by the Supreme Court's sentence no. 2512/1980, whereby the foreign trustee was authorised to request legal effect for the foreign adjudication of bankruptcy.

In requesting legal effect in Italy, the trustee must indicate the motive for the request. It is likely that a third party will be involved in the process, such as, for instance, an opposing party.

In order to be given legal effect in Italy, the adjudication of bankruptcy must be final and conclusive ("*res judicata*") and must not be contrary to any related judgment issued in Italy. Moreover, the adjudication must not be contrary to the principles of Italian public order, with reference to both the contents of the judgment and its effects. The adjudication could be considered contrary to public order if it is irregular in terms of the legal system under which it was issued or if significant differences arise between the Italian and foreign bankruptcy procedures. Based on the precedents in this field, it can be said that the limit of tolerance of the differences between Italian and foreign bankruptcy procedures has been set at different levels, and the principles of Italian public order have contributed to favouring the application of Italian jurisprudence. This is even true in cases where the application of foreign legislation in bankruptcy matters would not have gone against the principles of Italian public order.

It is worth pointing out that in order to obtain legal effect in Italy for a foreign adjudication of bankruptcy, the existence of a formal order of the foreign judge is not required, since it is sufficient to demonstrate that the judge in question issued a decision. This can be substantiated merely by an examination of the objective and subjective premises upon which the bankruptcy was adjudicated and by the fact of nomination of the trustee, which is a direct result of the adjudication.

It is therefore necessary to analyse, in terms of the applicable foreign legislation, whether the foreign judgment contains the essential decrees that would form the basis of an equivalent Italian judgment.

Requesting legal effect for a foreign judgment in Italy is the responsibility of the foreign trustee or, if permitted under the foreign law, of the bankruptcy office, regardless of whether that office is administrative or judicial in nature. In the latter case, the prosecuting attorney represents the foreign bankruptcy office before the appropriate Court of Appeals in filing the request for legal effect in Italy.

The procedure of giving legal effect is carried out by a panel of judges, without the parties being present, and results in a decision, thus providing a quicker and more efficient process without alienating the debtor's right to defend him/herself. There are two reasons for issuing a judgment at the end of the procedure: one is that the Italian system requires that the adjudication of bankruptcy be issued by means of a judgment; the other is that the issuing of a decision provides the irrefutable right of appeal before the Supreme Court for all foreign judgments given legal effect in Italy (with the exception of those that must be verified through regular preliminary investigation).

As already mentioned, through the process of giving legal effect the foreign trustee is "legitimised" to act in Italy. This means that he/she may recover the goods which are part of the debtor's estate and sell those which may be in his/her possession. By "legitimation" is meant the empowerment to initiate or to take part in legal action.

The process of giving legal effect is necessary to act upon the debtor's estate, to prevent other creditors suffering any loss, and in order to avoid a situation in which the value of the property is diminished. Legal effect is also necessary in order to allow all of the interested creditors to file a claim without the necessity of assessing on an individual basis the nature of each debt.

The judge of the state in which the bankruptcy has been filed must have already heard the debtor and must have granted him/her an appropriate term within which to file a defence. As already mentioned, the foreign judge's decision must be final and conclusive. In Italy, it is not possible to request legal effect for adjudications of bankruptcy pertaining to individuals or to non-commercial entrepreneurs, because such a judgment is incompatible with the provisions of Italian legislation in this field. It should be noted, however, that the Italian Supreme Court has ruled that a foreign adjudication of bankruptcy for an entrepreneur who had ceased the activity more than one year prior to the bankruptcy was not contrary to Italian public order, and could be given legal effect in Italy, provided it was not contrary to the legal principles of the nation of origin.[2]

The foreign trustee would be the person summoned in procedures regarding the debtor's ownership rights to assets included in the bankruptcy. It has been noted that the foreign trustee is fully legitimised to act following the granting of legal effect. In the absence of legal effect, however, it is possible for a foreign trustee to appear before an Italian court upon the presentation of the petition and his/her nomination to request a postponement until the adjudication has been made.

Under Italian law, upon the adjudication of bankruptcy, an "operating centre" is created to handle the related procedure. This is not the case when a foreign adjudication of bankruptcy is given legal effect in Italy. Rather, in cases where the debtor possesses immovable property in Italy, the foreign trustee must register the foreign adjudication, which has been given legal effect, and the resulting decision with the Registrar of Immovable Property. Once the trustee has completed this step, he/she may substitute him/herself for any creditor who has proven a debt in the foreign bankruptcy, in order to proceed with execution. In fact, if a creditor has not yet proven a debt in the foreign bankruptcy, the trustee can do this in his/her place.

Once the trustee has sold the assets of the debtor, he/she acts as a single creditor and collects the total amount due to the various creditors who have a proven credit in the bankruptcy. Once this step is completed, the trustee distributes the sums due to the creditors who have proven the debt in the foreign bankruptcy. Any amount remaining after this process is distributed to the creditors who previously failed to prove the debt, regardless of whether they were entitled to do so or not. At this point, any controversies that arise between the trustee and the creditors who failed to prove the debt in the foreign bankruptcy will be resolved by an Italian judge. Conversely, any controversies with creditors who have proven the debt will be resolved by the judge of the country where the bankruptcy proceedings were originally filed.

The trustee is also empowered to file for the revocation of payments made to creditors before the bankruptcy was adjudicated. This procedure, which is typical to the

[2] 9 January 1975, decision no. 42.

Italian system, consists in revoking payments made to creditors within a maximum two-year period preceding the filing of the bankruptcy petition, this term varying in terms of the motive for the payment in question.

The creditors subject to revocation must reimburse the sum they received, which is added to the contributory mass,[3] and then prove the debt in the bankruptcy after which they will receive payment once again in due course. The trustee may resort to this procedure in cases where the effect of a contract of which the debtor is a party and which has been signed in Italy is being contested. Another situation in which the trustee may revoke payment is when a declaration is made that a contract regarding goods located in Italy which are part of the debtor's estate, is void.

An adjudication of bankruptcy often has an immediate effect on any related pending procedures. Therefore when the bankruptcy is adjudicated in the country where the debtor is residing, domiciled, or carries on a business activity, he/she can no longer take any part or action in any company or cooperative of his/her ownership that operates in the same country, even if not headquartered there.

Generally speaking, the actions that a debtor in a bankruptcy that has been adjudicated overseas may take, through the trustee, must be aimed at increasing the estate, such as, for instance, beginning proceedings to repossess assets or oppose claims against assets. Finally, the granting of legal effect could also be requested by a person who is not a party to the bankruptcy, but rather has a personal interest in increasing the bankrupt estate.

For a third party to legitimise his/her involvement, he/she must be able to provide judicial means which will allow the recovery of some of the debtor's assets. In such a case, the request for legal effect is considered legitimate.

9.2.2 Effects of a foreign adjudication of bankruptcy on cases of insolvency verified in Italy — relevancy and effects of the foreign judgment — limitations on the adjudication of bankruptcy of a foreigner in Italy

According to current legislation in Italy, two conditions must exist in order to adjudicate a bankruptcy:

(a) the debtor must be an entrepreneur engaged in a medium to large private business activity;
(b) there must exist evidence of insolvency.

According to Article 9 of the Bankruptcy Law, the adjudication must be issued by the tribunal of the place where the entrepreneur's business is based.

The "real seat" of the business is the place in which the entrepreneur actually carries out the activities. If the entrepreneur's activities are spread out in various offices, the "main seat" is considered to be the place where the administrative functions and/or contractual relationships with third parties are carried out. Normally, the headquarters of a business are indicated in the by laws and in the registry of the tribunal where the company is registered. In cases where the registered headquarters are not the office where the actual operative functions of the activity take place, then

---

[3]Contributory mass is a term referring to those, usually liquid, assets used to play the creditors.

the "real seat" of the company is considered to be that where in fact such functions are actually carried out.

Based on this principle, Article. 9 of the Royal Decree 16 March 1942 (no. 267) — by which the legislation pertaining to bankruptcies became effective — provides:

> "The entrepreneur whose company is headquartered in another country can be adjudicated bankrupt in the Italian Republic even if an adjudication of bankruptcy has been declared overseas. This is true if no international conventions exist between the two countries providing otherwise."

Consequently, even if the foreign adjudication of bankruptcy has been issued but has not been given legal effect in Italy, it is possible to obtain a separate adjudication of bankruptcy in Italy, in accordance with Article. 9 of the Bankruptcy Law. Precedents demonstrate that an Italian judge may adjudicate the bankruptcy of a foreign company in two cases: either the company has assets in Italy which are likely to be levied, or the company has contractual obligations in Italy which it has not fulfilled.

Clearly, such cases diverge from the concept of the universality of the adjudication of bankruptcy ("*fallite sur fallite ne vaut*"), since, based on the principle that the company has an operative secondary branch in Italy, two adjudications of bankruptcy may be declared. It so happens, however, that many countries are party to conventions whereby a bankruptcy declared in one nation has executable effects in the other. In fact, very often such conventions provide that the jurisdiction in which the bankruptcy should be adjudicated is that in which the activity is headquartered.

Once again, the question of jurisdiction arises when the entrepreneur owns a number of companies in Italy and it is impossible to identify which is the most important. The general rule is that the tribunal in the area in which the headquarters of the company are located has jurisdiction. In the above mentioned case, however, jurisdiction is assigned to the first tribunal with which the bankruptcy petition is filed.

According to Article 24 of the Royal Decree 16 March 1942 (no. 267), the tribunal that has adjudicated the bankruptcy is also the appropriate forum for any ensuing controversies. Therefore, by law, any controversies deriving from the bankruptcy must be filed with the adjudicating tribunal. Clearly, the purpose of this provision is to avoid the situation in which matters relating to a single bankruptcy are fragmented in a number of cases heard by different tribunals.

The above provision does resolve the issue of territorial authority but has no effect on the matter of jurisdiction. As already stated, if the debtor is domiciled in any part of the Italian state, the bankruptcy would be adjudicated by an Italian tribunal. This does not hold true, however, if the debtor is domiciled overseas, since Article 24 is applicable only nationally.

It is therefore necessary to consult Article 9, which covers both the issues of territorial authority and jurisdiction. In fact, as already seen, Article 9 provides that the appropriate Italian tribunal may adjudicate the bankruptcy of a foreign entrepreneur, even if the activity is headquartered overseas and the debtor has already been adjudicated bankrupt in that country.

Controversies deriving from the bankruptcy are those — such as the revocation of payments to creditors, mentioned earlier — that originate from the state of insolvency of the debtor, or which are directly or indirectly influenced by the bankruptcy. In such cases, the disputes must be included in the bankruptcy proceedings in order to ensure the unity of the procedure and the *par condicio creditorum* (equal condition of the creditors).

During the proceedings, the main office of the company is that where administrative and operative activities were actually being carried out at the time of the adjudication of bankruptcy or at the time when operations ceased, even if officially or previously, headquarters existed elsewhere.

When a petition of bankruptcy is filed, the tribunal must ascertain its authority in the matter. If the tribunal finds that it has no authority, it cannot issue an adjudication, and, if it is possible to determine the appropriate forum, it must hand the file over to the tribunal concerned.

Territorial authority is not required for the adjudication of the bankruptcy to be valid, but serves to ensure that the matter is filed with the appropriate tribunal. In fact, there is virtually no legal basis on which we can establish the juridical relevance of the territorial authority of the tribunal that adjudicates the bankruptcy. The law merely states that the appropriate tribunal is the one located in the same area as the headquarters or main office of the business. The regional distribution of authority is aimed at ensuring the efficiency of the execution, and legally speaking, this advantage is not considered to be very significant if one considers the damages that creditors would suffer if the adjudication of bankruptcy were considered null and void if such a technicality were not complied with. Hence, the absence of any provision aimed at voiding an adjudication of bankruptcy based on lack of territorial authority.

In fact, as mentioned earlier, if more than one Italian tribunal adjudicates the bankruptcy of a single debtor, the ensuing conflict is resolved by assigning the matter to the tribunal where the case was first filed and voiding any subsequent adjudications. Should the same case have been filed with several tribunals simultaneously, then the issue of authority comes into play and the matter is submitted for examination to the Supreme Court which then decides the assignment. The same goes for cases in which more than one tribunal has found it had no authority.

According to Italian law, the request for the adjudication of bankruptcy may be filed by a number of persons, and, in fact, Article 6 of the Bankruptcy Law states that these include: the debtor, one or more of the creditors (who have filed a petition), the prosecuting attorney, or *ex officio*.

The decision in which the bankruptcy is adjudicated is fairly complex with regard to its contents because it provides the following:

- the nomination of the judge;
- the nomination of the curator (equivalent of the trustee in Italy);
- the date by which the evaluation of the total debt must be carried out, as well as the deadline for the creditors to file their claim, which may not exceed thirty days from the publication of the adjudication.

Moreover, in addition to the listed standard provisions, the judgment may also contain the order of arrest of the debtor and/or any other persons involved, should evidence exist that they have committed offences punishable by law.

The judgment of bankruptcy is immediately executable on an interim basis. Within 24 hours of being issued, the judgment, and in particular its contents, must be communicated to the debtor, the creditor(s), the prosecuting attorney, as well as the

Registry of Companies at the tribunal where the debtor was born or where the business was created. Within the same deadline, the extract of the judgment must be posted on the outside door of the tribunal and published in the Regional Publication of Legal Announcements.

In cases where it is necessary to repossess the assets of the debtor which are located overseas, or assets in Italy belonging to a foreign debtor, questions pertaining to the applicable law and to the authority of the judge are to be resolved under international private law.

From a technical and economical point of view, it would be preferable to apply one law, that of the place where the bankruptcy was adjudicated. However, given the diversity of jurisprudence in this field from one country to the next, it is inconceivable that a nation would favour foreign creditors to the disadvantage of its own citizens, be they creditors or other persons having rights in the bankruptcy. From a theoretical point of view, this difficulty could be overcome at least in part by means of a uniform bankruptcy law for all countries sharing similar legal and economic systems. No such multilateral convention exists, however, and it is therefore necessary that each country take into consideration the needs of foreigners or non-residents in carrying out the procedures required by law.

Until recently, the doctrine commonly followed was that if no norms existed regarding Italian jurisdiction in bankruptcy matters, the above mentioned Article 9 would be applied, by which territorial authority is determined on the basis of the place in which the business had its main office. The second subparagraph of the same article, regarding the adjudication of bankruptcy in Italy of a foreign company, makes no specific reference to territorial authority. It is in fact the absence of any such reference which has led to the interpretation of this subparagraph whereby, in order to be declared bankrupt in Italy, a foreign company must have at least one branch within the Italian state.

On the other hand, based on Article. 15 of the Bankruptcy Law, which is interpreted to provide that the eventual debtor must be summoned before the bankruptcy is adjudicated, the Constitutional Court has ruled, with its sentence of 16 July 1970 (no. 141), that the debtor should be considered as a defendant and, therefore, Article 4 of the Civil Procedure Code is applicable. Article. 4 concerns jurisdiction in cases involving foreigners, and provides that a foreigner can be summoned for trial in Italy when:

(a) he/she resides, is domiciled, has elected domicile, or is legally represented in Italy;
(b) he/she has accepted Italian jurisdiction (provided that the matter is not related to assets located overseas);
(c) the matter in question concerns assets located in Italy, the inheritance of an Italian citizen, wills probated in Italy, or obligations undertaken or to be fulfilled in Italy;
(d) the matter in question is related to another case pending before an Italian judge, or regards precautionary provisions which either are to be carried out in Italy or pertain to a case which may be heard by an Italian judge.

Conversely, a judge from the country of the foreigner may hear a case against an Italian citizen.

Therefore, domicile, residency or long-term representation in Italy are the conditions required in order to adjudicate the bankruptcy of the foreigner in Italy. In fact any company created overseas which has an administrative office in Italy can indeed be adjudicated bankrupt by an Italian court.

For companies that have a secondary branch in Italy regulated in accordance with Article 2506 of the Italian Civil Code, the office in question must operate with full decision-making autonomy. In this case, the branch is considered to be a representative, on a long-term basis, of the parent company, and bankruptcy can be adjudicated in Italy.

As mentioned earlier, the entrepreneur with an activity headquartered overseas may be declared bankrupt in Italy, even if the same adjudication has already been pronounced overseas. This norm should be interpreted in terms of Article 3 of the Civil Procedure Code, which states that when two cases regarding the same matter are pending before a foreign and an Italian tribunal, the former has no influence on the latter. One must consider, however, that an ordinary cognizance trial can be carried out simultaneously in two different nations with conclusions that reflect the influence of the relevant national legislation. In this case, one trial does not affect the other and there exists no provision preventing both from being carried out simultaneously. Problems may arise at the time of execution, however, since, under Italian law, particularly in cases of bankruptcy, execution cannot take place if its object is not located within the Italian territory. Therefore, if the estate of the debtor is the object of the collective execution, the principal of territoriality should prevail and as many adjudications of bankruptcy should be issued as there are nations in which the assets are distributed.

In the absence of an international convention regarding the uniform handling of bankruptcies, the alternative is that a foreign adjudication of bankruptcy issued under a legal system different from that used in Italy does not create any impediment to such an adjudication regarding the same debtor being issued by an Italian judge. Instead, the contrary occurs, and it is very difficult to establish when and why an adjudication of bankruptcy cannot be issued under Italian legislation, given the numerous norms applicable to this type of situation. Again, in this case, it is necessary to apply Article 9 of the Bankruptcy Law restrictively, taking into consideration the contents of Article 4 of the Italian Civil Procedure Code.

In fact, if the giving of legal effect can be obtained but is not requested and no case to this effect is pending in an Italian court, there is no reason why an adjudication of bankruptcy cannot be pronounced under Italian jurisdiction, provided the required conditions exist. If, on the other hand, a request has already been filed for legal effect, and this application must be granted, the bankruptcy cannot be adjudicated directly by an Italian court.

Finally, if an adjudication of bankruptcy is pronounced overseas and for some reason cannot be given legal effect in Italy, it becomes necessary to determine whether it is worthwhile filing a petition in Italy. In this case it is important to evaluate whether the tangible increase in the estate which is likely to result from a procedure in Italy makes further "complicating" the bankruptcy proceedings worthwhile.

The co-existence of bankruptcies makes the co-ordination of these essential in order to avoid having the same estate be the object of several procedures. In fact, theoretically, it is possible for a creditor to prove the debt in two or more bankruptcy proceedings regarding the same estate which have been filed in different nations. In such a case, considerable confusion may ensue, and this is where the need for co-ordination arises.

If there is no co-ordination of the two bankruptcies the problems that ensue can be resolved in two ways. One solution is to determine jurisdiction in terms of territoriality, in which case execution can be carried out only in the nation where the adjudication was originally pronounced. The other solution is that the foreign judge carry out the execution in order to recover and liquidate the estate of the debtor. The midpoint between these two extremes is to attribute a universal character to the bankruptcy and to the estate in question. In this way, a single adjudication of bankruptcy exists which is given legal effect in as many states as is required fully to recuperate all of the assets to be included in the estate.

By accepting the theory of universality of the bankruptcy, the curator's powers are vast enough to allow him/her to recuperate all of the debtor's assets in any nation where they may be located.

Considering the bankruptcy in light of a collective execution does not, however, extend its effects overseas, since each part of the execution is to be carried out on a regional basis. On the other hand, it is normally considered that the adjudication of bankruptcy issued in Italy or overseas does not imply that execution can be carried out either against third parties or for the release of the assets belonging to the estate. Therefore, the giving of legal effect does not empower the foreign trustee to recover the assets of the debtor that are under the control of third parties, or those belonging to others but resulting to the debtor. Rather, the trustee is thus empowered to recover only those assets already available and in the possession of the debtor.

In order to understand the effects of a foreign adjudication of bankruptcy, it may be useful to consider the said bankruptcy as a management of the liquidation procedure. The trustee replaces the debtor in the management function and furthermore is empowered to take actions that the debtor could not.

This substitution is the basis upon which the trustee is empowered to carry out the liquidation, and his/her functions are limited to the "transformation" of the estate, without, however, taking any action against an estate with which he/she is not concerned. Therefore, in this case, execution takes on the characteristics specific to voluntary, not involuntary, proceedings. The opposite of the concept of universality of the bankruptcy is that of territoriality, whereby the adjudication has effect only in the nation in which it is declared.

In conclusion, it can be stated that a uniform doctrine or jurisprudence regarding the topics covered herein is lacking and the need for multilateral conventions to this effect is ever more pressing.

9.2.3 Treatment of foreign creditors — recognition of foreign creditors — proving of a debt by a foreign creditor in Italy

As discussed in the preceding sections, once the bankruptcy is adjudicated, the estate of the debtor is expropriated in favour of the creditors. The judicial protection of the assets and of the relationships that are part of the estate does not concern so much the debtor as it does the creditors. Such protection is therefore handled by the curator who is responsible for the administration of the estate. Each creditor must have his/her claim verified for it to be included in the bankruptcy, in accordance with Article

52 of the Bankruptcy Law which states: "each credit, even if benefiting from the right of pre-emption, must be verified according to the provision of Title V, unless otherwise provided for by law." Title V includes provisions pertaining to the assessment of liabilities and the rights of third parties.

This verification is applicable to all creditors, including those who filed the petition for the bankruptcy, if that is the case, and those who have obtained a final and conclusive judgment regarding the legitimacy of their credit.

The verification of the credit is a crucial part of the bankruptcy procedure. Article 51 of the Bankruptcy Law provides that: "unless other provisions of the law exist, from the day that the bankruptcy is adjudicated, no individual entity may proceed with or take any action against the assets which are part of the estate."

The steps of the bankruptcy procedure can be summarised as follows:

(a) the custody of the estate and administration of bankruptcy procedures;
(b) verification of debts to be proven;
(c) liquidation of assets;
(d) distribution of assets to the creditors.

This section is specifically concerned with the verification of the debts to be proven, a step that is carried out by the judge delegate and does not involve cross-examination. The debtor, the curator and the creditors meet during the assembly of creditors which is presided over by the judge delegate, who is apprised of the global situation and is therefore able to carry out the appraisal. The judge delegate has vast powers, in that in evaluating each individual claim, he/she must bear in mind the differing interests of the creditors in order to avoid any subsequent opposition or court cases, since such cases would be carried out with cross-examination in the pattern of a normal trial. Claims presented before the assembly of creditors are eligible for verification. Those presented after the assembly are referred to as "late" claims.

At the time of the adjudication of bankruptcy, two dates are established. The first is that by which the creditors must present their claims and must be no more than 30 days following the publication of the adjudication. The second is that upon which the assessment of liabilities will take place, and must be no later than 20 days following the first deadline. The time and place where the assessment will be carried out is also established at the time of the adjudication. The curator communicates these matters by registered mail, to the creditors listed in the roll. For non-resident creditors, the communication is sent to whomever represents them in Italy. The deadlines are not final and can be modified when there are creditors who do not reside in Italy or who do not have a representative in the country.

The claims must be presented by all of the creditors whose credit arose before the bankruptcy was adjudicated. Even creditors who have obtained judicial recognition of their credit through a final and conclusive sentence are also obligated to file a claim. The claim must feature the first and last name of the creditor, the amount due, the reason for which the amount is due, the justification of any right of pre-emption and supporting documentation. If the creditor is not domiciled in the municipality where the tribunal is located, the claim must contain a domicile of choice in the municipality in question. If no domicile is chosen, all communications will be sent to the creditor care of the Registry of the tribunal.

By law, the claim has effect from the date upon which it is deposited. The Registrar makes a chronological list of all the claims received and sends the entire file to the judge delegate. The judge delegate and the curator review all of the claims and establish a preliminary assessment of total liabilities, in accordance with Article 96 of the Bankruptcy Law.

Once this step is completed, the next is the liquidation of assets, which consists of the conversion of the property of the debtor into cash which will then be used to pay the creditors. Article 104 of the Bankruptcy Law provides:

> "The curator must proceed with the sale of the property, under the direction of the judge delegate and after hearing the committee of creditors, if one has been created."

With regard to movables, Article 106 provides that once the judge has heard the curator and the committee of creditors, he/she is to establish the time and method of sale. The sale can be done either privately or by auction, following the procedure dictated by the judge. If necessary, the judge may request the assistance of an appraiser.

The sale of real property is carried out by order of the judge delegate in response to the curator's request. The sale takes place before the judge, unless the property is located in an area where another tribunal has jurisdiction, in which case this tribunal is empowered to act by delegation, as provided for in Article 108 of the Bankruptcy Law.

The distribution of cash assets is carried out in accordance with the order provided in Article 111:

(a) payment of expenses, including those covered temporarily by the Treasury, and of debts — contracts for the administration of the bankruptcy and for the continuation of business activities if this was allowed;

(b) payment of creditors having the right of pre-emption on sold property, in the order provided by law;

(c) payment of unsecured creditors, in proportion to the amount of each proven debt, including those mentioned under point (b) if the guarantee has not been liquidated or if the amount obtained from the sale was insufficient to cover the debt.

The payment of the creditors is necessarily regulated by the law of the place where this procedure occurs ("*lex fori*"). On the other hand, pre-emption which derives from real rights of guaranty is regulated by the law of the place where the property is located ("*lex rei sitae*"), as is the situation for real rights in general. In his/her investigation, the judge will identify those rights of pre-emption which are similar or identical to those provided for by Italian law and will apply the order indicated in the civil code. The judge must establish the *par condicio creditorum* (equal conditions amongst the creditors), who are classified according to equal rights of pre-emption. Creditors who do not have any right of pre-emption are classified according to other criteria.

There is no particular type of limitation to or discrimination against the rights of foreign creditors. With regard to the distribution of cash assets, employees who are owed up to the last six months of salary plus any severance pay due are considered to be privileged creditors. In order to proceed with distribution, it is not necessary to await the end of the liquidation process. Rather, the distribution is carried out gradually, in terms of the availability of cash assets.

From the date in which the bankruptcy is executable, and provided the judge has not established different terms, the curator must present a report of available cash assets and a distribution plan on a bi-monthly basis. Partial distributions must never exceed 90% of the sums available, since 10% must remain in order to cover unforeseeable expenses.

Partial distributions are carried out in two ways: by direct allocation of the amounts due; or by the creation of a contingency fund. The allocations are paid out to the creditors who have a proven debt at the time the distribution is decided.

The contingency fund is created for those creditors whose credit has yet to be proven, in accordance with Article 113 of the Bankruptcy Law. Such creditors are:

(a) creditors residing overseas, whose credit has not yet been proven because the deadline for doing so has been extended;
(b) creditors whose claim is provisionally admitted but who have yet to provide the instruments by which payment can be made; those who are subject to a suspensive condition which has yet to be fulfilled, including credits which cannot be recuperated directly from the bankrupt debtor without first attempting recovery from a principal debtor;
(c) creditors whose claim is provisionally admitted following an appeal of the judge's decision to decline the claim;
(d) creditors with a proven credit for whom a contingency fund has been ordered following the contesting by other creditors or the petition of revocation.

Finally, the curator's administrative report is reviewed by the judge delegate who ascertains its regularity, orders that it be deposited at the Registry and sets a hearing date, during which time all interested parties may state any observations. If no contestation arises during the hearing, the judge approves the report; otherwise he/she schedules another hearing before a panel of judges.

The final distribution of assets begins when any controversies are resolved and when the report is approved. The final distribution also includes the depositing in a bank of amounts due to creditors who do not appear or for those who cannot be found.

Thus far, everything that has been discussed is applicable in cases where the business is bankrupt. In some cases, however, it is possible lawfully to defer the adjudication of bankruptcy in order that the debtor can arrive at a settlement with the creditors and resolve his/her financial problems. In fact, legally speaking, this latter alternative is favoured, because in this way the entrepreneur may continue his/her activity, which is beneficial to the economy, and because the survival of the company means that production and employment will not be affected negatively.

The settlement agreement is collective in nature, and is concluded between the debtor and the majority of unsecured creditors. The agreement, however, is binding on all the creditors. In any case, the debtor must "deserve" the benefits which he/she is granted, and his/her eligibility is reviewed and decided upon by judicial authorities in terms of the debtor's professional integrity and the reasons leading to the insolvency. The prerequisites include: that the debtor has not been declared bankrupt in the five preceding years, that he/she has not already benefitted from composition, and that he/she has not been convicted of bankruptcy.

Until the conclusion of the agreement, the activity of the entrepreneur is carried out under the control of judicial authorities. Legal actions are suspended. Creditors are not entitled to claim rights of pre-emption, so that the *par conditio creditorum* is maintained. If no agreement is concluded, then the bankruptcy is declared following the procedure described earlier.

Alternatives to bankruptcy are also favoured because they are generally less costly than bankruptcy proceedings, revenues from private liquidation of assets are higher and the process is usually much faster. These alternatives, under Italian legislation, include the controlled administration of the debtor's estate and composition with the creditors. The first allows the debtor to become solvent again through the addition of assets to the estate. The second allows the debtor to repay all of the creditors.

Through composition, the debtor guarantees that he/she will pay a percentage of his/her debts which cannot be less than either the total value of his/her assets or the minimum provided by law. Alternatively, the debtor may transfer his/her assets to the creditors for liquidation, provided the amount obtained corresponds to the percentage stated above, and provided the creditors relinquish any further claim.

Through controlled administration, the creditors forego the option to take any further action and relinquish their right of pre-emption on the debtor's assets in order to facilitate the administration process. Essentially, the creditors grant a moratorium and the debtor renounces his/her liberty of management.

In either procedure, the creditors must be aware of the debtor's state of insolvency and must approve the process to be followed. Therefore, foreign creditors are entitled to the recognition of their rights and can prove their credit in Italy. The agreement is concluded only with the unsecured creditors whose credit arose within the two years preceding the proposal of composition. Successive creditors are excluded from the negotiations but are not to be prejudiced by the same.

Under controlled administration, in order to participate, the creditors must forego any rights deriving from privilege, guarantees or mortgages, and their credit becomes unsecured. In this way, their position is the same as that of the other creditors. In a composition agreement, the creditors are entitled to relinquish their guarantee only partially, provided the waived portion of said guarantee amounts to at least one third of the value of the total credit and related expenditures.

Even before the agreement is finalised, once the proposal is presented by the debtor, the bankruptcy cannot be declared and no alterations can be made to the position of the creditors and to the estate in general.

The appropriate judicial authority in this alternative procedure is the same as would oversee the bankruptcy proceedings, ie the tribunal of the place where the main branch of the company is located. The procedure begins with the presentation of a signed petition by the debtor, in which he/she must indicate the reasons behind the current state of insolvency, the reasons for the proposal, and the accounting books of the company.

If the tribunal rejects the proposal, it declares the bankruptcy *ex officio*. If, on the other hand, the tribunal accepts the proposal, it opens the procedure and nominates the persons who will oversee it (judge delegate, judicial commissioner). The tribunal also sets the date of the assembly of creditors, which is to be scheduled within 30 days of the opening of the procedure. The tribunal then determines the total amount which will be necessary for the procedure and sets an eight-day deadline within which the debtor must deposit said amount at the Registry of the tribunal.

During the procedure, either upon the request of one of the interested parties or *ex officio*, and following the assembly of creditors, the tribunal may entrust the judicial commissioner with all or part of the management of the business and the administration of the debtor's assets. At the end of the procedure, provided it is carried out in accordance with the law, the tribunal issues a temporarily enforceable ratification.

Given this brief overview of alternatives to bankruptcy, it can be said that in any case, the general provisions in either are quite similar, and the interests of the creditors, even those overseas, are protected. The difference, which may be significant to the creditors, lies in the fact that in the alternative procedure, the characteristics of the credit may be changed, as well as the amount recuperated.

Credits in foreign currency must be converted to an equivalent value in Italian Lire as this is the currency in which the creditors will be paid.

10

The New Insolvency Regimes in Russia and the Commonwealth of Independent States

Carol A. M. Patterson

Baker & McKenzie, Moscow, Russia

10.1 Introduction

Originally the scope of this chapter was to summarise the developments in 1992/93 in debtor-creditor, insolvency and secured lending legislation in Russia. This was the year in which comprehensive bankruptcy legislation was to have been adopted to fill a remaining gap in the rapidly assembled collection of new laws, including joint stock company laws, property reform laws, and privatisation laws which are necessary to accompany Russia's transformation to a market economy.

Bankruptcy law would seem to be urgently needed to provide a mechanism for winding down chronically unprofitable state enterprises. The instances of spiralling inter-enterprise debt, and the *de facto* insolvency of thousands of state-owned enterprises in Russia have been documented and well-publicised. Production has fallen, foreign debt repayments have been missed or re-scheduled, and financing and even sufficient ruble banknotes to make payrolls have been difficult for enterprises to obtain. With inflation, there has been a shortage of banknotes.

Yet the mere prospect of putting in place a legal framework to proceed with bankruptcy of these enterprises has frightened the legislators. When the draft bill, much revised and delayed, was presented to parliament for debate and approval in May 1992, it was rejected by the Supreme Soviet. During debate of the bill, fears were expressed by many delegates that almost every enterprise in the country would fail the solvency test defined by the bankruptcy bill, and the result of implementing it would be the loss of millions of jobs. The legislators were unwilling to take on that responsibility.

Thus, Russia is still without comprehensive bankruptcy legislation. This fact becomes even more striking in light of the fact that less "progressive", smaller republics of the former Soviet Union, notably Ukraine, Belarus and Kazakhstan have all adopted bankruptcy legislation in the last year and a half.

Current Issues in Cross-Border Insolvency and Reorganisations (E. B. Leonard, C. W. Besant, eds.; 1–85333–958–X; © International Bar Association; pub. Graham & Trotman/International Bar Association, 1994; printed in Great Britain), pp.191-203.

Therefore, in addition to discussing the current state of debtor-creditor law in Russia, this chapter will also review and compare the features of the bankruptcy legislation of these four former Soviet republics, in order to put Russian bankruptcy law in a current comparative context.

10.2 Bankruptcy legislation in four former Soviet Republics

(a) *Russia*: temporary legislation on bankruptcy, a presidential decree, was enacted 14 June 1992.
(b) *Kazakhstan*: the law on bankruptcy was passed 14 January 1992, and was effective as of February 1992.
(c) *Belarus*: the law on bankruptcy and insolvency was passed 30 May 1991.
(d) *Ukraine*: the law on bankruptcy was passed 14 May 1992.

It is surprising to observe the rather significant differences between the new bankruptcy legislation that has recently been adopted in these four former Soviet republics. In the past the four republics had mostly uniform law, and no law on bankruptcy, aside from rudimentary procedural guidelines on liquidating a state enterprise. Of course, in the past all four had the same state-controlled organisation of enterprises, and have to this day, an intertwined economy with inter-enterprise supply relationships and debt cutting across the borders of these four and the other 11 former republics.

Kazakhstan, the most Eastern of the four republics, has the most comprehensive and most "Western" bankruptcy legislation. This law was part of a larger package of legislation prepared with the advice of foreign, primarily English and American, advisers to the government of Kazakhstan, who advised on how to attract foreign investment in Kazakhstan's oil industry. While it is not nearly as detailed as some western bankruptcy codes the Kazakh law has most of the features of western bankruptcy law, and has an emphasis on winding-up businesses that are proved to be insolvent or bankrupt. The least comprehensive bankruptcy legislation, and most reminiscent of a socialist state-controlled system, is the newly-decreed temporary Russian decree on bankruptcy. As previously mentioned, the passage of a more comprehensive and stringent law was blocked by the Supreme Soviet prompted by fears that its adoption would result in massive unemployment. The insolvency test of "three months" inability to pay was felt to be too draconian, as it was perceived as a test that, if strictly enforced, would ensnare the majority of state enterprises.

Therefore, it was apparent by the end of May 1992, that passage of the legislation would be postponed, if not altogether blocked. Yet the International Monetary Fund was requiring bankruptcy legislation as one of the essential preconditions for providing its financial assistance package and membership to Russia. The result is a "decree" passed by President Yeltsin, virtually on the eve of his departure for the US and meetings with IMF officials in mid-June. In fact, the decree was published for the first time in the Russian press while President Yeltsin was in the US.

The Russian presidential decree, which sets out a "never-never plan" for reorganising companies, has been criticised in the press, and legal and government circles in Russia. The draft bankruptcy legislation is being redrafted, but has not yet been circulated for comments or reintroduced to the Supreme Soviet.

The new bankruptcy laws of Belarus and Ukraine fall somewhere in the middle of this spectrum. In particular, the law of Belarus seems to strike a middle ground with the introduction of a two-track procedure. It provides extensive creditor rights and a stringent procedure for winding-up insolvent companies in cases where there is adjudged to be fault, or no prospect for turning the debtor around financially. On the other hand, it provides flexibility and lots of time for reorganisation to those state enterprises that are adjudged to be capable of being reorganised and financially revived.

An outline of the essential features of the legislation in these four republics follows.

10.2.1 The Russian Bankruptcy Decree

The decree, adopted on 14 June is entitled "On Measures for Support and Recovery of Insolvent State Enterprises (Bankrupts) and Administration of Special Procedures Thereto". It is of a temporary nature, and is expressly stated to continue to be effective only pending the adoption of a law on bankruptcy.

Prior to the adoption of this decree, only government-instituted liquidation of a state enterprise was available as a means of dissolving an insolvent enterprise. The liquidation provisions were lacking in detail and difficult to invoke. requiring the consent of management, labour, staff and the government.

The new bankruptcy decree is closely tied to privatisation legislation and process which was commenced in Russia in July 1991. In the original Russian privatisation law of 3 July 1991, "liquidation" was stated to be one of the means of privatisation of a state enterprise. Although the other means of privatisation (corporatisation, auction or tender) had been extensively codified in subsequent regulation, the criteria or procedure for invoking liquidation and sell-off of the assets of a state enterprise had not been elaborated in the same fashion. The bankruptcy decree now achieves this goal.

The decree applies only to state enterprises, which are defined as all enterprises in which state ownership amounts to 50% or more of the equity. The stated purpose of the decree is to bring about the result that all state enterprises "which cannot honour their obligations to creditors or the [state] budget shall be proclaimed insolvent". The special liquidation procedures outlined in the decree will apply to bankrupt state enterprises, with a view to causing "state property assigned to state enterprises to be used efficiently".

The grounds for a declaration of bankruptcy being made are defined as:

(a) failure to meet liabilities to the [state] budget for three months;
(b) failure to meet the demands of companies or individuals with property claims against the enterprise within three months of the due date; [or]
(c) accumulation of debts exceeding double the value of assets of the enterprise.

Certainly, it is surprising to see a definition that allows debts to be double the value of assets, before insolvency can be declared. This rather lax definition was adopted to take into account the effects of inflation in Russia, where recently incurred debts will far exceed in stated value the book value of assets acquired before inflation began.

The adjudicator of whether a state enterprise will be declared bankrupt is to be the relevant privatisation (property management) authority. In Russia, there are three levels of state property: those administered on a nationwide level; those administered on the level of republics or autonomous regions within Russia; and those administered on the municipal or regional level. Privatisation authorities, named property management committees, have been set up across the country at each level to deal with privatisation of enterprises within their respective jurisdictions.

The bankruptcy process is commenced by presentation by a government ministry or state committee, a tax agency, a financial institution, bank or creditor of evidence of an enterprise's insolvency. The enterprise may itself commence bankruptcy proceedings. There is a mandatory obligation on tax and financial agencies, including banks, to report to the relevant state property management committee facts that constitute grounds for declaration of bankruptcy of a state enterprise. Conversely, it appears that ordinary creditors of an enterprise may have to exhaust all civil collection remedies against an enterprise before being able to commence bankruptcy proceedings. The report is presumably to be made in written sworn form although this is not detailed in the decree. Upon receipt of a report, the property management committee is to request and receive from the enterprise itself within one week information on the enterprise, including a full list of creditors and debtors, and the enterprise's most recent balance sheet. This information is to be reviewed by the committee, and will remain confidential unless a declaration of bankruptcy is subsequently made.

The refusal of an enterprise to provide such information shall result in an "unconditional declaration of such enterprise to be a bankrupt". Within one month of submission of information, the property management committee shall make a determination, resulting either in:

(a) a declaration that the enterprise is solvent (this is the case in event of an amicable settlement between the enterprise and its creditors); or
(b) a declaration that the enterprise is bankrupt, which shall constitute a decision to liquidate.

The enterprise may appeal a declaration of bankruptcy but the appeal does not suspend administration of liquidation procedures.

A bankrupt enterprise, immediately following the declaration of bankruptcy, passes under control of the property management committee which has made the declaration. The declaration is to be published and made known to the staff of the enterprise, the local council, and the anti-monopoly authority. The property management committee (including also ministry representatives, experts, creditors and enterprise staff), has a further one-month period within which to examine options for reorganisation of the enterprise, and its recovery. At the end of this period a recovery programme is to be adopted, consisting either of:

(a) transfer of the enterprise to independent management through competitive bidding; or
(b) the appointment of an administrative manager by the property management committee.

In the interim, the property committee is to secure the safe-keeping of the enterprise's property, its continued production, and the observance of the rights of its employees.

Only in very limited circumstances, if an enterprise has been stripped of its licence to engage in business, or if it is judged impossible to restore the solvency of the enterprise within a time period of as much as three years, shall a liquidation or asset sell-off process be invoked. In all other circumstances, a recovery programme is to be introduced.

The competitive bidding process for a candidate to implement the recovery programme is to be held within three weeks of the committee's decision to reorganise the enterprise. Bidding is instituted to find independent management and entrepreneurs who will compete for the right to use the enterprise for a term of six to 18 months. In doing so, they must guarantee that jobs will not be reduced by more than 30%, and undertake all obligations of the enterprise and all environmental safety obligations.

Foreigners are allowed to participate in the bidding process for bankrupt enterprises (an exception to the norm in the privatisation programme). Each bidder must make a deposit equal to 10% of the book value of the enterprise assets to secure its bid. The labour collective of the enterprise may bid on the same terms as others. The winner of the bidding process is the entrepreneur who has deposited the greatest pledge as financial guarantee for meeting liabilities of the enterprise.

If there are no bidders, or if the successful bidder fails to achieve recovery of the enterprise within the stipulated time, the enterprise shall be placed under direct management for a period of three to 12 months (or up to 18 months in the case of an agricultural enterprise). An administrative manager is to be appointed by the ministry with jurisdiction over the enterprise. The administrative manager may not be an official of the bankrupt enterprise and is accountable directly to the agency (ministry) that has appointed him and to the appropriate property management committee. He is to be paid pursuant to contract.

The successful bidder (or the appointed administrative manager) has the following rights during the period stipulated by the property management committee:

(a) to change the pattern of the enterprise's production;
(b) to appoint and dismiss employees, including managers, but not more than 30%;
(c) to manage property, including selling or pledging fixed and circulating assets (not buildings), provided that 80% of proceeds from such sale or pledge are used to cancel liabilities of the enterprise;
(d) to make decisions (together with the property management committee) to divide up the enterprise or convert it into a joint stock company;
(e) to manage production directly.

The property management committee may not interfere with day-to-day management of the enterprise while the bidder or administrative manager is in charge. The state is not liable for new obligations incurred by the enterprise during this period.

Within one week of expiry of the recovery period stipulated for the bidder or administrative manager, a report on the financial status of the bankrupt enterprise shall be submitted to the property management committee by the bidder or administrative manager. If the report establishes that measures to salvage an enterprise have not resulted in its recovery and that the grounds of bankruptcy remain, then (and only then) shall liquidation be commenced. The bidder for an enterprise that has not been successfully recovered shall lose its pledge, the proceeds of which shall be used to pay creditors of the enterprise.

If, on the other hand, recovery has taken place, the appropriate property management committee is to terminate the status of bankruptcy and the bidder who has salvaged the bankrupt enterprise becomes its owner. The bidder's equity is stated to consist of funds invested in the course of the recovery period, together with any profits, minus existing enterprise liabilities. The bidder's pledge is to be returned and used to increase equity in property of the enterprise. Likewise, an administrative manager who has salvaged an enterprise shall receive a bonus (paid from the enterprise) equal to 20 months' wages, and may be appointed director of the enterprise.

Liquidation and expungement from the state register of an enterprise will take place in the rare cases where recovery is not attempted, or (as will probably be more likely) if recovery under competitive bid conditions or an appointed administrative manager fails. There is an additional stipulation that enterprises which are put into bankruptcy a second time within one year of the first failure of a recovery plan will be liquidated.

In the event of liquidation, a liquidation commission is to be formed, including representatives of the enterprise's labour collective. Creditors are to submit claims within two months of announcement of liquidation, and a sale of the enterprise is to take place through competitive bidding, with terms of bidding to include:

(a) acquisition of the enterprise as whole;
(b) assumption of obligations of same; *and*
(c) assumption of obligations to ensure social guarantees.

Terms may also include:

● obligation to preserve primary form of business;
● preservation of at least 70% of jobs.

Only if these terms are not met in competitive bidding shall piecemeal sale of assets take place. Bidders in a liquidation sale must deposit a pledge equal to 50% of initial (book value) price of the enterprise, and if there is only one bidder, the sale will take place at the initial price. The sale proceeds from the liquidation auction are to be used to cancel obligations of the enterprise to the budget to meet creditors' claims to make payments to enterprise employees, and to pay costs of attempted recovery programmes. There are no provisions in the decree that provide for what payments will be made in the event there are not sufficient funds generated by the sale to pay off all claims in full. There is no attempt to classify creditors, and no statement that funds will be distributed on a pro rata basis.

Employees are guaranteed at least three months' wages in the piecemeal sale of property of an enterprise. Presumably, this obligation would be met out of the state budget, if there were not sufficient funds generated by the sale.

(a) Comments on the Russian Decree
In conclusion, there are many obvious deficiencies in the Russian Bankruptcy Decree. Creditors' rights are not specifically protected (in fact are harmed by the extensive recovery plan proposals), nor is their participation in the decision-making process provided for. There is no distinction or classification of creditors claims except for the provisions safeguarding jobs in the enterprise and ensuring severance payments if the enterprise is finally liquidated.

There is no clearly defined test or statement of what constitutes "recovery" under a competitive bidding programme or administrative manager. Even assuming that bidders do indeed bring about the successful recovery of an enterprise, their rights then to assume ownership and the conditions under which they shall do so are not set out in enough detail.

The enterprise has a seemingly endless stream of obligations, through two recovery periods, into a liquidation auction where bidders are once again sought to assume obligations and continuation of the enterprise.

The Decree seems to depend to an unrealistic degree on recovery programmes for these enterprises, and in particular ignores once again the advice already given by foreign advisers that insolvent or failed companies carrying with them obligations to maintain the workforce, will not be attractive to foreign investors.

The exact conditions and procedures (eg, reporting obligations and fiduciary duties for administrative managers) are not stipulated, but are left to be governed by individual contract. This will probably result in much uncertainty and abuse of management powers, as has already been apparent in other areas, for example in the early land purchase and privatisation attempts. Finally, the Decree is too limited in its application. It ignores the fact that joint ventures have now been in existence for almost five years and joint stock companies for two years, and that consequently, there are already a considerable number of private enterprises. Some of these enterprises are failing with no efficient mechanism for creditors or deadlocked partners to bring them to an end. These deficiencies become even more glaring when comparison is made to legislation already passed by other emerging independent states which were part of Soviet Union.

10.2.2 The Kazakhstan Bankruptcy Law

The scope of the Kazakh Bankruptcy Law is broader than the Russian decree, as it extends to individuals, any enterprises, both state and private, and banks. In contrast to the Russian Decree, the adjudicator of bankruptcy under the Kazakh Law is the court or arbitration tribunal with jurisdiction where the debtor's assets are located.

Grounds for bankruptcy are defined as "a persistent inability of the debtor, in view of a shortage of financial resources, to satisfy in time his creditors' claims and perform his obligations with respect to the state budget". The bankruptcy process may be commenced either by petition of the debtor, or a suit filed by a creditor. A creditor's petition must show proof that three months have elapsed after the due date of the debt, and that the debt is undisputed by the debtor.

As with the Russian Decree, the initial burden is placed on the debtor to provide full information regarding debts and assets. If the debtor fails to do so, the court may appoint a trustee to gather such information and charge the expense to the debtor. The claims of creditors are to be proved by supporting documents and verified by affidavit. The Law provides that once the bankruptcy process is commenced, a petition may not be withdrawn without leave of court, and that any settlement offered by the debtor to creditors must be approved by court.

With respect to state enterprises or banks, if the relevant property management committee or bank authority provides a guarantee to creditors, the court may grant a stay of proceedings in order to continue with rehabilitation of the debtor. However, in contrast to the Russian Decree, once a declaration of bankruptcy has been made by the court or arbitration tribunal, liquidation is the mandatory procedure to be followed, and will proceed through to a sale of assets.

The only remaining exception to mandatory liquidation is an amicable settlement proposed by the debtor which must provide for payment in full of all employee claims, damage claims and other similar claims enumerated in the class of top priority creditors, payment in full of all tax and state budget claims, and settlement terms acceptable to the majority of all remaining creditors. Such a settlement is additionally subject to the approval of the court. It may be nullified if a creditor subsequently proves that full disclosure was not made by the debtor. The liquidation of a bankrupt enterprise is to be conducted by trustee who is to be assisted by valuators in making a valuation of the debtor's assets. A creditors' committee is given the right to participate at all stages in the administration of the liquidation. Creditors and the debtor as well may appeal decisions of the trustee to the court which appointed the trustee. (In the Russian Decree, the right of appeal is ensured only for the debtor, and participation is ensured only for members of the enterprise labour collective.)

The trustee is given discretion to decide upon the timing and method of selling off the debtor's assets, provided notice of sale reaches the largest possible number of interested purchasers.

In administering distribution of the proceeds of liquidation, the trustee is to adhere to a scheme of distribution that differentiates between classes of creditors. Each class must receive compensation in full for its claims before distributions will be made (on a pro rata basis, if necessary) to the succeeding class of creditors.

Priorities are established as follows:

- *1st priority*: employee claims, damage claims, alimony claims, lawyers' claims for unpaid legal fees;
- *2nd priority*: state and local taxes, state budget payments, social insurance claims;
- *3rd priority*: secured creditors' claims, with bank secured claims taking precedence over other secured creditors in this class;
- *4th priority*: unsecured creditors' claims;
- *5th priority*: labour collective members' equity share claims; *and*
- *6th priority*: all other claims.

Once a sale of assets has occurred, an individual debtor shall be free and clear of debts and shall be discharged by the court, except in cases where he concealed property or essential information, or transferred a portion of his property to other persons within a year of the bankruptcy. A bankrupt enterprise will be struck off the state register once its assets have been distributed, and the trustee's report filed with the court.

(a) Comments on the Kazakhstan Law

This law is much more creditor friendly than the Russian Decree, and provides procedures to deal with failing enterprises. While proposals and amicable settlements are allowed, there are the safeguards of court supervision, and guaranteed payment of priority claims, before an enterprise will be allowed to continue. The state or bank authority may decide to intervene to save a state enterprise or bank, but must undertake the obligations of the enterprise or bank to other creditors in order to obtain a stay or deferment of the liquidation process.

In providing that private enterprises and individual debtors may avail themselves of the bankruptcy process, the Law is forward-looking, and provides a greater degree of certainty that there will be some established method of dealing with the failure of private businesses.

Of course, it remains to be seen how the Law will be enforced by the courts, whether professional trustees will develop, and whether creditors will avail themselves of legal protection. It is still too early to tell whether this western-inspired law will correspond to the realities in Kazakhstan.

10.2.3 The Belorussian Law on Economic Insolvency and Bankruptcy

The Bankruptcy Law in Belarus applies to all "subjects of economic activity", which are further defined to be state and private enterprises, and business partnerships, but not individuals. It thus falls between the Russian and Kazakh laws in the breadth of its jurisdiction.

Grounds for a declaration of bankruptcy are stated to be "an inability to pay debts on a current basis", an excess of debts over assets (this is stricter than the Russian Decree), or the debtor's own admission of insolvency. The courts of justice adjudicate and administer the bankruptcy law.

Once a petition is submitted by a creditor or the debtor itself, the court is obliged to appoint an expert to conduct an examination of the financial and economic performance of the debtor. "Experts" may include officials of the relevant committee for state property management, a person agreed upon by the parties (presumably the debtor and creditors), or an expert appointed by the court. The expert is to analyse the financial condition of the debtor, verify the validity of creditors' claims, and establish the cause of insolvency. He shall submit a report to the court, including an opinion and, if justified in his opinion, a plan for settling claims against the debtor.

A unique feature of this legislation is that it makes a distinction between "insolvency" and "complete insolvency", provides workout options for the former case and requires liquidation in the latter.

In the case of a creditor-initiated insolvency, the expert's report may propose priorities in satisfying claims, deferment of claims for up to one year, elaborate on pro rata payments to creditors, and measures to reorganise the debtor's business. More leeway is allowed in debtor-initiated insolvencies, where the plan may additionally include longer deferments (up to three years), provide for loans from special economic risk funds and for adoption of the debtor's own plan to settle creditors' claims.

Following receipt of the expert's report, the court will schedule a hearing of the bankruptcy petition. The court may make a determination on the claims of creditors and may reject claims as invalid. It may also award damages to the debtor against the creditor for "moral and material loss" if false claims have been submitted. Even if the creditors' claims are recognised, the court, in cases where the insolvency is determined to have been caused by objective reasons and is adjudged to be temporary in nature, may defer fulfilment of liabilities.

The court is also granted jurisdiction to "invalidate, terminate, or postpone the performance of economic agreements which have brought the debtor to insolvency".

This presumably could be used to invalidate contracts whose terms were highly unfavourable to former state enterprises, for example obligations to sell to the state at artificially low prices. If the court finds fault on behalf of the debtor or determines that the business cannot be carried on under changed economic conditions, it may order liquidation. The court may order a stay of liquidation for up to one year, provided that the debtor posts a deposit in an amount fixed by the court.

The court therefore has wide discretion in determining whether a debtor enterprise shall be granted a stay or allowed time to rehabilitate. However, once liquidation has been determined to be necessary, the law clearly provides that the prevailing principle is to be "the maximum possible satisfaction of the claims of creditors through the liquidation of insolvent companies".

To carry out liquidation, the court appoints a trustee ("a person or entity licensed to carry out this kind of work"). In the course of proceeding with liquidation, the court may be called upon to adjudicate on fraudulent transactions and preferences, and may invalidate "deals made within a year of the start of bankruptcy proceedings, with the aim of concealing property or avoiding payment of debts" and "[deals in which the debtor] has received considerably less than the economically justified price of property".

Creditors' rights are expressly provided for and include rights to be represented in court at all stages of the proceedings, to receive information, to oversee the trustees, and to appeal actions of the trustee to court. Two-thirds of the creditors must approve the liquidation plan.

As with the Kazakhstan law, the Belorussian law provides for priorities amongst the bankruptcy claimants, although the order of priorities is somewhat different:

- *1st priority*: secured creditors;
- *2nd priority*: wage claims, experts' fees and other costs of the bankruptcy;
- *3rd priority*: contractual obligations to pay for goods, work or services received by the enterprise, fines and penalties, taxes and state budgetary obligations;
- *4th priority*: unsecured bond and securities obligations and bank liabilities;
- *5th priority*: commitments to shareholders and partners; *and*
- *6th priority*: other obligations.

All sales of assets in the liquidation process must take place through public tender.

(a) Comments on the Belorussian Law

This Law, with its equal emphasis on reorganisation of debtor enterprises and deferment of claims if there are "objective" reasons for insolvency, and its provision for liquidation if not, attempts to strike a balance between the pressures that caused the Russian Parliament to balk from adopting a real bankruptcy law and the need to ensure creditor protection which is the focus of the western laws and the advice received from western advisers.

The law is notable for the broad powers given to the courts to award damages against creditors submitting invalid claims, to invalidate fraudulent conveyances and preferences and to cancel onerous contracts. Creditors' rights are protected. Trustees are established as administrators of the system. It should prove effective, and to date (it has been enacted for more than a year) has not resulted in a catastrophic flood of state enterprise failures.

10.2.4 The Ukrainian Law on Bankruptcy

The Law of Ukraine on Bankruptcy, passed on 14 May 1992 applies to legal business entities, both public and private. It is specifically stated not to apply to mortgage creditors, although this appears to be contradicted later by the inclusion of secured creditors as a class for distribution.

The grounds for a declaration of bankruptcy are the most stringent of the four republics under discussion, for debts that remain unpaid for more than one month may form the basis of a bankruptcy petition. This is the standard test that is applied in western jurisdictions, for example in Canada.

The arbitration courts are to administer enforcement of the Bankruptcy Law, and (as with Kazakhstan), must approve of the withdrawal of any petition or any compromise proposal.

Within one month of the bankruptcy process being commenced and publication in the press, the creditors must submit all claims and shall meet at a creditors' assembly at the end of the one month period to form a committee of creditors. If proposals are to be made, they must likewise be submitted within the one month period for the submission of claims.

The Law envisages that there may be proposals from related industries or creditors to assume or partially guarantee the liabilities of the debtor enterprise, and to thus gain control of its management and reorganisation. The labour collective of the debtor enterprise has the right to lease the assets of enterprise where it has been petitioned into bankruptcy, provided they assume the debts of the enterprise. This form of organisation, the "employee leasehold enterprise", has been one of the forms of quasi-privatisation that has flourished in Russia, and apparently in Ukraine in the past few years.

The Law provides that if such a proposal is forthcoming from either the labour collective or another entity which will step into the shoes of the debtor enterprise and assume its obligations, the court may discontinue the bankruptcy proceedings. Otherwise, the court will make a declaration of bankruptcy, and liquidation ensues.

In a liquidation, the liquidation committee is to be appointed by the court, drawing on representatives of the creditors' assembly, financial institutions, and the fund for state property if the debtor is a state enterprise. The liquidation committee discontinues any business activity of the debtor, and arranges for the sale of the debtor's assets. In the course of liquidation, the court has power to review transactions and to recognise as invalid any agreement for the sale of debtor property executed within three months before institution of bankruptcy proceedings, if it was executed in pursuance of the interests of the debtor.

Distribution of proceeds of liquidation is to be carried our in accordance with a priorities classification, as follows:

- *1st priority*: payment of bankruptcy expenses and claims of secured creditors (mortgage bonds);
- *2nd priority*: employee obligations;
- *3rd priority*: local taxes, social insurance;
- *4th priority*: ordinary creditors;
- *5th priority*: employee equity claims; *and*
- *6th priority*: other claims.

(a) Comments on the Ukrainian Law

This Law is similar to the Belorussian Law in that it tries to protect employee inter-ests and allow for reorganisation of state enterprises. One drawback, however, is that it is not as detailed and comprehensive as the Belorussian Law, with the reorganisa-tion provisions in particular being very general. It is also perhaps unrealistic to place reliance on other companies stepping forward to guarantee the liabilities of insolvent enterprises, in circumstances where their rights to control the business are not well defined.

10.3 Other developments in Russian debtor-creditor law

Although 1992/93 has not seen the introduction, as expected, of comprehensive bankruptcy law in Russia, on 29 May 1992, the long-awaited Law on Pledges was implemented.

The Law defines the concept of pledge as the right of a creditor to be satisfied out of the value of pledged property in priority to other creditors. It provides that pledges may secure:

> "any valid obligation, specifically a loan agreement, a banking loan, a contract of sale, a lease contract, a contract for the carriage of goods, and other contracts."

The security, or object of a pledge is not well defined, being stated as "items, secur-ities, and other property and property rights". It is understood to cover real property rights, rights to buildings, equipment, inventory, work in progress, choses in action, bonds, securities and other property rights.

The scope of a pledge extends to securing obligations to be incurred in future to a particular creditor (ie credit lines). As well, the law specifically provides that after-acquired property of the debtor may be pledged. The validity of the pledge is stated to be dependent on the validity of the indebtedness secured by the pledge. There are two types of pledged property outlined by the law: that remaining in property of the debtor; and that transferred to a creditor (pawned property).

There are requirements governing the content and form of a pledge, requiring that it be in writing and sworn before a notary public. Pledge contracts concerning land or buildings located in Russia, rolling stock, civilian aircraft, ships and space objects registered in Russia are to be governed by, and must comply with, the Russian Law of Pledges.

State registration of a pledge contract is mandatory with respect to pledges of property that is itself subject to state registration (eg, land and buildings). Registration is to take place at the state organ which registers the subject of the pledge. The procedure is not elaborated in further detail.

Additionally, an obligation is imposed on legal entities to keep a "pledge book" listing all pledges entered into by the legal entity. Damages may be awarded against an entity which fails to meet this obligation. The Law provides that recovery on the pledged property is to be governed by the individual pledge contract. While the Law stipulates that excess proceeds from sale of collateral are to be returned to the debtor, it does not elaborate a duty of care to be imposed on the secured creditor in realising on the pledged property. Security rights over pledged collateral continue in force upon transfer of collateral, with or without notice to the transferee or the creditor.

The new Law on Pledges provides a much greater degree of certainty than the Civil Code provisions which it supersedes, and should encourage more lending. There has been great reluctance to date, especially on the part of foreign financial institutions, in part owing to the practical impossibility of enforcing secured property rights. In the future, more guidelines for realisation on security, state registration of security over assets such as work in progress, inventory, equipment, and accounts receivable, and guidelines for resolution of conflicts between competing secured creditors will have to be enacted. In the meantime, this Law represents a step in the right direction, and should give much-needed assurance and increased security to both domestic and foreign lenders.

In conclusion, I would hope that as 1992/93 has seen the introduction of pledge law after two years of debate and revisions, that the next year will see the adoption of urgently needed bankruptcy legislation in Russia, perhaps following the precedents that have been established in 1992 by Belarus, Kazakhstan and Ukraine. If implementation of their bankruptcy laws does not prove to be too catastrophic to the economy of those countries, perhaps Russia will follow suit.

11

Shareholder Liability, Consolidation and Pooling

Christopher K. Grierson[1]
Lovell White Durrant, London and New York

In this chapter, two related areas are examined:

(a) the circumstances in which the English courts will render a holding company liable for the debts of its subsidiary; *and*

(b) the comparison between the US law of "substantive consolidation" and the legal basis on which the English courts will permit the assets and liabilities of related corporations to be "pooled". A recent example of "pooling" is the liquidation of Bank of Credit and Commerce ("BCCI") and this case will be examined by reference to decisions of the English courts.

11.1 Shareholder liability

The notion of separate legal corporate personality has been the cornerstone of modern English company law since the decision of the House of Lords in *Salomon v Salomon & Co*[2] and both the courts and Parliament have generally proved reluctant to derogate from the principle. The general attitude of the courts has been that it is appropriate to "pierce the corporate veil" only when special circumstances exist.

In 1844, Parliament enacted the first general Companies Act ("an Act for the Registration, Incorporation and Regulation of Joint Stock Companies") under which any company with transferable shares or comprising more than 25 members could obtain incorporation by registering a deed of settlement executed by its members containing the provisions set out in the Act. At that time, however, the "members" (ie shareholders) of the company could not escape or limit liability for its debts and contractual or other obligations. Although creditors of the company could not sue the shareholders personally, any judgment creditor of the company could, with the leave

[1]The author is an English solicitor and a partner in Lovell White Durrant, based at the firm's New York office.
[2][1897] AC 22.

Current Issues in Cross-Border Insolvency and Reorganisations (E. B. Leonard, C. W. Besant, eds.; 1–85333–958–X; © International Bar Association; pub. Graham & Trotman/International Bar Association, 1994; printed in Great Britain), pp. 205-231.

of the court, levy execution of a judgment against the company on the private property of any shareholder. In 1855, Parliament passed the Limited Liability Act whereby any company registered under the Act of 1844 could limit the liability of its shareholders for debts and obligations generally to the amount unpaid on their shares. This could only be done if the company adopted the word "Limited" as the last word of its name and satisfied certain other requirements. In 1856, Parliament passed the Joint Stock Companies Act which repealed the Acts of 1844 and 1855 and it made it possible for any company with seven or more shareholders to obtain incorporation and limited liability. The Act of 1856 was ultimately repealed and replaced by the Companies Act 1862 which has been amended by numerous subsequent Acts.

Just before the turn of the century, the House of Lords had to consider the issue of limited liability in *Salomon v Salomon & Co.*[3]

Salomon carried on business as a leather merchant and boot manufacturer. He wished to form a limited company to purchase his business but also to retain control over the conduct of that business. The shareholders of the company were Salomon and members of his family. The company was formed and he and six other members of his family became shareholders. He and two of his sons were appointed directors. A contract for the sale of his business to the company was entered into and completed. The business did not do well and when it was wound up a year later its liabilities exceeded its assets by £7,733. The liquidator claimed that the company's business was in reality still Salomon's, the company merely being a sham designed to limit Salomon's liability for debts and that Salomon should be ordered to indemnify the company against its debts. The trial judge found in favour of the liquidator. He held that the subscribers of the memorandum other than Salomon (ie the other shareholders who were members of his family), held their shares as mere nominees for him, and that Salomon's only purpose in forming the company was to run his business for him. The Court of Appeal also found in favour of the liquidator but on a different basis. Lord Justice Lopes held:

> "It was never intended that the company to be constituted should consist of one substantial person and six mere dummies, the nominees of that person, without any real interest in the company. The Act contemplated the incorporation of seven independent *bona fide* members, who had a mind and a will of their own, and were not the mere puppets of an individual who, adopting the machinery of the Act, carried on his old business in the same way as before, when he was a sole trader."[4]

Consequently, it was held that Salomon had incorporated the company for an unlawful purpose and that he was obliged to indemnify the company as a consequence of the formation of it with a view to obtaining a result not permitted by law.

The House of Lords unanimously reversed the decisions of the previous two courts and held that Salomon had no liabilities to the company or its creditors. Lord Halsbury, the then Lord Chancellor, held:

[3]*Ibid.*
[4][1895] 2 Ch 323 at p. 341.

"I must pause here to point out that the statute enacts nothing as to the extent or degree of interest which may be held by each of the seven [subscribers of the memorandum], or as to the proportion of interest or influence possessed by one or the majority of the shareholders over the others. One share is enough. Still less is it possible to contend that the motive of becoming shareholders or of making them shareholders is a field of enquiry which the statute itself recognises as legitimate. If they are shareholders, they are shareholders for all purposes; and even if the statute was silent as to the recognition of trusts, I should be prepared to hold that if six of them were the *cestuis que* trust of the seventh, whatever might be their rights *inter se*, the statute would have made them shareholders to all intents and purposes with their respective rights and liabilities, and, dealing with them in their relation to the company, the only relations which I believe the law would sanction would be that they were corporators of the corporate body."[5]

Lord Herschell observed:

"In a popular sense, a company may in every case be said to carry on business for and on behalf of its shareholders; but this certainly does not in point of law constitute the relation of principal and agent between them or render the shareholders liable to indemnify the company against the debts which it incurs."[6]

The principles decided in *Salomon* have endured, subject to the limited departure described below, for almost 100 years.

In 1985, in *Williams & Humbert Ltd v W. H. Trade Marks*[7] the Court of Appeal approved the principle that:

"... it is appropriate to pierce the corporate veil only when special circumstances exist that establish that the corporation is a mere facade concealing the facts."[8]

There are nonetheless some examples in case law and statute where, notwithstanding the principle of *Salomon*, the courts and Parliament have shown themselves willing to lift or, rather look behind, the veil of incorporation. The statutory exceptions are referred to later in this chapter.

The discussion of the case law that follows provides an insight into the legal theories which the courts have used to mitigate the rigours of the approach in *Salomon*.

It is not possible to lay down specific rules as to the circumstances in which the court will "lift the corporate veil", so as to regard two associated companies as one entity nor, notwithstanding remarks to the contrary in a number of textbooks, can an increasing tendency of the courts to lift the veil be identified. It seems, however, that there must be two elements before the court will even consider the issue:

(a) there must be some reason why the companies should as a matter of public policy be regarded as one entity; *and*
(b) there must be the fact of unity of control.

The expression "to pierce the corporate veil", although frequently used, is not in fact a term of art nor is it descriptive of any cause of action. The phrase is used in different senses to describe widely differing circumstances in which the court will look behind the corporate form to attribute status, acts, rights or liabilities to those who manage

[5][1897] AC 22 at p. 30.
[6]*Ibid* at p. 43.
[7][1985] 2 All ER 619.
[8]*Ibid* at p. 628.

or control the corporate entity. In some cases, such attribution has been to their advantage although more often to their disadvantage.

Cases in which the courts are willing to pierce the corporate veil to hold the controllers of a company liable for the acts or debts of the company fall into two groups: fraud and agency.

11.1.1 Fraud

It is well established that the courts will not allow "artificial" corporate entities to be used for the purposes of fraud, or as a device to evade a contractual or other legal obligation in circumstances amounting to fraud. Thus in *Gilford Motor Co Limited v Horne*,[9] Horne had covenanted with the appellant company not to solicit its customers after he had left its employment. On ceasing his employment, Horne formed a company to carry on a competing business and this company started to solicit the appellant's customers. The court granted an injunction to enforce the convenant against both Horne and the company he had formed to conduct his activities. The company was described in the judgment as "a device, a strategem," and a "cloak or a sham".[10]

A recent example can be found in the decision of the court in *Creasey v Breachwood Motors Limited*.[11]

Creasey worked for Breachwood Welwyn Limited ("Welwyn") which carried on the business of a garage trading in cars and other vehicles. Breachwood Motors Limited ("Motors") carried on similar businesses at other premises. Both Welwyn and Motors were controlled by the same persons. Creasey was the general manager of, and was summarily dismissed by Welwyn. He issued a writ against Welwyn claiming damages for wrongful dismissal. Welwyn then ceased trading and the next day Motors took over its business. Motors took over all the assets of Welwyn and paid all its debts but without making any provision for Creasey's claim if that were to succeed. After Creasey had obtained judgment in default against Welwyn, Welwyn was struck off the register as defunct and dissolved and Creasey then obtained an order substituting Motors as defendants which Motors appealed. Creasey argued, *inter alia*, that the judge should lift the corporate veil and not let the persons controlling Motors take the benefit of Welwyn's business by means of the informal transfer of the business and all of Welwyn's assets to Motors, leaving Creasey with a claim against a defendant with no assets.

The judge dismissed Motors' appeal and held that it was a case in which the court would be justified in lifting the veil and treating Motors as liable for the remaining liability of Welwyn.

The judge referred to the decision of the Court of Appeal in *Gilford Motor Co Limited v Horne*[12] and also to the judgment of the Court of Appeal in *Re a Company*.[13] In that case, as summarised by the judge in *Creasy*:

"The evidence established that the defendant [Dr Wallersteiner] had created a network of English and foreign companies and trusts through which he could dispose of his English

[9][1933] Ch 935.
[10]*Ibid* at p. 956.
[11][1992] BCC 638.
[12]*See* n. 9.
[13][1985] 1 BCC 99, 421.

assets and, when the insolvency of the plaintiffs was imminent and after the alleged fraud had been committed, he had used this network to dispose of his assets. In these circumstances the court would pierce the corporate veil in order to achieve justice and accordingly the order pertaining to the foreign companies and trusts was proper, subject to the limitation that it was restricted to those companies and trusts over which the defendant exercised substantial or effective control."[14]

The judge then referred to the judgment delivered by Lord Justice Cumming-Bruce:

"In our view the cases before and after *Wallersteiner v Moir* [1974] 1 WLR 991, CA show that the court will use its powers to pierce the corporate veil if it is necessary to achieve justice irrespective of the legal efficacy of the corporate structure under consideration. As Lord Denning MR said ([1974] 1 WLR 991 at p. 1013) the companies there identified were distinct legal entities and the principles of *Salomon v Salomon & Co Ltd* [1897] AC 22, HL *prima facie* applied. But only prima facie. On the facts of the Wallersteiner case, the companies danced to Dr Wallersteiner's bidding."[15]

It should be noted that, just as the courts may lift the corporate veil to prevent the promoters from perpetrating a fraud, they will not do so in order to assist them from escaping its consequences. In *R v Arthur*,[16] where a director, charged with fraudulent conversion of company property, claimed that he had acted with the consent of his co-director with whom he had shared the spoils and that the two of them and their wives were the only members, it was held that this was no defence as the company was a separate legal entity.

Another recent example is *Attorney-General's Reference (Number 2)*[17] where the two defendants were directors and sole shareholders of numerous companies and were charged with appropriating the company's funds for their own private use contrary to the Theft Act 1968. The evidence showed that they procured the companies to borrow large sums of money which they then applied for their own personal and extravagant expenditure. At the trial the judge ruled that there was no case to answer since the defendants as sole shareholders were in effect the company and could not be guilty of stealing from themselves. This decision was unanimously reversed by the Court of Appeal. Lord Justice Kerr held:

"... we do not consider that anything in *Salomon v A. Salomon & Co Ltd* [1897] AC 22 assists the defendants. One of the issues decided in that case can be summarised as follows: Where a solvent company enters into a transaction (in that case with one of the shareholders) with the knowledge and consent of all the shareholders and directors, all acting honestly and then becomes insolvent, the liquidator cannot subsequently seek to have the transaction set aside on the ground that it was fraud upon the company, or the shareholders, or the company's creditors. A similar conclusion was recently reached by a majority of the civil division of this court in *Multinational Gas and Petrochemical Co v Multinational Gas and Petrochemical Services Limited* [1983] Ch 258 ... However, neither *Salomon v A. Salomon & Co Limited* [1897] AC 22 nor the *Multinational Gas* case were concerned with allegations that the shareholders and directors had acted illegally or dishonestly in relation to the company. Where this is alleged the position is different ..."[18]

---

[14][1992] BCC at p. 646.
[15]*Ibid.*
[16][1967] Crim LR 298.
[17][1984] 1 QB 624.
[18]*Ibid* at p. 640.

11.1.2 Agency

Two basic propositions of the English law of agency are that:

(a) a person is liable for his engagements (and for his torts) even though he acts for another, unless he can show by the law of agency he is to be held to have expressly or impliedly negatived his personal liability by naming his principal as the person to be responsible; *and*

(b) an agent is entitled to an indemnity from his principal for liabilities incurred by him in execution of his authority.

If, therefore, a company carries on its business as agent for another company then, under English law, the parent could be liable to indemnify the subsidiary for the liabilities incurred. If the subsidiary were to go into liquidation, the parent could be liable to indemnify it for the net deficiency. Such a consequence does not involve disregarding the separate corporate status of the subsidiary, nor is it inconsistent with the principles of the *Multinational* case referred to below.

There is a right to such an indemnity under English law not only in a true agency situation (ie where a party acts for the disclosed or undisclosed principal entitled to intervene to enforce a contract for its own benefit) but in a case where a party enters into a contract as principal on the instructions of another for the purpose of benefiting that other, and thus acts as a mandatory. For example, a bank that on the instructions of a buyer of goods issues a letter of credit to the seller acts as principal; so far as the contract created by the letter of credit is concerned the buyer is not even an undisclosed principal. But the bank has entered into its contractual undertaking on the instructions of and for the benefit of the buyer so that the relationship between them is that of principal and agent and the bank is entitled to be indemnified against its liability. It is not necessary that the agency should be express.

> "...there is no reason why, in fact, a company should not act as an agent of its shareholders. Where there is an express agreement to this effect, no difficulty arises. But this will be a rare occurrence. More often the courts will be asked to infer an agency relationship and *Salomon's* case shows how difficult it will be to persuade them to draw this inference. Nevertheless, they have always shown less reluctance to do so where the inference they are asked to draw is that a subsidiary company has acted as agent for its holding company."[19]

The traditional view is that the mere fact that one company is the subsidiary of another, even a wholly owned subsidiary, is not of itself sufficient to make the subsidiary an agent of the holding company or to regard the two as one single entity.

The courts appear to be more ready to find the existence of an agency from evidence, which would not otherwise be sufficient, if the holding company owns all, or substantially all, of the subsidiary's shares. In *Firestone Tyre and Rubber Co Ltd v Lewellin*[20] it was the extent of the holding company's shareholding in the subsidiary that finally persuaded the court to lift the corporate veil.

In some cases the courts have found that, even in the absence of express agreement, there was an arrangement between the shareholders and a company so as to constitute the company the shareholders' agent for the purposes of carrying on the

---

[19]Gower, *Principles of Modern Company Law* (4th ed.), p. 123.
[20][1956] 1 All ER 693.

business and therefore to make the business that of the shareholders. In *Smith, Stone & Knight Ltd v Lord Mayor, Alderman and Citizens of the City of Birmingham*,[21] where a company acquired a partnership concern and, having registered it as a company, continued to carry on the acquired business as a subsidiary company, the profits of the new company were treated by the corporators as profits of the parent company and that company appointed the persons who conducted the business and were in effectual and constant control. It was held by the court that the subsidiary was not operating on its own behalf but on behalf of the parent company and that the profits of the subsidiary should properly be treated as those of the parent. The six relevant factors were determined to be the following:

(a) were profits of the subsidiary treated as profits of the parent?
(b) were the persons conducting the business appointed by the parent company?
(c) was the parent company the head and brain of the trading enterprise?
(d) did the parent govern the enterprise, decide what should be done and what capital should be invested in it?
(e) did the parent make the profits of the subsidiary by its skill and direction?
(f) was the parent company in effectual and constant control?

Notwithstanding the decision in *Smith Stone & Knight Ltd*, there is a strong presumption under English law that companies within a group are separate legal entities. More recently, however, increased attention has focused on situations involving subsidiary companies where the courts have been willing to treat a subsidiary company as an agent of the holding company and conducting the latter's business for it.

In *Littlewoods Mail Order Stores v IRC*,[22] the taxpayer company held a 99-year lease at an annual rent of £23,444. When the lease had 88 years to run it was surrendered for a lease of 22 years 10 days at a refund of £6 per year. The company assigned that lease to a wholly-owned subsidiary which granted an underlease for 22 years at a rent of £43,450 per annum. The subsidiary then assigned the headlease to the owner of the freehold and received the freehold reversion. It was claimed that the whole of the £42,450 was deductible as an expense of trade. The Court of Appeal held that the additional payments of £19,000 (the difference in rents under the original lease and underlease) were designed to acquire a capital asset and were not deductible. Counsel for the company argued that the subsidiary was to be treated as a separate entity. Lord Denning M. R., in declining to do so, said:

> "The doctrine laid down in *Salomon v Salomon & Co* has to be watched very carefully. It has often been supposed to cast a veil over the personality of a limited company through which the courts cannot see. But this is not true. The courts can and often do draw aside the veil. They can, and often do, pull off the mask. They look to see what really lies behind. The legislature has shown the way with group accounts and the rest. And the courts should follow suit. I think that we should look at [the subsidiary] and see it as it really is — the wholly-owned subsidiary of [the parent company]. It is the creature, the puppet, of [the parent company], in point of *fact*: and it should be so regarded in point of *law*."[23]

[21][1939] 4 All ER 116.
[22][1969] 1 WLR 1241.
[23]*Ibid* at p. 1254.

In a later case, *DHN Food Distributors Ltd v Tower Hamlets London Borough Council*,[24] Lord Denning expressed an equally broad view of the circumstances in which a court may lift the corporate veil. He said:

> "We all know in many respects a group of companies are treated together for the purpose of general accounts, balance sheet, and profit and loss account. They are treated as one concern. Professor Gower in *Modern Company Law* (3rd ed. 1969), p. 216 says: 'There is evidence of a general tendency to ignore the separate legal entities of various companies within a group, and to look instead at the economic entity of the whole group.'"[25]

The judgment of Lord Denning in that case has to be tempered by more cautious judgments delivered by other members of the Court of Appeal, which show that Professor Gower's "general tendency" may be more apparent than real. The expansive view of the willingness of the courts to lift the corporate veil was not shared by Lord Denning's colleagues in the *Littlewoods* case where Lord Justice Sachs said:

> "...at one stage it seemed as if the Crown might be on the verge of seeking to erode the principle that for tax purposes every company, whether it be a subsidiary or not, has its own separate legal identity.......Any attempt, however, thus to erode that important principle was firmly disclaimed by [Counsel] who without qualification agreed that [the subsidiary] and [the parent] were separate entities for the purposes of tax legislation; moreover, nothing in this judgment of mine is intended to have any such erosive effect."[26]

Equally cautious statements are to be found in the concurring judgment of Lord Justice Goff in the *DHN* case. He said:

> "...this is a case in which one is entitled to look at the realities of the situation and to pierce the corporate veil. I wish to safeguard myself by saying that so far as this ground is concerned, I am relying on the facts of this particular case. I would not at this juncture accept that in every case where one has a group of companies one is entitled to pierce the veil, but in this case the two subsidiaries were both wholly owned; further they had no separate business operations whatsoever; thirdly, in my judgment, the nature of the question involved is highly relevant, namely, whether the owners of this business have been disturbed in their possession and enjoyment of it."[27]

The views of Lords Justices Sachs and Goff are more representative of the majority of judicial opinion and in view of the trend of decisions since Lord Denning's judgments in the 1960s and 1970s it seems that the courts are likely to remain conservative when presented with requests to pierce the corporate veil. For example, in a Scottish decision, *Woolfson v Strathclyde Regional Council*,[28] the issue before the House of Lords, as in *DHN*, was a question relating to compensation for the compulsory acquisition of land. The judgment suggests that however unfortunate the outcome for the claimant, if that results from a decision by the claimant so to organise things as to produce what he considered the best way of securing his own interests, then he must accept the consequences of that policy. The judges declined to sanction corporate unveiling in this case and the decision of the Court of Session was upheld by the House of Lords.

[24] [1976] 1 WLR 852.
[25] *Ibid* at p. 860.
[26] [1969] 1 WLR 1241 at p. 1255.
[27] *See* n. 24, at p. 861.
[28] (1978) SLT 159.

11.1.3 The holding company as a director

Shareholders as such owe no duty of care to the company. It does not, however, follow that if shareholders engage in the management of a company, they cannot become liable as directors merely because they are shareholders.

It is well established in English law that a company can be a director of another company (*Re Bulawayo Market Limited*[29]) and that a person who is a *de facto* director — ie, who acts as a director even though not appointed as such — owes the same duties as a *de jure* director (*In Re Canadian Land Reclaiming and Colonising Co: Coventry and Dixon's Case*[30]). A parent company is not, however, to be treated as a director, or to be responsible on other grounds for the management of its subsidiary, merely because as parent it controls the composition of the board of the subsidiary, or because members of the parent board are also directors of the subsidiary. Nor does it suffice that the parent imposes on the subsidiary budgetary rules or policy or operational guidelines within which the subsidiary is required to conduct its business. The imposition of such rules and guidelines is a normal characteristic of group trading and does not make the parent a director of the subsidiary. The position is otherwise, however, where the parent disregards the legal management and structure of the subsidiary and intervenes substantially in the conduct of its affairs.

11.1.4 Shareholders' ratification of directors' conduct

In principle, the conduct of a company's affairs is of concern only to its shareholders. The directors and officers of a company owe a duty to act within the scope of their own powers, in the interest of the company with loyalty and good faith and with a degree of skill and diligence. These duties are owed solely to the company itself, not to any individual shareholder or to creditors (see *Foss v Harbottle*[31]). If the directors commit what would ordinarily be a breach of duty to the company and thereby cause a loss or damage then, subject to the exceptions described below, it is open to the members to approve or ratify their acts. No one except the members suffers from the breach of duty and no one else is entitled to complain of that breach. This is particularly relevant in a case where a parent company has acted as a director and purports to ratify its own acts *qua* shareholder. This principle was reaffirmed in *Multinational Gas and Petrochemical Co v Multinational Gas and Petrochemical Services Limited*.[32]

In *Multinational*, three multinational oil companies, incorporated in the USA, France and Japan caused the plaintiff ("Multinational") to be incorporated in Liberia to buy, transfer, store and sell liquified petroleum gas and other similar products. On the advice of tax counsel, the three oil companies procured the incorporation in England of the second wholly-owned subsidiary, Multinational and Petrochemical Services Limited ("Services"), to carry on the business of Multinational under an agency agreement. Multinational ceased trading in circumstances which, in the words of the court, amounted to a "financial disaster for the plaintiffs' creditors". In the course of the winding-up of the company, the liquidator was advised that there was evidence that Services had acted negligently in preparing budgets, forecasts and information for Multinational

[29][1907] 2 Ch 458.
[30](1880) 14 Ch D 660.
[31](1843) 2 Hare 461.
[32][1983] Ch 258.

and that the directors of Multinational — who, it was alleged, acted at all material times "in accordance with the directions and at the behest of" the three oil companies — had in turn been negligent in failing to appreciate the deficiencies in the materials supplied by Services and had made decisions negligently.

At the instance of its liquidator, Multinational commenced an action for damages for breaches of duty of care against Services and applied for leave, pursuant to the Rules of the English Supreme Court, to issue concurrent writs against the three oil companies and the directors of Multinational and to serve notice of those writs on the defendants outside the jurisdiction of the English court.

In an application for leave for notice of the writ to be served on a foreign defendant, where an action had properly been brought against Service within the jurisdiction, an order would not be made if the foreign defendant had a good defence to the action. The majority of the Court of Appeal held that, although Multinational had a separate existence from its shareholders, it existed for their benefit provided that they acted *intra vires* and in good faith, they could manage its affairs as they chose whilst it was solvent, and that the shareholders, who had no duty to third parties or to future creditors, had, by approving the directors' acts, made those acts the acts of Multinational, the plaintiff, and it could not now complain of the lack of commercial judgment of the directors in making the decisions.

Lords Justices Lawton and Dillon held, *inter alia*, that Multinational was "at law a different legal person from the subscribing oil company shareholders and was not their agent"[33]; that the oil companies and shareholders were not under any duty of care to the plaintiff; and that, as shareholders, the oil companies were not "liable to anyone except to the extent and the manner provided by the Companies Act 1948".[34] One of the key passages in the judgment of the Court of Appeal appears in the judgment of Lord Justice Lawton. He said:

> "The submission in relation to the defendants was as follows. No allegation had been made that the plaintiff's directors had acted *ultra vires* or in bad faith. What was alleged was that when making the decisions which were alleged to have caused the plaintiff loss and giving instructions to Services to put them into effect they had acted in accordance with the directions and behest of the three oil companies. These oil companies were the only shareholders. All the acts complained of became the plaintiff's acts. The plaintiff, although it had a separate existence from its oil company shareholders, existed for the benefit of those shareholders, who, provided they acted *intra vires* and in good faith, could manage the plaintiff's affairs as they wished. If they wanted to take business risks through the plaintiff which no prudent businessman would take they could lawfully do so. Just as an individual can act like a fool provided he keeps within the law so could the plaintiff, but in its case it was for the shareholders to decide whether the plaintiff should act foolishly. As shareholders they owed no duty to those with whom the plaintiff did business. It was for such persons to assess the hazards of doing business with them. It follows, so it was submitted, that the plaintiff as a matter of law, cannot now complain about what it did at its shareholders' behest.
>
> This submission was based on the assumption, for which there was evidence, that Liberian company law was the same as English company law and upon a long line of cases starting with [*Salomon*] and ending with the decision of this court in *In Re Horsley*

[33]*Ibid* at p. 269.
[34]*Ibid*.

& *Weight Limited* [1982] Ch 442. In my judgment these cases establish the following relevant principles of law: first, that the plaintiff was at law a different legal person from the subscribing oil company shareholders and was not their agent: see the *Salomon* case... Secondly, that the oil companies as shareholders were not liable to anyone except to the extent and the manner provided by the Companies Act 1948: see the same case... Thirdly, that when the oil companies acting together required the plaintiff's directors to make decisions or approve what had already been done, what they did or approved became the plaintiff's acts and were binding on it: see by way of examples *Attorney General for Canada v Standard Trust Company of New York* [1911] AC 498; *In Re Express Engineering Works Limited* [1920] 1 Ch 466 and *In Re Horsley & Weight Limited* [1982] Ch 442. When approving whatever their nominee directors had done, the oil companies were not, as the plaintiff submitted, relinquishing any causes of action which the plaintiff might have had against its directors. When the oil companies, as shareholders, approved what the plaintiff's directors had done there was no cause of action because at that time there was no damage. What the oil companies were doing was adopting the directors' acts and as shareholders, in agreement with each other, making those acts the plaintiff's acts.

It follows, so it seems to me, that the plaintiff cannot not complain about what in law were its own acts." [35]

There are cases where the members of a company cannot authorise or ratify improper conduct and therefore the principles established, *inter alia*, in *Multinational*, cannot apply, ie where the acts complained of:

(a) involve the company in unlawful conduct;
(b) are a fraud on the company; *or*
(c) are a fraud on creditors or affect the company's ability to discharge its debts or otherwise jeopardise its solvency.

11.1.5 Unlawful conduct

The members of a company cannot effectively approve or ratify conduct by the directors causing the company to perform acts which are either *ultra vires* or unlawful by statute or under the general law. In *Re Exchange Banking Co, Flitcroft's case*,[36] the directors of a banking company had for several years presented to the general meetings of shareholders' both reports and balance sheets in which various bad debts were shown as assets, thus recording an apparent profit when for some time the company had in fact been trading at a loss and dividends were improperly paid out of capital. In the winding-up, the liquidator applied for an order requiring the directors to repay the lost capital. The directors argued that they had derived no benefit from the improper payments after dividend, that no fraud had been proved and that they were at best guilty of a tort for which damages were not provable in the liquidation. The Court of Appeal held that the improper payment of dividends out of capital was a misapplication of the company's funds and a breach of trust and that, even if the shareholders had approved what was done with full knowledge of the facts, that would not have exonerated the directors. The Master of the Rolls held, *inter alia*:

"A limited company by its memorandum of association declares that its capital is to be applied for the purposes of the business. It cannot reduce its capital except in the manner

---

[35]*Ibid* at pp. 268–269.
[36](1882) 21 Ch D 519.

and with the safeguards provided by statute... A limited company cannot in any other way make a return of capital, the sanction of a general meeting can give no validity to such a proceeding, and even the sanction of every shareholder cannot bring within the powers of the company an act which is not within its powers."[37]

11.1.6 Fraud on a company

It is also clear that the members of a company cannot approve or ratify acts of the directors which constitute a fraud on the company. Here "fraud" bears an extended meaning.

"But a resolution of a general meeting cannot, either prospectively or retrospectively authorise the directors to act in fraud of the company. And, here again, "fraud" is used in a wider sense than deceit or dishonesty. If the directors have acted in their own interests or those of a third party rather than in the interests of the company, or have not directed their minds to the question whether what they are doing is in the best interests of the company, a resolution of the general meeting will not protect them."[38]

11.1.7 Fraud on or improper conduct injurious to creditors

Where the acts that the members purport to approve or ratify are a fraud on creditors or affect the company's ability to discharge its debts the approval or ratification is ineffective to protect the directors from liability. (In *Multinational*,[39] the judgment of the Court of Appeal was expressed as being on the basis that shareholders could manage a company's affairs as they chose *whilst it was solvent*.) If in such a case the company subsequently goes into *insolvent* winding-up, the liquidator may bring proceedings in the name of the company in respect of the wrongful acts of the directors despite the fact that those acts have been approved or ratified by the members. In taking such proceedings for the benefit of creditors the liquidator is not seeking to enforce a cause of action vested in the creditors themselves. He is simply asserting that the acts complained of have resulted in a loss to the company and cannot be approved or ratified by the members because the interest of *creditors* are also affected by such loss.

There are at least two cases in which creditors are clearly affected adversely by improper conduct on the part of the directors.

The first is where such conduct is a fraud on creditors, as where assets are deliberately transferred from the company with a view to placing them out of the reach of creditors. There are dicta in several English decisions to the effect that a fraud on creditors cannot be ratified or condoned by shareholders, for it is something the company itself cannot lawfully do: see, for example, *Re Halt Garage (1964) Ltd*[40] (*per* Mr Justice Oliver "Fraud opens all doors"[41]) and *Rolled Steel Products (Holdings) Ltd v British Steel Corporation*[42] where Lord Justice Slade observed:

[37]*Ibid* at p. 533.
[38]See Gower, *op cit*, p. 619, and see also *Attorney-General's Reference (Number 2) (see* n. 17).
[39]*See* n. 32.
[40][1982] 3 All ER 1016.
[41]*Ibid* at p. 1037.
[42][1986] 1 Ch 246.

"This last-mentioned principle [of consent or ratification by shareholders] certainly is not an unqualified one. In particular, it will not enable the shareholders of a company to bind the company itself to a transaction which constitutes a fraud on its creditors..."[43]

The second case where creditors are adversely affected by acts injurious to the company is where, at the time of the acts in question, the members were no longer the sole persons having an interest in the performance of the directors' duties to the company, because at the time of those acts, or as the result of them, the company was insolvent. This principle is described in two decisions of appellate courts in New Zealand and Australia and has been approved by the English Court of Appeal.

In the first, *Nicholson v Permakraft (NZ) Limited*[44] a company that had liquidity problems was restructured, and as part of the restructuring a substantial sum was paid to shareholders by way of distribution of a capital profit. The payment was approved by all the shareholders but upon the company subsequently becoming insolvent and going into liquidation, the liquidator instituted proceedings against the shareholders for recovery of the dividend on the ground that the directors had acted in breach of duty in causing it to be paid and that such breach could not be ratified by the shareholders. At first instance judgment was given in favour of the liquidator, but this was reversed by the New Zealand Court of Appeal on the ground that there were sound commercial reasons for the restructuring, the transaction was entered into in good faith and at the time of payment of the dividend the company's solvency was not in doubt. In the course of his judgment Mr Justice Cooke explained the principle in the following terms:

"The duties of directors are owed to the company. On the facts of particular cases this may require the directors to consider *inter alia* the interests of creditors. For instance creditors are entitled to consideration, in my opinion, if the company is insolvent or near-insolvent, or of doubtful solvency, or if a contemplated payment or other course of action would jeopardise its solvency.

...as a matter of business ethics it is appropriate for directors to consider also whether what they do will prejudice their company's practical ability to discharge promptly debts owed to current and likely continuing trade creditors.

To translate this into a legal obligation accords with the now pervasive concepts of duty to a neighbour and the linking of power with obligation. It is also consistent with the spirit of what Lord Haldane said. In a situation of marginal commercial solvency such creditors may fairly be seen as beneficially interested in the company or contingently so. On the other hand, to make out a duty to future *new* creditors would be much more difficult..."[45]

The other two members of the court agreed that wrongful acts of the directors at a time when the company is insolvent or which make it insolvent cannot be effectively ratified by the members, but preferred to express no view where the company was near insolvency or of doubtful solvency.

This decision was followed by the New South Wales Court of Appeal in *Kinsela & Anor v Russell Kinsela Pty Limited*.[46] In that case a company whose financial position was precarious granted a lease of premises at substantially below the market

---

[43]*Ibid* at p. 296.
[44](1985) 1 NZLR 242.
[45]*Ibid* at p. 249.
[46](1986) 10 ACLR 395.

rent with no provision for escalation during the term of the lease. The lessee was also given the option to purchase the premises at any time during the term at a price likely to be substantially below the market value. Shortly after the lease was executed the company went into liquidation. The liquidator obtained an order from the trial judge avoiding the lease on the ground that there had not been full disclosure to one share-holder but that if such disclosure had been made the directors could not be held to have been guilty of a breach of duty, as they would have acted with the consent of all the shareholders. On appeal the judgment was upheld but the Court of Appeal ruled that as the company was plainly insolvent at the time it granted the lease the transaction was voidable notwithstanding consent of all shareholders. The Chief Justice held:

> "In a solvent company the proprietary interests of the shareholders entitle them as a general body to be regarded as the company when questions of the duty of directors arise. If, as a general body, they authorise or ratify a particular action of the directors, there can be no challenge to the validity of what the directors have done. But where a company is insolvent the interests of the creditors intrude. They become prospectively entitled, through the mechanism of liquidation, to displace the power of the shareholders and directors to deal with the company's assets. It is in a practical sense their assets and not the shareholders' assets that, through the medium of the company, are under the management of the directors pending either liquidation, return to solvency, or the imposition of some alternative administration."[47]

The Chief Justice declined to formulate a general test of the degree of financial instability which would impose upon directors an obligation to consider the interests of creditors.

The remarks of the Chief Justice have been approved by the English Court of Appeal in *West Mercia Safetywear Limited v Dodd*[48] and *Lee Panavision Limited v Lee Lighting Limited*.[49]

On the question whether directors owe a duty to future creditors there are conflicting dicta. In the *Multinational* case Lord Justice Dillon said that "a solvent company owes no duty of care to future creditors".[50] On the other hand, Lord Templeman stated by way of obiter dictum in the decision of the House of Lords in *Winkworth v Edward Baron Development Co Ltd*[51]:

> "But a company owes a duty to its creditors, present and future. The company is not bound to pay off every debt as soon as it is incurred, and the company is not obliged to avoid all ventures which involve an element of risk but the company owes a duty to its creditors to keep its property inviolate and available for the repayment of its debts. The conscience of the company, as well as its management, is confided to its directors. A duty is owed by the directors to the company and to the creditors of the company to ensure that the affairs of the company are properly administered and that its property is not dissipated or exploited for the benefit of the directors themselves to the prejudice of the creditors."[52]

---

[47]*Ibid* at p. 401.
[48][1988] BCLC 250 at p. 252.
[49][1992] BCLC 22 at p. 30.
[50][1983] Ch 258 at p. 288.
[51][1986] 1 WLR 1512.
[52]*Ibid* at p. 1516.

11.1.8 Statutory exceptions to the principle in Salomon

The general duties of a director have been referred to above: a director must act *bona fide* and in the interests of the company (as a whole and not, for instance in the interests of one shareholder or group of shareholders). He must act honestly and in good faith. He must take such care as an ordinary man might be expected to take on his own behalf, but need only exercise skill and care to the standard to be expected of a person of *his* (or *its*) knowledge and experience. A company may become the director of another company and will thereby assume the duties of a director, even though not formally appointed.

Where a director has acted in breach of his duties he can be made to compensate the company for the resulting loss. Where he has made a secret profit, or improperly received a benefit, he can be required to disgorge it, or account to the company for it. He may only keep what he is entitled to keep under his agreement with the company. Where a director has misapplied company property, even if honestly and in good faith he, like a trustee, can be made to account to the company for the property and make up the loss. Where insolvency is an issue, a failure on the part of a director properly to perform his duties, resulting in a loss to the company, will mean that it is the creditors' interests which are then being prejudiced as well as those of the members. As long as the company pays its debts, creditors have no cause, nor any standing, to complain. In a liquidation, the liquidator will take action to get in and maximise the assets available to pay the creditors and breaches of directors' duties and their consequences may come to light when they would otherwise not do so.

In addition to the rights of action available at common law, or in equity, remedies have been created or re-enacted in the Insolvency Act 1986 which, if applied to a shareholder, whether an individual or a holding company, operate as exceptions to the rule in *Salomon*.

(a) Summary remedy — Insolvency Act 1986, section 212
In a winding-up there is a procedure whereunder not only a liquidator but any creditor (or contributory) can apply to the court for the examination of any person (including a corporation) who has been an officer of the company, and for an order compelling him to restore money or property to the company or to contribute money to it by way of compensation for breach of duty.

(b) Fraudulent trading — Insolvency Act 1986, section 213
This section provides that if, in the course of a winding-up it appears that the company's business has been carried on with intent to defraud creditors, or for any fraudulent purposes, the court, on the liquidator's application, may declare that anyone who was knowingly a party to the fraud, is liable to make such contribution to the company's assets as the court thinks proper.

(c) Wrongful trading — Insolvency Act 1986, section 214
Section 214 imposes a new and personal liability on directors to contribute to the assets of a company which has gone into insolvent liquidation. "Insolvent" for this purpose means that the company has gone into liquidation at a time when its assets are insufficient to pay its debts and other liabilities as well as the expenses of the winding-up. "Director" includes a person who occupies the position of director, even

though not formally appointed, or a shadow director, ie a person in accordance with whose directions or instructions the directors customarily act. (A "person" can be a company, including a foreign corporation.)

A director can be made liable for wrongful trading if at some stage before the commencement of the winding-up, he knew or ought to have concluded that there was "no reasonable prospect that the company would avoid going into insolvent liquidation" and he was a director or shadow director of the company at the time. There is no need to show any intent to defraud. The court may not make an order under section 214 if it is satisfied (but the burden of proof is on the director) that the director took "every step with a view to minimising the potential loss to the company's creditors as (assuming him to have known that there was no reasonable prospect that the company would avoid going into insolvent liquidation) he ought to have taken". For the purpose of assuming the director's state of mind, the facts which he ought to know or ascertain, the conclusions which he ought to reach, and the steps which he ought to take, are those which could be known, or ascertained or reached or taken, by a reasonably diligent person having both:

(a) the general knowledge, skill and experience that may reasonably be expected of a person carrying out the same functions as are carried out by that director in relation to the company; *and*
(b) the general knowledge, skill and experience which that director has.

Functions that are entrusted to a director but which he does not in fact carry out are deemed for this purpose to be included within those he actually carries out.

This means that there is an objective test and a subjective test and the director must meet the higher of the two in order to escape liability. This has particular implications for a director with greater responsibilities (eg a managing director or a finance director) or for one with particular experience (such as one who has much experience of rescuing companies and returning them to profitability), or indeed for a holding company.

Section 214 is compensatory and the amount to be contributed by the director (on being held liable) is that by which the company's assets could be seen to have been depleted by the director's conduct and which caused the court's discretion to become exercisable (ie failing to take every step to protect creditors).

Following the enactment of the Insolvency Act 1986, and in particular the provisions dealing with wrongful trading in section 214, the previous common law position is of less importance although it is possible for there to be circumstances in which a director, including a holding company, could be liable at common law or in equity but not under the section. Furthermore, there are some jurisdictions where English common law principles still apply (eg The Bahamas, Bermuda, the Cayman Islands) and where there is no legislation corresponding to the Insolvency Act 1986, in which a liquidator would still have to satisfy the court that it should not adhere the principle of *Salomon* in order to make a holding company liable for the whole or part of the debts of its subsidiary.

11.2 Substantive consolidation in US bankruptcies

Substantive consolidation is an equitable doctrine created in US bankruptcies by judges under their broad equity powers. The doctrine permits the court in a bankruptcy case involving one or more related companies to disregard the separateness of the corporate entities and to consolidate and pool the assets and liabilities, treating them as though held and incurred by one entity. In effect, substantive consolidation creates a single estate for the benefit of all of the creditors of the consolidation companies and combines all the creditors of the various companies into one creditor body.

The US Bankruptcy Code does not specifically empower Bankruptcy Courts to order substantive consolidation. Rather, courts find the power to impose substantive consolidation in the general "equity powers" provided for in section 105 of the Bankruptcy Code.

Substantive consolidation must be compared with joint administration which is a procedure by which the courts hear two or more related cases of companies that have filed bankruptcy petitions as a single case. The purpose of joint administration is to make case administration easier and less costly. Joint administration requires, however, that the estates of the companies be kept separate and distinct.

In determining whether substantive consolidation should be ordered (in essence whether the separate corporate existence of one entity should be ignored), the court will:

(a) analyse the pre-bankruptcy relationships of the companies in order to determine whether they justify the treatment of the separate corporate entities as a single unit;

(b) examine the relationships of creditors to the consolidated and separate entities; *and*

(c) ascertain whether substantive consolidation would result in undue hardship to any particular group of creditors.

The court will then balance the conflicting interests of creditors and grant substantive consolidation where it has been shown that the economic prejudice which would result from continued recognition of the separate corporate entities outweighs the prejudice which consolidation would cause. Bearing in mind the possibility of unfair treatment of creditors, the courts have invoked sparingly the power to order substantive consolidation and only after a detailed enquiry of all relevant factors.

Not all courts apply the same balancing test in determining whether substantive consolidation will be equitable in a particular case but most have examined the same components of the pre-bankruptcy relationships of the companies in order to determine whether they justify the treatment as separate corporate entities or as a single entity in bankruptcy. In recent years, US Bankruptcy Courts have focused on the following seven elements in determining the necessity for substantive consolidation:

(a) the presence or absence of consolidated financial statements;

(b) the unity of interest and ownership between the various companies;

(c) the existence of parent and inter-company guarantees or loans;

(d) the degree of difficulty in segregating and ascertaining individual assets and liabilities;

(e) the transfer of assets, without formal observance of corporate formalities;

(f) co-mingling of assets and business functions; *and*

(g) the profitability of consolidation at a single physical location.

No single element is deemed to be conclusive. Consolidation hinges on the balancing of equities favouring consolidation against equities favouring continuation of separate treatment of the companies. Where an objecting creditor relied upon the separateness of related companies in extending credit the court may be reluctant to order consolidation, in the absence of a strong case for the necessity of it.

It has been suggested that the seven factors are merely variants of two critical factors:

(a) whether the creditors dealt with the companies as a single economic unit and did not rely on their separate identity in extending credit; *or*
(b) whether the affairs of the companies are so entangled that consolidation would benefit all creditors.

As to the first factor, the expectations of creditors create significant equities — many creditors make loans on the basis of the financial status of a particular company and expect to be able to look to the assets of that company for repayment of a loan.

The second factor (entanglement of the debtors' affairs) is present in cases in which there has been a co-mingling of the two companies' assets and business functions. Substantive consolidation will, however, be used in such cases only after it has been determined that all creditors will benefit because untangling is either impossible or so costly as to consume the assets.

In *Chemical Bank New York Trust Co v Kheel*,[53] the Court of Appeals for the Second Circuit found that consolidation was warranted because the cost of untangling the "hopelessly" obscured financial records of the companies would exceed the benefit that would accrue from the records. The Court set a rigorous standard which couples expense and difficulty with the practical impossibility of restructuring the financial records before allowing consolidation. This standard requires the problem of disentanglement to be so egregious that it threatens the realisation of any assets.

Kheel involved the liquidation of eight shipping companies which one individual owned or controlled. In addition, the companies operated in disregard of any corporate distinctions. Chemical Bank, one of the creditors, argued that substantive consolidation was improper without a finding that a creditor dealt with a group of companies believing it to be a single entity. The Court observed that the companies shifted funds, made inter-company loans, regularly paid each other's obligations, and made withdrawals and payments from and to corporate accounts without sufficient recordkeeping. The Court upheld the consolidation because the expense of reconstructing the financial records of the company would extinguish any chance of recovery for the pre-petition creditors. In addition to avoiding the time and effort of disentangling the debtor's affairs, consolidation facilitated the previously impossible determination, allowance, and classification of the claims of creditors.

11.3 The English equivalent of substantive consolidation — pooling

Under English law there is no equivalent of the US doctrine of substantive consolidation. The closest to which the English courts come is "pooling", which does not

---

[53] 369 F 2d 845 (2nd Cir 1966).

involve a complete merger of the estates; rather a compromise between the liquidators of the companies who are parties to the arrangement.

The English courts had to consider the issue of pooling in the case of the BCCI which, on 5 July 1991, was closed in most countries in the world where there were BCCI operations.

There were two principal BCCI operating companies. Bank of Credit and Commerce International SA of Luxembourg ("BCCI SA") and Bank of Credit and Commerce (Overseas) Limited of the Cayman Islands ("BCCI Overseas"). Both of these companies were owned by a holding company in Luxembourg ("BCCI Holdings").

The BCCI Group could be split into three approximately equally-sized units:

(a) a network of over 40 branches of BCCI SA located in 13 countries, of which 24 were in the UK;
(b) over 60 branch of BCCI Overseas that were located in 28 countries and centered in the Cayman Islands; *and*
(c) the subsidiaries and affiliates of BCCI Holdings which operated over 250 banking offices in some 28 countries.

At closure the total number of employees in the BCCI group was approximately 12,000.

On the closure of the Bank, provisional liquidators were appointed over BCCI SA in England. Initially a receiver was appointed over BCCI Overseas in the Cayman Islands but by 22 July 1991 provisional liquidators had been appointed. In Luxembourg, BCCI Holdings and BCCI SA were placed under controlled management, although in 1992 the District Court of Luxembourg made orders for the winding-up of BCCI SA and BCCI Holdings and for the appointment of joint liquidators. In 1992 also, the courts of England and the Cayman Islands made winding-up orders and appointed liquidators in respect of BCCI SA and BCCI Overseas respectively.

Following the closure of the bank, the various provisional liquidators, and subsequently the liquidators, of BCCI SA both in Luxembourg and in England, and of BCCI Overseas in the Cayman Islands, entered into negotiations with the Government of Abu Dhabi (representing the majority shareholders of BCCI Holdings) with a view to agreeing on arrangements that would improve and accelerate the return to creditors of BCCI.

The parties eventually reached an agreement, subject to the satisfaction of certain conditions, not the least being the approvals of the courts having the governance of the liquidations. The agreements requiring approval were a contribution agreement and pooling agreements. The agreements were approved by the courts of England and the Cayman Islands but the pooling agreements only were approved by the Luxembourg Court. Notwithstanding the failure to obtain approval of the contribution agreement, the discussion which follows provides an interesting insight into the principles which the English courts will adopt.

As reflected in the judgment of the English Court of Appeal referred to below, the essence of the "contribution agreement" was that it was a compromise of cross-claims between the majority shareholders and certain other parties in Abu Dhabi associated with them (described by the Court and hereinafter as "the Abu Dhabi interests") and the liquidators in England, Luxembourg and the Cayman Islands of BCCI SA and

BCCI Overseas. The liquidators had claimed that, as the Abu Dhabi interests were the regulatory authorities in Abu Dhabi and had representation on the boards of BCCI SA and BCCI Overseas, they should have appreciated very much earlier the frauds which were being perpetrated on BCCI SA and BCCI Overseas by, in particular, Abu Dhabi citizens and should have intervened long ago. It was said that, because of those failures, the Abu Dhabi interests were liable, not only morally but also legally, to compensate the creditors for loss. Conversely, the Abu Dhabi interests put forward cross claims against BCCI SA and BCCI Overseas for a total of $2.2 billion on the basis, broadly, that the sums claimed were monies that belonged to one or more of the majority shareholders and were deposited with a body called ICIC Overseas, which were then fraudulently misappropriated by former officers of the BCCI group for the benefit of the BCCI group.

The pooling agreements provide for a pool of assets and liabilities of BCCI SA and BCCI Overseas so as to avoid, *inter alia*, lengthy and costly disputes between BCCI SA and BCCI Overseas over the ownership of assets and also to simplify the processing of creditors' claims.

On 12 June 1992, the English court (Sir Donald Nicholls VC) authorised the liquidators to enter into the agreements. He gave a nine-page judgment, the relevant parts of which are discussed in the context of the Court of Appeal decision referred to below. The granting of sanction was opposed by a number of creditors including a majority of the creditors' committee appointed in the English liquidation of BCCI SA.

Following the granting of sanction by Sir Donald Nicholls VC, certain creditors in the English winding-up appealed to the Court of Appeal. On 17 July 1992 the appeal was dismissed.[54]

In the Court of Appeal counsel for the dissenting creditors did not challenge the exercise by Sir Donald Nicholls VC of his discretion to approve the agreements. An appeal based on that ground would have been doomed to failure, given the judgment of the House of Lords in *Hadmor Productions Limited v Hamilton*,[55] which is authority for the rule that an Appeal Court should only disturb the exercise of the judge's discretion in exceptional circumstances.

Instead, counsel for the dissenting creditors founded his challenge on the ground that, on a true appreciation of the law, the Vice-Chancellor had no power to make the order he did. The appeal was therefore concerned with technical arguments of law. Whilst Sir Donald Nicholls' judgment was short and simple so that any depositor might read and understand it, the judgment of the Court of Appeal is lengthy and tightly argued.

The application to the Vice-Chancellor to approve the agreements and authorise the liquidators to carry them into effect was made under paragraphs 2 and 3 of Part I of Schedule 4 to the Insolvency Act 1986. These are in the following terms under the heading in "Part I — Powers exercisable with Sanction":

> "2. : Power to make any compromise or arrangement with creditors or persons claiming to be creditors, or having or alleging themselves to have any claim (present or future, certain or contingent, ascertained or sounding only in damages) against the company, or whereby the company may be rendered liable.

[54][1992] BCC 715.
[55][1983] AC 191.

3. : Power to compromise, on such terms as may be agreed —
    (a) : all calls and liabilities to calls, all debts and liabilities capable of resulting in debts, and all claims (present or future, certain or contingent, ascertained or sounding only in damages) subsisting or supposed to subsist between the company and a contributory or alleged contributory or other debtor or person apprehending liability to the company, and
    (b) : all questions in any way relating to or affecting the assets or the winding up of the company..."

The section conferring these powers is section 167 of the Insolvency Act 1986 which provides:

"Where a company is being wound up by the court, the liquidator may. . .

    (a) : with the sanction of the court or the liquidation committee, exercise any of the powers specified in Parts I and II of Schedule 4 to this Act (payment of debts; compromise of claims etc.; . . ."

Section 195 of the Insolvency Act 1986 provides:

"(1) The court may:
    (a) : as to all matters relating to the winding up of a company, have regard to the wishes of the creditors or contributories (as proved to it by any sufficient evidence), and
    (b) : if it thinks fit, for the purpose of ascertaining those wishes, direct meetings of the creditors or contributories to be called, held and conducted in such manner as the court directs, and appoint a person to act as chairman of any such meeting and report the result of it to the court."

The basis in law of the complaints of the appellants and of the other creditors who, before the Vice-Chancellor, opposed his approving the agreements, was primarily that he had wholly failed to have any regard to the views and wishes of the overwhelming majority of those creditors of BCCI SA, whose views were made known to him. On the contrary, and in spite of section 195 and, it was agreed, the settled practice which has developed in such matters, he had rejected the views of the overwhelming majority of those creditors and had substituted his own view that it was expedient in the interests of the creditors of BCCI SA that the agreements should be approved and be carried into effect.

It was urged, in particular, in relation to the pooling agreements that they seek to achieve something which can only be approved by a scheme of arrangement under section 425 of the Companies Act 1985 and could not be approved under the compromise powers described above. It was also argued in relation to the contribution agreement that certain aspects of it infringe the pari passu rule which, it was said, is so fundamental that the court was precluded from approving the contribution agreement either under the compromise powers or under any other power whatsoever.

Lord Justice Dillon recounted that:

"Part of the answer to those submissions put forward by the liquidators is that it is impracticable in the circumstances of this case, and in view of the overwhelming difficulties of a complex international fraud, to convene any meeting of the creditors of [BCCI] SA or class meetings in accordance with section 425, let alone also to convene, if that be necessary, comparable meetings of creditors of [BCCI] Overseas. The liquidators are supported on this and other submissions by the majority shareholders in

[BCCI] SA or, more strictly, its holding company, who are, in particular, the ruler of Abu Dhabi, the Crown Prince of Abu Dhabi and the government of Abu Dhabi."[56]

The technical legal arguments were not put forward by the appellants from academic interest, but because they argued that the terms of the contribution agreement were seriously inadequate and that they hoped that, if the agreements were rejected and if the majority shareholders and other Abu Dhabi interests were pressed by litigation and forced to give discovery, much more favourable terms of compromise would be put forward by the majority shareholders. As to the pooling agreement, the appellants conceded that pooling of assets and liabilities of BCCI SA and BCCI Overseas was probably necessary, but that there ought to be a further investigation before it was decided whether the pooling should be on a one for one rather than some other ratio.

Lord Justice Dillon referred to two important aspects of the proposed arrangements with the majority shareholders:-

"The first is that under the terms of the compromise only those creditors of [BCCI] SA and [BCCI] Overseas will be able to participate in the compensation sum who expressly assent to the compromise and release any individual claims they may have against the Abu Dhabi interests. This is mitigated in the case of those creditors who initially fail to respond to the terms of the offer of compromise, or who initially oppose but subsequently change their minds, by complicated provisions for catch-up payments in one of the supporting agreements. But it is the position that, although the compensation payment represents in part the unspecified value of an asset in [BCCI] SA, that is to say [BCCI] SA's claim for damages against the Abu Dhabi interests, creditors of [BCCI] SA or [BCCI] Overseas who do not assent to the compromise and do not release whatever individual claims they may have against the Abu Dhabi interests will not be able to participate in that asset. That is said to offend against the *pari passu* rule. It may be added that the problem of creditors assenting is complicated by the problem of ring fencing, to which I shall have to come."

The second aspect that would fall foul of the *pari passu* rule was that under the contribution agreement the proceeds of claims against certain third parties, and in particular two firms of accountants and one firm of solicitors, were to be shared equally between the Abu Dhabi interests and the liquidators.[57]

In considering the negotiating background, Lord Justice Dillon said:

"It is not in doubt that the terms of the Contribution Agreement represent the best that the liquidators have been able to achieve after protracted and difficult negotiations with the majority shareholders. It is not a question of being able to select some terms and reject others. The terms are a package and it is a question of "take it or leave it"."[58]

Lord Justice Dillon referred to the problem of "ring fencing" in the following terms:

"Under English law, as under the laws of Luxembourg and the Cayman Islands, realisations by the liquidators are applicable, subject to payment of preferential creditors (which is not an issue in this case), in paying all creditors worldwide *pari passu*. But in many other jurisdictions, for instance in states of the USA, that is not the law; in such jurisdictions, where a branch of an international company incorporated elsewhere is wound up, the proceeds of realisation of the assets of the branch may be applicable exclusively, after payment of preferentials, in paying off the creditors of that branch, in priority to all creditors

---

[56][1992] BCC 715 at p. 722.
[57]*Ibid* at pp. 723–724.
[58]*Ibid* at p. 724.

of other branches. That is conveniently called 'ring fencing' in that the branch is ring-fenced and isolated from other liabilities. There are other versions of ring fencing which may favour nationals or residents of a particular country at the expense of nationals of other countries. There is also the problem that in some countries, local branches of [BCCI] SA or [BCCI] Overseas have been sold by local banking authorities or local liquidators or have been merged with other local banks.

It is one of the provisions of the pooling agreement that local branches in the hands of local liquidators or administrators should be able to come into the pooling agreement. It is the hope of the liquidators that branches of [BCCI] SA in nine countries (including the United Kingdom and Luxembourg and including Gibraltar, where the branch seems to have been operated, before liquidation, as a branch of the United Kingdom operation) and branches of [BCCI] Overseas in seven countries including the Cayman Islands will come into the pooling agreement."[59]

Lord Justice Dillon referred to the creation of a creditors' committee in the English liquidation of BCCI SA with eight members and the fact that the creditors' committee voted by a majority of 7:1 against the implementation of the agreements. In this context he discussed the practicality of convening a meeting of creditors of BCCI SA (or of BCCI Overseas) or class meetings of creditors for the purposes of a scheme of arrangement under section 425 of the Companies Act 1985. More importantly for the present analysis, he also discussed the reason why it was said that there must be the pooling agreement.

From the reports before the Court, Lord Justice Dillon deduced that, combining the creditors of BCCI SA and BCCI Overseas, the total figure for creditors would be approximately 310,000. In addition, in many countries, because of banking secrecy laws, the English, Luxembourg or Cayman Island liquidators could not have access to the names and addresses of creditors who were depositors with the local branches of BCCI SA or BCCI Overseas. He also referred to timing problems because of the number of countries involved where meetings might have to be held, particularly in view of the strict time limits for approval of the agreements.

As for convening a meeting of creditors of BCCI SA, Sir Donald Nicholls VC had held as follows:

"There would be formidable practical difficulties in holding a meeting, but these would not be insurmountable. More importantly, creditors of each of the two companies fall into many different classes with different interests (for example, depositors in countries where there has been 'ring fencing' and depositors in countries where there has not). So a single vote at a single meeting would not be a sound guide to the creditors' views. But an attempt to hold a series of class meetings would encounter the feature which bedevils every step in this saga which has brought loss and misery to so many thousands of families throughout the world: the sheer complexity one meets at every turn will thwart any effort to proceed neatly along the normal legal paths."[60]

Lord Justice Dillon added that it was his personal view that it would be wholly impracticable to hold a creditors' meeting of the creditors of BCCI SA with appropriate classes because of conflicting interests, whether under a scheme under section

[59]*Ibid* atpp. 724–725.
[60]*Ibid* at p. 718.

425 of the Companies Act 1985 or under section 195 of the Insolvency Act 1986 (to ascertain the wishes of the creditors), or at all.

The Vice-Chancellor had said of the pooling agreements:

> "I am in no doubt that the agreements are so plainly for the benefit of the creditors that I should approve them without further ado. I am satisfied that the affairs of BCCI SA and BCCI Overseas are so hopelessly intertwined that a pooling of their assets, with a distribution enabling the like dividend to be paid to both companies' creditors, is the only sensible way to proceed. It would make no sense to spend vast sums of money and much time in trying to disentangle and unravel."[61]

Lord Justice Dillon said:

> "I entirely agree. I would reject the submission that there should first be further investigation as to whether *pari passu* distribution is the correct basis for pooling or not. In the complexities of this case I do not see that further investigation would be likely to be fruitful and the time taken would defeat the time limits of the contribution agreement."[62]

Lord Justice Dillon then turned to the law. This can be summarised under a number of headings.

11.3.1 Giving effect to majority votes of creditors

Lord Justice Dillon referred to a number of decided cases where there had been meetings of creditors, for example, to decide whether to approve a compromise, in particular in *Re Ridgway, ex parte Hurlbatt*.[63] In that case, Mr Justice Cave stated that he should give credit to the creditors for believing that their own opinion was the right one. The judge had said:

> "That being so and having no ground for thinking that the creditors have not honestly and *bona fide* striven to understand the matter and had their own interests in view, I think I should do wrong if I were to overrule their own decision in their own matter merely on the ground that the result they anticipate may not be realised and may not be so beneficial as they think it will be. In my opinion that was not the intention with which the Legislature gave the Court the power which it is now asked to exercise."[64]

Lord Justice Dillon emphasised that *Re Ridgway* was a case in which there had been a meeting of creditors to express an opinion on the compromise. Lord Justice Dillon stated:

> "But in the complexities of the present case it is not, in my judgment, practicable to convene a meeting of creditors with any necessary class meetings, and I do not believe that the judge is necessarily precluded by the views of the majority of the informal creditors committee, and those who happen to turn up and oppose at the hearing before him, from forming his own decision on the agreements. The word in section 195 [of the Insolvency Act 1986] is 'may' and not 'shall' and he has, in my judgment, a residuary discretion where there are 'special circumstances',... as there are, in my judgment, in the present case."[65]

---

[61]*Ibid* at p. 719.
[62]*Ibid* at p. 728.
[63](1889) 6 Morrell's Bankruptcy Reports 277.
[64]*Ibid* at p. 281.
[65][1992] BCC. 715 at p. 730.

11.3.2 The power to compromise with creditors and members

Lord Justice Dillon then turned to section 425 of the Companies Act 1985. One of the arguments by the appellants was that the proposed compromise with the majority shareholders could only be put into effect by means of the scheme of arrangement under section 425. Section 425 reads as follows:

"(1) : Where a compromise or arrangement is proposed between a company and its creditors, or any class of them, the court may on the application of the company or any creditor or member of it or, in the case of a company being wound up, of the liquidator, order a meeting of the creditors or class of creditors, or of the members of the company or class of members (as the case may be), to be summoned in such manner as the court directs.

(2) : If a majority in number representing three-fourths in value of the creditors or class of creditors or members or class of members (as the case may be), present and voting either in person or by proxy at the meeting, agree to any compromise or arrangement, the compromise or arrangement, if sanctioned by the court, is binding on all creditors or the class of creditors or on the members or class of members (as the case may be), and also on the company or, in the case of a company in the course of being wound up, on the liquidator and contributories of the company."

The appellants relied on the decision of Mr Justice Plowman in the matter of *In Re Trix Limited*.[66] In that case the liquidator of a company (one of a group of 12) had sought sanction of the court to a conditional agreement of compromise. The effect of the court sanction in that case would have been to enable a company's assets to be distributed in a way which might not have been strictly in accordance with the creditors' rights under the companies legislation and the winding-up rules. Mr Justice Plowman had held that the proper way to distribute the assets of a company other than strictly in accordance with creditors' rights was by a scheme of arrangement under the predecessor to section 245 of the Companies Act 1985.

Mr. Justice Plowman said:

"However convenient it may be for the liquidators to have a compromise sanctioned by the court, it is in my judgment wrong in principle to allow that course to be taken, for none of the persons affected has had any opportunity of being heard to challenge it — indeed the whole object is to preclude such a challenge."[67]

He also said:

"The method which has been adopted here puts the burden on the court of deciding whether a particular method of distribution is fair in all the circumstances and should be accepted. In my judgment, this is an unjustifiable burden, first because, under the machinery provided by section 206, the creditors alone ought to be asked to decide it, and secondly because I have not had the benefit of hearing any alternative point of view.

In my judgment, it would be unfair to non-assenting creditors to deal with the matter in the way proposed since it deprives them of the opportunity of airing their views and of the protection of the court's control over meetings, advertisement and circular under section 206."[68]

[66][1970] 3 All ER 397.
[67]*Ibid* at p. 398.
[68]*Ibid* at pp. 398–399.

By contrast, Lord Justice Dillon referred to the report decision in *Re Taylor*.[69] This was the decision of a Scottish court, the Inner House of the Court of Session. The case concerned two companies which carried on businesses at various farms and estates and a hotel. These businesses were carried on in such a way that did not enable the business transactions of the different entities to be distinguished and separated from each other. All the transactions for the hotel, the farms and the estates were conducted through one bank book. The official liquidator discovered that the liabilities of the companies and of one of the moving spirits behind the companies (a Mr Morris) were so intermingled that he was unable to ascertain which creditors had claims against which of the companies and which creditors had claims against the estate of Morris.

The Court of Session held when ruling on a section similar, referred to in Schedule 4 to the Insolvency Act 1986.

Lord McCluskey said:

> "In our view, if it is established that the assets of the companies and of the sequestrated estate are so confused that it is impossible separately to identify the assets of each and if also it appears that it is practically impossible to determine who are the true debtors for those creditors who have claims arising out of some business with the companies and/or the sequestrated estate, then it would be open to the noter [the liquidator] to enter into a compromise arrangement in conjunction with Robert Wight Wilson so as to enable an overall settlement to be reached with all the creditors."[70]

Lord Justice Dillon stated that the decision was a clear decision of the Inner House, first, that compromise powers are to be given a wide meaning and that they permit a liquidator to enter into any compromise arrangement with creditors that might have been entered into by the company itself; and that would cover a compromise by BCCI SA with BCCI Overseas to resolve all their mutual dealings.

Secondly, and importantly for the purpose of this chapter, it followed from *Re Taylor*[71] that if it is established that the assets of the estates were so confused that it is impossible to identify the assets of each and it is practically impossible to determine who the true debtors are, it would be open to the liquidator to enter into a compromise arrangement in the exercise of the compromise powers rather than by a scheme of arrangement under the predecessor of section 425 of the Companies Act 1985. Lord Justice Dillon held that in the circumstances prevailing in *Re Taylor*, the principle in *Re Trix*[72] was "set on one side".[73]

Lord Justice Dillon cited the judgment of Sir Donald Nicholls VC on this issue under the heading "An exceptional case" as follows:

> "The creditors' committee and others contended that I have no jurisdiction (that is, legal power) to approve these proposals on this application by the liquidators. The argument was that in several respects the proposals involve a variation in the rights of creditors and that such a variation can only be sanctioned so as to bind the creditors as part of a formal scheme of arrangement under section 425 of the Companies Act 1985.

---

[69][1992] BCC 440.
[70]*Ibid* at p. 444.
[71]*See* n. 69.
[72]*See* n. 66.
[73][1992] BCC 715 at p. 733.

I do not agree. The liquidators' powers under paragraphs 2 and 3 of Schedule 4 to the Insolvency Act 1986, exercisable with the approval of the court, are wide and they are wide enough to cover this case.

In so far as the package does involve departures from the simple and fundamental principle that an insolvent company's assets should be distributed equally among all its creditors, I would in normal circumstances expect the scheme of arrangement procedure to be followed. That procedure contains additional safeguards for creditors. But if that procedure is followed in this case the proposals will flounder and sink in a morass of elaborate legal procedures and niceties. That cannot be the right way to approach this exceptional case."[74]

Although the next sentence was not cited by Lord Justice Dillon, the Vice-Chancellor went on to say: "Exceptional circumstances call for exceptional treatment."[75]

Lord Justice Dillon held:

"It seems to me that, in the very similar circumstances of this case, *Re Taylor* is authority to warrant the conclusion at which the Vice-Chancellor arrived. Of course, in this case it is not possible to tell what the assets of [BCCI] SA and [BCCI] Overseas are, but it is possible, to some extent at any rate, to say who the creditors are.

But it is not practicable to hold meetings, let alone class meetings, to ascertain the wishes of the creditors. I therefore do not see any real difference between the present case and *Taylor*."[76]

11.3.3 Conclusion

The Court of Appeal agreed with the conclusion reached by the Vice-Chancellor. The court had a residual discretion not to follow the wishes of the creditors committee in the special circumstances of BCCI. Lord Justice Dillon went so far as to say that he would not interfere with the discretion which he held the Vice-Chancellor had to approve the agreements, notwithstanding the views of the majority of the creditors committee and notwithstanding that the pooling agreement was not put before the Vice Chancellor by way of a scheme of arrangement under section 425 for which it was impracticable to convene any meetings, and notwithstanding the incidental departures from the *pari passu* rule of distribution which were to be found under the contribution agreement.

The ruling by the Court of Appeal relating to pooling was based very firmly on the special considerations applying to BCCI, in particular the commingling of assets and liabilities. The result, if implemented, will not be a process amounting to substantive consolidation but the pooling seeks to address the same problems as those found in the *Kheel* case,[77] indeed it is more ambitious than the application of the US doctrine because the pooling involves the estates of companies administered under the laws of at least three separate jurisdictions. The pooling of the assets and liabilities of BCCI will be achieved under the liquidators' powers of compromise rather than by way of a formal scheme of arrangement, the implementation of which would, according to the English courts, have been impossible.

[74]*Ibid* at p. 733.
[75]*Ibid* at p. 720.
[76]*Ibid* at p. 733.
[77]*See* n. 53.

12

The Model International Insolvency Co-operation Act

Timothy E. Powers* and Rona R. Mears**
Haynes and Boone, LLP, Dallas, Texas, USA

John A. Barrett***
Fulbright & Jaworski, Houston, Texas, USA

Businesses have expanded their operations throughout the world and governments have followed diligently with harmonised trade regulations, tax treaties, and even judicial co-operation conventions. Creditors have loaned funds across borders, investors have started buying securities around the globe and around the clock, and accordingly international regulation of lending and securities transactions is being discussed, if not yet enacted.

The contrast in international insolvencies is dramatic. A multinational business that fails, or that tries to reorganise in response to impending insolvency, must face a maze of often conflicting insolvency laws in the several countries where its assets and creditors are located. Furthermore, it finds no international means to discipline and integrate domestic insolvency laws so that it may marshal all of its assets and satisfy all creditors in one proceeding, in one place. The multinational debtor's estate is often inequitably dismantled, as in one jurisdiction after another, creditors find favour in local courts and take local assets to satisfy their claims without regard to other

---

*Partner, Haynes and Boone, LLP, Dallas, Texas, USA., Chairman, Committee J–1, Subcommittee on International Co-operation in Bankruptcy Proceedings, Section of Business Law, International Bar Association.

**Partner, Haynes and Boone, LLP, Dallas, Texas, USA., Member of Committee J and Subcommittee J–1, Section of Business Law, International Bar Association, and principal drafter of the Model International Insolvency Co-operation Act.

***Partner, Fulbright & Jaworski, Houston, Texas, USA, Chairman, Committee J, Section of Business Law, International Bar Association.

Current Issues in Cross-Border Insolvency and Reorganisations (E. B. Leonard, C. W. Besant, eds.; 1–85333–958–X; © International Bar Association; pub. Graham & Trotman/International Bar Association, 1994; printed in Great Britain), pp. 233-243.

creditors or jurisdictions.[1] Thus, the fairness to debtor and creditors alike that is sought with such diligence in domestic proceedings, becomes an idle dream in most cross-border insolvencies. Such incongruity is embarrassment enough in itself. More troubling, however, is the uncertainty and lack of predictability in global commercial relations — and particularly lending — that is created by the absence of a framework for international insolvency law.

12.1 Cooperation or chaos

Insolvency lawyers, accountants and administrators need no further evidence of the dilemmas faced in conducting an international insolvency proceeding; they experience such problems routinely. What does deserve attention, however, is the prospect to be faced in this decade, and in the next century. More companies will be doing business worldwide — acquiring, borrowing, merging, buying and selling, lending and investing, across many borders. At the same time, a certain predictable proportion of these multinational companies will become insolvent, or, worse yet, a global economic disruption may trigger international insolvencies on a massive scale. In such circumstances, the frustration and inequity experienced now may grow into economic and legal chaos for creditors, debtors, and such innocent third parties as consumers, investors and governments.

By its nature, the problem of international insolvencies cannot be solved by independent action in individual nations without due consideration for the systems and statutes of other countries and without a fundamental commitment to the principle of universality.[2] Equitable results for all creditors and the multinational debtor will only come about by a central administration of the debtor's estate, with the aid and support of other jurisdictions. To pursue an isolated approach in individual countries, without co-operation, takes us no further than the current state of affairs in which the courts in many countries practice territoriality[3] with regard to foreign insolvency proceedings and only advocate universality when their courts are claiming the worldwide assets of a local debtor.[4]

A co-operative approach to cross-border insolvencies would seem to be the proper subject for a multilateral convention. A number of efforts have been undertaken historically to draft bilateral or multilateral conventions[5] but, with only

---

[1]See, eg, *In re McLean Industries, Inc, First Colony Farms, Inc, United States Lines, Inc, and United States Lines (S.A.), Inc, Debtors, Bankruptcy Nos. 86 B 12238-86 B 12241 (HCB)*, US Bankruptcy Court, SD New York, filed 24 November 1986, especially as discussed in Vogel, "There's No Word for Chapter 11 in Dutch", *Business Week*, 30 November 1987, p. 62. The variety and complexity of insolvency laws in various jurisdictions is evident in compilations such as R. Gitlin & R. Mears (eds.) *International Loan Workouts and Bankruptcies* (1989); J. Dalhuisen, *Dalhuisen on International Insolvency and Bankruptcy* (1984).

[2]"Universality" generally presumes that a local bankruptcy adjudication will have full international effect, and envisions a single bankruptcy administration of the entire estate at the domicile of the debtor. See Powers & Mears, "Protecting a US Debtor's Assets in International Bankruptcy: A Survey and Proposal for Reciprocity", 10 *N.C.J. Int'l L. & Comm. Reg.* 303 (1985), pp. 305–306.

[3]"Territoriality" rejects the extraterritorial effect of bankruptcy adjudication and requires the administration of bankruptcy proceedings in each country where the debtor's assets are found. See Powers & Mears (*see* n. 2), p. 306.

[4]See, eg, Powers & Mears (*see* n. 2), pp. 309–340. Nearly all of the jurisdictions surveyed evidence this anomaly to some extent.

[5]Among the most notable attempts at insolvency treaties are: an EEC draft bankruptcy convention (Draft, Convention on Bankruptcy, Winding-Up, Arrangements, Compositions and Similar Proceedings (1980), reprinted in 3 *Common Mkt. Rep.* (CCH) para. 6111 (31 March 1981)), and a US–Canada draft bilateral treaty (Draft of United States of America-Canada Bankruptcy Treaty, 29 October 1979, reprinted in J. Dalhuisen (*see* n. 1), App. D–6A–1 to 6A–13).

several limited exceptions,[6] such efforts have been unsuccessful. Many reasons have been given for the failure of treaty proposals on international insolvency. Insolvency is perceived in most societies as a substantially private matter, not one that requires government intervention beyond providing local proceedings to settle the affairs of a local debtor or creditor. Governments have no compelling interest in giving the time and attention to delicate international negotiations required for a treaty on insolvency: no revenues will result; no wars will be prevented; no fundamental protections enhanced. Multinational businesses, like their domestic counterparts, assume that they will succeed and cannot be persuaded to lobby for international protection in the event that they become insolvent. Likewise, multinational lenders are uninterested, as they assume that their lending decisions are fundamentally sound and that a relatively small proportion of their borrowers will become insolvent. Finally, agreement on a unified approach to insolvency as the basis for a workable multilateral convention requires so much specificity and the resolution of so many issues and policies, that most drafts become impossibly detailed and complex, and therefore unworkable.[7]

Another avenue must be found for encouraging and implementing the co-operation of nations so that the central administration of international insolvencies based on universality will become routine and thus predictable. One solution that has been proposed is a Model International Insolvency Co-operation Act ("MIICA" or "Model Act")[8] that may be adopted through legislation in each jurisdiction, and will create a network of reciprocal co-operation for international insolvency proceedings. In essence, the enactment of MIICA throughout the world would result in a single, or at least central, proceeding in a single place, collecting and administering the debtor's entire estate, treating equitably all creditors worldwide and binding all by the debtor's discharge, or alternatively, allowing the debtor to make a fresh start in worldwide reorganisation.

12.2 In the beginning: What MIICA is (and is not)

If multinationals, lenders and governments are not interested in advocating cross-border insolvency co-operation, then who is? Certainly one answer is the lawyers, accountants, administrators and others who must provide counsel and manage proceedings in international insolvencies. Therefore, it is not surprising that the Model Act currently proposed was born out of the practical problems and frustrations of practitioners participating in international insolvency proceedings on behalf of their debtor or creditor clients. A series of discussions were held by these practitioners during 1986–88, at international insolvency institutes and meetings of the International

---

[6]eg, the Scandinavian Convention, 7 November 1933, 155 LNTS 136; the Bustamente Code of Private International Law, 20 February 1928, 86 LNTS 362 (chapter on bankruptcy).
[7]See, e.g., Powers & Mears (*see* n. 2), pp. 347–348.
[8]Model International Insolvency Co-operation Act, Third Draft, 1 November 1988 (hereafter "MIICA"), prepared and printed by Committee J, International Bar Association, London, UK. MIICA and its Official Comment are published in the International Business Lawyer (July/August 1989). Copies may also be obtained by writing to Timothy E. Powers, Haynes and Boone, LLP, 3100 NationsBank Plaza, 901 Main Street, Dallas, Texas 75202, USA, Telephone: (214) 651–5610; Fax: (214) 651–5940.

Bar Association ("IBA") Committee J.[9]A consensus was reached: drafting and nego-tiating a treaty on international insolvency would be a long, and perhaps unsuccessful process; meanwhile something must be done to encourage cross-border co-operation and provide help to those conducting international insolvencies.

Initially, the practitioners agreed that the primary principle that should govern international insolvencies is universality, the vision of a single insolvency adminis-tration, protecting and marshalling the debtor's estate and providing for a reorganisa-tion or distribution of assets with regard to all creditors everywhere. Later discussions focused on what types of relief and help should be available in countries outside the site of a central insolvency proceeding, and the results were predictable: the stay or dismissal of local proceedings, the production of records and access to testimony, the turnover of assets, the recognition and enforcement of judgments and orders, and the recognition of a representative of the debtor's estate. Flexibility in procedures and more than a modicum of consideration for local policies and laws were also identified as keys to successful co-operation, but always within the context of a reciprocal duty to co-operate.

Based on a number of considerations, including a proposal for reciprocity that had been raised in a 1985 law journal article,[10] a continued disenchantment with treaty proposals, and an interest in the mechanism of the US section 304 proceeding,[11] an official body was organised by Committee J of the IBA to conduct an international insolvency co-operation project[12] and to draft a model statute that could be adopted as domestic legislation in individual countries, yet provide a reciprocal and unified method for handling cross-border insolvencies.

An initial draft of MIICA[13] was circulated in February 1988 to members of Committee J who formed country committees of insolvency practitioners that reviewed and commented on the first and subsequent drafts.[14] Revisions were made to drafts in direct response to those country comments that received a significant

[9]Among the meetings at which the seminal discussions occurred were: American Bar Association National Institutes on "International Loan Workouts and Bankruptcies," New York City, 1985 and 1987; International Bar Association ("IBA") Biennial Conference, Meeting of Committee J (Creditors' Rights, Insolvency, Liquidation and Reorganisation), chaired by Ronald de Ruuk and John A. Barrett, New York City, 1986; IBA Section on Business Law Biennial Conference, Meeting of Committee J, chaired by Ronald de Ruuk and John A. Barrett, London, 1987; IBA Biennial Conference, Meeting of Committee J, chaired by John A. Barrett, Buenos Aires, 1988; and IBA Section on Business Law Biennial Conference, Meeting of Committee J, chaired by John A. Barrett, Strasbourg, 1989.

[10]See Powers & Mears (see n. 2), pp. 346–350.

[11]Bankruptcy Code, s 304, 11 USC s 304 (1979) (hereafter "section 304"). See generally Powers, "section 304: The US Model for Recognition of Foreign Bankruptcy Proposals," reprinted in R. Gitlin & R. Mears (see n. 1), pp. 83–108; Gitlin & Flaschen, "The International Void in the Law of Multinational Bankruptcies", 42 Bus. Law. 307 (1987), pp. 315–322; and Powers & Mears (see n. 2), pp. 341–346.

[12]Although originally organised on an ad hoc basis, the group was established in early 1988 as Subcommittee J–1 on International Co-operation in Bankruptcy Proceedings (the "Subcommittee on International Co-operation").

[13]The first draft of MIICA, dated 1 February 1988, was drafted by members of the Subcommittee on International Co-operation, including the authors. A second draft was prepared by the Subcommittee in response to comments and dated 1 July 1988 (hereafter the "Second Draft").

[14]The original country committees participating in the MIICA project were from: Australia, Canada, England, Federal Republic of Germany, Israel, Italy, Japan, Nigeria, Scotland, Switzerland and the US. More recently country commentators have been added from Argentina, Brazil, Denmark, France, Mexico, Norway, Portugal, South Africa, Spain and Uruguay.

amount of support. Thus, the current draft of MIICA[15] belongs to no particular authors and to no one jurisdiction.

Certainly none of its authors or commentators would claim that MIICA is necessarily the ultimate solution to handling international insolvencies. Other approaches will be followed simultaneously, most notably by those who continue to advocate a treaty. But MIICA is at least a starting point and an occasion to focus attention on the dire circumstances of cross-border insolvencies. In its almost pristine simplicity, MIICA offers a manageable framework that helps us to imagine a world in which international insolvency co-operation is a reality; by doing so, the Model Act fosters the spirit of co-operation it envisions.

12.3 The Model Act: principles and provisions

12.3.1 Principles

An Official Comment to the Model Act[16] begins by stating the general principles on which MIICA is based. It underscores the central role of universality in the thinking of its authors and commentators:

"Insofar as possible, ... universality should be the guiding principle of all efforts toward international insolvency co-operation, for it alone is truly compatible with the realisation of equal treatment of all creditors, debtors, assets and liabilities, and the swift and effective administration of the estate. Within the parameters of this overarching principle, mechanisms must be provided for the recognition of foreign representatives, the stay of local proceedings, the production of documents and testimony, the integration of asset distribution and other forms of ancillary relief. In a world of increasing global integration and growth of true multinational business entities, these principles are the indispensable elements in attaining equity and fairness in international insolvency proceedings."[17]

All of the specific provisions of MIICA flow from this statement of principle, utilizing ancillary cases as the primary means to obtain relief and mandating co-operation based on reciprocity. Although appearing almost naive on its face, MIICA's concept, and the provocative image it creates, has already evoked a stimulating response from the eighteen country committees currently involved in the project.[18]

---

[15]The current draft, dated 1 November 1988, resulted from revisions made after comments were received at the meeting of Committee J held in Buenos Aires in October 1988.

[16]Official Comment to Model International Insolvency Co-operation Act, Third Draft, 1 November 1988 (hereafter "Official Comment"), prepared by Committee J, International Bar Association, London, England. Copies of the Official Comment may be obtained by writing to Timothy E. Powers, Haynes and Boone, LLP, 3100 NationsBank Plaza, 901 Main Street, Dallas, Texas 75202, USA, Telephone: (214) 651-5610; Fax: (214) 651-5940.

[17]*Ibid*, p. 1.

[18]Country committee comments on MIICA from the participating jurisdictions have been collected by the Subcommittee on International Co-operation and reproduced by Committee J for distribution and discussion purposes as "Proposal for Consultative Draft of Model International Insolvency Co-operation Act for Adoption by Domestic Legislation With or Without Modification," dated 15 March 1989 (hereafter the "Country Reports Compilation"). Each of the reports includes a general response to MIICA, specific observations and comments, and proposals for promoting MIICA and harmonising it with existing statutes.

12.3.2 Provisions

The substantive provisions of MIICA[19] are concisely contained in seven sections that cover three major topics: duties of the local court to assist foreign insolvency proceedings, procedures for providing such assistance and insolvency treaty override of the Model Act. The Official Comment sets out, with regard to each section, its purposes and sources, and a brief explanation that elaborates on how the section is intended to work and on any difficult issues or problems the section has raised in preliminary considerations of MIICA.

(a) Duties of the local court

Section 1 imposes on the local court in a jurisdiction that adopts MIICA (the local or recognising court is referred to hereafter as the "court" or "local court"), three fundamental duties in insolvency matters. The court must:

(a) recognise a foreign representative of a debtor;
(b) "act in aid of and be auxiliary to" a foreign proceeding that is underway in a country that has adopted domestic legislation substantially the same as MIICA; *and*
(c) provide such aid to foreign proceedings in any other country if:
    (i) that locale is a proper and convenient forum, and
    (ii) it is in the overall interest of the creditors to administer the estate there.[20]

The Official Comment clearly identifies the significance of section 1 by asserting that it "supplies a foundation for the entire model act and its principle of universality".[21] The terms "in aid of" and "auxiliary to" are described as portraying the "ideal role"[22] of the local court with regard to foreign insolvency proceedings, while the recognition of the foreign representative provides an entry point for the debtor and its estate into the court. The preliminary clause of section 1 that sets out the types of foreign proceedings to which the Model Act applies is purposely broad, to include all types of insolvency matters, and in particular to include reorganisations and related mechanisms designed to rehabilitate rather than liquidate the debtor.

Although similar on its face to the methodology of the US Bankruptcy Code section 304 proceeding, sources for section 1 named in the Official Comment also include English, Australian and Canadian law.[23] Several features of MIICA distinguish it from the US section 304 proceeding, including the strict reciprocity requirement of section 1(b) that mandates co-operation of the local court with its counterpart in a foreign country which has also adopted MIICA or similar domestic legislation, and, secondly, the limited enumeration of issues to be considered by the court in deciding whether to provide co-operation to a court located in a non-reciprocal jurisdiction.[24] Among the unresolved issues raised by the Official Comment to section 1 is whether in many jurisdictions the court would go so far in providing aid as to recognise and enforce foreign revenue (tax) or penal claims, both of which are seldom recognised or enforced

---

[19]References throughout the text and footnotes to "sections" and "subsections" refer to sections and subsections of MIICA.
[20]Section 1.
[21]Official Comment, section 1, Explanation.
[22]*Ibid.*
[23]Official Comment, section 1, Sources.
[24]Contrast, eg, section 1 provisions and section 304 provisions as discussed in references cited in n. 11.

now. As with other similar considerations, it is submitted here that this issue must be resolved by each jurisdiction as it adapts MIICA prior to enactment.[25]

(b) Ancillary cases

Once recognised by the local court, the foreign representative's primary means for obtaining relief is to commence in the local jurisdiction a case ancillary to the foreign proceeding, as provided in section 2. The ancillary case may be commenced for purposes of obtaining one or more of the types of assistance enumerated in section 2, or "obtaining any other appropriate relief".[26] The breadth in scope of the relief available is underscored at the close of subsection 2(a): the local court is authorised to exercise "such additional powers with respect to the matter as it could exercise if the matter had arisen within its own jurisdiction".[27] In response to the anxieties of commentators that this provision may be misused, the Official Comment adds in its explanation: "... however, this provision is not intended to provide the Court with discretion to favour local creditors or other local parties in interest."[28]

In order to ensure that all proceedings in the local jurisdiction are administered together in aid of the foreign jurisdiction, section 2(b) of MIICA provides that as soon as an ancillary case has been commenced, any pending proceedings related to the debtor's insolvency will be consolidated with the ancillary case. Thus, for instance, if local creditors have acted independently to enforce their claims, such actions would be consolidated and administered through the ancillary case.

Once again, the similarity of the ancillary case to the US section 304 proceeding is obvious. In the description of sources appearing in the Official Comment, however, the characteristics that distinguish MIICA are described and the sources to which this section is attributed include, in addition to the US provision, legislation in both Canada and Switzerland.[29]

(c) Separate proceedings as an alternative

Section 3 allows the foreign representative an alternative course of action if the local court denies the commencement of an ancillary case: the representative may petition for a full insolvency proceeding in accordance with the laws of the local jurisdiction. The most common use of this alternative would presumably be by foreign representatives from non-reciprocal jurisdictions who are denied aid based on the discretion of the local court under subsections 1(c)(i) or (ii). The Official Comment to section 3 points out that the foreign representative must first apply for relief by petitioning for an ancillary case, and may not in his or her discretion, choose to commence a full proceeding instead.[30] In response to objections that the foreign representative should have discretion in the first instance to commence a full separate proceeding, the drafters respond that the primary goal of MIICA is to create a central administration and that the sacrifice of such discretion is necessary to attain that goal.[31]

---

[25]Official Comment, section 1, Explanation.
[26]Subsection 2(a)(v).
[27]Subsection 2(a).
[28]Official Comment, section 2, Explanation.
[29]Official Comment, section 2, Sources. Regarding parallels to the US section 304 proceeding, see section 304 (*see* n. 11) and references cited in n. 11.
[30]Official Comment, section 3, Explanation.
[31]*Ibid.*

(d) Applicable law

In administering an insolvency proceeding related to a foreign insolvency, the local court must determine what substantive insolvency law to apply. Section 4 distinguishes the ancillary case from the full separate proceeding that may be commenced as an alternative avenue of relief under section 3. With regard to the full proceeding, the local court is to apply the substantive insolvency law of the local jurisdiction.[32] However, if a foreign representative commences a case ancillary to a foreign proceeding, the local court is to apply the substantive insolvency law of the jurisdiction where the foreign proceeding is being conducted, unless the court is constrained from doing so by considerations of private international law or conflict of laws principles.[33] The Official Comment asserts that whenever possible, ancillary cases should be governed by the substantive insolvency law of the foreign jurisdiction and that application of local substantive law "should only occur in isolated and infrequent instances when the application of the substantive insolvency law of the foreign proceeding would violate public policy".[34] Regarding procedural matters, the Official Comment observes that "presumably" in ancillary cases procedure would be governed by the laws and rules of procedure of the local recognising jurisdiction.[35] Participants in the MIICA project have remarked on the great difficulties that may occur in requiring the local court to apply foreign substantive law, and the likelihood that this provision would not be acceptable in many adopting jurisdictions.[36]

(e) Treaty override

In recognition of the continuing efforts toward drafting a treaty on international insolvency co-operation, and the dedication of some practitioners to this approach, section 7 was added rather late in the drafting process.[37] This section provides that if such treaty comes into force and has been ratified by the local jurisdiction, the treaty will override MIICA. Authors of the Official Comment, mindful of the ongoing efforts for a draft treaty, and the objections of some that the enactment of MIICA may stall such efforts, have concluded in the explanation to section 7:

> "Enactment of the model act is not to be construed as prohibiting or deterring the adoption and ratification of such treaties or conventions; on the contrary, section 7 explicitly addresses the issue of how to reconcile the later ratification of such a treaty by a country which has previously adopted the model act."[38]

(f) Miscellaneous provisions

In addition to the sections discussed above, other sections of MIICA supply definitions of "foreign representative" and "foreign proceeding",[39] and provide that an appearance by a foreign representative under the Model Act does not submit the rep-

---

[32]Subsection 4(b).
[33]Subsection 4(a).
[34]Official Comment, section 4, Explanation.
[35]*Ibid.*
[36]See generally Country Reports Compilation (*see* n. 18).
[37]Section 7 was added to the Second Draft just prior to its publication in July 1988.
[38]Official Comment, section 7, Explanation. English Country Committee chairman, Michael Prior, London, England, has suggested that MIICA provides the "headlines" of international insolvency co-operation and that the details of implementation must be provided later by treaty. English Country Report, Country Reports Compilation (*see* n. 18).
[39]Section 6.

resentative to jurisdiction of the local courts for other purposes.[40] The issue of proper jurisdiction of the foreign court is dealt with obliquely in the definition of "foreign proceedings". In order to meet the definition of "foreign proceeding", the foreign court must have proper jurisdiction. The Official Comment explains that the determination of proper jurisdiction is made by the local court, and the authors assert that they assume the court would use a forum *nonconveniens* approach, conceding jurisdiction based on "greater contacts with the debtor and its estate".[41] In response to objections that MIICA might encourage debtors to select a forum most favourable to their interests, the Official Comment remarks that the local court may consider whether there has been improper forum selection or "shopping" when making its assessment of proper jurisdiction.[42]

(g) Current status

MIICA was endorsed by the governing body of the International Bar Association in June 1989, for adoption by domestic legislation with or without modification. Twenty-one countries are currently developing legislation for the adoption of domestic legislation in their countries similar to MIICA.[43] MIICA is also available in seven languages.[44] However, although its fundamental principles are inarguable and its procedural mechanisms quite simple, MIICA faces major hurdles in its adoption. In the US, for example, it is anticipated that problems will arise because of the omission of the qualification factors set forth in section 304(c). In addition, a "wait and see" attitude is being taken in the European Community in the face of the Strasbourg Convention and the implementation of 1992 principles. Others are postponing actively advocating MIICA within their countries until at least one of the major countries formally adopts or incorporates MIICA into its bankruptcy law. Additional problems are presented in countries having adopted internal legislation of their own which may overlap or compete with the effect of MIICA.[45]

12.4 A world with MIICA: vision and reality

In contemplating the possibilities raised by MIICA for international insolvency practice, and for the administration of multinational estates, the vision is in stark

---

[40]Section 5.
[41]Official Comment, section 6, Explanation.
[42]*Ibid.*
[43]The countries currently considering the adoption of MIICA legislation include: Argentina, Australia, Brazil, Canada, Denmark, England, France, Germany, Israel, Italy, Japan, Mexico, Nigeria, Norway, Portugal, Scotland, South Africa, Spain, Switzerland, US and Uruguay.
[44]MIICA is available in seven languages: Danish, Dutch, English, German, Japanese, Norwegian and Spanish. Copies of the translations of MIICA are available from Timothy E. Powers, Haynes and Boone, LLP, 3100 NationsBank Plaza, 901 Main Street, Dallas, Texas 75202 USA-3714, Telephone: (214) 651-5610; Fax: (214) 651-5940.
[45]See eg, Swiss Federal Code on Private International Law (CPIL), effective 1 January 1989. This statute provides for the recognition of a foreign bankruptcy decree (if the decree is enforceable in the country where it is issued), (a) there is no ground for denial under Art 25 (generally, Art 25 of the Statute relates to proceedings preempted by an already commenced Swiss action ordered between the same parties and having the same object, or to orders obtained abroad in violation of fundamental notice/fairness concepts); and (b) if the country where the decree was issued grants reciprocity. However, the recognition of a foreign bankruptcy decree requires as a rule the application of the bankruptcy law consequences under Swiss law for the foreign debtor's assets located in Switzerland. See also s 426 of the English Insolvency Act 1986.

contrast to reality. At its best, the vision of a world with MIICA includes adoption of the Model Act in substantially its model form, and in at least a sizeable number of major trading nations. This alone would provide a significant step towards establishing a network of reciprocal international insolvency co-operation. The extent to which MIICA is supported, and the ingenuity of local practitioners in adapting MIICA and harmonising its provisions with existing local laws will play major roles in determining whether, and how broadly, MIICA is adopted. The vision of universality — and a conviction that MIICA has a role in making it a worldwide reality — is one that must be held by insolvency practitioners in many countries of the world, if the MIICA project is to succeed. Such conviction must exist in the face of formidable obstacles.

The reality is that while some jurisdictions may adopt MIICA, others will not. Those that do adopt MIICA will — and indeed are expected to — adapt the form of the Model Act to make it work in their individual jurisdictions, and to make it sufficiently acceptable to be enacted. A long process of advocacy and negotiation will have to occur, country by country, except in those rare instances where integrated legal systems may provide the opportunity for adoption at a multinational level covering a number of jurisdictions, as in the integrated European Community.

In the process, significant issues will be raised, and dilemmas will inevitably occur. Some civil law jurisdictions may find the entire ancillary case procedure unamendable to their legal structure. More fundamentally, some jurisdictions may be unable to adopt MIICA because of the preference for local creditors or the dominance of local self-interest generally that permeates their legal and policy regimes. Others will argue that the theory and substance of MIICA is not sufficiently jurisdiction–neutral ever to be taken seriously in their own or other jurisdictions.

Finally, perhaps the most difficult question has already been put forward: are we able to envision accurately how MIICA will really work, even in the hypothetical best situation in which it is adopted widely and in essentially its model form? And if so, will MIICA enhance the "overall effectiveness" in handling international insolvencies, rather than simply extending the individual powers secured for the foreign representative? In formulating this query, one commentator concludes:

> "Our main goal must be to improve the global system as a whole; with that in mind, [we must] see whether there has been a net, positive effect or whether new problems have been substituted for old."[46]

12.5 Conclusion

Insolvency practitioners and administrators around the world must concern themselves with the prospects for handling international insolvencies in the twenty-first century. Without their active involvement in the MIICA project now underway, international insolvency law may languish for yet another century, perpetuating the inequitable results now prevalent in multinational insolvency liquidations and reorganisations. If no one else will come forward to undertake the task, the insolvency professionals must, and in fact they may be uniquely suited to do so.

---

[46]Ralph D. McRae, Vancouver, British Columbia, in letter to Timothy E. Powers, Subcommittee on International Co-operation chairman, dated 15 August 1988.

It is much too early to assess the prospects for MIICA's success, although the prospective involvement and support of international organisations is a welcome move toward a broader dialogue and enactment in some jurisdictions. To suggest, however, that MIICA is the only avenue to international insolvency co-operation, or even the single best approach, is to miss the point. MIICA is a framework that for now appears to be workable and useful as a focus for discussion and action; one that has the support of a significant number of insolvency practitioners worldwide who are in a position to advocate its adoption and generate an international environment in which insolvency co-operation may evolve, if not in this decade, perhaps in the next century.

Finally, the effort that has been undertaken to conceptualise and draft the Model Act has been in itself an extraordinary one. The authors and commentators have gained much from one another as they have shared their aspirations for international co-operation. They have argued and counter-argued both the content and wording of MIICA, testing and prodding one another to see new views of insolvency issues, forcing one another to step out of their local venues and look squarely at the world of insolvency as a whole. It bodes well that the effort that has produced MIICA was itself one of genuine international collaboration and co-operation.

13

Effects of Foreign Bankruptcy Judgments and Powers of Foreign Receivers — A French Perspective

Laurent Gaillot
Lebray, Gaillot & Gravel, Paris, France

13.1 Introduction

International bankruptcies have become increasingly frequent in recent years. Because of the internationalisation of the economy and the growth of international trade, furthered in particular by numerous multilateral regional or worldwide trade or investment treaties, enterprises have developed their activities abroad. As a result, the enterprises' assets have been increasingly spread out over the territories of various countries.

A second reason is that the severe economic conditions that have prevailed recently and that led to numerous domestic bankruptcies clearly have also affected enterprises with multinational activities.[1]

International bankruptcies give rise to complex legal difficulties.[2] These difficulties are especially acute in the French legal environment for two reasons.[3] First, French law does not contain any statutory or regulatory provisions on the international aspects of bankruptcies. The recently enacted French Bankruptcy Law is on

---

[1]Coviaux, *"Redressement et liquidation judiciaires, Procédures collectives en droit international"*, *Jurisclasseur Droit International, Fascicule* 568, p. 1 (1989) (hereinafter cited as Coviaux); Vaisse, *"Les effets internationaux de la faillite en droit français"*, *1989 Revue de droit des affaires internationales (Rev. de dr. des aff. intern.)*, pp. 349 and 350.

[2]*Ibid.*; see generally *Coviaux; Trochu, Conflits de lois et conflits de juridictions en matière de faillite* (1967) (hereinafter cited as Trochu); Loussouarn & Bredin, *Droit du Commerce International* (1969), pp. 676 *et seq* (hereinafter cited as Loussouarn & Bredin). See also Ridruejo, *"La faillite en droit international privé"*, *Rec. Cours A. La Haye*, 1977-II-174; Didier, *"La problématique du droit de la faillite internationale"*, *1989 Rev. de dr. des aff. intern.* 201.

[3]Coviaux, p. 4.

Current Issues in Cross-Border Insolvency and Reorganisations (E. B. Leonard, C. W. Besant, eds.; 1–85333–958–X; © International Bar Association; pub. Graham & Trotman/International Bar Association, 1994; printed in Great Britain), pp. 245-257.

this issue as lacunary as the previous French bankruptcy statutes.[4] In addition, France has not yet entered into any multilateral conventions on bankruptcy.[5] France is only a party to bilateral treaties, and even the number of those treaties is limited. Solutions therefore result from the application of general private international law principles. In addition, French case law on international bankruptcies is scarce and often the decisions on these matters are early decisions.

Secondly, French courts have not made a clear choice between the two alternative concepts that may govern international bankruptcies.[6] Under the unity or universality principle, a bankruptcy decision rendered in one state should have effect in every country where the debtor has property or creditors. As a result, a simple set of proceedings may be followed.[7] Under the territoriality principle, however, bankruptcy declarations may be made in each of the states where the "insolvency" of the debtor has been established and theoretically, make it possible to have bankruptcy proceedings commenced in every country where the debtor has assets.[8]

French case law has tended to adopt the territoriality principle.[9] Indeed, French courts may commence bankruptcy proceedings in France against a foreign person and the law governing this bankruptcy shall be the *lex fori*.

French courts, however, have also taken into account the unity principle. For example, courts hold that a bankruptcy commenced against a person or entity whose domicile or registered seat is situated in France shall have extraterritorial effects. Also, French courts recognise effects in France of bankruptcy judgments rendered abroad and powers of foreign receivers[10] appointed further to these judgments.[11]

Recent leading judicial decisions have substantially amended the previous case law on this latter issue and significantly illustrated and/or developed the combined

---

[4]Law 85–98 of 25 January 1985 relating to judicial reorganisations (*redressements*) and liquidations, 1985 *Journal Officiel de la République Française* (JO), 26 January 1985, 1097. See generally Ripert & Roblot, *Traité de Droit Commercial* (13th ed., 1992), pp. 2846 *et seq* (hereinafter cited as Ripert & Roblot); Gaillot & Carton in Gitlin & Mears, *International Loan Workouts*, "Questionnaire on Creditors' Rights Against Business Debtors" (1989), pp. 321 *et seq*.

[5]Upon the date of the submission of this article, France has signed but not yet ratified the European convention relating to certain international aspects of bankruptcy. See generally BOTTIAU, "*La Convention européenne sur certains aspects internationaux de la faillite adoptée par le Conseil des Ministres lors de sa 434ème réunion des 19–23 février 1990*", 1990 *Revue des Procédures collectives*, pp. 97 *et seq*.

[6]See generally Loussouarn & Bredin, pp. 678 *et seq* Trochu, pp. 47 *et seq* Trochu, "*Encyclopédie Dalloz*", *Droit International, Faillite* (1969), pp. 3 *et seq* (hereinafter cited as Trochu Dalloz). Case law as to the application of the territoriality principle rather than the unity principle or vice versa does not necessarily follow a consistent pattern. Courts adopt a pragmatic approach which seems guided by the protection of creditors. *Ibid*, p. 12; Loussouarn & Bredin, p. 691.

[7]Coviaux, p. 679.

[8]*Ibid*; Trochu Dalloz, p. 7.

[9]Coviaux, p. 18; Ripert & Roblot, p. 2913; Mayer, *Droit international privé* (3rd ed., 1987), p. 659 (hereinafter cited as Mayer). In its 1988 annual report, the Supreme Court declares, however, without nuance, that French courts have adopted the territoriality principle. See Vasseur, note to Court of Appeals, Paris, 8 July 1992, *1992 Recueil Dalloz Sirey-Jurisprudence (Dalloz)* 476 at p. 478 note (1) (hereinafter cited as Vasseur).

[10]The term "receiver" is used in a broad sense and covers *inter alia* the notion of administrators as well as of liquidators.

[11]Coviaux, p. 18; see generally Grasman, "*Effets nationaux d'une procédure collective étrangère (Redressements ou liquidations judiciaires, faillite, concordat)*", 1990 *Revue Critique de Droit International Privé (RCDIP)* 421.

application by French courts of the territoriality and unity principles. This chapter analyses the effects of foreign bankruptcy decisions and the powers of foreign receivers in France in light of these recent developments, with a view toward acquainting the non-French reader with the main underlying principles of French case law on international bankruptcies.

It first examines the effects of these decisions and powers of these receivers in the absence of any applicable bankruptcy treaty. These effects and powers vary depending upon whether *exequatur* of the foreign judgment has been accorded (*see* **13.2**).[12] It then reviews the rules applicable to such effects and powers under the bilateral treaties on bankruptcy into which France has entered (*see* **13.3**).

13.2 Effects of foreign bankruptcy decisions and powers of foreign receivers in the absence of applicable bankruptcy treaties

Foreign bankruptcy judgments produce as of right certain effects in France.[13] These effects and the powers of foreign receivers are, however, limited when these judgments have not been submitted to *exequatur* (*see* **13.2.1**). Such effects and powers may become significantly broader after the *exequatur* of the foreign bankruptcy judgment has been accorded (*see* **13.2.2**).

13.2.1 Effects and powers prior to exequatur

French courts refuse to declare the foreign bankruptcy judgment enforceable unless this judgment has been granted *exequatur*.[14] The foreign bankruptcy judgment is nevertheless deemed to create a new legal situation and will have certain effects in France[15] although these effects remain limited.[16]

(a) Effects
Courts have consistently and repeatedly held that the foreign bankruptcy judgment evidences the powers of the foreign receiver and in particular its powers to represent creditors.[17] Accordingly, the foreign receiver is entitled to initiate *judicial*

---

[12]Art 509 of the New Code of Civil Procedure provides that "judgments rendered by foreign courts... are executory in the territories of the Republic in the manner and in the cases foreseen by the law." Art 2123 of the Civil Code states that execution can be held upon foreign judgments after they have been "declared executory by a French court". This declaration of executory force takes the form of an *exequatur*. See generally Battifol & Lagarde pp. 172 *et seq*; Mayer, pp. 389 *et seq*.

[13]Loussouarn & Bredin, p. 681.

[14]Coviaux, p. 96; *Contra Trib. de première instance, Saint-Pierre et Miquelon*, 26 October 1990, 1991 *Revue de Jurisprudence Commerciale (RJC)* 176.

[15]Battifol & Lagarde, p. 745; Loussouarn & Bredin, p. 688; Remery, note to Cass. civ., 25 February 1986, 1987 *Jurisclasseur Périodique, La Semaine Juridique (JCP)* II 14969 (hereinafter cited as Remery).

[16]*Ibid*, p. 358.

[17]Cass. civ., 21 June 1870, 1971 DP, 1, 294; Court of Appeals, Poitiers, 20 December 1972, 1974 RCDIP 118. Effects of bankruptcy judgments are in this respect similar to those of certain types of judgments, in particular, judgments respecting status and capacity. Indeed, such judgments are accorded some effects without an *exequatur* being required. Commentators refuse, however, to establish a parallel between bankruptcy judgments and judgments regarding status and capacity on the grounds that traditionally, under French bankruptcy law, there is no incapacity of the debtor as a result of the bankruptcy judgment. See eg Ripert & Roblot, p. 2913. The foreign bankruptcy judgment will evidence the powers of the foreign receiver provided that the commencement of bankruptcy proceedings and the appointment of this receiver are not disputed. Coviaux, p. 99.

proceedings in France.[18] He may also seek provisional remedies[19] and request the *exequatur* of the foreign bankruptcy judgment.[20]

Certain commentators also express the view that, should French bankruptcy proceedings have been commenced in France, the foreign receivers may file the claims of the foreign creditors in France.[21] Courts, however, must first verify that the foreign receiver has the necessary powers to this effect. In any event, foreign creditors should be allowed to file their claims independently from the foreign receiver.[22]

Finally, certain commentators citing early decisions argue that, subject to the limitations discussed below, foreign receivers should be able to exercise all the actions of the debtor[23] and, for example, collect the claims of the debtor.[24]

(b) Limitations

Before the foreign bankruptcy judgment has been granted *exequatur*, the foreign bankruptcy judgments will have limited effects and the powers of the foreign receiver will face serious limitations. These limitations result from the application of the territoriality doctrine as well as of the general principle pursuant to which a foreign judgment has not *res judicata* effects in France and may not be enforced in France until after *exequatur* has been accorded.[25]

The application of these principles as to foreign bankruptcy judgments and powers of foreign receivers lead to the following consequences:

(a) Prior to the *exequatur*, the debtor is not divested in France of his powers to administer and dispose of his assets. As a result, French courts have traditionally held that the debtor may freely dispose of his assets located in France.[26]

This debtor's freedom shall be curtailed only by the possible subsequent *exequatur* by French judges of the foreign bankruptcy judgment or the commencement of bankruptcy proceedings in France against the debtor and the possible ensuing avoidance of the debtor's actions during the so-called suspect period pursuant to French bankruptcy provisions.

(b) The foreign bankruptcy judgment does not affect creditors' rights in France. Creditors may bring actions in France to collect their claims.[27] The debtor may effect payments to his creditors and set off between the respective creditors' and debtors' claims may occur.[28] The debtor's debts, however, do not become due in France as a result of the foreign bankruptcy judgment. Also, creditors may initiate bankruptcy proceedings in France.[29]

---

[18]See eg Cass. civ., 21 June1870 (*see* n. 17); Cass. civ., 25 February 1986, 1987 JCP 14969; Court of Appeals, Paris, 8 July 1992, 1992 Dalloz 476.
[19]Coviaux, p. 100.
[20]Cass. civ., 7 November 1978, 1980 RCDIP 345.
[21]Coviaux, p. 100. See however Trochu Dalloz, ap. 30.
[22]*Ibid.*
[23]Coviaux, p. 101.
[24]Court of Appeals, Toulouse, 17 April 1883, 1883 *Journal du Droit International (Clunet)* 161.
[25]Loussouarn & Bredin, p. 689; Battifol & Lagarde, p. 745.
[26]Court of Appeals, Colmar, 10 February 1864, 1864 Sirey 2, 122; Court of Appeals, Poitiers, 20 December1972 (*see* n. 17).
[27]Cass. req., 12 November 1873, 1873 Sirey 1, 17.
[28]Cass. civ., 26 June 1905, 1905 Sirey 1, 433; *see* however 13.2.2 (b).
[29]Court of Appeals, Paris, 3 March 1878, 1878 Clunet 606.

(c) Generally, foreign compositions, arrangements between the debtor and his creditors (*concordats*) or similar proceedings do not produce effects in France.[30] Certain early decisions have therefore concluded that a creditor may initiate judicial proceedings in France against the debtor even though the arrangement between the debtor and creditors has been approved by the foreign bankruptcy court and such creditor has adhered to this arrangement. This case law, however, has been criticised by commentators.[31]

(d) Forfeiture of the debtor's rights further to the foreign bankruptcy judgment or more generally measures ordered by the foreign bankruptcy judges against the debtor's managers do not apply in France.[32]

(e) The foreign receiver may not take any executory measures over the debtor's assets in France and seek the sale of such assets.[33]

(f) The foreign receiver may not exercise any further actions should bankruptcy proceedings have been commenced in France. Powers of the French administrator and/or the French liquidator are then exclusive.[34]

The question thus revolves around the criteria on the basis of which French courts may have jurisdiction and commence bankruptcy proceedings in France.

Courts have consistently exercised jurisdiction when the domicile or the registered seat of the debtor is located in France.[35] To this effect, courts control whether the debtor's registered seat is indeed the seat where its activities are carried out. French courts assert jurisdiction when the debtor's registered seat abroad is fictitious and the corporate management actually operates on French territory.[36]

In addition, French courts have exercised jurisdiction in cases where the debtor had in France only a place of activity distinct from his domicile or registered seat. Under such circumstances, courts note the presence in France of a "branch", a "commercial establishment", a "commercial seat" and a "distinct establishment".[37] Further, French courts have commenced bankruptcy proceedings against foreign debtors (even when such debtors did not have any establishment in France) on the grounds of the business

---

[30]Cass. civ., 21 July 1903, 1904 Clunet 138.

[31]See eg Battifol & Lagarde, p. 746.

[32]*Ibid*, p. 745, note 8.

[33]Loussouarn & Bredin, p. 689. In a 1991 decision, the Paris Court of Appeals held that the *exequatur* of a foreign judgment does not constitute an executory measure as such and that the commencement of bankruptcy proceedings in France does not prevent the issuance of the *exequatur* order. Court of Appeals, Paris, 4 July 1991, 1992 Clunet 705.

[34]Cass. com., 19 January 1988, 1988 Dalloz 565; Coviaux, p. 101. Any creditors of the bankrupt, irrespective of their nationality, may file their claims with the French bankruptcy authorities. Cass. civ., 11 March 1913, 1914 Dalloz 1.185; Cass. com., 19 January 1988, cited above in this note.

[35]Cass. req., 26 April 1932, 1932 Gazette du Palais. 2, 145.

[36]Court of Appeals, Paris, 9 July 1960 as cited in Coviaux, p. 31. Cass. civ., 21 July 1987, 1987 Bulletin des Arrêts de la Cour de Cassation (Chambres civiles) (Bull. civ.) I No. 242.

[37]Cass. com., 19 January 1988 (*see* n. 34); Cass. req., 5 July 1897, 1897 DP 1, 515.

relationships entered into in France by these debtors,[38] the presence in France of a debtor's agent[39] or the location in France of certain of the debtor's assets.[40]

Finally, in certain cases, French courts have even resorted to the exclusive bases of jurisdiction provided for by Article 14 (French nationality of the plaintiff) and by Article 15 (French nationality of the defendant) of the Civil Code to institute bankruptcy proceedings against foreign debtors.[41]

The decisions recently rendered in connection with the Bank of Credit and Commerce International (BCCI) matter illustrate certain of the blocking effects for foreign receivers of the commencement of bankruptcy proceedings in France.[42]

The BCCI French bank was a branch of BCCI Ltd Overseas, a company whose registered seat was in the Cayman Islands. The BCCI French bank was based in Paris and had agencies in Marseille, Cannes and Monaco. The Paris Tribunal of Commerce commenced bankruptcy proceedings against the BCCI French bank. The liquidators of BCCI Overseas Ltd brought an appeal against this decision on the grounds, *inter alia*, that the Paris Tribunal of Commerce did not have jurisdiction.

The liquidators sought to avoid the opening of bankruptcy proceedings in each country where BCCI assets were situated and organise the distribution of these assets to the BCCI creditors on a worldwide basis. The liquidators argued that the BCCI liquidation judgment rendered in the Cayman Islands should apply universally and accordingly, that the Paris Tribunal of Commerce lacked jurisdiction to commence separate bankruptcy proceedings against the BCCI Paris branch.[43] The Paris Court of Appeals approved the decision rendered by the Paris Tribunal of Commerce.[44]

The Court of Appeals first pointed out that the decision appointing the BCCI liquidators in the Cayman Islands had not been submitted to *exequatur* in France and that this decision could not be recognised directly in France in the absence of any treaty between France and the Cayman Islands. Accordingly, the Court declared that standard rules as to international jurisdiction should be applied and domestic rules as to venue should be transposed in the international sense.[45]

---

[38]See eg Court of Appeals, Colmar, 10 May 1932, 1934 Clunet 98; Cass. com., 19 March 1979, 1981 RCDIP 525.

[39]Cass. civ., 12 July 1962, 1963 Clunet 1056.

[40]Court of Appeals, Colmar, 10 May 1932 (*see* n. 38). Such bases of jurisdiction may appear debatable in light of Art 1 of the French bankruptcy law. It shall be recalled that, under this provision, the *redressement judiciaire* (reorganisation proceedings) aims at: (a) saving the enterprise; (b) maintaining the enterprise's activities and the jobs it provides; and (c) satisfying the creditors' claims (*apurement du passif*). See Argenson & Toujas, *Traité theorique et pratique des procédures collectives* (1987) p. 113.

[41]Court of Appeals, 17 July 1877, 1878 Clunet 271; Court of Appeals, Colmar, 10 May 1932 (*see* n. 38). This case law has been criticised by several commentators. See eg Trochu Dalloz, p. 19. As noted by commentators, under the underlying circumstances of certain of such cases, competence of the courts which asserted jurisdiction on the grounds of Art 14 and 15 may be justified on other bases such as the presence in France of a debtor's establishment. Coviaux, p. 40.

[42]Court of Appeals, Paris, 8 July 1992 (*see* n. 18); Trib. com., Paris, 23 July 1991, 1992 Dalloz 232.

[43]Vasseur, p. 478.

[44]1992 Dalloz 476, p. 477.

[45]*Ibid*. Generally, courts refer *inter alia* to the standard domestic rules as to territorial jurisdiction to determine whether or not they have jurisdiction to adjudicate a dispute of an international character. Cass. civ., 19 October 1959, 1960 Dalloz 37. See generally Battifol & Lagarde, pp. 673 *et seq*.

The Court of Appeals then recalled that under Article 1 of the Decree of 27 December 1985,[46] bankruptcy proceedings must be commenced before the tribunal in the jurisdiction of which the debtor's registered seat is located, and when this office is located abroad, proceedings must be commenced before the tribunal in the jurisdiction in which the debtor's main establishment is situated.

After having noted that the registered seat of BCCI Ltd Overseas was located abroad, the Court held that, among the BCCI Ltd Overseas branches in France and Monaco, the Paris branch, due to its importance in comparison with that of the other French or Monaco branches, constituted the main BCCI branch on the French territory and therefore fell within the scope of Article 1 of the 1985 Decree. As a result, the Court held that the Paris Tribunal of Commerce had validly exercised jurisdiction in order to pronounce bankruptcy proceedings in France.[47]

13.2.2 Effects and powers after exequatur

Subject to certain conditions, exequatur may be sought and accorded to bankruptcy judgments.

(a) *Exequatur* — conditions

(i) PROCEDURAL ASPECTS
(a) Any person who has an "interest" to do so may file a request for *exequatur*.[48] Clearly, the foreign receiver will meet this requirement. Other persons, however, may have interest in initiating *exequatur* proceedings. These might include:
  - the debtor himself. For example, it may be in the debtor's interest to claim the benefit in France of a reduction of debts obtained under a settlement arrangement entered into by the debtor with his creditors further to a foreign bankruptcy judgment[49];
  - the public prosecutor. Traditionally, courts have recognised the right of the public prosecutor to request the *exequatur* of the foreign bankruptcy judgment in order to enforce in France the sanctions imposed upon the debtor.[50] Commentators express the view that the public prosecutor should be entitled to initiate *exequatur* proceedings even when the foreign bankruptcy court has not imposed any sanction[51];
(b) Pursuant to standard procedural rules, execution proceedings are brought before the court in the jurisdiction in which the centre of the debtor's activities (or in lack of such, the debtor's assets), are situated[52];

[46]Decree No. 85–1388 of 27 December 1985, JO 29 December 1985, 15281.
[47]The Paris Court of Appeals therefore considers the presence in France of a branch as a sufficient element to commence bankruptcy proceedings under Art 1 of the 1985 Decree regardless of whether this branch might not be necessarily characterised as the "main" establishment in light of the global debtor's organisation. This holding is in line with early decisions of the Supreme Court. See eg Remery, note to Trib. com., Paris, 23 July 1991, 1992 Dalloz 232, p. 234. The validity of this holding, however, has been disputed by certain commentators. See Vallens, 1993 RJC 6, p. 9.
[48]Coviaux, p. 111.
[49]Cass. civ., 17 May 1983, 1983 Bull. civ. I No. 147.
[50]Court of Appeals, Paris, 8 July 1880, 1880 Clunet 581.
[51]Loussouarn & Bredin, p. 690; Coviaux, p. 111.
[52]Loussouarn & Bredin, p. 690.

(c) Proceedings are initiated by a summons (*assignation*) directed to the defending party and are adversary (even if the foreign bankruptcy judgment has been rendered further to an *ex parte* motion).[53] Admittedly, certain lower courts have held that *exequatur* might be granted further to an *ex parte* motion.[54] This solution, however, has been criticised by commentators and set aside by the Supreme Court in a 1986 decision.[55]

(ii) REQUIREMENTS

In order to be granted *exequatur*, the foreign bankruptcy judgment must meet the five standard basic requirements imposed to this effect by current case law.[56]

The first three requirements pertain to the necessity that the rendering court have adjudicatory jurisdiction in the international sense. Namely, competence of the foreign court shall be recognised in France for *exequatur* purposes provided that:

(a) under French conflict-of-jurisdiction rules, French courts do not have exclusive jurisdiction;
(b) the asserted jurisdictional basis is acceptable in view of the connection of the parties and the underlying transaction with the court of origin;
(c) the choice of the foreign forum is not fraudulent.

In addition, the rendering court must be competent under its own law and must have applied the law indicated by French choice-of-law rules. Also, the judgment and the procedure in the foreign court must conform to French conceptions of *ordre public* (public policy), and the judgment must be free of fraud. French courts may review issues of fact as well as law only for the purposes of determining whether or not these five conditions are met.

The satisfaction of jurisdiction test does not usually give rise to difficulties as, in the case of international bankruptcies, the criterion for exercising jurisdiction based on the debtor's registered office, domicile or main offices, is widely accepted.[57] Difficulties may arise, however, when jurisdiction is derived from the presence of the debtor's assets or the seeking by the debtor of credit facilities in the country of the rendering bankruptcy court.

Case law on this issue is not entirely consistent. It can only be noted that, generally, certain courts tend solely to prevent patent frauds. Others declare, however, that the dispute must be sufficiently connected with the country in which proceedings are brought and that the choice of this jurisdiction must neither be arbitrary, artificial nor fraudulent.[58]

In addition, the foreign bankruptcy decision must conform to French conceptions of *ordre public* . The notion of public policy for purposes of the *exequatur* of foreign

[53]*Ibid*; Coviaux, p. 114.
[54]See eg *Tribunal de Grande Instance*, Avesnes sur Helpe, 7 May 1987, 1988 RCDIP 368. Commentators explain this solution on the grounds that a foreign receiver may initiate *exequatur* proceedings only for the purpose of avoiding the commencement of bankruptcy proceedings in France and not for taking enforcement measures. Loussouarn & Bredin, p. 690.
[55]*Ibid*; Cass. civ., 12 November 1986, 1986 Bull. civ. I No. 257.
[56]There exist no statutory provisions regulating the recognition and enforcement of foreign judgments. See generally Battifol & Lagarde, pp. 717 *et seq.*
[57]Loussouarn & Bredin, p. 690.
[58]Court of Appeals, Paris, 10 November 1971, 1973 Clunet 239.

bankruptcy decisions has been rather narrowly construed. For example, *exequatur* was granted to bankruptcy decisions rendered against persons which under French bankruptcy laws might not have been subjected to bankruptcy proceedings. Under such circumstances, however, courts have granted *exequatur* provided that this *exequatur* purported to seek enforcement measures limited to the debtor's assets in France and did not aim at the commencement of bankruptcy proceedings in France.[59]

Also, the Supreme Court has held that the debtor's actions may be avoided prior to the bankruptcy judgment for periods longer than those allowed under French bankruptcy law and that such periods were not incompatible with French public policy.[60]

(b) *Exequatur* — consequences

As a result of the *exequatur*, the foreign bankruptcy *judgment* will be *res judicata* and be enforceable in France.[61] No bankruptcy proceedings may then be commenced against the debtor in France. The *exequatur* order will entail significant consequences in time and space.

(i) "RETROACTIVE" EFFECTS OF THE *EXEQUATUR* ORDER

The main difficulties as to the consequences of *exequatur* have evolved recently around whether the bankruptcy judgment becomes effective in France as of the date of the *exequatur* decision or whether such decision applies retroactively and produces effects as of the rendering date.

Until recently, courts had traditionally held that the foreign judgment may produce effects in France only as of the date of the *exequatur* order.[62] A leading decision rendered by the Supreme Court in 1986, however, has substantially amended the previous case law on this issue.[63] The facts underlying this decision may be summarised as follows.

A Danish company distributed in Denmark the products of a French company. Bankruptcy proceedings were commenced against the Danish company. The French company that held a claim against the Danish company filed its claim in Denmark with the Danish bankruptcy authorities and attached in France certain immovable assets owned by the Danish company. In order to seek the avoidance of this attachment, the Danish receiver requested and obtained the *exequatur* of the Danish

---

[59]Cass. civ., 20 1967, 1967 Bull. civ. I No. 172. See also Cass. civ., 29 June 1971, 1973 RCDIP 343. Commentators have construed the latter decision as a refusal by the French Supreme Court, in respect of real estate, to give effects in France to the English rule pursuant to which ownership of the debtor's assets is transferred to the trustee in bankruptcy. Battifol & Lagarde', p. 745, note 4.

[60]Cass. civ., 15 July 1975, 1975 Clunet 875. Recently, on two occasions, the Supreme Court resorted to the notion of public policy to set aside actions initiated by creditors to collect claims which had accrued prior to the bankruptcy judgment or arbitral awards rendered in connection with such actions. Specifically, on 5 February 1991, the Supreme Court held that, in case of bankruptcy, the stay of creditors' actions and divestiture of the debtor are of a public policy nature. Cass. civ., 5 February 1991, 1991 Bull. civ. 1 No. 44. Also, on 4 February 1992, the Supreme Court held that violation of the rule imposing equal treatment of the creditors who are part of the general body of creditors would not conform to public policy. Cass. civ., 4 February 1992, 1992 Bull. civ. I No. 38.

[61]Standard appeals procedures apply. The decisions granting exequatur to foreign bankruptcy judgments are not subject to the specific appeals procedures applicable in case of bankruptcy judgments. Cass. civ., 15 July 1975, 1975 Clunet 847.

[62]Cass. civ., 26 June 1905, 1905 Sirey 1, 433.

[63]Cass. civ., 25 February 1986 (*see* n. 18).

bankruptcy judgment. Further to the *exequatur*, the court of lower instance and the Court of Appeals set aside the actions initiated in France by the creditors to collect their claims and declared the attachment of the immovable assets obtained by the French company unenforceable.

The Supreme Court held that the question at issue was whether the attachment of the debtors' assets subsequent to the foreign bankruptcy judgement was enforceable as against the general body of creditors and that this problem was to be governed by the law applicable to the bankruptcy. The Court approved the decision of the Court of Appeals which set aside the separate action brought by the creditor. The Supreme Court declared that: "nothing prevents judges from taking into consideration certain effects that the foreign bankruptcy law ascribes to the decision which has been held enforceable in France" provided that such effects are in conformity with the French conception of international public policy.

In that particular case, the Court noted that the relevant domestic law (ie specifically Danish law) prohibited creditors from seeking provisional remedies and from bringing actions to collect their claims against the debtor after the bankruptcy judgment and further remarked that the same solutions were provided for under French law.[64] The Supreme Court admits that, once *exequatur* has been granted, two of the most important and traditional consequences of a bankruptcy — ie the debtor's divesture of his power of control over his assets and the prohibition for creditors to collect claims — shall take effect as of the date when the foreign bankruptcy judgment has been rendered.[65]

The impact of this leading decision has been much debated.[66] In particular, the question arises as to whether the solution adopted by the Supreme Court applies only to creditors who have filed their claims with the foreign bankruptcy authorities or instead to all creditors including those who, in the absence of any advertising in France, were not informed of the foreign bankruptcy proceedings.[67] Commentators, on several grounds, tend to favour a broad construction of the Supreme Court's holding. First, this holding does not limit its application to creditors who are aware of the bankruptcy proceedings.[68] Second, this solution is favourable to the security of international trade in preventing the taking of separate actions by creditors and thus the breaching of equality among creditors.[69] Third, and most significantly, this solution is in line with the principle of unity and universality which supports international bankruptcy conventions.[70]

(II) APPLICATION OF THE LAW OF THE BANKRUPTCY

The second main consequence of the *exequatur* resides in the application in France of the foreign bankruptcy law. As a result of the *exequatur*, a foreign bankruptcy which has been commenced abroad and is declared enforceable in France shall remain subject to the law of the country where this bankruptcy has been pronounced.[71]

---

[64]*Ibid*, 354.
[65]See Jacquemont, Note to Cass. civ., 25 February 1986; 1988 Clunet 425, 434.
[66]See Remery, p. 357.
[67]*Ibid*.
[68]*Ibid*.
[69]*Ibid*.
[70]Coviaux, p. 127; Remery, p. 358.
[71]Cass. com., 25 February 1981, 1981 Bull. civ. IV No. 110.

Determining the scope of application of the law of the bankruptcy when such law conflicts with the *lex rei sitae*, the *lex contractus* or the *lex societatis* may give rise to numerous and delicate issues.[72] Mention shall only be made of the recent case law regarding the rules as to conflicts between the law of the bankruptcy, the *lex rei sitae* and the *lex contractus* in respect of the enforceability as against the general body of creditors of securities obtained by creditors prior to or after the rendering of the foreign bankruptcy judgment.

In the leading 1986 decision mentioned earlier, the Supreme Court held, in regard to a provisional judicial mortgage granted after the bankruptcy judgment, that the law of the bankruptcy had to be combined with the *lex rei sitae*.[73] The Court clearly declared that the enforceability of the judicial mortgage as against the general body of creditors was to be governed by the law of the bankruptcy while the validity of the creation of the mortgage was subject to the *lex rei sitae*.[74]

In a 1990 decision, after having recalled that under Article 24 of the France/Italy Bankruptcy Treaty the admission of creditors' claims are governed by the law of the country where bankruptcy proceedings have been pronounced, and noted that, under the circumstances of the particular case, bankruptcy proceedings had been commenced in Italy, the Supreme Court approved the Court of Appeals holding which had subjected to the law of the bankruptcy the conditions under which a creditor could claim set off as against the Italian bankruptcy authorities.[75]

Finally, in 1991, the Supreme Court held that, in case of the buyer's bankruptcy, the conditions under which the seller may claim goods subject to a retention-of-title clause must be governed by the law of the bankruptcy, irrespective of what the law governing the validity or the enforceability in general of the retention-of-title clause might be.[76] Specifically, the Court approved the Court of Appeals decision which had set aside the action brought by a German company to claim goods which were not any further in kind at the debtor's premises and therefore applied Article 121, paragraph 2 of the French Bankruptcy Law.[77]

Although the 1990 decision involves the France/Italy Bankruptcy Treaty and the 1991 decision was rendered in connection with French bankruptcy proceedings, certain commentators take the position that the Supreme Court has laid down, in these three decisions, a general conflict-of-laws rule which subjects to the law of the bankruptcy the conditions under which securities or guarantees claimed by creditors should be enforceable as against the general body of creditors.[78]

---

[72]Coviaux, p. 128.
[73]Cass. civ., 25 February 1986 (*see* n. 18), 355.
[74]*Ibid.*
[75]Cass. civ., 6 June 1990, 1991 Dalloz 137.
[76]Cass. civ., 8 January 1991, 1991 Dalloz 276.
[77]*Ibid.*
[78]Remery, note to Cass. civ., 6 June 1990, 1991 Dalloz 137, p. 139; Remery, note to Cass. civ., 8 January 1991, 1991 Dalloz, p. 276.

13.3 Effects of foreign bankruptcy decisions and powers of foreign receivers under international bankruptcy treaties

As mentioned, at present, France is not a party to any multilateral convention on bankruptcy; it has only entered into bilateral treaties. Such treaties have been entered into with Belgium (8 July 1899),[79] Italy (3 June 1930),[80] Monaco (13 September 1950)[81] and Austria (27 February 1979).[82] The treaty entered into with Switzerland was abrogated in 1992.[83]

All these treaties adopt and apply the principle of unity and universality in regard to relations between the contracting states.[84] Standard private international rules apply and separate bankruptcies may be pronounced, however, in the case where the domicile or the registered office of the debtor is situated in a third country.[85] The principle of unity inspires in particular the provisions of these treaties regulating the effects of the foreign bankruptcy judgments and the powers of the foreign receivers.[86]

13.3.1 France/Belgium Treaty

A judgment rendered in one contracting state is *res judicata* in the other contracting state (Article 8, paragraph 2). The *res judicata* effect is subject to the following conditions: the rendering court must have jurisdiction; rights of the defence must have been respected; and the judgment must be compatible with public policy.[87]

Subject to these conditions, the foreign bankruptcy judgment prior to its *exequatur* will produce effects in the other contracting state. For example, bankruptcy proceedings will entail termination as of right in the other contracting state of the powers granted by the debtor.[88] Also, the receiver may "take any provisional and management measures and exercise any actions as representative of the bankrupt or the general body of creditors" (Article 8, paragraph 2).

Enforcement measures only require *exequatur* (Article 8, paragraph 3).

---

[79] 1900 JO 5029.
[80] 1933 JO 11846.
[81] 1953 JO 5133.
[82] 1980 JO 1570.
[83] Decree 92-174 of 25 February 1992, 1992 JO.
[84] Coviaux, p. 133.
[85] See eg Art 8 of the France/Belgium Treaty.
[86] Determining the scope of application of these treaties especially in regard to those of other bilateral or multilateral conventions into which France has entered may raise difficulties. A decision recently rendered by the Supreme Court may clarify certain of these difficulties. As one knows, bankruptcy, winding up, arrangements, composition or similar proceedings are excluded from the scope of the Brussels' Convention of 27 September 1968 on Jurisdiction and the Enforcement of Judgments in Civil and Commercial Matters. In a 1992 decision, to define the scope of this exclusion, the Supreme Court adopted the same criteria as those previously developed by the EC Court of Justice to this effect. E.C. Court of Justice, *Gourdain ès qualités v Nadler*, 22 February 1979, 1979 RCDIP 657. Specifically, the Supreme Court declared that Art 1 of the Brussels's Convention excludes any actions which derive directly from the bankruptcy and closely fits within the framework of the bankruptcy proceedings. Cass. civ., 13 April 1992, 1992 RCDIP 67. Under the particular circumstances of the case, the Supreme Court declared that *exequatur* of the judicial decision which holds the receiver liable for the payment of supplies ordered after the commencement of the bankruptcy proceedings should be granted under the Brussel's Convention. See generally Remery, note to Cass. civ., 13 April 1992, 1993 RCDIP 68 *et seq.*
[87] Coviaux, p. 153.
[88] Trib. civ., Nancy, 20 June 1905, 1906 Clunet 1124.

A recent decision rendered by the Paris Court of Appeals illustrates the powers of a foreign receiver under Article 8, paragraph 2 of the France/Belgium Treaty.[89] The Paris Court of Appeals declared that the divesture of the Belgium debtor directly applied to his assets located abroad and held that the remittance to the Belgium receiver of sums deposited on behalf of the debtor in a bank account in France did not constitute an execution measure implying coercion or the use of force and therefore should not be treated as an enforcement measure. Accordingly, such remittance did not require the prior *exequatur* in France of the Belgium bankruptcy judgment.[90]

13.3.2 France/Italy Treaty

In principle, a judgment validly rendered in one contracting state will be effective as of right in the other contracting state.[91] Prior to *exequatur*, the foreign receiver may take in the other contracting state all provisional and management measures and exercise any actions as representative of the bankrupt or the general body of creditors (Article 21).

The foreign bankruptcy judgment shall be effective in the other contracting state provided, however, that this judgment meets the requirements set forth in Article 1 of the Convention and in particular that this judgment be final.[92]

In 1958, the Supreme Court approved a Court of Appeals decision which denied the action of a receiver appointed further to an Italian judgment on the grounds that this judgment was a default judgment and might be still under possible attack in Italy and that the time period within which an appeal against this judgment could be brought had not expired.[93]

13.3.3 France/Monaco Treaty

The effects of a bankruptcy pronounced in one contracting state by a court having jurisdiction apply in the other contracting state. The receiver appointed further to this bankruptcy may exercise in both states all actions as a representative of the bankrupt or the general body of creditors and in particular request provisional remedies (Article 3, paragraph 2). Executory measures require the prior *exequatur* of the bankruptcy decision (Article 3, paragraph 3).

Bankruptcy judgments become *res judicata* in the other contracting state as of the date when these decisions become *res judicata* in the state where these decisions have been rendered (Article 8).

13.3.4 France/Austria Treaty

The judicial decisions rendered in one contracting state by courts having jurisdiction are recognised as of right in the other contracting state provided that these decisions are compatible with public policy and the rights of defence have been respected (Article 7).

Exequatur is only required to take enforcement measures over immovables (Articles 8 and 10). As a result, the receiver may dispose of the debtor's movable assets without having first to submit the bankruptcy judgment to *exequatur* (Article 8).[94]

---

[89]Court of Appeals, Paris, 30 March 1990 (Juris-Data No. 021572).
[90]*Ibid.*
[91]Coviaux, p. 155.
[92]*Ibid.*
[93]Cass. civ., 4 January 1958, 1958 Bull. civ. I No. 9.
[94]Coviaux, p. 156.

Appendix 1

Proposal For Consultative Draft of Model International Insolvency Co-operation Act For Adoption by Domestic Legislation With or Without Modification

Prepared by members of the International Bar Association, Section on Business Law, Committee J
(Creditors' Rights, Insolvency, Liquidation and Reorganisations),
Subcommittee on International Co-operation
in Bankruptcy Proceedings

Introduction

The concept of a Model International Insolvency Cooperation Act (MIICA) received its initial impetus at the meeting of SBL Committee J (Creditors" Rights, Insolvency, Liquidation and Reorganisations) during the IBA Biennial Conference in New York in September 1986. Subsequently, Country Groups comprised of Committee J members were established in several countries and these groups, through their Country Chairmen, reported on the concept at the SBL"s London Conference in September 1987. The discussion and consideration given to the concept in New York and in London led to the development of the Model International Insolvency Co-operation Act. No other organisation or country is drafting and proposing such a model provision.

The "Consultative Draft of MIICA for Adoption by Domestic Legislation With or Without Modification" is a model statute, proposed for adoption in jurisdictions throughout the world, that provides mechanisms by which courts may assist and act in aid of insolvency proceedings being conducted in other jurisdictions. The fundamental principle underlying MIICA is universality which envisions a single administration of the insolvent debtor"s estate, providing protection of the estate and a equitable distribution of assets among both domestic and foreign creditors in liquidation, or equitable administration in a reorganisation or rehabilitation proceeding. It is contemplated that the Consultative Draft of MIICA may be adopted with considerable modification in order to be effectively integrated with existing domestic legislation in some countries.

An initial draft of MIICA was submitted to designated Country Chairmen for comment in February 1988 and was revised as of 1 July 1988 in response to these comments. Thereafter, at the meeting of Committee J during the IBA's Biennial Conference in Buenos Aires in September 1988, additional comments on MIICA and

Current Issues in Cross-Border Insolvency and Reorganisations (E. B. Leonard, C. W. Besant, eds.; 1–85333–958–X; © International Bar Association; pub. Graham & Trotman/International Bar Association, 1994; printed in Great Britain), pp. 259-268.

the prospects for its adoption were submitted in reports given by Country Chairmen. A few additional revisions to MIICA were agreed, resulting in the third draft dated 1 November 1988. In Buenos Aires, Committee J determined to submit MIICA to the Councils of the International Bar Association and the Section on Business Law for approval at their meetings in Helsinki, 9 and 10 June 1989, prior to commending the task of implementing jurisdictional adoption to designated members of Committee J. We are happy to report that the third draft of MIICA which follows was approved by both Councils.

John A. Barrett
Fulbright & Jaworski, London
Chairman, Committee J

Timothy E. Powers
Haynes & Boone
Dallas, Texas
Chairman, Committee J,
Subcommittee on International Co-operation
in Bankruptcy Proceedings

Third draft 1 November 1988: Model International Insolvency Co-operation Act

Section 1

In all matters of insolvency, including bankruptcy, liquidation, composition, reorganisation or comparable matters, a Court, in accordance with the provisions of this Act,

(a) shall recognise a foreign representative of the debtor or estate, provided that such foreign representative complies with the orders of such Court;
(b) shall act in aid of and be auxiliary to foreign proceedings pending in the courts of all countries that provide substantially similar treatment for foreign insolvencies as that provided by this Act; and
(c) shall act in aid of and be auxiliary to foreign proceedings pending in the courts of all other countries, if the Court is satisfied that:
   (i) the court or administrative agency having jurisdiction over the foreign representative is a proper and convenient forum to supervise administration of the property of the debtor; and
   (ii) the administration of the property of the debtor in the pertinent jurisdiction by the foreign representative is in the overall interests of the creditors of the debtor.

Section 2

(a) A foreign representative may commence a case ancillary to a foreign proceeding by filing a petition under this Act for purposes of:
   (i) obtaining an order to turn over to the foreign representative any property of the debtor or the estate in this jurisdiction;

   (ii) staying or dismissing any action or proceeding concerning the debtor or estate in this jurisdiction;

   (iii) obtaining testimony or production of books, records or other documents relating to an insolvency;

   (iv) obtaining recognition and enforcement of a foreign judgment or court order; or

   (v) obtaining any other appropriate relief.

The Court may exercise such additional powers with respect to the matter as it could exercise if the matter had arisen within its own jurisdiction.

(b) Upon the commencement of an ancillary case, any currently pending related insolvency proceedings in this jurisdiction shall be consolidated with such ancillary case.

Section 3

In the event that ancillary proceedings pursuant to Section 2 are unavailable or denied, a foreign representative of the estate in a foreign proceeding concerning a person may commence an insolvency proceeding against such person in this jurisdiction in accordance with the provisions of the applicable laws of this jurisdiction.

Section 4

(a) In any case commenced ancillary to a foreign proceeding as provided in Section 2, a Court shall apply the substantive insolvency law of the foreign court having jurisdiction over the foreign proceeding, unless after giving due consideration to principles of private international law and conflict of laws, the Court determines that it must apply the substantive insolvency law of this jurisdiction.

(b) A Court shall apply the substantive insolvency law of this jurisdiction in any insolvency proceeding brought by a foreign representative as provided in Section 3.

Section 5

An appearance in a Court by a foreign representative in connection with a petition or request under this Act does not submit such foreign representative to the jurisdiction of any Court in this jurisdiction for any other purpose.

Section 6

(a) "Foreign representative" means a person who, irrespective of designation, is assigned under the laws of a country outside of this jurisdiction to perform functions in connection with a foreign proceeding that are equivalent to those performed by a trustee, liquidator, administrator, sequestrator, receiver, receiver-manager or other representative of a debtor or an estate of a debtor in this jurisdiction.

(b) "Foreign proceeding" means an insolvency proceeding, whether judicial or administrative, in a foreign country, provided that the foreign court or administrative agency conducting the proceeding has proper jurisdiction over the debtor and its estate.

Section 7

Any treaty or convention governing matters of insolvency cooperation, which has been ratified by this country and the country in which a foreign proceeding is pending, shall override this Act with regard to such matters between such countries, unless the treaty or convention shall otherwise provide.

Third draft 1 November 1988: Official comment to Model International Insolvency Co-operation Act:

Statement of General Principles

The ultimate goal of model legislation for international insolvency cooperation is universality, which envisions a single administration providing protection of the insolvent debtor"s estate from dismemberment, and an equitable distribution of assets among both domestic and foreign creditors in liquidation, or the equitable administration of the estate in a reorganisation, composition or rehabilitation proceeding. Insofar as possible, such universality should be the guiding principle of all efforts toward international insolvency cooperation, for it alone is truly compatible with the realisation of equal treatment of all creditors, debtors, assets and liabilities, and the swift and effective administration of the estate. Within the parameters of this overarching principle, mechanisms must be provided for the recognition of foreign representatives, the stay of local proceedings, the production of documents and obtaining of testimony, the integration of asset distribution and other forms of ancillary relief. In a world of increasing global integration and growth of true multinational business entities, these principles are the indispensable elements in attaining equity and fairness in international insolvency proceedings.

Statutory comments

Section 1

PURPOSES

The purposes of Section 1 are to provide assurance and predictability that the foreign representative will be recognised by the Court; to require the foreign representative to comply with orders of the Court; to ensure that the Court will aid foreign proceedings in countries where a form of the model act (or similar legislation) has been adopted; and to encourage the Court to aid foreign proceedings in other countries, where the model act has not been adopted, provided that only two limited and very basic qualifications are satisfied.

SOURCES

Subsection 1(a) is derived from principles found in provisions of the laws of England (case law) and the United States Bankruptcy Code §304(a) and §306. Subsections 1(b) and (c) are similar in form to §29(2)(a) and (b) of the Australian Bankruptcy Act. The specific qualifications enumerated in Subsections 1(b) and (c) are similar to those in §§316(5)(a) and (b) of the provisions on international insolvencies included in two recent bankruptcy bills introduced, but not adopted, in Canada (the "Canadian Bill"). The omission of a third qualification in the Canadian Bill was based upon comments in Report of the Canadian Committee Special Project on International Cooperation in Bankruptcy Proceedings, IBA/SBL Committee J., 1987 (the "Canadian Report") at pp. 46–47.

EXPLANATION
Section 1 supplies a foundation for the entire model act and its principle of universality by providing for recognition of foreign representatives, and by providing that the Court shall act in aid of and by auxiliary to foreign proceedings in all matters of insolvency. The scope of matters is sufficiently broad to include debtor rehabilitation as well as liquidation. The terms in aid of and "auxiliary to" clearly set forth the ideal role of the Court in relation to foreign proceedings and the recognition of the foreign representative establishes the point of entry into the Court for that foreign proceeding and its representative. Subsection 1(a) requires the Court to recognise foreign representatives so that, even though the Court may have discretion in responding to the requests of the foreign representative, that representative is assured of recognition in order to place the request before the Court. The sole qualification to such recognition is that the foreign representative must comply with any Court orders; the Court could withdraw recognition if the foreign representative did not so comply.

Subsection 1(b) requires the Court to act in aid of and be auxiliary to courts in countries which have adopted the model act. This reciprocity provision will provide an incentive for countries to adopt the model act, or substantially similar treatment, so that its representatives will have a basis for depending upon the receipt of aid in those jurisdictions which have likewise adopted the model act.

Subsection 1(c) provides that the Court shall provide aid to courts of countries which have not adopted the model act, but which satisfy two fundamental qualifications: that the foreign proceeding is a proper and convenient forum and that administration in that proceeding is in the overall interests of the general body of creditors of the debtor. Such qualifications in no way provide special consideration for local parties, but rather establish a basic threshold of fairness and equity which is central to the concept of international insolvency cooperation. Certain additional factors which would arguably provide the Court with greater discretion to deny aid to the foreign proceeding, such as those found in United States Bankruptcy Code §304 and Canadian Bill §316(5), have not been included in the model act. Such omission is in response to commentaries received from a number of jurisdictions which criticise the United States provisions for giving too much discretion to the Court by enumerating multiple factors which the Court may consider, and thus allowing many alternatives for determining to deny aid to foreign proceedings.

Section 1 generally raises the issue of whether a Court would act in aid of and by auxiliary to foreign proceedings with regard to recognition and enforcement of foreign revenue (tax) or penal claims that are not currently recognised or enforced in many jurisdictions. The resolution of the issue must be left to the individual jurisdictions adapting to model act for adoptions.

Section 2

PURPOSES
The purposes of Section 2 are to provide the framework for aid to a foreign proceeding by establishing the mechanism of a case ancillary to a foreign proceeding, in which the foreign representative may seek several types of relief; to set forth four of the most commonly sought types of assistance which foreign representatives may request; to ensure flexibility by allowing the foreign representative in an ancillary case to obtain any other appropriate relief in addition to the four enumerated types of

aid; and to provide that any separate related proceedings pending in the jurisdiction shall be consolidated with the ancillary case.

SOURCES
Section 2 is similar conceptually and in form to §304 of the United States Bankruptcy Code, which similarly provides for cases ancillary to foreign proceedings without the commencement of separate bankruptcy proceedings. The model act deviates significantly from §304, however, by omitting the six factors to be considered by the Courts in determining whether to grant ancillary judicial assistance. No such factors are set forth in Section 2 of the model act. Such omission responds to the criticism of some bankruptcy practitioners that §304, as currently enacted, provides too much discretion to the Court by setting forth such criteria. Instead, the model act enumerates the types of aid which the foreign representative may seek in the ancillary case, once the Court has determined to act in aid of the foreign proceeding in accordance with limited guidelines set out in Section 1. The specific types of relief listed are derived from the comments of bankruptcy practitioners in response to the Special Project on International Cooperation and Bankruptcy Proceedings, IBA Committee J, 1987, and from certain statutory and other sources. Subsections 2(a), (b) and (c) are similar to types of relief enumerated in the Canadian Bill at §316(3). Subsection 2(d) is derived from the Federal Statute on Private International Law Tenth Chapter: Bankruptcy and Composition Law of Switzerland, Articles 159 ff, and was stressed, along with Subsection 2(a), by the Switzerland Commentary on the Special Project on International Cooperation and Bankruptcy Proceedings, IBA/SBL Committee J, 1987.

EXPLANATION
Whereas some statutes provide that foreign representatives may "seek orders", others provide that foreign representatives may "obtain recognition of foreign decrees", or may "seek necessary relief". Such provisions do not provide a flexible framework within which foreign representatives may obtain aid of many types and in many different forms, depending upon the needs which are generated by the foreign proceeding. The United States model of the "case ancillary to a foreign proceeding" provides just such a flexible mechanism within which the foreign representative may then take any number of actions and seek any number of different types of relief depending upon the particular needs of the estate. In addition, the concept of an "ancillary case" reemphasises the universality principle by distinguishing this special type of case allowed for the particular purposes of aiding and being auxiliary to the foreign proceeding which remains the dominant and central administration for the debtor"s estate. The enumeration of types of relief to be sought provides a starting point, based largely upon comments of bankruptcy practitioners with regard to the goals which foreign representatives are likely to bring to the ancillary case. The four enumerated types of relief will cover a very significant portion of the actions sought in ancillary cases, but Subsection 2(a)(v) provides the additional flexibility to foreign representatives to seek any other kind of appropriate relief. The last sentence of Subsection 2(a) provides the Court with full powers to provide relief and act in aid of the foreign representative and the foreign proceeding; however, this provision is not intended to provide the Court with discretion to favour local creditors or other local parties in interest. Subsection 2(b) is based upon the recognition that creditors or other parties in interest may commence either involuntary insolvency proceedings or related judicial or

administrative proceedings in the recognising jurisdiction, prior to the commencement of a case ancillary to a foreign proceeding. A foreign representative had the discretion to either allow such action to proceed, or to commence a case ancillary to the foreign proceeding, in which case, under the terms of Subsection 2(b), the separate proceeding brought by the creditor or other party in interest shall be consolidated with the ancillary case. Upon such consolidation with the ancillary case, the separate proceeding will be fully integrated into a single administration of the estate, and will be governed by the provisions of the model act. It is the intent of this provision to allow consolidation of any future actions similarly brought, following commencement of the ancillary cases.

Section 3

PURPOSES
The purposes of Section 3 are to provide a further means for foreign representatives to enter the Court and seek relief, if the ancillary case is unavailable or is denied by the Court; and to ensure the broadest possible access of the foreign representative to the Court by allowing a full proceeding to be commenced in accordance with the laws of the Court's jurisdiction in the event that such proceeding is deemed necessary.

SOURCES
The United States Bankruptcy Code §303(b)(4) similarly allows a foreign representative to commence full proceedings in the United States. The Canadian Report at p. 46 strongly recommends such a provision and commends the United States Bankruptcy Code for so providing.

EXPLANATION
The primary thrust of the model act is toward a central administration of the estate in one jurisdiction with ancillary cases in other jurisdictions as necessary. However, in the event that the Court declines to act in aid of a foreign proceeding and refuses to allow an ancillary case (under the provisions of Section 1(c)), this Section provides the foreign representative with an alternative course in which a full proceeding may be commenced against the debtor in accordance with the domestic provisions of the applicable statute of the jurisdiction. Section 3 has been drafted to clearly indicate the necessity of the foreign representative first considering and seeking to obtain ancillary relief under Section 2, and only in the event that it is unavailable, proceeding to initiate a full proceeding under Section 3. This construction further buttresses the universality principle and the emphasis which the model act places upon a central administration.

Section 4

PURPOSES
The purposes of Section 4 are to provide guidance to the Court with regard to the applicable substantive insolvency law for proceedings under the model act; to distinguish between the ancillary case and the full proceedings, by providing that the substantive insolvency law of either the foreign or local jurisdiction may be applied in an ancillary case whereas the substantive insolvency law of the local jurisdiction is applicable to the full proceedings; to encourage recognition of the law of the foreign jurisdiction insofar as possible in ancillary cases, but to provide for the possibility that such law may be improper in the local jurisdiction and thus not subject to being

utilised; and to further confirm that a full proceeding initiated by the foreign representative is subject to the substantive insolvency law of the local jurisdiction and that such law will be applicable law for the full proceeding.

SOURCES
Subsection 4(a) reflects a principle noted in the English Commentary to the Special Project on International Cooperation and Bankruptcy Proceedings, IBA/SBL Committee J, 1987 regarding Section 426 of the Insolvency Act 1986 of England. Subsection 4(b) sets forth the generally accepted principle of utilising local substantive law when the benefits of a full local proceeding are sought by the person initiating the proceeding.

EXPLANATION
It is clear that if a foreign representative has been denied the assistance of the Court in initiating an ancillary case, and has initiated a full bankruptcy proceeding under the laws of the local jurisdiction, then the applicable substantive law should be that of the local jurisdiction. In an ancillary case, the issue of applicable substantive law is more complex. Ideally, following the principle of universality in its purest form, the substantive law of the foreign court would govern the entire proceedings, including ancillary cases, whereas procedural matters would presumably be governed in the ancillary cases by the procedural law of the recognising jurisdiction. However, the constraints of public policy or strongly supported local bankruptcy principles in the Court''s own jurisdiction, may require that this basic principle be modified and, in some instances, that local substantive law be applied. The intention of the model act is that the Court should, whenever possible in ancillary cases, apply the substantive insolvency law of the jurisdiction of the foreign proceeding, and that the application of local substantive insolvency law should only occur in isolated and infrequent instances when the application of the substantive insolvency law of the foreign proceeding would violate public policy.

Section 5

PURPOSES
The purpose of Section 5 is to allow the foreign representative to appear in the Court for the limited purposes of obtaining ancillary relief, without the fear of being subject to the jurisdiction of the Court for other purposes.

SOURCES
Section 5 is patterned closely after United States Bankruptcy Code §306.

EXPLANATION
In order to encourage foreign representatives to seek relief by initiating cases ancillary to the foreign proceeding, or, if necessary, to initiate a full proceeding, this section provides protection of foreign representatives from the Court assuming jurisdiction for other purposes. Such protection is limited to actions of the foreign representative prior to the commencement of the ancillary proceeding, and is not intended to prevent subjecting the foreign representative to claims or counterclaims validly raised after commencement of the ancillary proceeding. The intention of the model

act is not only to provide access to the Court for the foreign representative, but to provide an efficient, equitable and safe mechanism for the foreign representative to use, in order to encourage a central administration of the estate and to foster the principle of universality. The protections which this section affords the foreign representative are important aspects of this effort.

Section 6

PURPOSES

The purposes of Section 6 are to define "foreign representative" and "foreign proceeding" clearly; to frame such definitions with sufficient flexibility to cover the various types of proceedings and the various roles which administrators may play under the laws of a variety of jurisdictions; and to allocate to the Court responsibility for determining that there is proper jurisdiction in the foreign proceeding.

SOURCES

The definition set forth in Section 6(a) is closely patterned after §316(1) of the Canadian Bill. The definition set forth in Section 6(b) is derived in part from United States Bankruptcy Code §101(22).

EXPLANATION

It is the intention of the model act to include within the term "foreign representative" at Subsection 6(a) all of those persons who perform substantially equivalent functions in a foreign insolvency. Note, for instance, that the breadth of this definition allows it to include such unique concepts as the "debtor-in-possession" under the provisions of the United States Bankruptcy Code. Subsection 6(b) defines "foreign proceeding" with sufficient breadth to include all types of judicial and administrative proceedings that exist in jurisdiction throughout the world. "Foreign proceeding" does not include private non-judicial receiverships or similar actions that are not under the control of a judicial or administrative body. To meet the definition of "foreign proceeding" under the model act, the foreign court or agency conducting the proceedings must have proper jurisdiction. Determination that proper jurisdiction exists, and therefore that the proceeding is a "foreign proceeding" under the terms of the model act must be made by the Court. An underlying assumption of the model act is that the Court, guided by a forum non-conveniens approach, would concede jurisdiction to the foreign court or administrative agency in a jurisdiction having greater contacts with the debtor and its estate. In making its jurisdictional determination, the Court should be accorded maximum flexibility so that, for instance, it may consider whether improper forum selection or "shopping" has occurred in the choice of forum made by the debtor.

Section 7

PURPOSES

The purposes of Section 7 are to recognise that treaties or conventions may be adopted and ratified to govern the subject matter of the model act, and to provide that in such instance, the treaty or conventions shall override the model act with regard to international insolvency matters between the ratifying countries.

SOURCES
Section 7 was drafted in response to comments of bankruptcy practitioners, some of whom advocate the adoption and ratification of treaties or conventions to effect international insolvency cooperation, and some of whom simply seek to clarify the relation of such treaty and the model act in those instances in which a treaty or convention is ratified following the enactment of the model act.

EXPLANATION
Section 7 provides that if a treaty or convention is effected with regard to international insolvency cooperation, it will override the model act with regard to such matters between the ratifying countries. This new provision explicitly recognises that bilateral or multilateral treaties or conventions may be effected as alternative means for establishing arrangements concerning international insolvency cooperation between countries. Enactment of the model act is not to be construed as prohibiting or deterring the adoption and ratification of such treaties or conventions; on the contrary, Section 7 explicitly addresses the issue of how to reconcile the later ratification of such a treaty by a country which has previously adopted the model act.

Miscellaneous comments

1. Meaning of "insolvency".

The term "insolvency" has been used in the title of the model act, and throughout its text and official comment, to mean all of those various proceedings under all types of law and in various jurisdictions worldwide, applicable to actions regarding financial failure generally, including insolvency, bankruptcy, reorganisation, composition, rehabilitation and any other such proceeding by whatever name.

2. Venue

A provision governing venue with respect to cases commenced ancillary to a foreign proceeding has not been included in the model act. It is presumed that venue will be determined by the Court in accordance with the applicable laws of the Court"s jurisdiction.

3. Effects of multi-jurisdiction

Although no marshalling provision has been included in the model act, the principles of universality and single insolvency administration dictate an equitable worldwide distribution. Thus, if a creditor receives payment or other satisfaction of a claim in a foreign proceeding, such creditor should not receive any payment in the Court's jurisdiction until other holders of claims who are entitled to share equally with such creditor, have received payment equal in value to the consideration already received by the creditor in the foreign proceeding. This comment is derived substantially from United States Bankruptcy Code §508(a).

Appendix 2

Model International Insolvency Co-operation Act: Spanish Translation of the Third Draft of the Act and Commentary as of 1 November 1988

Acta modelo de cooperacion internacional en casos de insolvencia

Sección 1

En todos los casos de insolvencia, incluyendo la quiebra, la liquidación, el convenio, la reorganización o asuntos similares, un Tribunal, de acuerdo con las provisiones de este Acta,

(a) reconocerá a un representante extranjero del deudor o de la masa (patrimonio), siempre que tal representante extranjero cumpla con las ordenes de ese Tribunal.
(b) asistirá y auxiliará en los procedimientos extranjeros pendientes en los tribunales de aquellos paises que proporcionen un trato sustancialmente similar a las insolvencias extranjeras al que proporciona este Acta; y
(c) asistirá y auxiliará en los procedimientos extranjeros pendientes en los tribunales de todos los demás países, si se acredita que:
   (i) el tribunal u órgano administrativo que tiene jurisdicción sobre el representante extranjero es un foro apropiado y conveniente para supervisar la administración de la masa (patrimonio) del deudor; y
   (ii) la administración de la masa (patrimonio) del deudor en la jurisdicción pertinente por el representante extranjero se realiza en interés general de los acreedores del deudor.

Sección 2

(a) Un representante extranjero puede iniciar un procedimiento auxiliar de un procedimiento extranjero instando una petición al amparo de este Acta a los fines de:
   (i) obtener una orden de entregar al representante extranjero cualquier propiedad del deudor o de la masa en esta jurisdicción;
   (ii) la suspensión o desestimación de cualquier acción o procedimiento referente al deudor o a la masa en esta jurisdicción;
   (iii) obtener testimonio de los libros, registros, actas u otros documentos relacionados con una insolvencia;
   (iv) obtener el reconocimiento y ejecución de una sentencia o resolución de un tribunal extranjero, u

Current Issues in Cross-Border Insolvency and Reorganisations (E. B. Leonard, C. W. Besant, eds.; 1–85333–958–X; © International Bar Association; pub. Graham & Trotman/International Bar Association, 1994; printed in Great Britain), pp. 269-286.

(v) obtener cualquier otra prestación conveniente.

El Tribunal puede ejercer dichos poderes adicionales con respecto al asunto en las mismas condiciones y con las mismas facultades que si el asunto se hubiera iniciado dentro de su propia jurisdicción.

(b) Al comenzar un procedimiento auxiliar, se unirá al mismo cualquier procedimiento pendiente relativo a insolvencia que exista en esa jurisdicción.

Sección 3

En el caso de que sean inviables o de que se denieguen los procedimientos auxiliares previstos en la Sección 2, un representante extranjero de la masa en un procedimiento extranjero relativo a una persona, puede iniciar un procedimiento de insolvencia contra tal persona en esta jurisdicción de acuerdo con las leyes aplicables en esa jurisdicción.

Sección 4

(a) En cualquier procedimiento comenzado como auxiliar de un proceso extranjero según lo dispuesto en la Sección 2, el Tribunal aplicará la Ley sustantiva de insolvencia del tribunal extranjero que tenga jurisdicción sobre el proceso extranjero, a no ser que, después de considerar los principios de la Ley internacional privada y del conflicto de leyes, el Tribunal determine que debe aplicarse la Ley sustantiva de insolvencia de esa jurisdicción.

(b) Un Tribunal aplicará la Ley sustantiva de insolvencia de esta jurisdicción en cualquier proceso de insolvencia entablado por un representante extranjero según la Sección 3.

Sección 5

La comparecencia ante un Tribunal por parte de un representante extranjero en conexión con una petición o una solicitud realizadas según este Acta no somete a tal representante extranjero a la jurisdicción de ningún Tribunal de esa jurisdicción para cualquier otro fin.

Sección 6

(a) "Representante extranjero" quiere decir una persona que, con independencia de su designación, está facultada por las leyes de otro país fuera de esta jurisdicción para realizar funciones en conexión con un proceso extranjero equivalentes a las que realiza un fideicomisario, liquidador, administrador, embargador, administrador judicial interventor u otro representante de un deudor o de la masa de un deudor en esta jurisdicción.

(b) "Proceso extranjero" quiere decir un proceso de insolvencia, bien judicial o administrativo, en un país extranjero, siempre que el tribunal u órgano administrativo extranjero que lleve el proceso tenga jurisdicción sobre el deudor y su patrimonio.

Sección 7

Cualquier tratado o convenio que regule los asuntos de cooperación en materia de insolvencia, que haya sido ratificado por este país y por aquél en que hay un procedimiento extranjero pendiente, prevalecerá sobre este Acta en cuanto a tales asuntos entre tales países, a no ser que se indique otra cosa en dicho tratado o convenio.

Comentario oficial al acta modelo internacional de ooperacion ante la insolvencia

Declaración de principios generales

El objetivo final de la legislación modelo para la cooperación internacional en asuntos de insolvencia es la universalidad que tiende a una única administración que proteja la propiedad del deudor insolvente del desmenbramiento, y una distribución equitativa del activo entre los acreedores (tanto nacionales como extranjeros) en la liquidación, o la administración equitativa de la propiedad en un proceso de reorganización, composición o rehabilitación equitativa de la propiedad en un proceso de reorganizacizón, composición o rehabilitación. En lo posible, tal universalidad será el principio inspirador de todos los esfuerzos hacia una cooperación internacional en casos de insolvencia, pues dicha universalidad es perfectamente compatible con un trato igual para todos los acreedores, deudores, activos y pasivos, y la rápida y eficaz administración de la propiedad. Dentro de los parámetros de este principio comprensivo, se deben proporcionar los mecanismos para el reconocimiento de los representantes extranjeros, la suspensión de actuaciones locales, la producción de documentos y testimonios, la integración de la distribución del activo y otras formas de ayuda auxiliar. En un mundo de integración y crecimiento global de entidades comerciales multinacionales, estos principios son los elementos indispensables para el logro de la equidad y justicia en los procedimientos de insolvencia internacional.

Comentarios estatutarios

Sección 1

PROPÓSITO

Los propósitos de la sección 1 son porporcionar la seguridad y previsibilidad de que el Tribunal reconocerá al representante extranjero; de obligar al representante extranjero a cumplir con las órdenes del Tribunal; de asegurar que el Tribunal colaborará en actuaciones extranjeras en países donde se ha adoptado una forma del acta modelo (o legislación parecida); y de estimular al Tribunal a colaborar en actuaciones extranjeras que se lleven a cabo en otros países, donde no se ha adoptado el acta modelo, siempre que sa satisfagan solo dos cualificaciones limitadas y muy básicas.

FUENTES

Se deriva la Subsección 1(a) de los principios encontrados en las disposiciones de las leyes de Inglaterra (Ley empírica) y el Código de Quiebra de los Estados Unidos §29(2)(a) y (b) del Acta Australiana de Quiebra. Las cualificaciones específicas enumeradas en Subsecciones 1(c)(i) y (ii) son similares a las de §§316(5)(a) y (b) de las disposiciones sobre insolencias internacionales incluidas en dos poryectos de ley recientes sobre la quiebra que se introdujeron, pero que no se adoptaron, en Canadá (el "Proyecto de Ley Canadiense"). La omisión de una tercera cualificación en el Proyecto de Ley Canadiense se basó en unos comentarios en el Informe del Comité Canadiense - Proyecto Especial sobre la Cooperación Internacional en Actuaciones de Quiebra, IBA Comité I, 1987 (el "Informe Canadiense") páginas 46-47.

EXPLICACIÓN

La Sección 1 proporciona una base para todo el acta modelo y su principio de universalidad al disponer el reconocimiento de universalidad al disponer el reconocimiento de prerestentantes extranjeros, y al prescribir que el Tribunal actuará en la ayuda de y será auxiliará en procedimientos extranjeros en todos los asuntos de insolvencia. El ámbito de aplicación es lo bastante amplio como para incluir tanto la rehabilitación del deudor como la liquidación. Los términos "asistirá" y "auxiliará en" proponen claramente el papel ideal del Tribunal en relación al as actuaciones extranjeras, y el reconocimiento del representante extranjero establecen en el momento de entrada para aquel proceso extranjero y su representante. La Subsección 1(a) obliga al Tribunal a reconocer a los representatnes extranjeros para que, aunque el Tribunal pueda tener discreción a la hora de responder a las peticiones del representante extranjero, a dicho representante se le asegure el reconocimiento para presentar la petición ante el Tribunal. La única cualificación a tal reconocimiento es que el representante extranjero cumpla con cualquier orden que reciba del Tribunal; pudiendo el tribunal retirar el reconocimiento si el representante extranjero no actúa en tal sentido.

La Subsección 1(b) obliga al Tribunal a actuar en ayda de y a auxiliar a los tribunales en países que hayan adoptado el acta modelo. Esta disposición de reciprocidad proporcionará un incentivo a los países para que adopten el acta modelo, o un trato sustancialmente parecido, a fin de que sus representantes tengan una base para depender de la recepción de aydua en aquellas jurisdicciones que han adoptado asimismo el acta modelo.

La Subsección 1(c) dispone que el trinbunal proporcionará ayuda a los tribunales de países que no hayan adoptado el acta modelo, pero que satisfagan dos cualificaciones fundamentales: que el proceso extranjero tiene lugar en un foro competente y adecuado, y que la administración en ese proceso se realiza en interés general de los acreedores del deudor. Tales cualificaciones de ninguna manera proporcionan un tratamiento especial para las partes locales, sino que establecen u marco básico de justicia y equidad que es consustancial al concepto de la cooperación internacional ante la insolvencia. No se han includio en el acta modelo ciertos factores adicionales, que discutiblemente proporcionarían al tribunal una mayor discreccíon para negar auxilio al proceso extranjero, como los que se encuentran en el Código de Quiebra §304 de los Estados Unidos y el Proyecto de Ley Canadiense §316(5). Esta omisión se debe a los comentarios recibidos de un número importante de jurisdicciones que critican las disposiciones norteamericanas por dar demasiadà discreción al Tribunal al enumerar los múltiples factores que el Tribunal puede tener en cuenta y por lo tanto, facilitando muchas alternativas para determinar la negación de ayuda a las actuaciones extranjeras.

La Sección 1 generalmente plantea el tema de si un Tribunal actuaría "en ayuda de" y sería "auxiliar en" procedimientos extranjeros en cuanto al reconocimiento y ejecución de los litigios de ingresos extranjeros (impuestos) o penales que no se reconocen ni ejecutan actualmente en muchas jurisdicciones. Se debe dejar la resolución de este asunto a cada jurisdicción al adaptar el acta modelo.

Sección 2

OBJETIVOS

Los objetivos de la Sección 2 son proporcionar un marco para la ayuda a un proceso extranjero al establecer el mecanismo de un caso subordinado a un proceso extranjero, dentro del cual el representante extranjero puede buscar varios tipos de auxilio; exponer cuatro de los tipos de ayuda más comúnmente buscados que los representantes extranjeros puedan pedir; asegurar una flexibilidad al permitir al representante extranjero en un caso subrodinado obtener cualquier otro auxilio apropiado, además de los cuatro tipos de ayuda mencionados; y disponer que se una cualquier proceso relacionado con el caso subordinado que se esté tramitando en la jurisdicción de que se trate.

FUENTES

La Sección 2 es arecida en concepto y en forma la §304 del Código de Quiebra de los EEUU, que prevé los procedimientos auxiliares de actuaciones extranjeras sin el comienzo de un procedimiento de quiebra independiente. Sin embargo, se aparta de modo significativo del §304, al omitir los seis factores que e Tribunal tendrá en cuenta al determinar si se concede ayuda judicial subordinada. No figura ningún factor de este tipo en la Sección 2 del acta modelo. Esta omisión responde a la crítica de algunos especialistas en quiebra que señalan que el §304, en su actual recacción, proporciona demasiada discreción al Tribunal al establecer tales criterios. En su lugar, el acta modelo enumera los tipos de ayuda que el representante extranjero puede solicitar en el procedimiento auxiliar, una vez que el Tribunal haya decidido actuar en ayuda del proceso extranjero de acuerdo con las directivas limitadas establecidas en la Sección 1. Los tipos específicos de ayuda enumerados obedecen a comentarios de especialistas en quiebra en respuesta al Proyecto Especial sobre la Cooperación Internacional y Actuaciones de la Quiebra, IBA, Comité J, 1987, y a ciertas fuentes estatutorias. La Subsección 2(a) proporciona tipos de auxilio parecidos a los del Proyecto de Ley Canadiense en §316(3). Se deriva la Subsección 2(b) del Estatuto Federal sobre la Ley Privada Internacional, Capítulo Décimo: La Quiera y la Ley de Acomodamiento de Suiza, Articulos 159 ff., así como junto con la Subsección 2(a), del Comentario Suizo sobre el Proyecto Especial sobre la Cooperación Internacional y Actuaciones de Quiebra, IBA Comité J, 1987.

EXPLICACIÓN

Mientras que algunos estatutos disponen que los representantes extranjeros pueden "solicitar órdenes", otros disponen que los representantes extranjeros pueden "obtener el reconocimiento de sus títulos extranjeros" o pueden "buscar el auxilio necesario". Tales disposiciones no proporcionan un marco flexible dentro del cual los representantes extranjeros puedan obtener auxilio de muchos tipos y en formas diferentes, según las necesidades que el proceso extranjero genere. El modelo americano del "caso auxiliar de un proces extranjero", proporciona justamente este tipo de mecanismo flexible dentro del cual el representante extranjero puede tomar cualquier tipo de iniciativa y buscar todo tipo de auxilio según las necesidades particulares del patrimonio del deudor. Además, el concepto de un "caso auxiliar" vuelve a dar énfasis al principio de universalidad al distinguir este tipo especial de asunto permitido para los objetivos de ayudar y ser auxiliar en un proceso extranjero que permanece como la administración dominante y central de la propiedad del deudor.

La lista de tipos de auxilio que se puede buscar proporciona un punto de partida, basado en gran parte en los comentarios de expertos en quiebra en relación a los posibles objetivos que los representantes extranjeros pretendan conseguir en el caso auxiliar. Los cuatro tipos de auxilio mencionados cubrirán una porción muy significativa de las acciones buscadas en asuntos auxiliares, pero la Subsección 3(a)(v) dipsone una flexibilidad adicional a los representantes extranjeros para que soliciten cualquier otro tipo de auxilio apropriado. La última frase de la Subsección 2(a) otorga al Tribunal plenos poderes para proporcionar ayuda y actuar en ayuda del representante extranjero y el proceso extranjero; sin embargo, la intención de esta disposición no es proporcionar al Tribunal la discreción de favorecer a acreedores locales su otras partes locales en interés. Se basa la Subsección 2(b) en el reconocimiento de que los acreedores u otras partes en interés pueden comenzar o bien una actuación de insolvencia involuntaria, o una actuación judicial, o una actuación administrativa, dentro de la jurisdicción de reconocimiento, con carácter previo al comienzo de un caso auxiliar a un proceso extranjero. Un representante extranjero tiene la facultad de instar tal acción, o bien comenzar un caso auxiliar del proceso extranjero, en cuyo caso, bajo las condiciones de la Subsección 2(b), se consolidará con el caso auxiliar el proceso separado entablado por el acreedor u otra parte en interés. Al producirse tal consolidación con el caso auxiliar, se integrará el proceso separado en una sola administración del patrimonio, y se regirá por las provisiones del acta modelo. Es la intención de esta disposición permitir la acumulación de cualquier acción futura entablada de la misma manera, después del comienzo del caso subordinado.

Sección 3

OBJETIVOS
Los objetivos de la Sección 3 son proporcionar otro medio para que los representantes extranjeros soliciten auxilio del Tribunal, si no es posible iniciar el caso auxiliar o si se lo niega el Tribunal; y para asegurar el acceso más amplio posible del representante extranjero al Tribunal al permitir que inicie un proceso de acuerdo con las leyes de la jurisdicción del Tribuna en el caso de que se estime que tal proceso es necesario.

FUENTES
El Código §303(b)(4) asimismo permite que un representante extranjero comience un proceso pleno en EEUU. El Informe Canadiense en la p. 46 recomienda una disposición de este tipo (disposición que recoge el Código de Quiebra Americano).

EXPLICACIÓN
El acta modelo se orienta hacia una administración central del patrimonio en una jurisdicción determinada, existiendo casos subordinados en otras jurisdicciones. Sin embargo, en el caso de que el Tribunal se niegue a actuar en ayuda de un proceso extranjero y deniegue admitir un caso auxiliar (bajo las disposiciones de la Sección proporciona al representante extranjero una via alternativapor la cual se puede comenzar un proceso pleno contra el deudor según las disposiciones de la Ley aplicable de la jurisdicción. Se ha redactado la Sección 3 para indicar claramente la necesidad de que el representante extranjero primero solicite el auxilio subordinado según las disposiciones de la Sección 2, y solo en el caso de que esto no sea posible, proceda a iniciar un proceso pleno según lo dispuesto en la Sección 3. Esta

construcción apoya aún más el principio de universalidad y el énfasis que el acta modelo hace sobre una administración centralizada.

Sección 4

OBJETIVOS

Los objetivos de la Sección 4 son: proporcionar directivas al Tribunal en cuanto a la ley de insolvencia aplicable a los procedimientos de conformidad conel acta modelo; distinguir entre el caso subordinado y el proceso pleno, al disponer que se pueda aplicar la ley de insolvencia sustantiva de la jurisdicción bien sea extranjera o local en un caso subordinado, mientras que se aplica la ley de la jurisdicción local al proceso pleno; potenciar el reconocimiento de la Ley de la jurisdicción extranjera, en cuanto sea posible, en los casos subordinados, si bien previendo la posibilidad de que tal ley pueda no ser la propia en la jurisdicción local y por tanto no proceda su aplicación; y, confirmar que un proceso pleno iniciado por el representante extranjeros está sujeto a la ley de la jurisdicción local y que tal ley será la ley aplicable para el proceso pleno.

FUENTES

La Subsección 4(a) refleja un principio anotado en el Comentario Inglés al Proyecto Especial sobre la Cooperación International y Actuaciones de Quiebra, IBA Comité J, 1987, con respecto a la Sección 426 del Acta de INsolvencia 1986 de Inglaterra. La Subsección 4(b) sienta el principio acceptado generalmente de que debe aplicarse la ley sustantiva local cuando la persona que inicie el proceso busca los beneficios de un proceso local pleno.

EXPLICACIÓN

Está claro que si a un representante extranjero se le ha negado la asistencia del Tribunal en la iniciación de un caso subordinado, y él ha iniciado un proceso de quiebra según las leyes de la jurisdicción local, la ley sustantiva aplicable debería ser la de la jurisdicción local. En un caso subordinado, el tema de la ley sustantiva aplicable es más complejo. Siguiendo el principio de la universalidad en su forma más complejo. Siguiendo el principio de la universalidad en su forma más pura, la ley sustantiva del tribunal extranjero gobernaria todas las actuaciones, incluyendo los caso subordinados, mientras que los asuntos procesales presumiblemente se gobernarian por la ley procesal de la jurisdicción del reconocimiento. Sin embargo, los imperativos de orden público o los principios de quiebra locales pueden requerir que se modifique este principio básico y, que e aplique (en algunas instancias) la ley sustantiva local. La intención del acta modelo es que el Tribunal, cuando se posible en los casos subordinados, aplique la ley de la jurisdicción del proceso extranjero, yu que se publique la ley sustantiva local (solo en instancias aisladas e infrecuentes) cuando la aplicación de la ley sustantiva del proceso extranjero suponga una violación del orden público.

Sección 5

OBJETIVOS

El objetivo de la Sección 5 es permitir que el representante extranjero comparezca ante el Tribunal a los fines de obtener auxilio subordinado, sin el temor de ser sujeto a la jurisdicción del Tribunal para otros fines.

FUENTES
La Sección 5 sigue el ejemplo del Código de Quiebra §306 de los Estados Unidos.

EXPLICACIÓN
Para alentar a los representantes extranjeros a solicitar auxilio mediante el inicio de casos subordinados al proceso extranjero, o si fuera necesario, el inicio de un proceso entero, esta sección proporciona protección a los representantes extranjeros del Tribunal que asuma jurisdicción para otros fines. Se limita tal protección a las acciones del representante extranjero anteriores al comienzo del proceso subordinado, sin que trate de evitarse el sometimiento del representante extranjero a las demandas o reconvenciones presentadas válidamente después edel comienzo del proceso subordinado. La intención del acta modelo no es sólo proporcionar acceso al Tribunal para el representante extranjero, sino proporcionar también un mecanismo eficiente, para fomentar una administración central de la propiedad y promover el pincipio de universalidad. Las protecciones que esta Sección proporciona al representante extranjero son aspectos importantes de este esfuerzo.

Sección 6

OBJECTIVOS
Los objetivos de la Sección 6 son definir claramente "representante extranjero" y "proceso extranjero"; enmarcar tales definiciones con suficiente flexibilidad para cubrir los diferentes tipos de procesos y los diferentes papeles que pueden desempeñar los administradores bajo las leyes de diversas jurisdicciones; y asignar al Tribunal la responsabilidad de determinar que haya la debida jurisdicción en el proceso extranjero.

FUENTES
La definición indicada en la Sección 6(a) toma como ejemplo el §316(1) del Proyecto de Ley Canadiense. La definición de la Sección 6(b) proviene en parte, del Código de Quiebra de los Estados Unidos §101(22).

EXPLICACIÓN
Es la intención del acta modelo incluir dentro del término "representante extranjero", Subsección 6(a), todas aquellas personas que realicen funciones sustancialmente equivalentes en una insolvencia extranjera. Nótense, por ejemplo, que la amplitud de esta definición le permite incluir conceptos tales como "deudor-en posesión" bajo las disposiciones del Código de Quiebra de los EEUU.

La Subsección 6(b) define "proceso extranjero" consuficiente amplitud como para incluir todos los tipos de actuaciones judiciales y administrativas que existen en las jurisdicciones por todo el mundo. El "roceso extranjero" no incluye procedimientos concursales extra-judiciales o actuaciones similares que no están bajo el control de un ente judicial o administrativo. Para cumplir con la definición de "procesco extranjero" tal y como dispone el acta modelo, el Tribunal u órgano extranjero que realice el proceso debe tener la jurisdicción debida. El Tribunal debe determinar que existe la debida jurisdicción, y por lo tanto, que el proceso es un "proceso extranjero" bajo los términos del acta modelo. El acta modelo presupone que, el Tribunal, guiado por un planteamiento "*forum non-conveniens*", concedería la jurisdicción al Tribunal u órgano administrativo extranjero en aquel foro que tenga mayor conexión con el deudor y su patrimonio. El Tribunal para determinar su jurisdicción, tendrá máxima flexibilidad para que, por ejemplo, pueda considerar si se está ante un supuesto de selección indebido del foro, o "shopping" por parte del deudor.

Sección 7

OBJECTIVOS
El objectivo de esta Sección 7 es el reconocimiento de que puedan ser adoptados y ratificados tratados o convenios que regulen las materias contempladas por el acta modelo asf como el carácter preferente de lo dispuesto por el acta modelo en cuanto a los asuntos internacionales de insolvencia entre los paises que la ratifiquen.

FUENTES
Se redactó la Sección 7 en respuesta a los comentarios de expertos en quiebra, algunos de los cuales abogaron por la adopción y ratificación de tratados o convenios en materia de cooperación internacional en supuestos de insolvencia, algunos de los cuales pretendian aclarar la relación entre un tratado de este tipo y el acta modelo en aquellas instancias en que se ratifica un tratado o convenio tras la promulgación del acta modelo.

EXPLICACIÓN
La Sección 6 dispone que, si se efectúa un tratado o convenio relativo a la coopración internacional sobre insolvencia, anulará el acta modelo en cuanto a las materias previstas entre los paises que lo hayan ratificado. Esta nueva disposición reconoce explicitamente que se ueden efectuar tratados o convenios bilaterales o multilaterales como un medio alternativo para establecer soluciones a la cooperación internacional en materia de insolvencia. No se debe interpretar la promulgación internacional en materia de insolvencia. No se debe interpretar la promulgación del acta modelo como una prohibición o disuasión de la adopción y ratificación de tales tratados y convenios; al contrario, la Sección 7 señala explicitamente sobre como reconciliar la ratificación posterior de un tratado de este tipo por parte de un pais que haya adoptado anteriormente el acta modelo.

Comentarios diversos

1. Significado de "Insolvencia"

Se ha usado el término "insolvencia" en el titulo del acta modelo, asf como en el texto y comentario oficial del mismo, para signficar todas aquellas actuaciones que, bajo las distintas leyes y en las distintas jurisdicciones de todo el mundo, aplicables al as acciones relativas a desequilibrios financieros en general, entre las que se incluyen la insolvencia, la quiebra, la reorganización, la composición, la rehabilitación y cualquier otro proceso similar cualquiera que sea su denominación.

2. La Competencia

No se ha incluido en el acta modelo una disposición que regule la competencia referente a los casos iniciados como subordinados de un proceso extranjero. Se presume que el Tribunal determinará su competencia de acuerdo con la ley aplicable en la jurisdicción del Tribunal.

3. Los Efectos de la Distribución de la Multijurisdicción

Aunque no se haya incluido una disposición de ordenamiento (marshalling) en el acta modelo, los principios de universalidad y de una administración única de la insolvencia imponen una distribución mundial equitativa. De esta forma, si un acreedor recibe el pago a cualquier otra satisfacción a su pretensión en un proceso extranjero, tal acreedor no debe recibir ningún pago igual en valor al ya recibido por este acreedor en el proceso extranjero. Este comentario proviene esencialmente del Código de Quiebra de los Estados Unidos §508(a).

Ley modelo de cooperacion internacional en materia de insolvencias

Sección 1

En todos los casos de insolvencia, incluyendo la quiebra, la liquidación, el convenio, la reorganización o asuntos similares, un Tribunal, de acuerdo con las provisiones de esta Ley,

(a) podrá reconocer a un representante extranjero del deudor or de la masa de la quiebra, siempre que tal representante extranjero cumpla con las ordenes de ese Tribunal.

(b) podrá actuar en ayuda de y auxiliará a los procedimientos pendientes en los tribunales de aquellos países que proporcionen un trato a las insolvencias extranjeras sustancialmente similar al que proporciona la presente Ley; y

(c) podrá actuar en ayuda de y auxiliará a los tribunales de todos los demás países en los procedimientos que se tramiten en el extranjero, si se acredita que:

    (i) el tribunal u órgano administrativo que tiene jurisdicción sobre el representante extranjero es un fuero apropiado y conveniente para supervisar la administración de los bienes del deudor, y

    (ii) la administración por el representante extranjero de los bienes del deudor en la jurisdicción pertinente se lleva a cabo teniendo en cuenta los intereses de todos los acreedores del deudor.

Sección 2

(a) Un representante extranjero puede iniciar un procedimiento judicial relacionado con otro tramitado en el extranjero presentando una petición al amparo de esta Ley a los fines de:

    (i) obtener una orden de entrega a dicho representante extranjero de cualquier bien del deudor en esta jurisdicción;

    (ii) conseguir la suspensión o desestimación de cualquier acción o procedimiento, en esta jurisdicción en relación con el deudor o con la masa de acreedores.

    (iii) obtener testimonio de los libros, registros, actas u otros documentos relacionados con un caso de insolvencia;

    (iv) obtener el reconocimiento y ejecución de una sentencia o resolución de un tribunal extranjero, o

    (v) alcanzar cualquier otra reparación apropiada. A este respecto, el Tribunal podrá ejercer las mismas facultades que hubiera ejercido si la cuestión hubiera surgido dentro de su propia jurisdicción.

(b) Una vez iniciado un procedimiento secundario cualquier otro procedimiento que esté relacionado con el anterior se acumulará a éste.

Sección 3

En el caso de que sean inviables o de que se denieguen los procedimientos secundarios previstos en la Sección 2, el representante extranjero de la masa de acreedores en un procedimiento tramitado en el extranjero relativo a una persona, podrá iniciar un proceso de insolvencia contra tal persona en esta jurisdicicción de acuerdo con las leyes aplicables en esta jurisdicción.

Sección 4

(a) En cualquier proceso secundario instado según lo dispuesto en la Sección 2, el Tribunal aplicará la Ley sustantiva de insolvencia del tribunal extranjero que tenga jurisdicción sobre el proceso extranjero, a no ser que, después de considerar las normas del Derecho Internacional Privado y de conflictos de leyes, el Tribual determine que debe aplicarse la Ley sustantiva de insolvencia de esta jurisdicción.

(b) El Tribunal aplicará la Ley sustantiva de insolvencia de esta jurisdicción en cualquier proceso de insolvencia entablado por un representante extranjero según la Sección 3.

Sección 5

La comparecencia ante un Tribunal por parte de un representante extranjero en conexión con una petición o una solicitud realizadas según esta Ley no somete a tal representante extranjero a la jurisdicción de ningún otro Tribunal de esta jurisdicción para cualquier otro fin.

Sección 6

(a) "Representante extranjero" será aquella persona que, con independencia de su designación, esté facultada por las leyes de otro país fuera de esta jurisdicción para realizar funciones en conexión con un proceso tramitado en el extranjero equivalentes a las desempañadas por un fideicomisario, liquidador, administrador, embargante, administrador judicial, interventor u otro representante de un deudor o del patrimonio de un deudor en esta jurisdicción.

(b) "Proceso extranjero" será un proceso de insolvencia, bien judicial o administrativo, tramitado en un país extranjero, siempre que el tribunal u órgano administrativo extranjero que conozca de dicho proceso tenga jurisdicción sobre el deudor y su patrimonio.

Sección 7

Cualquier tratado o convenio que regule los asuntos de cooperación en materia de insolvencia, que haya sido ratificado por este país y por aquel en que hay un procedimiento pendiente, prevalecerá sobre esta Ley en lo que se refiere a aquellas cuestiones surgidas entre dichos países, a no ser que se indique otra cosa en dicho tratado o convenio.

Comentario oficial a la ley modelo de cooperacion internacional en materia de insolvencias

Exposición de Motivos

El principal objetivo de esta ley modelo para la cooperación internacional en asuntos de insolvencia es la universalidad que tiende a una única administración que evite la disgregación de los bienes del deudor insolvente, y a una distribución equitativa del activo entre los acreedores (tanto nacionales como extranjeros) en la liquidación, o la administración equitativa de los bienes en proceso de reorganización, composición o rehabilitación. En lo posible, tal universalidad será el principio inspirador de todos los esfuerzos hacia una cooperación internacional en casos de insolvencia, pues dicha universalidad es perfectamente compatible con un trato igual para todos los acreedores, deudores, activos y pasivos, y la rápida y eficaz administración de los bienes. Dentro de los parámetros de este principio protector, se deben arbitrar los mecanismos para el reconocimiento de los representantes extranjeros, la suspensión de procedimientos locales, la obtención de documentos y testimonios, la integración de la distribución del activo y otras formas de ayuda relacionadas con el proceso. En un mundo de integración y crecimiento global de entidades comerciales multinacionales, estos principios son los elementos indispensables para el logro de la equidad y justicia en los procedimientos de insolvencia internacional.

Comentarios a La Ley

Sección 1

FINES

Los fines de la Sección 1 son: asegurar que el Tribunal reconozca al representante extranjero; obligar a éste a cumplir con las órdenas del Tribunal; asegurar que el Tribunal colabore en los procesos que se tramitan en países donde se hays adoptado esta Ley modelo (o regulación legal similar); y estimular al Tribunal a colaborar en procesos que se lleven a cabo en otros países, donde no se haya adoptado la Ley modelo, siempre que se satisfagan los dos requisitos básicos que se especifican.

FUENTES

El apartado (a) de la Sección 1 deriva de principios recogidos en el sistema legal inglés (Jurisprudencia) y el Código Concursal de los Estados Unidos {S}304(a) y {S}306). Los apartados (b) y (c) son similares al {S}29(2)(a) y (b) de la Ley Concursal Australiana. Los requisitos enumeratos en los apartados 9(c)(i) y (ii) se perecen a los de {S}316(5)(a) y (b) de las disposiciones sobre insolvencias internacionales incluidas en dos recientes proyectos de ley sobre la quiebra pendientes de aprobación, en Canadá (el "Proyecto de Ley Canadiense"). La omisión de un tercer requisito en el Proyecto de Ley Canadiense se baso en los comentarios contenidos en el Informe del Comité Canadiense — Proyecto Especial sobre la Cooperación Internacional en Procedimientos Concursales, IBA Comité J, 1987 (el "Informe Canadiense") páginas 46–47.

INTERPRETACIÓN

La Sección 1 es la base para toda la Ley modelo y su principio de universalidad al establecer el reconocimiento de representantes extranjeros, y al determinar que el Tribunal actue en aydua y auxilie a procedimientos extranjeros en todos los asuntos de insolvencia. El ámbito de aplicación es lo bastante amplio como para incluir la rehabilitación de deudor y la liquidación. Los términos "en ayuda de" y "auxiliar a" definen claramente el papel ideal del Tribunal en relación con los procesos extranjeros, y el reconcocimiento del representante extranjero establece el momento de entrada al Tribunal para aquel proceso extranjero y su representante. El apartado

(a) obliga al Tribunal a reconocer a los representantes extranjeros para que presenten la petición ante al Tribunal, aunque éste pueda tener discreción a la hora de responder a las peticiones del representante extranjero. El único requisito a tal reconocimiento es que el representante extranjero cumpla con cualquier orden del Tribunal; pudiendo éste retirar el reconocimiento si el representante extranjero no la cumple.

El apartado (b) obliga el Tribunal a actuar en ayuda de y a auxiliar a los tribunales de países que hayan adoptado la Ley modelo. Este principio de reciprocidad proporcionará un incentivo a los países para que adopten la Ley modelo, o un trato sustancialmente paracido, a fin de que sus representantes tengan una base para exigir ayuda en aquellas jurisdicciones que hayan adoptado asimismo la Ley modelo.

El apartado (c) dispone que el Tribunal proporcionará ayuda a los tribunales de países que no hayan adoptado la Ley modelo, pero que cumplan dos requisitos fundamentales: que el proceso extranjero tiene lugar en un fuero competente y adecuado, y que la administración en ese proceso se realiza en interés general de los acreedores del deudor. Tales requisitos de ninguna manera proporcionan un tratamiento especial para las partes locales, sino que establecen un marco básico de justicia y equidad que es consustancial al concepto de la cooperación internacional ante la insolvencia. No se han incluido en la Ley modelo ciertos factores adicionales, que discutiblemente proporcionarían al Tribunal una mayor discreción para denegar ayudas a los procesos extranjeros tales como los contemplados en el Código Concursal de los Estados Unidos {S}304 y el Proyecto de Ley Canadiense {S}316(5). Esta omisión se debe a los comentarios recibidos de un número de jurisdicciones que critican las disposiciones norteamericanas por dar una amplia facultad discrecional al Tribunal por los múltiples factores que el Tribunal debe considerer y por lo tanto, facilitando muchas alternativas para la denegación de ayuda a los procesos extranjeros.

La Sección 1 en general plantea el tema de si un Tribunal "actuaría en ayuda de" y "auxiliaría a" procedimientos extranjeros en cuanto al reconocimiento de ingresos obtenidos en el extranjero (impuestos) o asuntos penales que no se reconocen actualmente en muchas jurisdicciones. Se debe dejar la resolución de este asunto a cada jurisdicción al adoptar la Ley modelo.

Sección 2

FINES
Los fines de la Sección 2 son: proporcionar un marco para la ayuda a un proceso extranjero estableciendo los mecanismos de un procedimiento secundario a un proceso extranjero, en el que el representante extranjero puede procurar varios tipos de ayuda; establecer cuatro de los tipos de asistencia más comúnes que los representantes extranjeros puedan pedir; asegurar una flexibilidad permitiendo al representante extranjero en un procedimiento secundario obtener cualquier otro auxilio apropiado, además de los cuatro tipos de ayuda mencionados; y disponer que se acumule cualquier procedimiento secundario al proceso que se esté tramitando en la jurisdicción de que se trate.

FUENTES
La Sección 2 es parecida en concepto y en forma al {S}304 del Código Concursal de los Estados Unidos, que regula de forma similar los procedimientos secundarios a los

procesos extranjeros sin el comienzo de un procedimiento de quiebra independiente. Sin embargo, se aparta de modo significativo del {S}304, al omitir los seis criterios que el Tribunal tendrá en cuenta al determinar si se concede ayuda judicial relacionada. No figura ningúna de estos criterios en la Sección 2 de la Ley modelo. Esta omisión responde a la crítica de algunos especialistas en quiebra que señalan que el {S}304, en su actual redacción, proporciona demasiada discreción al Tribunal al establecer tales criterios. Por el contrario, la Ley modelo enumera los tipos de ayuda que el representante extranjero puede solicitar en el procedimiento secundario, una vez que el Tribunal haya decidido actuar en ayuda del proceso extranjero de acuerdo con los limites establecidos en la Sección 1. Los tipos específicos de ayuda enumerados obedecen a comentarios de especialistas en quiebra en respuesta al Proyecto Especial sobre la Cooperación Internacional y Procedimientos Concursales, IBA, Comité J, 1987, y de ciertas fuentes legales. El apartado (a) establece tipos de ayuda parecidos a los del Proyecto de Ley Canadiense en {S}316(3). Deriva el apartado (b) del Estatuto Federal de Derecho Internacional Privado, Capítulo Décimo: Derecho Concursal Suizo, Artículos 159 y siguientes, y junto con el apartado (a), se ve reforzado por el Comentario Suizo sobre el Proyecto Especial sobre la Cooperación Internacional y Procedimientos Concursales, IBA Comité J, 1987.

INTERPRETACIÓN

Mientras que algunas leyes disponen que los representantes extranjeros pueden "solicitar órdenes", otras disponen que los representantes extranjeros pueden "obtener el reconocimiento de decretos extranjeros" o pueden "procurar la ayuda necessaria". Tales disposiciones no proporcionan un marco flexible dentro del cual los representantes extranjeros puedan obtener distintos auxilios y en formas diferentes, según las mecesidades que el proceso extranjero genere. El modelo de los Estados Unidos del "procedimiento secundario a un proceso extranjero", proporciona justamente este tipo de mecanismo flexible dentro del cual el representante extranjero puede tomar cualquier tipo de iniciativa y buscar todo tipo de auxilio según las necesidades particulares de la masa de acreedores. Además, el concepto de un "procedimiento secundario" vuelve a dar énfasis al principio de universalidad al distinguir este tipo especial de asunto permitido para los objetivos de ayudar y auxiliar a un proceso extranjero que mantiene la administración dominante y centralizada de los bienes del deudor. La lista de tipos de ayuda que se puede buscar proporciona un punto de partida, basada en gran parte en los comentarios de expertos en quiebra en relación a los objetivos que los representantes extranjeros probablemente presenten en el procedimiento secundario. Los cuatro tipos de ayuda mencionados cubrirán una porción muy significativa de las acciones procuradas en los procesos secundarios, pero el apartado (a)(v) dispone una flexibilidad adicional a los representantes extranjeros para que soliciten cualquier otro tipo de ayuda apropiada. La última frase del apartado (a) otorga al Tribunal plenos poderes para proporcionar auxilio y actuar en ayuda del representante extranjero y del proceso extranjero; sin embargo, la intención de esta disposición no es proporcionar al Tribunal la discreción de favorecer a acreedores locales u otras partes locales interesadas. Se basa el apartado (b) en el reconocimiento de que los acreedores u otras partes interesadas puedan comenzar o bien un proceso de insolvencia involuntaria, o un proceso judicial, o una actuación administrativa, dentro de su jurisdicción, con carácter previo al comienzo de un procedimiento secundario a un proceso extranjero. Un representante extranjero tiene la facultad de instar tal acción, o bien comenzar un procedimiento secundario al proceso extranjero, en cuyo caso, bajo las condiciones del apartado (b), el proceso separado entablado por el acreedor u otra parte interesada se acumulará al procedimiento secundario. Al producirse tal acumulación se integrará el proceso separado en una sola administración de los bienes del deudor, y se regirá por las disposiciones de la Ley modelo. Es la intención de esta disposición permitir la acumulación de cualquier acción futura entablada de la misma manera, después del comienzo del procedimiento secundario.

Sección 3

FINES

Los fines de la Sección 3 son: proporcionar otro medio para que los representantes extranjeros se personen ante el Tribunal y soliciten ayuda del mismo, si el procedimiento secundario es inviable o resulta denegado pro el Tribunal; y asegurar el acceso más amplio posible del representante extranjero al Tribunal al permitirle que inicie un proceso de acuerdo con las leyes de la jurisdicción del Tribunal en el caso de que se estime que tal proceso es necesario.

FUENTES

El Código Concursal de los Estados Unidos {S}303(b)(4) asimismo permite que un representante extranjero comience un proceso pleno en Estados Unidos. El Informe Canadiense en la p. 46 recomienda expresamente una disposición de este tipo y alaba al Código Concursal de los Estados Unidos por haberlo establecido asi.

INTERPRETACIÓN

La Ley modelo se orienta básicamente hacia una administración central de los bienes del deudor en una jurisdicción determinada, con procedimientos secundarios en otras jurisdicciones si fueran necesarios. Sin embargo, en el caso de que el Tribunal se niegue a actuar en ayuda de un proceso extranjero y deniegue admitir un procedimiento secundario (en virtud de las disposiciones de la Sección 1(c)), esta Sección proporciona al representante extranjero una vía alternativa por la cual se puede comenzar un proceso pleno contra el deudor según las disposiciones de la Ley aplicable en esa jurisdicción. Se ha redactado la Sección 3 para indicar claramente la necesidad de que el representante extranjero primero considere y solicite la ayuda subordinada según las disposiciones de la Secctión 2, y solo en el caso de que esto no sea posible, proceda a iniciar un proceso pleno según lo dispuesto en la Sección 3. Esta interpretación apoya aún más el principio de universalidad y el énfasia que la Ley modelo hace sobre una administración centralizada.

Sección 4

FINES

Los fines de la Sección 4 son: proporcionar directrices al Tribunal en cuanto a la legislación sustantiva aplicable a los procedimientos de conformidad con la Ley modelo; distinguir entre el procedimiento secundario y el proceso pleno, disponiendo que en un procedimiento secundario se pueda aplicar la Ley sustantiva de insolvencia tanto de la jurisdicción extranjera como local, mientras que se aplica la ley de la jurisdicción local al proceso pleno; potenciar el reconocimiento de la Ley de la jurisdicción extranjera, en cuanto sea posible, en los procedimienttos secundarios, si bien previendo la posibilidad de que tal Ley pueda no ser la propia en la jurisdicción local y por tanto no proceda su aplicación; y, confirmar que un proceso pleno iniciado por el representante extranjero esté sujeto a la ley de la jurisdicción local y que tal ley será la ley aplicable para el proceso pleno.

FUENTES
El apartado (a) refleja un principio anotado en el Comentario Inglés al Proyecto Especial sobre la Cooperación Internacional y Procedimientos Concursales, IBA Comité J, 1987, con respecto a la Sección 426 de la Ley de Insolvencia 1986 de Inglaterra. El apartado (b) sienta el principio aceptado generalmente de que debe aplicarse la ley sustantive local cuando la persona que inicie el proceso pretende los beneficios de un proceso local pleno.

INTERPRETACIÓN
Está claro que si a un representante extranjero se le ha negado la asistencia del Tribunal en la iniciación de un procedimiento secundario, y él ha iniciado un proceso de insolvencia según las leyes de la jurisdicción local, la Ley sustantiva aplicable debería ser la de la jurisdicción local. En un procedimiento secundario, el tema de la ley sustantiva aplicable es más complejo. Utopicamente siguiendo el principio de la universalidad en su forma más pura, la ley sustantiva del Tribunal extranjero regularía todas las actuaciones judiciales, incluyendo los procesos secundarios, mientras que los aspectos procesales presumiblemente se regularían por la ley procesal de la jurisdicción que los reconoce. Sin embargo, los imperativos de orden público o los principios concursales locales, vigentes en la jurisdicción del Tribunal, puden requerir que se modifique este principio básico y, que se aplique (en algunas instancias) la ley sustantiva local. La intención de la Ley modelo es que el Tribunal, cuando sea posible en los procesos secundarios, aplique la ley sustantiva de la jurisdicción del proceso extranjero, y que la ley sustantiva local de insolvencias se aplique solo en instancias aisladas e infrecuentes cuando la aplicación de la ley sustantiva del proceso extranjero suponga una violación del orden público.

Sección 5

FINES
Los fines de la Sección 5 son permitir que el representante extranjero comparezca ante el Tribunal a los limitados fines de obtener ayuda secundaria, sin el temor de quedar sometido a la jurisdicción del Tribunal para otros fines.

FUENTES
La Sección 5 sigue el ejemplo del Código Concursal de los Estados Unidos {S}306.

INTERPRETACIÓN
Para alentar a los representantes extranjeros a solicitar ayuda mediante el inicio de procedimiento secundario al proceso extranjero, o si fuera necessario, el inicio de un proceso pleno, esta sección establece protección a los representantes extranjeros de la posibilidad que el Tribunal asuma jurisdicción para otros fines. Se limita tal protección a las acciones del representante extranjero anteriores al comienzo del procedimiento secundario, sin que trate de evitarse el sometimiento del representante extranjero a las

demandas o reconvenciones presentadas válidamente después del comienzo de la procedimiento secundario. La intención de la Ley modelo no es sólo proporcionar acceso al Tribunal para el representante extranjero, sino establecer también un mecanismo seguro, justo y eficiente al servicio del representante extranjero, para fomentar una administración central de los bienes del deudor y promover el principio de universalidad. Las protecciones que esta Sección proporciona al representante extranjero son aspectos importantes de este esfuerzo.

Sección 6

FINES

Los fines de la Sección 6 son definir claramente "representante extranjero" y "proceso extranjero"; enmarcar tales definiciones con suficiente flexiblidad para cubrir los diferentes tipos de procesos y los diferentes papeles que pueden desempeñar los administradores bajo las leyes de diversas jurisdicciones; y asignar al Tribunal la responsabilidad de determinar su competencia en el proceso extranjero.

FUENTES

La definición establecida en el apartado (a) de la Sección 6 sigue el ejemplo del {S}316 del Proyecto de Ley Canadiense. La definición del apartado (b) deriva en parte del Código Concursal de los Estados Unidos {S}101(22).

INTERPRETACIÓN

Es las intención de la Ley modelo incluir dentro del término "representante extranjero", Sección 6(a), todas aquellas personas que realicen funciones sustancialmente equivalentes en una insolvencia extranjera. Nótese, por ejemplo, que la amplitud de esta definición permite incluir conceptos únicos tales como "deudor en posesión" bajo las disposiciones del Código Concursal de los Estados Unidos.

El Apartado (b) define "proceso extranjero" con suficiente amplitud como para incluir todos los tipos de actuaciones judiciales y administrativas que existen en las jurisdicciones de todo el mundo. El "proceso extranjero" no incluye procedimientos concursales extra-judiciales o actuaciones similares que no están bajo el control de un ente judicial o administrativo. Para cumplir con la definición de "proceso extranjero" tal y como dispone la Ley modelo, el Tribunal u órgano extranjero que conozca el proceso debe tener competencia. El Tribunal debe determinar que existe competencia, y por lo tanto, que el proceso es un "proceso extranjero" bajo los términos de la Ley modelo. La Ley modelo presupone que, el Tribunal, guiado por un planteamiento "forum non-conveniens", podría conceder competencia al Tribunal u órgano administrativo extranjer en aquel fuero que tenga mayor conexión con el deudor y su patrimonio. El Tribunal para determinar su competencia, tendrá máxima flexibilidad para que, por ejemplo, pueda considerar si se está ante un supuesto de selección indebido del fuero, o "shopping" por parte del deudor.

Sección 7

FINES

Los fines de esta Sección 7 son reconocer que los tratados o convenios pueden ser suscritos y ratificados para regular el objeto de la ley modelo y establecer que en tal caso, el tratado o convenio prevalecerá sobre la ley modelo en lo que respecta a cuestiones de insolvencia internacional habidas entre los países que los ratifican.

FUENTES

Se redactó la Sección 7 en respuesta a los comentarios de especialistas en asuntos concursales algunos de los cuales abogaron por la celebración y ratificatión de tratados o convenios para llevar a cabo la cooperación international en supuestos de insolvencia, y algunos de los cuales pretendían aclarar la relación entre un tratado de este tipo y la ley modelo en aquellos casos en que se ratifica un tratado o convenio tras la promulgación de la ley modelo.

EXPLICACIÓN

La Sección 7 dispone que, si se celebra un tratado o convenio relativo a la cooperación internacional sobre insolvencia, aquél prevalecerá sobre la ley modelo en cuanto a las materias habidas entre los países que lo hayan ratificado. Esta nueva disposición reconoce explícitamente que se pueden suscribir tratados o convenios bilaterales o multilaterales como un medio alternativo para establecer soluciones a la cooperación internacional en materia de insolvencia. No se debe interpretar la promulgación de la ley modelo como una prohibición o disuasión de la adopción y ratificación de tales tratados y convenios; al contrario, la Sección 7 recoge explícitamente como reconciliar la ratificación posterior de un tratado de este tipo por parte de un país que haya adoptado anteriormente le ley modelo.

Comentarios Diversos

1. Significado de "Insolvencia"

Se ha usado el término "insolvencia" en el título de la ley modelo, así como en el texto y comentario oficial del mismo, para significar todas aquellas actuaciones, bajo las distintas leyes y en las distintas jurisdicciones de todo el mundo, aplicables a las acciones relativas a desequilibrios financieros en general, entre los que se incluyen la insolvencia, la quiebra, la reorganización, la composición, la rehabilitación y cualquier otro proceso similar cualquiera que sea su denominación.

2. Sede del Tribunal

No se ha incluido en la ley modelo una disposición que regule la sede del Tribunal en casos ya iniciados y subordinados a un proceso extranjero. Se presume que el Tribunal determinará su sede de acuerdo con la ley aplicable en la jurisdicción del Tribunal.

3. Los Efectos de la Distribución de la Mulitjurisdicción

Aunque no se haya incluido una disposición de vigilancia en la ley modelo, los principios de universalidad y de una administración única de la insolvencia imponen una distribución mundial equitativa. De esta forma, si un acreedor recibe el pago o cualquier otra satisfacción a su pretensión en un proceso extranjero, tal acreedor no debe recibir ningún pago en la jurisdicción del Tribunal hasta que otros demandantes que tengan créditos de igual rango que el de dicho acreedor hayan recibido un pago igual en valor al ya recibido por esta acreedor en el proceso extranjero. Este comentario proviene esencialmente del Código Concursal de los Estados Unidos 508(a).

Appendix 3

Model International Insolvency Co-operation Act: Norwegian Translation of the Third Draft of the Act and Commentary as of 1 November 1988

Model for internasjonal ov om samarbeid i insolvenssaker

§ 1

I alle saker vedrørende insolvens, herunder personlig konkure og selskapskonkurs, akkord, gjeldsforhandling eller lignende forhold, skal Retten i henhold til bestemmelsene i denne lov

(a) godkjenne en utenlandsk reprsentant for debitor eller boet forutsaat at vedkommende utenlandske representant er villig til á rette seg etter avgjørelsene tatt av denne Rett;

(b) bistá og være til hjelp under utenlandske, verserende rettsforhandlinger ved domstoler i de land som i det vesentlige behandler utenlandske insolvenssaker pá samme máte som er beskrevet i denne lov; og

(c) bistá og vare til hjelp under utenlandske, verserende rettsforhandlinger ved domstoler i alle land, dersom Retten finner det godtgjort at:

   (i) domstolene eller det administrative organ under hvis jurisdiksjon den utenlandske representant arbeider, er egnet og passende til á ha tilsynet med forvaltningen av debitors formue; og

   (ii) forvaltningen av debitors formue ved en utenlandsk representant under nevnte jurisdiksjon er i kreditorfellesskapets interesse.

§ 2

(a) En utenlansk representant kan forfølge en sak i tilknytning til en utenlandsk rettsforhandling ved á ta rettslige skritt i henhold til denne lov i den hensikt á:

   (i) oppná en rettsavgjørelse for á overføre et hvilket som helst formuesgode som tilhører debitor i Rettens jurisdiksjonsområde til vedkommende utenlandske representant:

   (ii) utsette eller avvise ethvert rettslig skritt eller søksmål vedrørende debitor eller boet under vedkommene Retts jurisdiksjon;

   (iii) oppná vitneprov eller fremleggelse av regnskap, referater eller andre dokumenter som har tilknytning til en insolvenssak;

   (iv) oppná godkjennelse eller fullbyrdelse av enutenlandsk dom eller rettslig avgjørelse; eller

   (v) oppná annen hensiktsmessig bistand.

Current Issues in Cross-Border Insolvency and Reorganisations (E. B. Leonard, C. W. Besant, eds.; 1–85333–958–X; © International Bar Association; pub. Graham & Trotman/International Bar Association, 1994; printed in Great Britain), pp. 287-295.

Retten kan utøve ytterligere beføyelser i sakens anledning som vedkommende Rett kunne ha utøvet, hvis saken hadde ligget under dens eget jurisdiksjonsområde.

(b) Ved tilleggssøksmål knyttet til utenlandsk rettsforhandling, skal enhver annen verserende rettaforhandling med tilknytning til vedkommende insolvenssak innenfor eget jurisksjonsområde, forenes med dette tilleggssøksmål.

§ 3

Dersom det ikke er mulig á reise et tilleggssøksmál i henhold til § 2 eller forsøk pá á reise et slikt tilleggssøksmál blir avvist, kan ved personlig gjeldsorfølgning en utenlandsk representant starte selvstendig gjeldsforfølgning mot en slik person i overensstemmelse med gjeldende rett innenfor vedkommende Jurisdiksjonsområde.

§ 4

(a) Ved ethvert tilleggssøksmál med tilknytning til utenlandske rettsforhandlinger i henhold til § 2, skal Retten anvende de materielle insolvensrettslig regler som gjelder innen det jurisdiksjonsområde vedkommende utenlandske domstol arbeider, med mindre man finner at internasjonale privatrettslige regler eller regler for motstrid mellom rettsregler, fører til at Retten beslutter á anvende de materielle insolvensrettslige regler som gjelder innen eget jurisdiksjonsområde.

(b) En Rett skal anvende de materielle insolvensrettslige regler som gjelder innen eget jurisdiksjonsområde i alle insolvenssaker som er initiert av en utenlandsk representant i henhold til bestemmelsene i § 3.

§ 5

En utenlandsk representant som møter i en Rett i forbindelse med en begjæring eller rettsanmodning i henhold til denne lov, skal ikke være underlagt noen domstol innen vedkommende Retts jurisdiksjonsområde i noen annen henseende.

§ 6

(a) Med "utenlandsk representant" menes en person som uavhengig av tittel, i henhold til hans eget lands rettsregler, er bemyndiget til á ta seg av tilsvarende funksjoner som dem som utøves av en bobestyrer, akkordkommissær, leder av gjeldsnemnd eller annen representant for debitor eller bo i dette jurisdiksjonsområde.

(b) Med "utenlandsk rettsforhandling" menes forhandlinger vedrørende insolvens, uansett om disse forhandlinger er underlagt domstolene eller et administrativt organ i et fremmed land, sá sant vedkommende domstol eller adminstrative organ som leder forhandlingene, har full jurisdiksjon over debitor og hans bo.

§ 7

Alle traktater eller konvensjoner som regulerer samarbeidspørsmål vedrørende insolvens og som er ratifisert báde av eget land og det land hvor insolvens-forhandlingene har sitt utspring, skal være overordnet denne lov i slike saker med mindre traktaten eller konvensjonen bestemmer noe annet.

Offisielle kommentarer til modell for lov om internasjonalt samareide i insolvenssaker

Uttalelse om alminnelige prinsipper

Det endelige mål for lovgivningen om samarbeide i internasjonal insolvens, er underversialitet som muliggjør *én* administrasjon av insolvensboet, som forhindrer oppsmuldring av debitors formue, som muliggjør en rimelig og rettferdig fordeling av boets aktiva blant sável innenlandske som utenlandske kreditorer, eller som muliggjør en rimelig og rettferdig administrasjon av boer under gjeldsforhandling, akkord eller annen form for reorganiseringsforhandlinger. Sá langt som mulig bør slik underversialitet være det retningsgivende prinsipp i alt arbeid som angár internasjonalt insolvenssamarbeide, idet dette prinsipp alene er det eneste som er forenlige med lik behandling av alle kreditorer, debitorer, aktiva og passiva, samt en hurtig og effektiv administrasjon av insolvensboet. Innenfor rammen av dette overordnede prinsipp má det fremskaffes mekanismer som godkjenner en utenlandsk representant for insolvensboet, opprettholdelsen av lokal bobehandling, fremskaffelse av dokumenter og bevis, integrasjon ved fordeling av aktiva, og andre former for bistand. I en verden med økende global integrasjon og fremvekst av multinasjonale foretak er disse prinsipper ufravikelige elementer, i det man má søke á oppná en rimelig likebehandling i internasjonale invsolvensforhandlinger.

Kommentarer til de enkelte bestemmelser

§ 1

FORMÁL

Formálet med § 1 er á sikre at en utenlandsk representant vil bli anerkjent av retten, at den utenlandske representaten vil opptre i overensstemmelse med rettens beslutninger, og sikre at retten vil bistá ved forhandlinger i land hvor modell-loven eller lignende lovgivning er vedtatt, og á tilskynde retten til á bistá i forhandlinger i andre land hvor modell-loven ikke er vedtatt, forutsatt at to begrensede, men meget grunnleggende krav er tilfredsstillet.

KILDER

§ 1 a er utledet fra prinsippene i engelsk rett og fra US konkurslov § 304 (a) og § 306. § 1 b og c er en parallell til § 29 (2), (a) og (b) i den australske konkurslov. De spesielle krav nevnt i § 1 c, i) og ii) er en parallell til § 316 (5) (a) og (b) i en nylig foreslått, men ikke vedtatt, lov om internasjonal insolvens i Canada (det canadiske lovforslag). Utelatelse av det 3.krav i det canadiske lovforslag var basert pá kommentarer i rapport fra den canadiske komite — spesielt prosjekt for internasjonalt samarbeide i konkursforhandling, IBA komit J 1987 (den canadiske rapport) sidene 46–47.

FORKLARING

§ 1 uttrykker grunnlaget for hele modell-loven og dens prinsipper for underversialitet, ved á forutsette anerkjennelse av en utenlandsk representant, og ved á forutsette at retten skal bistá ved alle former for utenlandsk insolvensbehandling. Rammen er tilstrekkelig begrenset ved á inkludere savel debitors rehabilitering som hans likvidasjon. "Bistand" understreker rettens ideelle forpliktese i forhold til utenlandske rettsforhandlinger, og rettens godkjennelse av den utenlandske representant er selve poenget for utenlandsk rettergang og den utenlandske representaten. § 1 (a) krever at retten anerkjenner den utenlandske representant slik at denne kan, selv om retten kan utøve skjønn ved avgjørelse av den utenlandske representants a anmodninger, være sikret anerkjennelse slik at anmodninger derved kan fremmes for retten. Det eneste krav som stilles til den utenlandske representaten er at denne må forholde seg i overensstemmelse med alle beslutninger retten treffer, idet retten ellers kan trekke anerkjennelsen tilbake.

§ 1 (b) forplikter retten til á bistá rettsinstanser i land som har anerkjent modell-loven. Denne bestemmelse om gjensidighet innebæer et insentiv for land som ikke har anerkjent modell-loven, eller lignende bestemmelser, til á gjøre det samme, slik at disse lands representanter skal fá et grunnlag til á forvente bistand i de juristriksjoner som har anerkjent modell-loven eller lignende bestemmelser.

§ 1 (c) forutsetter at retten skal bistá domstolene i land som ikke har anerkjent modell-loven (eller lignende bestemmelser), men som tilfredsstiller to fundamentale krav: at den utenlandske behandling foregár i tilfredsstillende og ubetenklige former, og at administrasjonen av den utenlandske behandlingen er av vesentlig interesse for debitors kreditorfellesskap. Slike betingelser gir ikke grunnlag for spesielle overveielser for lokale parter, men etablerer en terskel av rimelighet som er nødvendig for á etablere et internasjonalt insolvenssamarbeide. Spesielle tilleggsfaktorer som uten tvil ville gi retten anledning til større skjønn ved spørsmálet om á nekte bistand til utenlandsk rettergang, f.eks. de som er inntatt i US knonkursklov § 304 og det canadiske lovforslag § 316 (5) er utelatt. Denne utelatelse er gjort pá grunn av mottatte kommentarer fra en rekke juristriksjoner som kritiserer US bestemmelser for á gi retten for stor diskresjoner adgang til á behandle en rekke faktorer, og sáledes fá muligheten til á avvise utenlandske anmodninger om bistand. § 1 reiser generelt spørsmálet om hvorvidt retten skal bistá utenlandsk behandling med hensyn til anerkjennelse og tvangsfullbyrdelse av utenlandske skatter/avgifter og/eller krav oppstátt av straffbar handling, og som ikke automatisk vil bli anerkjent eller tvangsfullbyrdet i mange juristriksjoner. Avgjørelsen i disse spørsmál má overlates til den enkelte juristriksjon som godtar modell-loven.

§ 2

FORMÁL
Formálet med § 2 er á lage en ramme for bistand til utenlandsk behandling ved á etablere en mekanisme for tilleggsbehandling til den utenlandske behandling, innenfor hvilken den utenlandske representant kan oppná andre passende løsninger i tillegg til de fire opplistede omráder, og á muliggjøre at ethvert annet uavgjort tvistespøsmál i juristriksjonen skal kunne behandles i den tilsluttede saken.

KILDER
§ 2 er i form og innhold en parallell til § 304 i US konkurslov, som pá samme máte ápner adgang for rettergang i tillegg til den utenlandske behandling, uten á pábegynne separat konkursbobehandling. Modell-loven fraviker imidlertid klart fra § 304 ved á utelate de 6 faktorer som retten i henhold til den nevnte bestemmelse má vurdere nár spørsmálet om á garantere tilsluttet judisiell bistand skal avgjøres. Ingen slike faktorer er inntatt i § 2 i modell-loven. Denne utelatelse er en følge av kritikk

som er reist fra praktiserende konkursadvokater, og som går på at § 304 gir retten for stor adgang til á anvende skjønn i adgangen til á ta hensyn til slike kriterier. Modellloven har i stedet oppregnet de typer av bistand som den fremmede representant kan anmode om i tilleggsbehandlingen, sá snart retten har besluttet á bistá den utenlandske behandling i overensstemmelse med de begrensede retningslinjer som er gitt i § 1. De spesielt oppregnede typer av bistand er utledet fra kommentarer fra praktiserende konkursadvokater, gitt til den spesielle arbeidsgruppe om internasjonalt samarbeide og konkursbehandling, IBA komite J 1987, og fra enkelte lovbestemmelser og andre kilder. § 2 (a) lister opp de samme områder hvor bistand skal gis som det canadiske lovforslag § 316 (3). § 2 (b) er utledet av kap.10, art.159 ff, i de føderale bestemmelser om internasjonal privatrett i den sveitsiske konkurs — og akkordlov, bestemmelser som forøvrig ble understreket i forbindelse med § 2 (a) av den sveitsiske kommentar til det spesielle prosjekt om internasjonalt samarbeide og konkursbehandling, IBA komite J 1987.

FORKLARING

Enkelt ulike bestemmelser i ulike land forutsetter at det den utenlandske representant kan "begjære Kjennelser", andre at den utenlandske representant kan "fá anerkjent utenlandske avgjørelser", eller "anmode om nødvendig bistand". Slike bestemmelser gir imidlertid ikke en tilstrekkelig fleksibel ramme innen for hvilken den utenlandske representant kan oppná bistand i ulike former og grader, alt avhjengig av hvilke behov som matte oppsta og bli utledet av den utenlandske behandlingen. Den valgte løsning i US "sak tilsluttet den utenlandske behandling" gir en slik fleksibel mekanisme som gjør det mulig for den utenlandske representant á foreta de rettergangsskritt, og á søke den type bistand som er relevant i forhold til de enkelte spesielle boer. I tillegg understreker igjen konseptet med "tilsluttet sak" det forannevnte universelle prinsipp, den utenlandske behandling er den dominerende og sentrale lovadministrajon, og at den "tilsluttede sak" er en spesiell "hjelpesak". Oppregningen av de typer av bistand som kan søkes gir et utgangspunkt som i det alt vesentlige er bygget på kommentarer fra praktiserende konkursadvokater, gitt ved henvisning til de spørsmål en utenlandsk representant sannsynligvis vil bringe inn i den "tilsluttede sak". De fire oppregnede "bistandstilfeller" dekker de fire vesentligste omrader i en "tilsluttet sak" hvor bistand blir søkt, men § 2 (a) 2.ledd forutsetter ogsá at den utenlandske representanten kan oppná annen relevant bistand. 2.ledd i § 2 (a) gir hjemmel for at retten med "full styrke" kan bistá den utenlandske representant og den utenlandske behandling. Dog er det forutsatt at denne bestemmelse ikke skal lede til at retten skjønnsmessig favoriserer lokale kreditorer eller andre lokale parter som har interesse i saken. § 2 (b) er basert pá det faktum at kreditorer eller andre interesserte parter kan komme til á begjære enten ufrivillig insolvensbehandling eller annen relatert domstol/administrativ behandling innenfor den samme juristriksjon, før begjæring om á ápne tilsluttet sak til en utenlandsk behandling er innkommet til retten. En utenlandsk representant har anledning til enten á tillate at slik rettergang blir innledet, eller á begjære "tilsluttet behandling" til den utenlandske behandling. For det siste tilfelle vil, i henhold til § 2 (b) den separate behandling som mátte være krevet av kreditorer eller andre interesserte parter, bli forenet med den tilsluttede sak. Ved slik forening vil den separat begjærte behandling bli fullt integrert i én adminstrasjon av boet, og vil bli undergitt reglene i modell-loven. Intensjonene med denne bestemmelse er á tillate forening av den tilslutte behandling og enhver lignende senere innbrakt sak.

§ 3

FORMÁL

Formálet med § 3 er á gi den utenlandske representant ytterligere en mulighet til á fá bistand dersom en tilsluttet sak ikke er mulig, eller avvist av retten. Bestemmelsen gir den utenlandske representaten rett til á kreve ápnet full insolvensforhandling i overensstemmelse med juristriksjonens gjeldende rett.

KILDER

US Konkurslov § 303 (b) (4) gir lignende adgang for en utenlandsk representant til á begjære full insolvensbehandling i USA. Den canadiske rapporten anbefaler pá side 46 sterkt en slik bestemmelse, og gir sin fulle tilslutning til at US konkurslovgivning innehar en slik bestemmelse.

FORMÁL

Den overordnede hensikt med modell-loven er á fá til *én* sentral administrasjon av boet i én juristriksjon, kombinert med tilsluttede behandlinger i andre juristriksjoner. Imidlertid, for det tilfelle at retten avslár á gi bistand til utenlandsk behandling, og avslar tilsluttet behandling, gir bestemmelsen den utenlandske representant et alternativ, derved at full bobehandling kan bli ápnet i debitors bo i overensstemmelse med de lokale rettsregler. Bestemmelsen or á betrakte som en "nødutgang", idet den utenlandske representant først má søke á fá bistand i henhold til § 2, og først nár slik bistand er konstatert ikke oppnáelig, kan § 3 anvendes. Denne systematikk og konstruksjon uthever ytterligere vektleggingen av modell-lovens underversialitetsprinsipp og *én* sentral administrasjon.

§ 4

FORMÁL

Formálet med § 4 er á gi retningslinjer til retten med hensyn til hvilke selvstendige rettsregler som skal anvendes ved behandling etter modell-loven. Det skilles mellom "tilsluttet sak" og hovedsak (administrasjon), og hovedreglen er at den fremmede (hovedadministrasjonens) rett skal anvendes. Dette for á oppmuntre til anerkjennelse av fremmed rett, selv om retten kan avslá á anvende fremmed rett dersom denne ikke finnes á være forenlig med egen rett. Videre bekrefter bestemmelsen ytterligere at nár den utenlandske representant begjærer full (lokal) bobehandling, (jfr. § 3), skal den lokale rett anvendes.

KILDER

§ 4 (a) gjengir et prinsipp som ble anført i den engelske kommentar til spesialprosjektet for internasjonalt samarbeide og konkursbehandling IBA komite J 1987. Det ble ogsá henvist til § 426 i den engelske konkurslov av 1986. § 4 (b) gjengir det generelle aksepterte prinsipp om á anvende den lokale internrett nár fullstendig behandling lokalt er begjært.

FORKLARING

Det er ápenbart at dersom en utenlandsk representant av retten har fátt avslátt anmodningen omn á ápne en tilsluttet sak, og den utenlandske representanten har begjært full konkursbehandling, må den lokale internrett anvendes. I en tilsluttet sak er spørsmålet om lovanvendelsen mer kompleks. Det ideelle er, og ved á følge prinsippet om underversialitet, á anvende de utenlandske rettsregler for hele behandlingen, inkludert de tilsluttede saker. De anvendbare prosessuelle regler derimot má være de som gjelder for den lokale juristriksjon. Imidlertid vil disse grunnleggende prinsipper mátte modifiseres pá grunn av de enkelte lands spesielle ufravikelige regler i konkurslovgivningen og/eller offentlig interesse. For slike tilfeller má egen internrett anvendes. Hensikten med modell-loven er at retten skal, i sá stor utstrekning som overhodet mulig, anvende den fremmede rett i en tilsluttet sak (hovedadminis-trasjonens rett), kun anvende egen internrett hvor de materielle internrettslige regler er uforenlige med de utenlandske (er i strid med egen "public policy").

§ 5

FORMÁL
§ 5's formál er á gi en utenlandsk representant adgang til á møte i retten i anledning spørsmålet om á oppná bistand pá et begrenset område, uten á mátte frykte for á bli trukket inn i andre forhold.

KILDER
§ 5 er en parallell til US' konkurslov § 306.

FORKLARING
For á kunne oppmuntre den utenlandske representanten til á anmode om rettens bistand ved á begjære ápnet tilleggsbehandling til utenlandsk hovedforhandling, eller hvis nødvendig, á begjære full lokal behandling, forutsetter bestemmelsen at den utenlandske representanten av retten ikke kan trekkes inn under dennes juristriksjon i andre saker. Beskyttelsen er dog begrenset til rettslige skritt som ligger forut for den tilsluttede behandling, og bestemmelsen har ikke til hensikt á beskytte den utenlandske representant i forhold som har oppstátt i anledning den tilsluttede sak, det være seg søksmál eller motsøksmál.

Intensjonene med modell-loven er ikke bare á ápne adgang til retten for den utenlandske representant, men á gi en effektiv, rimelig og sikker mekanisme som den utenlandske representant kan bruke i den hensikt á oppmuntre til en sentral administrasjon av boet, og á søke á fá gjennomført underversielle prinsipper. Den beskyttelse som denne bestemmelse gir den utenlandske representant er viktig i denne forbindelse.

§ 6

FORMÁL
Formálet med § 6 er á definere uttrykket "utenlandsk representant" og "utenlandsk behandling" sá klart som mulig. Det er formálet á gi en ramme som er tilstrekkelig fleksibel til á dekke de ulike behandlingsmáter og de ulike roller som administratorer har i de enkelte land, og á overlate til retten ansvaret for á avgjøre om det er en betryggende juristriksjon i den utenlandske behandlingen.

KILDER
§ 6 (a) er en parallell til § 316 (1) i det canadiske lovforslag. § 6 (b) er delvis utledet fra US' konkurslov § 101 (22).

FORKLARING

Det er modell-lovens intensjon med § 6 (a) á fá frem at uttrykket "utenlandsk representant" inkluderer alle personer som har en selvstending og likeartet stilling i utenlandsk insolvens. Det er á bemerke at definisjonen inkluderer et sápass spesielt konsept som "debitor i eierposisjon" som nevnt i bestemmelser i US' konkurslov.

§ 6 (b) definerer "utenlandsk behandling" med sá stor bredde at begrepet inkluderer alle typer av rettslig og administrativ behandling som eksisterer innenfor de enkelte juristriksjoner verden over. "Utenlandsk behandling" inkluderer ikke privat gjeldsforhandling e.l . som ikke stár under kontroll av en rettslig eller administrativ institusjon. For á bli omfattet av definisjonen "utenlandsk behandling" i henhold til modell-loven, má den rett eller institusjon som har saken til behandling ha den nødvendige juristriksjon (i henhold til institusjonens internrett). Avgjørelsen om nødvendig juristriksjon er tilstede, og som følge herav om behandlingen er "utenlandsk behandling" i henhold til modell-lovens definisjon, má avgjøres av retten. En underliggende forutsetning i modell-loven er at retten bør innrømme juristriksjon til den utenlandske rett eller administrative institusjon til den utenlandske rett eller administrative institusjon pá det sted som har den nærmeste tilknytning til debitor og hans formue, og dermed har for øye spørsmálet om den utenlandske juristriksjon er det passende forum... Nár retten skal ta sin avgjørelse, skal retten være gitt maksimal fleksibilitet slik at den f.eks. kan vurdere om det foreligger et tilfelle hvor debitor bevisst har valgt en juristriksjon for sin insolvens (forumshopping) som fremstár som uakseptabel og ikke i overensstemmelse med "debitors og hans formues nærmeste tilknytning".

§ 7

FORMÁL

Formálet med § 7 er á anerkjenne at traktater og konvensjoner som er vedtatt og ratifisert skal gjelde for de tilfeller modell-loven omhandler, og at traktaten eller konvensjonen for dette tilfelle er overordnet modell-loven med hensyn til internasjonale insolvensspørsmál i det land som har ratifisert traktaten eller konvensjonen.

KILDER

§ 7 ble utformet som følge av kommentarer fra praktiserende konkursadvokater, delvis pá grunnlag av anførsler om at vedtagelse og ratifikasjon av traktater og konvensjoner vil effektivisere det internasjonale konkurssamarbeide, og delvis pá grunnlag av behovet for á klargjøre forholdet mellom modell-loven og ratifiserte traktater/konvensjoner i de land hvor modell-loven er vedtatt.

FORKLARING

§ 7 Forutsetter at hvor en traktat eller konvensjon er effektiv med hensyn til internasjonal insolvens-samarbeide, er denne traktat eller konvensjon overordnet modell-loven i de ratifiserende land. Denne nye bestemmelsen erkjenner eksplisitt at bilaterale eller mutilaterale traktater eller konvensjoner skal være et effektivt alternativ for á etablere ordninger som vedrører internasjonalt insolvens-samarbeide mellom flere land. Vedtagelse av modell-loven skal ikke oppfattes som et forbud mot á adoptere og á ratifisere slike traktater eller konvensjoner, snarere tvert imot, § 7 gir eksplisitt uttrykk for hvordan ratifikasjon av traktater i land som allerede har adoptert modell-loven blir á behandle.

Diverse kommentarer

1. Innholdet av "insolvens"

Uttrykket "insolvens" er anvendt i modell-lovens tittel, i dens lovtekst og i de offisielle kommentarer på en slik máte at uttrykket fanger opp de varierende behandlingsmáter i de ulike retts-systemer verden over, og kan anvendes på aksjoner mot feilslått økonomisk virksomhet generelt, inkludert konkurs, akkord, gjeldsforhandling, reorganisering, rehabilitering og andre lignende instiutter hva de enn måtte være benevnt.

2. Verneting

Modell-loven har ingen bestemmelser om verneting forsávidt angár saker tilsluttet en utenlandsk behandling. Det er forutsatt at vernetinget má bli á fastsette av retten i overensstemmelse med internrettens bestemmelser.

3. Effekten av distribusjon via mulitijuristriksjon

Selv om modell-loven ikke har noe preseptoriske regler om fordeling av debitors adktiva, henviser prinsippet om underversialitet og en insolvensadministrasjon til en rimelig underversiell fordeling. Sáledes hvis en kreditor har mottatt betaling eller tilfredsstillende oppgjør for sitt krav i en utenlandsk behandling, skal en slik kreditor ikke motta ytterligere betaling i den lokale behandling før andre kreditorer med samme type krav har mottatt betaling eller oppgjør tilsvarende kreditoren i den utenlandske behandlingen. Denne kommentar er utledet fra US' konkurslov § 508 (a).

Appendix 4
Model International Insolvency Co-operation Act: Dutch Translation of the Third Draft of the Act as of 1 November 1988

Model wet tot regeling van internationale samenwerking inzake van faillissement

Sectie 1

In alle zaken betreffende de toestand van te hebben opgehouden te betalen, met inbegrip van faillissement verefefning, accoord, reorganisatie en vergelijkbare aangelegenheden zal een gerecht, in overeenstemming met de bepalingen van deze wet:

(a) een buitenlandse curator erkennen die is aangewezen tot vertegenwoordiging van een schuldenaar of een boedel, mits deze zich houdt aan de voorzieningen en bevelen gegeven door dat gerecht;

(b) handelen tot bijstand van en behulpzaam zijn bij buitenlandse procedures aanhangig bij de gerechten van alle staten die soortgelijke behandeling geven aan buitenlandse faillissementen zoals voorzien bij deze wet; en

(c) handelen tot bijstand van of behulpzaam zijn bij buitenlandse procedures aanhangig bij de gerechten van alle andere staten, indien het gerecht heeft vastgesteld dat:

   (i) het gerecht of het ambtelijke orgaan die zeggenschap en rechtsmacht heeft over de genoemde buitenlandse curator, de juiste instantie is om te worden belast met het toezicht op het beheer van het vermogen van de schuldenaar; en

   (ii) het beheer van het vermogen van de schuldenaar in de betreffende staat of jurisdictie door de bedoelde buitenlandse curator in het belang is van de schuldeisers van de schuldenaar.

Sectie 2

(a) Een buitenlandse curator is bevoegd tot het instellen van een vordering als een hulpvordering verbonden aan een buitenlandse procedure door het indienen van een verzoek ingevolge deze wet teneinde:

   (i) een bevel te verkrijgen om de buitenlandse curator in het bezit te stellen van alle vermogensbestanddelen of van de boedel van de schuldenaar in het land van het gerecht;

   (ii) opschorting of beëindiging te verkrijgen van elke actie of procedure in het land van het gerecht betrekking hebbende op de schuldenaar of de boedel;

Current Issues in Cross-Border Insolvency and Reorganisations (E. B. Leonard, C. W. Besant, eds.; 1–85333–958–X; © International Bar Association; pub. Graham & Trotman/International Bar Association, 1994; printed in Great Britain), pp. 297-299.

(iii) het verkrijgen van getuigenis of van overlegging van boeken, notulen en andere bewijsstukken betrekking hebbende op faillissement of vergelijkbaar instituut;

(iv) erkenning en tenuitvoerlegging te verkrijgen van een buitenlands vonnis of gerechtelijk bevel; of

(v) te verkrijgen elke andere passende gerechtelijke maatregel.

het gerecht is bevoegd tot het toepassen van elke verdere maatregel als tot zijnbeschikking zou staan indien de zaak vanuit het eigen land zou zijn aangebracht.

(b) Zodra een hulpprocedure als onder a. bedoeld aanhangig wordt gemaakt, zal deze worden gevoegd met een reeds aanhangige faillissementsprocedure in het eigen land.

Sectie 3

In het geval dat een hulpprocedure overeenkomstig sectie 2 niet bestaat of afgewezen wordt, kan een buitenlandse curator die als zodanig is benoemd in een buitenlandse procedure om het beheer te voeren over de boedel van een persoon, tegen diezelfde persoon een procedure tot faillietverklaring aanvangen, overeenkomstig de toepasselijke wet van het land.

Sectie 4

(a) In alle zaken waarin een hulpprocedure als bedoeld in sectie 2 is ingesteld, zal het gerecht het materiële faillissementsrecht toepassen van het buitenlandse gerecht dat bevoegd is in de buitenlandse procedure, tenzij het gerecht beslist dat het, in aanmerking genomen de regels van internationaal privaatrecht en conflictenrecht, het eigen recht moet toepassen.

(b) Het gerecht zal het eigen materiële faillissementsrecht toepassen op alle faillissementsprocedures die worden ingesteld door een buitenlandse curator overeenkomstig sectie 3.

Sectie 5

De verschijning in rechte door een buitenlandse curator in verband met enige vordering of verzoek ingevolge deze wet heeft niet tengevolge dat die curator onderworpen is aan de rechtsmacht van de gerechten in dat land voor enig ander doel.

Sectie 6

(a) Met "buitenlandse curator" wordt aangeduid de persoon die, ongeacht de wijze van zijn benoeming, is aangewezen onder de wetten van een land buiten het eigen land om in verband met een buitenlandse procedure de taken en bevoegdheden uit te oefenen gelijk of gelijkwaardig aan die van een trustee, vereffenaar, bewindvoerder, sequester, curator al dan niet met bevoegdheid tot beheer, of enige andere vertegenwoordiger van een schuldenaar of de boedel van een schuldenaar in het eigen land.

(b) Met "buitenlandse procedure" wordt aangeduid elke procedure overeenkomstig het faillissementsrecht, hetzij gerechtelijk hetzij administratief, in enig buitenland, mits het buitenlandse gerecht of administratief orgaan voor wie deze procedure wordt gevoerd rechtsmacht heeft over de schuldenaar en zijn boedel.

Sectie 7

Elk verdrag of internationale overeenkomst betreffende samenwerking in zaken van faillissementsrecht, dat is geratificeerd door het eigen land en door het land waar de buitenlandse faillissementsprocedure hangende is, zal voorrang hebben boven deze wet voorzover betrekking hebbende op dergelijke zaken, tenzij dat verdrag of die overeenkomst anders bepaalt.

Appendix 5

Model International Insolvency Co-operation Act: Japanese Translation of the Third Draft of the Act as of 1 November 1988

Current Issues in Cross-Border Insolvency and Reorganisations (E. B. Leonard, C. W. Besant, eds.; 1–85333–958–X; © International Bar Association; pub. Graham & Trotman/International Bar Association, 1994; printed in Great Britain), pp. 301-315.

第3草案

1988年11月1日

国際倒産協力モデル法案

第1条 破産、清算、和議、再建又はこれに類するものを含む倒産に関する全ての事項につき、本法の規定に従って、裁判所は、

(a) 債務者又は財団についての外国管財人(representative)を承認しなければならない、外国管財人(representative)はその裁判所の命令にしたがわなければならない。

(b) 倒産について裁判管轄権を有するすべての国の裁判所に係属している外国手続(foreign proceedings)に対して、その相手国が外国倒産手続について本法に定めるところと実質的に同様な取扱をしているかぎりは、これに助力し、補助として行動しなければならない。また、

(c) 次に該たるときは、倒産について裁判管轄権を有するすべての国の裁判所に係属している外国手続に対して、助力し、補助として行動しなければならない。

　(i) 外国管財人について裁判管轄権を有するその裁判所又は行政機関が、債務者の財産についての管財業務を監督するのに適切で都合のよい場所(a proper and convenient forum)に存し、かつ

　(ii) その裁判管轄地(jurisdiction)において、その外国管財人が債務者の財産について管財業務(administration)を行うことが、その債務者の債権者の全体の利益に適合すること。

第2条 (a) 外国管財人は本法による申立をすることによって、次の目的のために外国手続に対する補助(ancillary)手続を開始することがで

きる。

(i)　補助手続を開始する裁判管轄地(jurisdiction)に存する債務者の財産又は財団財産をその外国管財人に引き渡す命令を取得すること。

(ii)　補助手続を開始する裁判管轄地における債務者又は財団に対する訴訟や手続(any action or proceeding)を停止され又は棄却させること。

(iii)　倒産に関する証言を取得し、又は、帳簿その他の記録の提出命令(production)を得ること。

(iv)　外国判決又は外国裁判所の決定(foreign judgement or court order)の承認決定と執行決定を得ること。

(v)　その他の適当な救済を求めること。

裁判所はその裁判管轄地内で生じた事項に関して、さらにこれらに加えてその有する権限を行使することができる。

(b)　補助手続が開始されたときは、その国において現に係属している倒産手続は、その補助手続に併合される。

第3条　第2条の補助手続の申立ができず、またはその申立が却下された場合には、外国管財人は、その相手国においてその国の法に基づき、当該の債務者に対する倒産手続を開始することができる。

第4条　(a)　第2条により開始された補助手続において、裁判所は、国際私法と抵触法の原則を配慮した結果、その補助手続を行う国の実体法を適用しなければならないと決定した場合を除いて、その倒産手続について裁判管轄権を有する外国の実体法を適用しなければならない。

(b)　第3条により外国管財人の申立により開始された倒産手続については、その相手国の裁判所はその相手国の実体法を適用しなければならない。

第5条　本法による申立に関連して外国管財人が相手国の裁判所に出頭したとしても、その出頭はその外国管財人をその他の目的のためにそ

の相手国の裁判権に服せしめることにはならない。

第6条 (a) 「外国管財人(representative)」とは、相手国以外の外国の法に基づき、その外国における倒産手続に関して、管財人(trustee)、清算人(liquidator)、管理人(administrator)、強制管理人(sequestrator)、収益管理人(receiver)、収益管理人兼業務執行者(receiver-manager)その他の債務者又はその財団の代表者・代理人(representative)が行うべき任務と同様な任務を遂行するために選任された者であって、その名称の如何を問わない。

(b) 「外国手続(foreign proceedings)」とは、司法的行政的とを問わず、外国で行われる倒産手続をいう。但し、その外国裁判所又は行政庁がその債務者又は財団について手続を執行するための適正な管轄権を有することを要する。

第7条 外国手続が係属中の国との間で締結され批准された倒産協力について定める条約は、その条約が別異に定める場合を除き、締約国間の倒産協力事項について、本法に優先して適用される。

第3草案

1988年11月1日

国際倒産協力モデル法案についての公式説明

一般原則

国際倒産協力のためのモデル法の究極の目的は、倒産債務者の財団がばらばらに解体されてしまうことを防止する単一の倒産管理、および、清算手続においてはその資産の国内と外国の双方の債権者に対するに衡平な分配、ならびに、更生、和議、再建手続にあっては財団の衡平な管理を目指す普及主義である。その普及主義こそが国際倒産協

力に向けてのすべての努力にあたり可能なかぎりよるべき指導原理である。それだけが真に、すべての債権者、債務者、資産、負債の平等取扱を実現させ、財団の迅速で効果的な管理(administration)を可能とする。この深遠な原則のパラメーターとして、外国管財人(representative)の承認、ローカルな手続の停止、文書や証言の取得、資産分配の統一、および、その他の補助的救済方法のための仕組みが定められるべきである。地球的規模での統合が促進され、真に多国籍企業が成長しつつある世界において、国際倒産手続における衡平と公正を達成するために、これらの諸原則は欠くことができない。

逐 条 説 明

〔第1条〕

目　的

　第1条の目的は、その外国管財人がその裁判所の命令に服することを要求しつつも、外国管財人が全ての目的のために相手各国の裁判所によって承認されることを確実にし、それが期待できるようにし、このモデル法(又は類似の法)を採用した国々での外国手続に対して相手国の裁判所が補助を行うことを確実にし、さらにこのモデル法を未だ採用していないが二つの限定的で基礎的な要件を満たす他の国々の外国手続に対しても補助を与えることを助長するためのものである。

淵　源

　第1条a項は、英国法(判例法)と合衆国破産法304条a項、306条の規定の定める原則に由来する。b項とc項はオーストラリア破産法の29条2項a号b号に類似している。b項とc項に特定されている要件は、カナダで提案されているが、未だ立法には至っていない二つの最近の法案に含まれている国際倒産規定である316条5項a号b号に類似している。カナダ法案における第3の要件を排除したのは、1987年のIBAのJ委員会「国際倒産協力についての特別プロジェクト」におけるカナダ委員会の報告に依拠するものである(カナダ法案における第3の要件とは、前

出第1章第2節3掲記のカナダ新法案第316条5項c号である―訳者注)。

説　明

　第1条は、外国管財人を承認すべきこと、および、裁判所はすべての倒産事件についての外国手続に助力し、その補助として行動しなければならないと定めることによって、モデル法全体の基本と普及主義の原則を提供する。その事件の範囲は、債務者の再建と清算を含む充分に広範なものである。「助力し(in aid of)」と「補助として(auxiliary)」という用語は、外国手続に関する裁判所の理想的な役割を明確に表現したものであり、外国管財人の承認は、その外国手続の管財人のための相手国裁判所への入口を示したものである。a項は、外国管財人の各種申立に応えるかどうかについて裁判所が裁量権を有するとしても、裁判所に対して外国管財人が(各種の個別の―訳者注)申立をするための(適格についての―訳者注)承認が得られることについて確信できるようにするために、裁判所が(まず―訳者注)外国管財人を承認すべきことを求めたものである。この承認のための唯一の要件は外国管財人は承認裁判所の命令にしたがわなければならないことであって、もし外国管財人がしたがわないときは、その裁判所は承認を取消すことができる。

　b項は、裁判所が、モデル法を採用した国々の裁判所のために助力を与え補助として行動すべきことを求めたものである。この相互主義的規定は、モデル法あるいはそれと実質的に同様な取扱を採用することの促進剤となり、かくして、外国管財人がモデル法を採用した国々において共助を得られることの根拠をもつこととなる。

　c項は、未だモデル法を採用していないが、その外国手続が適切で都合のよい場所で行われており、かつその手続がその債務者の一体としての債権者の全体の利益に適合するという、二つの基礎的な要件を備える国々の裁判所に対して、裁判所は補助を供しなければならないこ

とを定める。これらの要件は、ローカルな関係者について特別な配慮をなすべきことを求めたものではなく、むしろ国際倒産協力の中心的な理念である公正と衡平の基礎的出発点を確立するものである。合衆国法304条やカナダ法案316条5項にあるような、これ以外の要件は、おそらく裁判所に対して、外国手続への補助を否定するための広範な裁量権を与えることになることは間違いないと思われるが、このモデル法では採用しなかった。これを排除したのは、合衆国法の規定が裁判所が考慮すべき多くの要件を列挙し、その結果、外国手続に対する補助を否定する決定をなすことができる多くの途を残してしまったが、このような広過ぎる裁量の余地を裁判所に与えていることについて、多くの国から寄せられた批判に応えたためである。

第1条はおそらく、裁判所は、多くの国々においては現に承認又は執行すべきものとされてはいない、外国歳入権(租税)又は刑事罰としての請求権の承認や執行に関する外国手続に助力し、その補助として行動すべきか、という問題を提起することになろう。この問題は、このモデル法を採用するにあたって、各国において解決されるべき問題として残さざるを得ない。

〔第2条〕

目　的

第2条の目的は、外国管財人が各種の救済を求める補助手続の仕組みを形造ることによって、外国手続に対する助力のための構造を規定することである。外国管財人が求めることがもっとも多い四つの種類の助力を規定し、補助手続において外国管財人がこの列挙された四つの種類の救済に加えて他の救済方法を求めることができるようにして柔軟性を持たせ、さらに承認国においてすでに係属している別の関連手続をその補助手続に併合すべきものとした。

淵　源

第2条は、独立の倒産手続を開始しないで外国手続の補助手続を行

うものとする合衆国破産法304条に、その概念と形式が類似している。モデル法は304条にかなりの程度に由来するが、外国手続が補助的な司法共助を受けさせるかどうか決定するにあたって裁判所が考慮しなければならない六つの要件を排除している点において異なっている。モデル法の第2条はこれらの要件を採用していない。この排除は、現行の304条がこのような要件を規定することによって、裁判所に広過ぎる裁量権を与えているとする実務家の重要な批判に直接に応えるものである。それに代えてモデル法は、いったん裁判所が第1条に規定された限定的指針にしたがって外国手続の補助として行動することを決定したときは、外国管財人が補助手続において求めることができる助力の型を列挙した。この列挙された救済の類型は、1987年のIBAのJ委員会「国際倒産協力についての特別プロジェクト」における実務家の意見と制定法の規定等によるものである。a項b項c項はカナダ法案316条3項に列挙されている型に似ている。d項は、スイス連邦国際私法第10章破産和議159条ffに由来し、a項とともに、1987年のIBAのJ委員会「国際倒産協力についての特別プロジェクト」におけるスイスの意見において強調されていたものである。

説　明

　いくつかの制定法が、外国管財人は、「命令を求める(seek orders)」ことができると定めているのに対して、他の制定法は、外国管財人は、「外国決定の承認を取得(obtain recognition of foreign decrees)」し、あるいは「必要な救済を求める(may seek necessary relief)」ことができる旨を規定している。このような規定は、外国管財人がその中において、外国手続から生ずる必要性に基づき、多くの異なった方法により沢山の種類の助力を得るための柔軟な構造を提供するものではない。合衆国型の「外国手続に対する補助(ancillary)手続」は、まさにその手続中において、外国管財人が、財団の具体的な必要性に応じて、いろいろな手続をとり、またいろいろな異なった種類の救済を求めるための

柔軟な仕組みを提供するものである。加えて、「補助(ancillary)手続」という概念は、その外国手続が、債務者の財団についての、なお優位に立ちかつ中心的な管理(dominant and central administration)であるままとしつつ、個別的な助力を与え、補助として存することを可能とするための特別の種類の手続として区別することによって、普及主義の原則を再確認することになる。列挙した種類の救済の型は出発点を示したに過ぎず、外国管財人が補助手続において求めるであろう事柄の到達点については、実務家の意見をまつものであるが、a項(v)は外国管財人が他の種類の適当な救済を求めることができるよう柔軟性を加えたものである。a項の最後の文章は、裁判所はその全ての権限を以て、外国管財人と外国手続に対して助力を与え、補助として行動すべきであると定めるが、この規定は裁判所がlocal債権者や利害関係人を利するように裁量権を行使することを意図しているのではない。b項は、債権者またはその他の利害関係人が、承認国において、外国手続に対する補助手続が開始される前に、非自己申立倒産手続または関連司法又は行政手続を開始することを認めることを前提としている。外国管財人はそのような動きを進むにまかせるか、あるいは外国手続に対する補助手続を開始するかの裁量権を有する。後者の場合には、b項に基づき、債権者や利害関係人の申立により開始された別の手続は、補助手続に併合されるべきこととなる。補助手続との併合により、別の手続は財団の単一の管財業務に完全に統合され、モデル法の規定によって律せられることになる。この規定の趣旨は、補助手続の開始後に同様に始められたその後の手続は全て、補助的に統合するというものである。

〔第3条〕

目 的

第3条の目的は、補助手続を行うことができず、あるいはそれが相手国の裁判所によって否定された場合において、外国管財人が相手国の裁判所に入って救済を求めるための他の手段を提供し、外国管財人

に必要とあらば相手国の法に基づく完全な倒産手続(full proceeding)を始めることを許すことにより、相手国の裁判所を最大限に利用することができるようにしたものである。

淵　源

　合衆国破産法303条b項４号は、同様に外国管財人が合衆国において完全な(full)倒産手続をとることを認めている。カナダ報告書46頁は、このような規定を設けることを強くすすめており、合衆国破産法がかく規定していることを賞賛している。

説　明

　モデル法の主要な目的は、一つの国における財団の集中的な管理と、もし必要ならば他の国における補助手続を行うことに向けられている。しかし、相手国の裁判所が、外国手続に助力することを断ったり、(第１条c項により)補助手続を拒絶したときには、本条は、外国管財人に、相手国の破産法の規定に基づく完全(full)な倒産手続を開始するというもう一つの途を提供するものである。第３条は、まず外国管財人は第２条により補助手続を求めることを第一に考えるべきものとし、それができない場合においてのみ、第３条により完全な(full)手続を開始するための手続をとるべきことを明らかにしている。この構造はさらに普及主義の原則を補強し、モデル法が倒産管理の集中に主眼を置いていることを強調するものである。

　〔第4条〕

目　的

　第４条の目的は、モデル法に基づき適用される倒産実体法について裁判所に基準を提供するものである。補助手続と完全な(full)手続とを区別し、完全な手続にはローカルな倒産実体法が適用されるが、補助手続には外国法とローカル法の倒産実体法の両方が適用されることとしている。補助手続においては可能なかぎりは外国法を承認することを奨励するが、外国法が適当でないときにはそれには拘束されないこ

ととしている。さらに外国管財人によって開始される完全手続はローカル倒産実体法によるものであって、ローカル法が完全(full)手続に適用される法であることを確認している。

淵　源

　a項は、1986年英国倒産法426条に関する、1987年のIBAのJ委員会「国際倒産協力についての特別プロジェクト」における英国の意見中にあった原則によっている。b項は、ローカルの完全倒産手続に訴えることが求められたときには、ローカル倒産実体法を適用するとの一般的に受け入れられた原則を規定している。

説　明

　外国管財人が、補助手続を開始することにより補助を得ることを相手国の裁判所に断られた場合において、ローカル法に基づく完全な倒産手続を開始した場合には、準拠すべき倒産実体法はローカル法であることは明らかである。補助手続においては、準拠すべき倒産実体法の問題はより複雑である。理想的には普及主義の原則を純粋に適用して、外国裁判所の所在地の実体法が補助手続を含む全体の手続を律すべきこととなろうが、一方補助手続における手続的な事項については承認国の手続法が適用されることとなろう。しかし相手国の公序の強い要請とローカルな倒産法についての確立した原則が、この基本原則を修正し、いくつかの場合において、ローカル実体法を適用すべきことを求めることになろう。モデル法の意図は、補助手続においてもできるだけ外国倒産実体法を適用すべきであって、ローカル倒産実体法を適用するのは、その外国法を適用することが公序に反することとなるような稀な場合に限られるべきであるというにある。

〔第5条〕

目　的

　第5条の目的は、外国管財人が、その他の目的のためにその相手国裁判所の裁判権に服せしめられてしまうという懸念を持つことなく、

相手国の裁判所に補助手続による救済を求めるという限られた目的のためにだけ、出頭することを認めたものである。

淵　源

第5条は合衆国破産法306条を模倣したものである。

説　明

本条は、外国管財人が外国手続の補助手続の開始による救済を求め、あるいは必要とあらば完全な手続の開始申立ができるようにするために、相手国の裁判所が他目的のために裁判権があるとしてしまうことから、外国管財人を保護している。この保護は、補助手続が開始される以前の訴訟等に限られており、補助手続開始後に有効に発生した債権又は反対債権に外国管財人が服することを妨げることまでも意図するものではない。モデル法の意図するところは、外国管財人に対して相手国の裁判所に対するアクセスを提供するだけでなく、財団の中央管理を助長し普及主義の原則の発達を促すために、外国管財人にとって効果的で衡平で安全な仕組みを提供することにある。本条が外国管財人に付与している保護はこの努力の重要な側面である。

〔第6条〕

目　的

第6条の目的は、「外国管財人(representative)」と「外国手続(foreign proceeding)」を明確に定義することであり、いろいろな種類の手続といろいろな国の法に基づきadministratorsが果たしているいろいろな役割を含められるように、十分に柔軟な定義を構成し、さらに、外国手続について適正な裁判管轄権があるかどうかを決定する責任が承認国の裁判所にあるものとした。

淵　源

第6条a項の定める定義は、カナダ法案316条1項を模倣したものである。第6条a項の定める定義は、部分的には合衆国破産法101条22号に由来するものである。

<u>説　明</u>

　モデル法は第6条a項によって、外国倒産手続において実質的に同等の役割を遂行するすべての人を「外国管財人」の用語の中に含ませることを意図している。例えば、この広範な定義には、台衆国破産法の規定による「占有を継続する債務者 "debtor-in-possession"」（台衆国破産法第11章の再建手続においては、原則として債務者が権限を失うことなく、しかも否認権や未履行契約の引受拒絶権など、管財人の重要な権限を有する。―訳者注）なる特異な概念も含まれる。

　第6条b項は、「外国手続(foreign proceeding)」に、世界中の国々で行われているすべての種類の司法的行政的手続を含められるように幅広く定義している。「外国手続」には、司法手続によらない私的なレシーバーシップ(non-judicial private receivership)、あるいは、司法又は行政官署によって管理されないこれと類似の手続を含まない。モデル法による「外国手続」の定義に合致するためには、手続を処理する外国の裁判所又は機関は、適正な裁判管轄権を有していなければならない。適正な裁判管轄権を有していることの決定、およびそれ故にその手続がモデル法の定義する「外国手続」である旨の決定は、承認国の裁判所によってなされなければならない。モデル法は、承認国の裁判所が、forum-non-conveniensの処理を適用して、外国の裁判所や行政機関が債務者と財団により大きなcontactsを有する場合には、それに管轄権を譲るであろうとの前提に立っている。管轄についての決定をなすにあたって、裁判所は、例えば、債務者が管轄地を選択するにあたって不適当な選択や "shopping" をしていなかったかどうかなどを配慮できるように、最大限に柔軟性がなければならない。

　〔第7条〕

<u>目　的</u>

　第7条の目的は、モデル法の主題事項を律するために締結され批准されるであろう条約等を承認し、そのような場合には、その条約等が

締約国間の国際倒産事項に関してモデル法に優先して適用されるとしている。

淵　源

　第7条は、国際倒産協力に有効な条約の締結や批准を支持し、モデル法の立法後に条約等が批准された場合における条約とモデル立法との関係を明確にすべきであると主張する何人かの倒産実務家の意見に応えて起草されたものである。

説　明

　第7条は、もし国際倒産協力事項に関する条約等が発効した場合には、その条約等が締約国間のそのような事項に関してモデル立法に優先して適用されることを定める。この新規定は、二国間又は多国間条約等が国家間の国際倒産協力に関する調整を確立するもう一つの手段として有効であることを明白に承認するものである。モデル法の立法は、そのような条約等の採用と批准を禁止又は妨げるものと解釈されてはならず、反対に、第7条は、モデル法を既に採用している国がその後にそのような条約を批准した場合に、いかに調和を図るかを明示的に言及したものである。

Miscellaneous Comments

1．"Insolvency" の意味

　"Insolvency" という用語は、あらゆる種類の法に基づき世界中の各国において、財政的危機状態において一般的に適用される倒産、破産、更生、和議、再建などその他その名称の如何を問わずあらゆる種類の手続を指すものとして、モデル法の表題とその条文ならびに公式説明全体を通じて使用されている。

2．裁判地(Venue)

　外国手続に付随して開始される手続について土地管轄に関する規定は、このモデル法には含まれていない。土地管轄は承認国の裁判所がその国の法に基づき決定すべきものである。

3. 他国への配当の効力

モデル法には統合規定は含まれていないが、普及主義と単一管理の原則は、世界中での公平な配当へと導く。かくして、もし債権者が外国手続において債権に対する弁済その他の満足を得たときには、その債権者は、同等に配分に与かる権限を有する他の債権者が同等の額の満足を受けるまでは、承認国において支払を受けられない。この注釈は合衆国破産法508条a項に実質的に由来するものである。

Appendix 6
Model International Insolvency Co-operation Act: Danish Translation of the Third Draft of the Act as of 1 November 1988

Model til lov om samarbejde I internationale insolvenssager

§ 1

I alle insolvenssager, herunder konkurs, likvidation, akkord, rekonstruktion og lignende anliggender skal retterne i overensstemmelse med bestemmelserne i denne lov:

(a) anerkende en udenlandsk repræsentant for skyldneren eller boet på betingelse af, at han opfylder retternes forskrifter,

(b) yde bistand i udenlandske sager, der behandles ved retterne i ethvert land, der i udenlandske sager vedrørende insolvens yder en bistand, der i alt væsentligt svarer til den i denne lov omhandlede,

(c) yde bistand i udenlandske sager, der behandles ved retterne i ethvert andet land, dersom det godtgøres over for dem:

    (i) at den ret eller forvaltningsmyndighed, under hvis myndighedsområde den udenlandske repræsentant hører, er kompetent til og forsvarligt kan varetage tilsynet med forvaltningen af skyldnerens ejendele,

    (ii) at det er i samtlige fordringshaveres interesse, at forvaltningen af skyldnerens ejendele inden for den pågældende retskreds varetages af den udenlandske repræsentant.

§ 2

(a) En udenlandsk repræsentant kan anlægge sag i tilslutning til en løbende udenlandsk sag ved indgivelse af stævning eller begæring i medfør af denne lov med henblik på:

    (i) indsættelse i besiddelsen af skyldneren eller boet tilhørende ejendele inden for den rets virkekreds, for hvilken sagen indbringe,

    (ii) udsættelse eller afvisning af søgsmål eller behandling af sager ved den pågældende ret,

    (iii) optagelse af vidneforklaringer eller fremlæggelse af bøger, optegnelser eller andre dokumenter vedrørende insolvenssagen,

    (iv) opnåelse af anerkendelse og tvangsfuldbyrdelse af udenlandske domme eller andre retsafgørelser, eller

    (v) benyttelse af ethvert andet hensigtsmæssigt retsmiddel.

Retten kan udøve de samme yderligere beføjelser i sagen, som den ville kunne udøve, dersom sagen faldt inden for dens egen virkekreds.

Current Issues in Cross-Border Insolvency and Reorganisations (E. B. Leonard, C. W. Besant, eds.; 1–85333–958–X; © International Bar Association; pub. Graham & Trotman/International Bar Association, 1994; printed in Great Britain), pp. 317-318.

(b) Ved anlæg af en sag i tilslutning til en løbende udenlandsk sag skal eventuelle sager vedrørende insolvens, der har forbindelse med denne, og som løber ved den pågældende ret, forenes med den førstnævnte sag.

§ 3

Dersom der ikke er mulighed for anlæg af sag i medfør af § 2 i tilslutning til en løbende udenlandsk sag, eller dersom en sådan sag nægtes fremmet her i landet, kan en udenlandsk repræsentant for boet under en løbende udenlandsk sag vedrørende en person indlede insolvenssag her i landet i overensstemmelse med de i dette gældende bestemmelser.

§ 4

(a) I sager anlagt i tilslutning til udenlandske sager i medfør af § 2 skal retterne anvende de materielle retsregler om involvens, der gælder ved den udenlandske ret, der er kompetent i den udenlandske sag, medmindre de efter grundsæt- ningerne i den internatnionale privatret og om lovkonflikter finder at burde anvende de her i landet gældende materielle retsregler om insolvens.

(b) I enhver insolvenssag, der anlægges af en udenlandsk repræsentant i medfør af § 3, skal retterne anvende de her i landet gældende materielle retsregler om insolvens.

§ 5

At en udenlandsk repræsentant giver møde for en ret i forbindelse med en stævning eller begæring indgivet i medfør af denne lov, medfører ikke, at han i andre henseender underkastes nogen rets kompetence her i landet.

§ 6

(a) Ved en "udenlandsk repræsentant" forstås enhver, der uden hensyn til stillingsbetegnelse er beskikket i medfør af lovgivningen i et fremmed land, til i forbindelse med sager at udføre hverv, der svarer til dem, der her i landet udføres af en kurator, likvidator, bobestyrer, midlertidig, bobestyrer, inkassator eller anden repræsentant for en skyldner eller et bo.

(b) Ved "udenlandske sager" forstås insolvenssager, der behandles af forvaltnings- myndigheder eller retter i et fremmed land, under forudsætning af at den udenlandske ret eller forvaltningsmyndighed, der forestår sagsbehandlingen, er almindeligt kompetent til at behandl sager mod skyldneren eller behandle hans bo.

§ 7

Alle traktater eller overenskomster om samarbejde i insolvenssager, som er indgået mellem dette land og det land, hvori en udenlandsk sag løber, går forud for denne lov i anliggender mellem disse lande, medmindre andet er bestemt i den pågældende traktat eller overenskomst.

Appendix 7
Model International Insolvency Co-operation Act: German Translation of the Third Draft of the Act and Commentary as of 1 November 1988

Modell eines Kooperationsgesetzes für Internationale Insolvenzen

§ 1

In allen Insolvenverfahren unter Einschluß von Konkurs-, Liquidations-, Vergleichs-, Reorganizations- oder vergleichbaren Verfahren soll ein Gericht in Übereinstimmung mit den Bestimmungen dieses Gesetzes,

(a) den ausländischen Vertreter eines Gemeinschuldners oder eines Nachlasses anerkennen, wenn der ausländische Vertreter in Übereinstimmung mit den Beschlüssen eines solchen Gerichtes handelt;

(b) ausländische Verfahren unterstützen, die vor Gerichten eines Staates eröffnet wurden, dessen Recht ausländische Insolvenzverfahren im wesentlichen ähnlich behandelt wie dieses Gesetz es vorsieht; und

(c) ausländische Verfahren unterstützen, die vor Gerichten anderer Staaten eröffnet wurden, wenn das Gericht festgestellt hat, daß

   (i) das Gericht oder die Verwaltungsbehörde, welcher den ausländischen Verwalter unterworfen ist, ein zuständiges und geeignetes Forum ist, und die Verwaltung des Vermögens des Schuldners zu ¨bewachen; und

   (ii) die Verwaltung des Schuldnervermögens im betreffenden Gerichtsstaat durch den ausländischen Verwalter im Gesamtinteresse der Gläubiger des Schuldners ist.

§ 2

(a) Ein ausländischer Verwalter kann ein das ausländische Verfahren unterstützendes Nebenverfahren einleiten, indem er nach Maßgabe dieses Gerichtes beantraft:

   (i) die gerichtliche Anordnung der Herausgabe jeglichen im Gerichtsstaat belegenden Vermögens des Schuldners oder des Nachlasses an den ausländischen Verwalter;

   (ii) die Uterbrechung eines inländishchen Verfahrens oder die Abweisung einer im Inland erhobene Klage, die den Schuldner oder den Nachlaß betreffen;

   (iii) die Vernehmung von Zeugen oder die Vorlage von Büchern, Aufstellungen oder anderer Dokumente, die mit einer Insolvenz zusammenhängen;

   (iv) die Anerkennung und Vollstreckbarkeitserklärung eines ausländischen Urteils oder einer gerichtlichen Anordnung; oder;

   (v) die Gewährung jeder anderen geeigneten Unterstützung.

Current Issues in Cross-Border Insolvency and Reorganisations (E. B. Leonard, C. W. Besant, eds.; 1–85333–958–X; © International Bar Association; pub. Graham & Trotman/International Bar Association, 1994; printed in Great Britain), pp. 319-328.

(b) Von der Eröffnung eines Nebenverfahrens an soll ein etwaiges und in Zusammenhang stehendes inländisches Insolvenzverfahren mit dem Nebenverfahren konsolidiert werden.

§ 3

Kann ein Nebenverfahren gemäß § 2 nicht eröffnet werden oder wird die Eröffnung eines Nebenverfahrens abgelehnt, kann ein ausländischer Verwalter einer Vermögensmasse dann, wenn das ausländische Verfahren eine Person betrifft, die Eröffnung eines Insolvenzverfahrens gegen diese Person im Gerichtsstaat in übereinstimmung mit den Vorschriften beantragen, die nach den Gesetzen der Gerichtsstaaten anwendbar sind.

§ 4

(a) In einem Nebenverfahren gemäß § 2 soll ein Gericht das materielle Insolvenzrecht des ausländischen und zuständigen Konkurseröffnungsstaates angewendet werden, wenn das Gericht nicht unter angemessener Berücksichtigung der Prinzipien des Internationalen Privatrechts zu dem Ergbnis kommt, daß das inländische materielle Insolvenzrecht anzuwenden ist.

(b) Ein Gericht soll in einem vom ausländischen Verwalter nach § 3 beantragten Insolvenzverfahren das materielle Insolvenzrecht der eigenen Gerichtsstaaten anwenden.

§ 5

Erscheint der ausländische Verwalter in Zusammenhang mit einem Antrag oder einem Ersuchen gemäß diesem Gesetz vor einem inländischen Gericht, so unterwirft er sich damit nicht der Zuständigkeit eines inländischen Gerichts für andere Zwecke.

§ 6

(a) Ein "ausländischer Verwalter" ist eine Person, die, ungeachtet ihrer Bezeichnung, nach ausländischem Recht berechtigt ist, Funktionen im Zusammenhang mit ausländischen Verfahren wahrzunehmen, welche den Funtionen eines trustee, Liquidators, Verwalters, Sequestrator, Vermögensverwalters, Vermögensverwalters mit Geschäftsführungsbefugnissen oder eines anderen Vertreters des schuldners oder des Nachlasses eines Schuldners im Gerichtsstand entsprechen.

(b) Unter einem "ausländischen Verfahren" ist ein gerichtliches oder verwalterungsrechtliches Insolvenzverfahren eines ausländischen Staates zu verstehen, wenn das ausländische Gericht oder die Verwaltungsbehörde, vor der dieses Verfahren stattfindet, zuständig ist.

§ 7

Eine Vereinbarung oder Konvention, die sich mit Fragen der Zusammenarbeit auf dem Gebiet von Insolvenzen befaßt und von diesem und dem Staat, in dem das ausländische Verfahren schwebt, ratifiziert wurde, geht diesem Gesetz hinsichtlich solcher Angelegenheiten zwichen diesen Staaten vor, wenn die Vereinbarung oder die Konvention nichts anderes vorsieht.

Offizielle Erläuterungen zum Modell des Kooperations: gesetzes für internationale Insolvenzen

Darlegungen der allgemeinen Prinzipien

Das Endziel einer Modellgesetzgebung für die Kooperation bei internationalen Insolvenz ist die Universalität, die eine einzige Verwaltung anstrebt, welche den Schutz der Vermögensmasses des insolventen Schuldners vor Zerspliterung und eine gleichmäßige Verteilung des Vermögens an inländische und ausländische Gläubiger in einer Liquidation, oder die gerechte Verwaltung einer Vermögensmasse in einem Reorganizations-, Vergleichs- oder Rehabilitationsverfahren vorsieht. Soweit als möglich sollte eine solche Universalität das leitende Prinzip aller Anstrengungen in Richtung einer Kooperation bei internationalen Insolvenzen sein, weil es allein wirklich in der Lage ist, die Gleichbehandlung aller Gläubiger, des Schuldners, der Forderungen und Verbindlichkeiten, sowie die schnelle und effecktive Verwaltung der Masse zu bewirken. Im Rahmen dieses überragenden Prinzips müssen Mechanismen für die Anerkennung fremder Verwalter, die Unterbrechung örtlicher Verfahren, die Vorlage von Dokumenten und die Einholung von Zeugenaussagen, die Integration der vermögensverteilung und andere Formen unterstützender Maßnahmen vorgesehen werden. In einer Welt der Zunahme globaler Integration und wahrer multinationaler Geschäftsunternehmen sind diese Prinzipien unabdingbare Elemente, um Gerechtigkeit und Fairneß in internationalen Insolvenzverfahren zu erreichen.

Gesetzeserläuterungen

§ 1

ZWECKE

Mit § 1 soll versichert und vorhersehbar gemacht werden, daß der ausländische Verwalter vom Gericht anerkannt wird; daß der ausländische Verwalter in Übereinstimmung mit den Beschlüssen des Gerichts handelt; daß das Gericht ausländische Verfahren in Staaten unterstützt, in denen eine Form dieses Modellgesetzes (oder eine ähnliche Gesetzgebung) übernommen wurde; zudem soll das Gericht ermutigt werden, ausländische Verfahren anderer Staaten, die dieses Modellgesetz nicht übernommen haben, zu unterstützen, soweit nur zwei beschränkte und sehr grundsätzliche Voraussetzungen erfüllt sind.

QUELLEN

§ 1(a) entstammt den Prinzipien, die sich in den Bestimmungen des englischen Rechts (Fallrecht) und § § 304(a) und 306 des US-amerikanischen Konkursgesetzes finden. § 1(b) und (c) weisen Ähnlichkeiten zu § 29 (2)(a) und (b) des australischen Konkursgesetzes auf. Die spezifischen Voraussetzungen, die §§ 1(b) und (c) aufzählt, ähneln den Bestimmungen über internationale Insolvenzen, die in zwei kürzlichen Gesetzesentwürfen in Kanada ("Canadian bill") vorgestellt aber nicht verabschiedet wurden. Die Auslassung einer 3. Voraussetzung des kanadischen Gesetzesentwurfs gründet sich auf anmerkungen im Bericht des kanadischen Komitees — Special Project on International Co-operation in Bankruptcy Proceedings, IBA Committee J, 1987 (der "Kanadische Bericht", S. 46–47.)

ERLÄUTERUNG

§ 1 schafft das Fundament für das gesamte Modellgesetz und seines Prinzips der Universalität, in dem es die Anerkennung ausländischer Verwalter vorsieht und bestimmt, daß das Gericht ausländische Verfahren in allen Angelegenheiten einer Insolvenz unterstützt. De Bereich der Angelegenheiten ist genügend weit, und die Rehabilitation des Schuldners ebenso wie die Liquidation des Schuldnervermögens zu umfassen. Die Begriffe "Unterstützung" und "Hilfestellung" legen deutlich die ideale Rolle des Gerichts im Zusammenhang mit ausländischen Verfahren da und die Anerkennung des ausländischen Verwalters eröffnet den Zugang für das ausländische Verfahren und seinem Verwalter zu dem Gericht. § 1(a) verlangt die Anerkennung des ausländischen Verwalters durch das Gericht, so daß, wenn das Gericht auch Ermessen in der Behandlung der Anträge des ausländischen Verwalters haben mag, sichergestellt ist, daß der Verwalter insoweit anerkannt wird, als er vor dem Gericht antragsbefugt ist. Die alleinige Voraussetzung für eine solche Anerkennung ist, daß der ausländische Verwalter in übereinstimmung mit den Beschlüssen des Gerichtes handeln muß; das Gericht könnte die Anerkennung versagen, wenn der ausländische Verwalter diesen zuwider handelt.

§ 1(b) verlangt, daß das Gericht ausländische Gerichte, die dieses Modellgesetz übernommen haben, unterstützt. Dieses Gegenseitigkeitserfordernis soll anderen Staaten einen Anreiz geben, das Modellgesetz anzunehmen oder ein grundsätzlich ähnliches Verfahren vorzusehen, so daß die Verwalter eine Grundlage haben, um sich auf die Gewährleistung von Hilfe in solchen Staaten verlassen zu können, die ihrerseits das Modellgesetz übernommen haben.

§ 1(c) sieht vor, daß das Gericht solchen Gerichten fremder Staaten Hilfe gewährt, die daß Modellgesetz nicht übernommen haben, aber zwei fundamentale Voraussetzungen erfüllen: Das ausländische Verfahren muß in einem geeigneten Forum eröffnet und die Verwaltung in diesem Verfahren im Gesamtinteresse der Gläubigergemeinschaft des Schuldners sein. Diese Voraussetzungen dienen nicht der vorrangigen Berücksichtigung lokaler Gläubiger, sondern schaffen eine grundsätzliche Schwelle der Gerechtigkeit und Fairneß, die den Mittelpunkt des Konzepts der Kooperationen bei internationalen Insolvenzen darstellen. Bestimmte zusätzliche Faktoren, die dem Gericht möglicherweise bei der Ablehnung der Unterstützung ausländischer Verfahren einen größeren Ermessensspielraum einräumen würden, wie dies etwa in § 304 des US-amerikanischen Konkursgesetzes und § 316(5) des kanadischen Entwurfes zu finden ist, sind in das Modellgesetz nicht übernommen worden. Die Nichtübernahme erfolgte im Hinblick auf Kommentare aus einer Reihe von Staaten, die die US-Bestimmungen kritisieren, weil dort die Aufzählung vieler Faktoren, die berücksichtigt weden können, dem Gericht einen zu großen Ermessensspielraum einräumen und deshalb viele Möglichkeiten zulassen, die Unterstützung von ausländischen Verfahren abzulehnen.

Bei § 1 stellt sich generell die Frage, ob ein Gericht ausländische Verfahren im Hinblick auf die Anerkennung und Vollstreckbarkeit ausländischer öffentlich-rechtlicher (steurrechtlicher) oder strafrechtlicher Forderungen, die gegenwärtig in vielen Staaten nicht anerkannt oder vollstreckt werden können, unterstützen sollte. Die Lösung dieser Frage muß den verschiedenen Gerichtsbarkeiten überlassen bleiben, deren Staaten das Modellgesetz übernehmen.

§ 2

ZWECKE

§ 2 soll den Rahmen der Unterstützung eines ausländischen Verfahrens durch Schaffung eines dem ausländischen Verfahrens untergeordneten Verfahrens herstellen, in welchem der ausländische Verwalter verschiedene Arten der Unterstützung beantragen kann; es sollen die vier gebräuchlichsten Arten der Unterstützung, die ausländische Verwalter benötigen, dargelegt werden, es soll Flexibilität hergestellt werden; indem dem ausländischen Verwalter gestattet wird, in einem Nebenverfahren jede andere Unterstützung zusätzlich zu den vier aufgezählten Arten der Unterstützung zu beantragen; und es soll sichergestellt werden, daß jedes gesonderte im Zusammenhang stehende Verfahren, daß vor den Gerichten des Staates schwebt, mit dem Nebenverfahren konsolidiert wird.

QUELLEN

§ 2 ist in Form und Konzept § 304 des US-amerikanischen Konkursgesetzes nachgebildet, der in ähnlicher Weise den ausländischen Verfahren untergeordnete Verfahren vorsieht, ohne eigenständige Insolvenzverfahren einzuleiten. Das Modellgesetz weicht jedoch deutlich von § 304 ab, in dem es die sechs Faktoren ausläßt, die die Gerichte bei der Beantwortung der Frage zu berücksichtigen haben, ob sie gerichtliche Unterstützung gewähren sollen. Keiner dieser Faktoren findet sich in § 2 des Modellgesetzes. Die Nichtübernahme ist eine Reaktion auf die Kritik einiger Konkurspracticker, denen zufolge § 304 in seiner gegenwärtigen Form dem Gericht durch diese Kriterien einen zu großen Ermessensspielraum einräumt. An Stelle dessen zählt das Modellgesetz die Arten der Unterstützung auf, die der ausländische Verwalter im Verfahren beantragen kann, wenn das Gericht beschlossen hat, das fremde Verfahren in Übereinstimmung mit den in § 1 vorgesehenen beschränkten Richtlinien zu unterstützen. Die aufgezählten besonderen Arten der Unterstützung gründen sich auf die Kommentare von Konkurspraktikern im Zusammenhang mit dem Special Project on International Cooperation in Bankruptcy Proceedings, IBA Committee J, 1987 und auf bestimmte Besetze und andere Quellen. § 2(a), (b) und (c) ähneln den Arten der Unterstützung, die in § 316(3) des kanadischen Entwurfs aufgezählt sind. § 2(d) lehnt sich an Artikel 159 ff. des schweizerischen Bundesgesetzes über das internationale Privatrecht, 10. Kapital[1]: Konkurs- und Nachlaßvertrag, dessen Wichtigkeit zusammen mit § 2(a) vom schweizerischen Kommentator beim Special Project on International Co-operation in Bankruptcy Proceedings, IBA Committee J, 1987 betont wurde.

ERKLÄRUNG

Während einige Gesetze vorsehen, daß der ausländische Verwalter "Beschlüsse beantragen" kann, bestimmen andere, daß der ausländische Verwalter "die Anerkennung ausländischer Urteile", oder "die notwendige Unterstützung" beantragen darf. Solche Bestimmungen führen nicht zu einem flexiblen Rahmen, innerhalbdessen der ausländische Verwalter die vielen Arten und die zahlreichen verschiedenen Formen der Unterstützung erhält, die die Bedürfnisse des fremden Verfahrens verlangen. Das US-Modell des Nebenverfahrens sieht einen solchen flexiblen Mechanismus vor, mit dem der ausländische Verwalter jede Klage erheben

[1] Jetzt: Arts 161 *et seq*, Kapitel 11.

und jede Unterstützung werden einen sehr signifikanten Teil der Anträge abdecken, die in Nebenverfahren verfolgt werden, §2 (a)(v) sorgt für zusätzliche Flexibilität, wenn ausländische Verwalter andere geeignete Arten der Unterstützung wünschen. Der letzte Satz von § 2(a) stattet das Gericht mit der Befugnis aus, dem ausländischen Verwalter und dem ausländischen Verfahren Unterstützung zu gewähren, jedoch beabsichtigt diese Bestimmung nicht, dem Gericht die Befugnis zu geben, die Interessen lokaler Gläubiger oder anderer lokaler Beteiligter zu begünstigen. § 2(b) basiert auf der Erkenntnis, daß Gläubiger oder andere interessierte Beteiligte die Eröffnung entweder eines Konkursverfahrens oder eines ähnlichen Gerichts — oder Verwaltungsverfahrens im Anerkennungsstaat vor der Einleitung eines Nebenverfahrens beantragen können. Es steht im Ermessen des Konkursverwalters, ein solches Verfahren entweder zu dulden oder ein Nebenverfahren einzuleiten, im letzteren Fall wird unter den Voraussetzungen von § 2(b) das von dem Gläubiger oder einem anderen Beteiligten eingeleitete eigenständige Verfahren mit dem Nebenverfahren konsolidiert. Durch die Konsolidation mit dem Nebenverfahren wird das eigenständige Verfahren völlig in die einzige Verwaltung der Masse integriert und unterfällt den Bestimmungen des Modellgesetzes. Die Bestimmung beabsichtigt die Konsolidation von nach Einleitung des Nebenverfahrens aus ähnlichen Gründen eröffneten Verfahren zuzlassen.

§ 3

ZWECKE

Mit § 3 soll ausländischen Verwaltern eine weitere Möglichkeit gegeben werden, mit Hilfe des Gerichts Unterstützung für den Fall zu erhalten, daß ein Nebenverfahren nicht eröffnet werden kann oder die Eröffnung vom Gericht abgelehnt wurde; außerdem soll dem ausländischen Verwalter der weitestmögliche Zugang zu Gericht ermöglicht werden, in dem die Eröffnung eines eigenständigen Verfahren in Übereinstimmung mit den Bestimmungen des Gerichtsstaates zugelassen wird, wenn ein solches Verfahren notwendig erscheint.

QUELLEN

§ 303(b)(4) des US-amerikanisches Konkursgesetzes gestattet einem ausländischen Verwalter in ähnlicher Weise, die Eröffnung eines eigenständigen Verfahrens in den USA zu beantragen. Der kanadische Bericht, s 46, empfiehlt eine solche Bestimmung mit Nachdruck und begrüßt, daß das US-amerikanische Konkursgesetz dieses vorsieht.

ERKLÄRUNG

Das primäre Ziel des Modellgesetzes geht in Richtung einer zentralen Verwaltung der Vermögensmasse in einem Staat mit Nebenverfahren in den anderen Staaten, in denen diese notwendig sind. In dem Fall jedoch, in dem das Gericht die Unterstützung eines ausländischen Verfahrens verweigert und die Eröffnung eines Nebenverfahrens ablehnt (gemäß den Bestimmungen von § 1(c)), versetzt diese Bestimmung den ausländischen Verwalter in die Lage, alternativ die Eröffnung eines eigenständigen Verfahrens gegen den Schuldner in Übereinstimmung mit den innerstaatlichen Bestimmungen des anwendbaren Rechtes des Jurisdiktionsstaates zu beantragen. § 3 wurde entworfen, um die Notwendigkeit deutlich zu machen, daß der ausländische Verwalter zunächst erwägt und versucht, unterstützende Maßnahmen nach § 2 zu erlangen, und nur in dem Fall, daß diese versagt werden, die Einleitung eines eigenständigen Verfahrens nach § 3 beantragt. Diese Konstruktion betont überdies das Universalitätsprinzip und den Stellenwert, den das Modellgesetz einer zentralen Verwaltung beimißt.

§ 4

ZWECKE

Mit § 4 sollen Richtlinien für das Gericht vorgesehen werden im Hinblick auf das anwendbare materielle Insolvenzrecht für Verfahren nach diesem Modellgesetz; es soll unterschieden werden Zwischen Nebenverfahren und eigenständigen Verfahren, indem vorgesehen wird, daß in einem Nebeverfahren das materielle Insolvenzrecht entweder des fremden oder des eigenen Staates angewandt werden darf, hingegen auf das eigenstädige Verfahren das materielle Insolvenzrecht de eigenen Staates Anwendung findet; es soll bei Nebenverfahren zur Anerkennung des Rechts des fremden Staates soweit als möglich ermutigt werden, zugleich aber für die Möglichkeit Vorsorge getroffen wird, daß die Anwendung dieses Rechts im eigenen Staat ungeeignet sein kann und deshalb nicht zur Anwendung kommen soll. Ferner soll klargestellt werden, daß sich ein vom ausländische Verwalter initiiertes eigenständiges Verfahren nach dem materiellen Insolvenzrecht des eigenen Staates richtet und dieses Recht auf das eigenständige Verfahren Anwendung findet.

QUELLEN

§ 4(a) reflektiert ein Prinzip, das sich im englischen Kommentar zum Special Project on International Co-operation in Bankruptcy Proceedings, IBA Committee J, 1987 im Hinblick auf § 426 des englischen Konkursgesetzes von 1986 findet. § 4(b) knüpft an das allgemein akzeptierte Prinzip an, nach dem das lokale materielle Recht anzuwenden ist, wenn die Vorteile eines eigenständigen lokalen Verfahrens von der Person in Anspruch genommen werden, die das Verfahren initiiert hat.

ERLÄUTERUNG

Es liegt auf der Hand, daß, wenn einem ausländischen Verwalter die Hilfe des Gerichts durch Einleitung eines Nebenverfahrens verwehrt wurde und der ausländische Verwalter ein eigenständiges Insolvenzverfahren nach den Gesetzen des lokalen Gerichtsstaates beantragt hat, das anwendbare materielle Recht das Recht dieses lokalen Gerichtsstaates sein sollte. In einem Nebenverfahren ist die Frage nach dem anwendbaren materiellen Recht komplexer. Legt man das Prinzip der Universalität in seiner reinsten Form zugrunde, so entspräche es Idealvorstellungen, wenn das materielle Recht des Konkurseröffnungsstaates die gesamten Verfahren, einschließlich der Nebenverfahren, beherrschen würde, während sich Verfahrensfragen in den Nebenverfahren vermutlich nach dem Verfahrensrecht des anerkennenden Gerichtsstaates richten sollten. Es ist jedoch möglich, daß die Einschränkungen des ordre public oder wesentliche örtliche Konkursprinzipien des eigenen Gerichtsstaates die Modifikation dieses Grundprinzipes verlangen und, in einigen Fällen, daß das örtliche materielle Recht angewandt wird. Nach der Intention des Modellgesetzes soll ein Gericht, wenn immer möglich, in Nebenverfahren das materielle Insolvenzrecht des Gerichtsstaates des ausländischen Verfahrens anwenden. Die Anwendung des örtlichen materiellen Insolvenzrechts sollte sich auf besondere Fälle beschränken, in denen die Anwendung des materiellen Insolvenzrechts, dem das ausländische Verfahren unterliegt, den ordre public verletzen würde.

§ 5

ZWECKE

§ 5 soll dem ausländischen Verwalter die Möglichkeit geben, zum begrenzten Zweck der Erlangung unterstützender Maßnahmen vor Gericht aufzutreten, ohne befürchten zu müssen, sich damit der Gerichtsbarkeit des Gerichts für andere Zwecke zu unterwerfen.

QUELLEN

§ 5 ist § 306 des US-amerikanischen Konkursgesetzes nachgebildet.

ERLÄUTERUNG

Um ausländische Verwalter zu ermutigen, Unterstützung durch Einleitung von Nebenverfahren oder soweit nötig durch Einleitung eines eigenständigen Verfahrens zu suchen, schützt diese Bestimmung ausländische Verwalter, indem dem Gericht verwehrt wird, seine Gerichtsbargeit für andere Zwecke auszuüben. Der Schutz beschränkt sich auf Handlungen des ausländischen Verwalters, die vor der Einleitung des Nebenverfahrens liegen, es ist nicht beabsichtigt, den ausländischen Verwalter vor Klagen oder Widerklagen zu schützen, die nach Einleitung des Hilfsverfahrens erhoben wurden. Das Modellgesetz beabsichtigt nicht nur, dem ausländischen Verwalter Zugang zum Gericht zu verschaffen, sondern auch, dem ausländischen Verwalter einen effizienten, fairen und sicheren Mechanismus zur Verfügung zu stellen, um zu einer zentralen Verwaltung der Vermögensmasse zu ermutigen und das Prinzip der Universalität zu fördern. Die Schutzmechanismen, die diese Bestimmung dem ausländischen Verwalter zuteil werden läßt, sind wichtige Aspekte dieser Bemühung.

§ 6

ZWECKE

Mit § 6 sollen die Begriffe "ausländischer Verwalter" und "ausländisches Verfahren" klar definiert werden; die Definitionen sollen flexibel genug sein, um die verschiedenen Typen der Verfahren und die verschiedenen Rollen, welche Verwalter nach den Gesetzen einer Reihe von Staaten haben können, zu erfassen; zudem soll dem Gericht die Prüfung der Frage zugewiesen werden, ob die das Verfahren im Ausland eröffnende Stelle tatsächlich zuständig ist.

QUELLEN

Die in § 6(a) niedergelegte Definition ist § 16(1) des kanadischen Entwurfs nachgebildet. Die in § 6(b) niedergelegte Definition ist teilweise § 101(22) des US-amerikanischen Konkursgesetzes entnommen.

ERLÄUTERUNG

Mit dem Begriff "ausländischer Verwalter" in § 6(a) sollen nach der Intention des Modellgesetzes all die Personen erfaßt werden, die im wesentlichen gleichwertige Funktionen in einem ausländischen Insolvenzverfahren haben. Beachtenswert erscheint zum Beispiel, daß die Weite dieser Definition es erlaubt, so einmalige Konzepte wie das des "Debtor-in-Possession" des US-amerikanischen Konkursgesetzes su erfassen.

§ 6(bb) definiert das "ausländische Verfahren" genügend weit, um alle gerichtlichen und verwaltungsrechtlichen Verfahren zu erfassen, die weltweit existieren. Das "ausländische Verfahren" umfaßt nicht private außergerichtliche Vermögensverwaltungen oder ähnliche Tätigkeiten, die nicht unter gerichtlicher oder verwaltungsrechtlicher Kontrolle stattfinden. Um unter die Definition des "ausländischen Verfahrens" diese Modellgesetzes zu fallen, muß das ausländische Gericht oder die Verwaltungsbehörde, die das Verfahren führt, zuständig sein. Die Frage, ob eine solche Zuständigkeit besteht und deshalb das Verfahren ein "ausländisches Verfahren" nach den Bestimmungen des Modellgesetzes ist, obliegt dem Gericht. Dem Modellgesetz liegt die Annahme zugrunde, daß das Gericht unter Berücksichtigung der forum-non-conveniens Lehre das ausländische Gericht oder die Verwaltungsbehörde als zuständig ansehen würde, weil diese engere Kontakte zum Schuldner oder seinem Nachlaß aufweisen. Bei der Prüfung der Zuständigkeit sollte dem Gericht größtmögliche Flexiblität eingeräumt werden, so daß zum Beispiel Raum für die Frage bleibt, ob der Schuldner rechtsmißbräuchlich oder ein ungeeignetes Forum gewählt hat.

§ 7

ZWECKE

§ 7 erkennt an, daß Verträge oder Konventionen, die den Gegenstand des Modellgesetzes regeln, angenommen und ratifiziert werden können und sieht für einen solchen Fall vor, daß das Abkommen oder die Konvention diesem Modellgesetz im Hinblick auf Angelegenheiten der internationalen Insolvenz zwischen den rativizierenden Staaten vorgeht.

QUELLEN

§ 7 wurde als Reaktion auf Kommentare von Konkurspraktikern entworfen, von denen einige die Annahme und die Ratifikation von Abkommen oder Konventionen empfohlen haben, um eine Kooperation bei internationalen Insolvenzen zu bewirken, und andere lediglich das Verhältnis eines solchen Abkommens zum Modellgesetz klarstellen wollten, wenn ein Abkommen oder eine Konvention nach der Inkraftsetzung des Modellgesetzes ratifiziert wird.

ERLÄUTERUNG

§ 7 sieht vor, daß dann, wenn ein Abkommen oder eine Konvention über die Kooperation bei internationalen Insolvenzen zustande kommt, diese dem Modellgesetz im Hinblick auf solche Angelegenheiten zwischen den Vertragsstaaten vorgehen. Diese neue Bestimmung erkennt ausdrücklich an, daß der Abschluß bilateraler oder multilateraler Abkommen oder Konventionen als alternatives Mittel in Betracht kommt, sich hinsichtlich der Kooperation bei internationalen Insolvenzen zu arrangieren. Die Inkraftsetzung des Modelgesetzes bedeutet nicht, daß der Abschluß und die Ratifikation solcher Vereinbarungen oder Konventionen untersagt oder von einem solchen Abschluß abgehalten wird. Im Gegenteil, § 7 spricht ausdrücklich an, wie im Fall der späteren Ratifikation einer Vereinbarung durch ein Land zu verfahre ist, welches zuvor das Modellgesetz übernommen hat.

Verschiedene Bemerkungen

1. Bedeutung einer "Insolvenz"

Der Begriff "Insolvenz" findet sich im Titel des Modellgesetzes, in seinem Text und seinen offiziellen Erläuterungen und umfaßt alle die verschiedenen Verfahren unter allen Arten des Rechts und in den verschiedenen Rechtsordnungen der Welt, anwendbar auf Tätigkeiten, die generell finanzielle Mißerfolge betreffen unter Einschluß von Insolvenzverfahren, Konkursverfahren, Reorganizationsverfahren, Vergleichsverfahren, Rehabilitationsverfahren und aller anderen vergleichbaren Verfahren ungeachtet ihrer Bezeichnung.

2. Zuständigkeit

Eine Regelung, die die örtliche Zuständigkeit für Nebenverfahren bestimmt, ist im Modellgesetz nicht vorgesehen. Es wird angenommen, daß das Gericht die örtliche Zuständigkeit in Übereinstimmung mit dem eigenen Verfahrensrecht bestimmt.

3. Auswirkungen einer staatenübergreifenden Masseverteilung

Auch wenn das Modellgesetz keine Bestimmungen über die Verteilung der Masse enthält, verlangen die Prinzipien der Universalität und der einheitlichen Insolvenzverwaltung eine weltweit gleichmäßige Verteilung. So darf ein Gläubiger, der Zahlungen oder eine anderweitige Befriedigung seiner Forderung in einem ausländischen Verfahren erhalten hat, keine Zahlungen im Gerichtsstaat erhalten, bevor nicht andere Gläubiger, die mit diesem Gläubiger gleichberechtigt sind, Zahlungen erhalten haben, die wertmäßig der Befriedigung entsprechen, die dieser Gläubiger im ausländischen Verfahren erlangt hat. Diese Kommentierung entstammt im wesentlichen § 508(a) des US-amerikanischen Konkursgesetzes.

Appendix 8
MIICA Country Chairmen

Argentina : Guillermo E. Matta y Trejo
Estudio Matta y Trejo
Buenos Aires, Argentina

Australia : David Bennett, Q. C.
Wentworth Chambers
Sydney, NSW Australia

Brazil : Walter Douglas Stuber
Amaro Stuber Street & Seybold
São Paulo , Brazil

Canada : E. Bruce Leonard
Cassels Brock & Blackwell
Toronto, Canada

Denmark : Advocat Ole Borch
Berning Schluter Hald
Copenhagen, Denmark

Jorgen Pedersen
Povl Jantzen & Co, Lawfirm
Copenhagen, Denmark

England : Michael W. Prior
Nabarro Nathanson
London, England

France : Jean-Louis Freyria
Ste d'Avocats SABLE
Lille, France

Germany : Dr Hans-Jochem Lüer
Lüer & Görg
Cologne, Germany

Current Issues in Cross-Border Insolvency and Reorganisations (E. B. Leonard, C. W. Besant, eds.; 1–85333–958–X; © International Bar Association; pub. Graham & Trotman/International Bar Association, 1994; printed in Great Britain), pp. 329-331.

Israel	:	Yoav Salomon Avniel, Salomon & Co. Haifa, Israel
Italy	:	Dr Angelo Pesce Pesce, Frignani Pastore & Ruben Milan, Italy
Japan	:	Koji Takeuchi, Chairman Sakura Kyodo Law Offices Tokyo, Japan
		Hideyuki Sakai (Vice Chairman) Blakemore & Mitsuki Tokyo, Japan
		Shinjiro Takagi (Chairman Emeritus) Judge of Tokyo High Court Tokyo, Japan
Mexico	:	Enrique A. González C González Calvillo y Forastieri, SC Mexico City, Mexico
Nigeria	:	Pius J. O. Anigboro Orieoghene Chambers Warri, Delta State, Nigeria
Norway	:	Advokat Jan Schjatvet Advokatene Schjatvet m.fl. Lillestrom, Norway
Portugal	:	Dr Vasco Soares da Veiga Advogado Lisbon, Portugal
Scotland	:	Alex M. Hamilton McGrigor Donald Glasgow, Scotland
South Africa	:	J. C. Vogel King William's Town South Africa
Spain	:	Dr Fermando Pombo Gómez-Acebo & Pombo Castellana 164 Madrid, Spain

Switzerland   :   Dr Karl Arnold
                     Pestalozzi Gmuer & Patry
                     Zürich, Switzerland

United States   :   Timothy E. Powers
                     Haynes and Boone
                     Dallas, Texas, USA

Uruguary   :   Jonas Bergstein
                     Estudio Bergstein
                     Montevideo, Uruguay

European
Community
Co-ordinator   :   Louis Lafili
                     Lafili & Van Crombrugghe
                     Brussels, Belgium

Appendix 9
MIICA Translation Working Group

Danish   :   Advokat Ole Borch
                     Berning Schluter Hald
                     Copenhagen, Denmark

                     Jorgen Pedersen Povl
                     Jantzen & Co, Lawfirm
                     Copenhagen, Denmark

Dutch   :   Rudolph Hulsenbek
                     Wieringa Advocaten
                     Herengracht 429
                     Amsterdam, The Netherlands

                     Louis Lafili
                     Lafili & Van Crombrugghe
                     Brussels, Belgium

French   :   Jacques Ferry, *Chairman*
                     Ferry & Associés
                     Paris, France

                     Louis Lafili
                     Lafili & Van Crombrugghe
                     Brussels, Belgium

                     Denis St-Onge
                     Desjardins Ducharme
                     Desjardins & Bourque
                     Montreal, Quebec, Canada

German   :   Dr Karl Arnold, *Chairman*
                     Rechtanswalte Pestalozzi Gmuer & Patry
                     Zürich, Switzerland

Current Issues in Cross-Border Insolvency and Reorganisations (E. B. Leonard, C. W. Besant, eds.; 1–85333–958–X; © International Bar Association; pub. Graham & Trotman/International Bar Association, 1994; printed in Great Britain), pp. 333-335.

Louis Lafili
Lafili & Van Crombrugghe
Brussels, Belgium

Dr Hans-Jochem Lüer
Lüer & Gorg
Cologne, Germany

Italian : Dr Angelo Pesce
Pesce, Frignani, Pastore & Ruben
Milan, Italy

Louis Lafili
Lafili & Van Crombrugghe
Brussels, Belgium

Japanese : Koji Takeuchi, *Chairman*
Sakura Kyodo Law Offices
Tokyo, Japan

Hideyuki Sakai
Blakemore & Mitsuki
Tokyo, Japan

Shinjiro Takagi
Judge of Tokyo High Court
Tokyo, Japan

Nowegian : Advokat Jan Schjatvet
Advokatene Schjatvet m.fl.
Lillestrom, Norway

Portuguese : Dr Vasco Soares da Veiga
Lisbon, Portugal

Walter Douglas Stuber
Amaro Stuber Street & Seybold
São Paulo SP, Brazil

Spanish : José de la Rosa
de la Rosa & Asociados
Seville, Spain

Enrique A. González C.
González Calvillo y Forastieri, SC
Mexico City, Mexico

Guillermo E. Matta y Trejo
Estudio Matta y Trejo
Buenos Aires, Argentina

Swedish   :   Magnus Ekberg, *Chairman*
                   Advokatfirman Ekberg HB
                   Jonkoping, Sweden